LIFE AND DEATH

LIFE AND DEATH

The Story of a Hospital

INA YALOF

RANDOM HOUSE NEW YORK

All rights reserved under International and Pan-American Copyright Conventions.
Published in the United States by Random House, Inc., New York and
simultaneously in Canada by Random House of Canada Limited, Toronto.

Library of Congress Cataloging-in-Publication Data

Yalof, Ina L.,
Life and death.

1. Columbia-Presbyterian Medical Center.
2. Hospitals—New York (N.Y.)—Staff—Interviews.
3. Medical personnel—New York (N.Y.)—Interviews.
I. Title.
RA982.N5C649   1989   362.1'1'097471   88-42671
ISBN 0-394-56215-1

Manufactured in the United States of America

98765432

FIRST EDITION

Book design by Carole Lowenstein

To my mother, with love

Here on this site we propose to build a
monument more lasting than bronze, which shall
testify alike to the growing power of human
knowledge to minister to the physical and
mental ills of man and to the zeal of civilized
man to help and cure his less fortunate
fellows.

—Nicholas Murray Butler
 speaking at the ground-breaking ceremony
 Columbia-Presbyterian Medical Center
 January 31, 1925

Our patients belong to us. They are ours and we are theirs. Forever.

—Tom Hickey, *physician's assistant,*
 from an interview,
 Columbia-Presbyterian Medical Center
 October 2, 1985

Acknowledgments

In a project of this magnitude, it is hard to imagine, early on, how many people will ultimately play an important part. I am deeply indebted to the medical staff and the employees of Columbia Presbyterian Medical Center for a kindness and patience that exceeded any reasonable expectation.

It was not easy deciding whom to include in this book. Clearly, for every person I selected, there were twenty more, equally engaging, whom I left out. If it had been possible, I would have gone on and on, as I see now that I have only scratched the surface. Having to draw the line in the interest of brevity was a main frustration throughout my research.

To list everyone who helped me along the way would be an impossible task. I do, however, need to single out some people. I met Joann Lamb and Dr. Keith Reemtsma two years before the inception of this book when I paid a professional visit to the Presbyterian Hospital heart transplant unit. Both of them so impressed me as to start me thinking about this project. I owe them an immeasurable debt of gratitude. Carol Rinzler, my agent, has been wonderful. She supported me when my courage wavered and has guarded my best interests with diligence and foresight. Susan Parker was my hospital appointed liaison, but she was also a lifeline and, more often than I care to remember, a panic button. She was right on target with her advice and suggestions and helped me to see the hospital through her many years of experience. She became and will always be a friend. Richard Zucker, director of public interest, was my conscience. He insisted that things be done "by the book," and after working within his high standards, I realize that there really is no other way. He and Michael Meyer spent innumerable hours reviewing the manuscript and I am grateful for their intelligent suggestions.

Particular thanks are due to Dr. Harold Fox, who made it possible for me to spend time in labor and delivery, to Dr. Robert Glickman, who took me along on medical rounds, and to Dr. Mehmet Oz, a surgical intern who introduced me to the rigors of night time in the emergency room.

I am especially indebted to the following people who generously gave of their valuable time, assisting me in my understanding of the dynamics of the hospital and illuminating areas that would otherwise have remained obscure: doctors Harold Fox, Sadek Hilal, Linda Lewis, Jack Maidman, Jay

P. Mohr, and Daniel Sciarra; nurses Martha Haber, Mary Jane Lomanto, May McDonald, Karen O'Grady, Colette Schafran, Trudy Schmidt, and Hannefore Zuckerman; and Dominick Agostini, William Dix, Viola Gaines, Patrick Greer, Willie Herriott, Tina Kister, Carmel Mahan, Lisa Morrone, Rochelle Moche, Richard Padilla, Jay Porter, Cynthia Ramirez, Thomas Rosemond, Sam Soutter, Lee Suszycki, Tom Taylor, Austin Van Putten, Damaris Vazquez, Robert Wright, and Nancy Wexler.

This book was read in its entirety by Leslie Yalof Garfield, Ellen Stern, and Susan Kogan and in early draft by Dr. Victor Parsonnet. I very much appreciate their useful comments. Ruth Harrison, David Cantor, and Audrey Smith were meticulous in transcribing the tapes. I often marveled at their ability to hear the words above background noises that included ambulance sirens, jackhammer drills, ringing telephones, and wailing babies.

To Dr. Thomas Morris, I owe the largest debt of gratitude for believing in me and in this project and for opening all the doors so that I could pass freely within the halls of the hospital he so ably leads.

Finally, I offer my profound appreciation to the people in this book who shared with me their experiences and their dreams. Gustave Ekstein has called words man's most precious gift. These people gave me their words. They meant everything to me.

Author's Note

The names of the people interviewed here are real, except one. However, to protect the privacy of the patients and others who appear in this book, certain names, descriptions and identifying characteristics have been changed.

Contents

Introduction

A warming breeze left over from summer was blowing across the Hudson
River when I first approached Columbia-Presbyterian medical center in
late September 1985. As I walked through the enclosed garden that leads
to the hospital's side entrance, a maintenance man walking near me paused
and knelt at a flower bed and studied a geranium with the care of a jeweler
examining a gem. He picked off a few dead leaves and continued on his
way. Several groups of medical students, deep in conversation, were scattered about the lawn eating lunch. Other people sat on cement benches,
soaking in the last rays of summer. If it had not been for the steady stream
of doctors in white coats and nurses in uniform, the park-like setting could
have been anywhere. Moreover, with the sun shining on the flowers edging
the lawn, it was hard to imagine that just outside the garden's stone walls
lay the gray, concrete landscape of New York City.

Entering through a small doorway, I found myself in a dimly lit vestibule
that led toward the lobby. I walked past a bank of elevators where staff
and people wearing visitors' badges waited impatiently. Continuing down
a long corridor, I fell into step behind an orderly who was pushing a
wheelchair piled high with folded towels. As he turned a corner, I stopped
at a set of swinging doors. The sign above them read: AREA A. I pushed
open one of the doors and entered, for the first time, the emergency room.

It was as though I had entered another world. Area A, one of four
emergency stations in the hospital, provides treatment for trauma victims
and people with acute illnesses. The waiting area resembles a make-shift
meeting room, with rows of molded plastic chairs on two sides of a narrow
aisle. Almost every chair was filled. Most people were waiting for a doctor;
some were waiting for a patient to return; and a few, as I later found out,
were there just to feel they belonged somewhere. Their eyes, staring
blankly at the backs of the people in front of them, reflected the long hours
of waiting. Those who glanced up as I passed by did so without interest.
I slipped into an empty seat in the far corner. And I watched.

At one point, a heavy-set woman, about sixty or so, labored through the
doorway. Her left arm was draped heavily around the slight frame of a
young girl; her right hand clutched her blouse over her heart. Two nurses
immediately rushed from behind the reception desk to aid the woman,

who seemed on the verge of collapse. Ignoring the girl, they took the woman into the treatment area in the back; the child took a seat among the rest of us.

For a while she sat, head bowed, hands clasped in her lap. Except for her age, she appeared very much like the others around her. And, like the others, she looked up sharply in expectation whenever a name was called or a person in a white coat walked by. Her patience did not last long, though, and soon she began to shift restlessly in her seat. Finally, unable to sit still any longer, she slid down from her chair, edged past the rows of waiting people, and tentatively approached a tall, moustached security guard leaning indifferently against the entrance to the treatment area. "Mister," she said in a soft voice, "my grandmother was s'posed to buy me McDonald's. Could you go in there, please, and tell her to come on?"

The guard turned and walked to the back where the wheels of a stretcher protruded from beneath a striped curtain. As he pulled back the curtain, I caught a glimpse of doctors and nurses working feverishly over the woman. The guard paused, shoved a hand into his pocket and returned to the front area and the waiting girl. He knelt down until their eyes were level, took his fist full of change, and put it into her small, cupped hands. "Your grandmother wants you to go down the hall and get some lunch," he said. "And then you come right back here and wait for her, okay?"

It was one of those isolated moments that, even as they happen, you know will be embedded in your memory forever. I am still not sure if it was the look on the little girl's face as she took the money, the unexpected sweetness of the officer, or that there, in the midst of pain and poverty, a stranger helped another stranger. Whatever it was, at that moment I knew the direction this book would take, and I knew I had come to the right place.

Presbyterian Hospital, with more than twelve hundred beds and a staff of nearly six thousand people, is one of the largest hospitals in the United States. For over a century, it has been regarded as one of the best. When the original hospital opened its doors in 1872, it was located at Seventieth Street and Park Avenue, having been founded by James Lenox, a businessman and philanthropist. History has it that a friend of Lenox's, Dr. Oliver White, had been called to attend the elderly black servant of a prominent New York family. He found her extremely ill and in urgent need of hospitalization, but, because of her race, he was unable to admit her to any hospital he felt was adequate. Furious, he told Lenox that what the city needed was a hospital "broad enough to admit patients without regard to color or creed." Thus was established the fundamental principle behind what was to become Presbyterian Hospital. In fact, above the entrance to the original hospital was an engraved cement slab with the words, "For the Poor of New York without Regard to Race, Creed, or Color." In 1928, the tablet was relocated to the present hospital.

In 1911, the trustees of Presbyterian Hospital and Columbia University's 104-year-old College of Physicians and Surgeons decided to combine their institutions. This venture, which was the brainchild of Presbyterian Hospital trustee Edward Harkness, ultimately led to the establishment of the nation's first medical center, which would thereafter be known as Columbia-Presbyterian Medical Center. A unique mixture of clinical practice, teaching and research, the merger has had a profound influence on the way medicine is taught and practiced in this country.

In 1928, the new medical center opened its doors. Under various arrangements, the hospital formed alliances with other hospitals and clinics farther downtown. Over the years, Vanderbilt Clinic, Sloane Hospital for Women, and Neurological Institute joined Harkness Pavilion within the original building. Eventually the New York Orthopaedic Hospital, Babies' Hospital, and the Eye Institute, with separate but connected buildings, all became part of the complex.

What exists today is a sprawling compound covering more than twenty acres along the Hudson River, bordered by Broadway, Riverside Drive, and West 163rd and West 168th streets. Although several large structures have since been added, the original building still serves as the core of the compound. From the eighteenth floor of the hospital building, looking north through the windows of operating room six, you can see a river of cars flowing across the George Washington Bridge. To the west, construction continues on the newest building, a modern structure that will eventually rise ten stories above the river. North and south, the neighborhood is alive with Latin American shops and restaurants, and four express stops away, due south on the A train, is Times Square.

So vast is this hospital, it is difficult to grasp the magnitude of its activities. There are 2,000 doctors and approximately 1,600 nurses. In 1987, 44,000 patients from fifty states and thirty-five foreign countries were admitted; 9,500 operations were performed, and 6,000 babies were born. Doctors in the outpatient clinic examined 488,000 patients, and more than 133,000 people walked or were wheeled through the doors of the emergency room, a statistic that translates to one patient every four minutes.

In a single day, the kitchen produces over 8,000 meals, half of which are served to patients and half to staff and visitors. The laundry has an output of 30,000 pounds; 15 telephone operators field calls to 8,000 telephones; and 16 mail-room clerks sort and deliver 19,000 pieces of mail, an amount equal to that delivered daily in South Orange, New Jersey, or Burbank, California.

To pay for all this, the hospital has an operating budget of $315 million, something of a rise since 1872, when expenses for the year totaled $35,000. The cost to a patient for one day in a deluxe private room in Harkness Pavilion is $860, which is more than it cost to run the entire hospital for one week in the year it was founded.

The purpose of this book is to tell the story of an inner-city hospital in the late 1980s. It is also a book about hospital people, what they do all day and how they feel about their jobs. But primarily, this is a book about a single hospital, its triumphs, its tragedies, its growing pains. I selected Presbyterian for several reasons. First, I wanted to write about a large metropolitan hospital. Second, I wanted a hospital in a lower socioeconomic neighborhood because people in such areas tend to work near their homes and I suspected they kept their jobs longer and would be able to recount firsthand some of the hospital's history. And this, in fact, turned out to be true. Finally, and most important, I wanted to write about an institution known for state-of-the-art medicine. What I got as a bonus was an institution with a luminous reputation, a grand tradition, and an affiliation with one of the finest medical schools in the country.

My original plan was to draw up a list of departments or physical areas in the hospital, and then select from each a number of people who were doing what I considered interesting or representative jobs. That plan, however, was short lived. Early on, I interviewed Leona Vincent, an orthopedic technician, sometimes known as "the Bone Lady." At the end of our interview, Leona suggested I see a friend of hers who she thought had the most unusual job in the hospital. "She teaches medical students to tie stitches on rats! Can you imagine that?" she said. I couldn't, so I proceeded to meet the woman. Rosemary Martino teaches the techniques of microsurgery (operating under a microscope, using needles and sutures practically invisible to the naked eye). In the course of our conversation, she told me about the time she saw her efforts translated into a life-saving event, as she watched a woman's severed arms being reattached by several of the surgeons she had taught. Fascinated by that image, I sought out one of the surgeons on the team that had performed that spectacular operation. And so it went . . .

Certain themes kept recurring. People talked a lot about how they got their jobs and how they felt about the patients. Many recalled how the murder of a young staff physician had affected them. There were frequent references to the forty-five-day hospital strike, and excitement about the new 750-bed facility under construction. AIDS was a prevalent subject, and as the months passed and the incidence of this disease increased, more and more people began to comment on it. Mostly, though, people wanted to talk about how one person, by doing his job, could make a difference. "I'm a spoke in a wheel," said the registrar in the emergency room, "and if my co-workers and I are strong together, the wheel spins quickly and the patient's life is saved."

Few of the interviews were conducted in offices. Instead, the narrators led me into their world through endless, dimly lit tunnels, up back stairways and down crowded corridors. We wove around patients on stretchers and pressed our way through a packed emergency room. I wore "scrubs" in the OR suite, "whites" in the food area, and a hospital gown in the neonatal intensive care unit. I walked in the rain with the gardener and shared pastries in the kitchen with the baker. I had a mini-lesson in microsurgery, watched the sun come up with the heart transplant team, and spent eight hours in the labor and delivery suite as thirteen new people entered this world. But the most captivating experience I had was the night I spent in the emergency room, watching the heroics of ordinary people whose singular concern was saving a life.

The day I conducted my first interview, the ground for the new facility was being cleared. As I worked, so did the construction crews, and as this book is completed, the brick is going up on the ten-story building. I know that the new hospital building has been eagerly awaited, but I have grown to love the old place, and I will miss it. After spending so much time here—three years to be exact—I have begun to feel at home within the walls and with the people.

As a medical writer for over ten years, I have found few other institutions that are as impressive as Presbyterian in patient care, education, and research. I think, though, that what impresses me the most is that this hospital had the confidence in its staff and facilities to open its doors to an outsider with a tape recorder, to know that it could stand up to close scrutiny, and that, warts and all, it would still emerge as the extraordinary place that it is.

LIFE AND DEATH

I
THE EMERGENCY ROOM

Friday evening. A steamy start to a summer holiday weekend. Traffic on the George Washington Bridge is leveling off. On the sidewalk outside the emergency entrance to the hospital, a young man in T-shirt and jeans leans against a parked car, tapping his foot as his radio blares Madonna.

Less than fifteen yards away, beyond the doors to the emergency room, is area A, the trauma area. The waiting room, painted a murky yellow, is large and well lit; a long counter, behind which sit the ER personnel, runs along one wall. The far end of the counter stops just at the double doors that lead to the rear, which is where the treatment rooms are. Tonight, perhaps because of the holiday, only half the chairs in the waiting room are occupied. Scanning the sparsely filled room and then the clock on the wall, which reads 9:10, the receptionist remarks to the triage nurse, "Isn't it amazing how quiet it is?" "It should only stay like this," the other woman answers.

Across from the reception counter, in the first row of chairs, an obese man with his arm in a sling is nodding off to sleep. Several empty chairs away sits an elderly, gray-haired woman in a flowered dress, grasping a cane between her knees. She whispers something in the ear of the young boy seated next to her, who is holding an ice-filled towel on his eye. Behind them a man rocks his whimpering young son in a stroller.

A surgical intern appears, picks up two charts from the end of the counter, and calls out: "Randy Gaines. Homer Carp." Both boys come forward. Randy, accompanied by his father, is seven years old and has a fishhook caught in his finger. Homer, a teenager in a bloody T-shirt and a Yankee cap, has slammed two fingers in a car door. As the intern leads the patients to a back room, he comments over his shoulder to the triage nurse, "Quiet, tonight. Maybe we'll get lucky."

As soon as he disappears, the phone at the desk rings, its sound jarring the baby in the stroller. It's the dispatcher from EMS (emergency medical service). The nurse listens intently, cradling the phone on her shoulder as she jots notes on a pad. She hangs up the phone and turns to the receptionist. "We've got a jumper on the way! I knew it couldn't last."

As if a button were pushed, the emergency room immediately springs to life. Two nurses and a resident head for the outside ramp to await the ambulance. The clerk inside the treatment area is alerting specialists in the hospital to stand by.

A "jumper," in emergency room slang, is a person who has traveled from the roof of a building to the street, bypassing stairs and elevators. To the emergency room staff, a jumper represents the archetype of the multiple trauma patient. Injuries are usually severe, often involving internal organs. A jumper may appear almost unhurt to the naked eye and yet be moments from death. A cracked rib may have punctured a lung or pierced the heart; a ruptured spleen may have caused massive internal bleeding; a fractured skull may have produced bleeding within and fatal compression of the brain. Action must be fast, efficient and coordinated.

In the crash room, the trauma surgery operating room at the rear of the treatment area where the most serious cases are taken, attendants begin setting up for the arrival of the patient. Outside, following the sounds of its own siren, the ambulance screetches to a halt in front of the ER. The doors swing open and the ER nurses get their first look at the patient, a young man who appears to be in his late twenties. He has dark hair, is slight of build, and is wearing jeans, T-shirt, and sneakers. The accompanying emergency medical technicians (EMTs), who know the layout of the ER almost as well as those who work there, quickly place the stretcher on a gurney and run it through the doors toward the crash room. The nurse outside runs alongside the patient, followed by the nurse at the top of the ramp, the doctor at the front door, and the security guards. It is a comet of activity, trailing a tail of white-coated people.

Once in the crash room, the EMTs will step aside, leaving the patient to the emergency-room staff. Because the patient is unconscious, there is no opportunity to get a history. For the time being, the staff will have to work blind.

As soon as the young man is transferred from the stretcher to the examining table, two nurses go to work cutting his clothes off with large shears. One doctor puts in an intravenous line while another listens to the patient's chest; a third draws blood for typing and cross matching, and a nurse hangs the intravenous bags. The X-ray machine is set and ready to go. The clock on the wall reads 10:05. No one knows who this man is or exactly what happened to him.

Outside the door a doctor talks with the EMS driver. "Have you been able to get anything on him? Any allergies? Any medical history we should know?" The EMT is unable to help, other than to say that it appears the man jumped or fell from the roof of a six-story building to the pavement. No one actually saw it happen. The man was unconscious when they arrived.

In a trauma case, it is standard procedure to evaluate the patient first, stabilize him, and then assess the damage. Evaluation begins with the ABCs: the airway (is it clear?), the breathing, and the circulation. In this case, the man's airway is clear and his respiration is only slightly labored. Suddenly the nurse taking his blood pressure calls out above the crowd, "His pressure's falling! Let's get that IV going!" Color is slowly draining from the patient. Because there are no visible signs of external hemorrhage, he may be bleeding internally. The crucial question is, where is it coming from? It could be from anywhere; the chest, the abdomen, or the muscles of the back or of the thighs.

Intravenous fluids are rapidly pushed into the patient to raise his blood pressure. When his pressure finally goes up, the nurse heaves a sigh of relief. Immediately, the doctors begin to assess the man's injuries, scanning him quickly from head to toe. There appears to be a skull fracture, at least one broken rib, a broken leg, and a broken nose, in addition to lacerations all over his body.

A nurse announces from the doorway to say that the man's mother has arrived. Mrs. Elizabeth Stockwell, a frail, gray-haired woman, still wearing her apron, has been brought to the ER by a friend of her son. "He couldn't have jumped from that roof," she says to the nurse. "He *wouldn't* have done that! He goes up there lots of nights when it's hot. He's a happy boy. He wouldn't have done that . . ." As she answers the nurse's questions, a picture of the jumper begins to emerge. His name is Robert Stockwell. He's twenty-seven, single, works in a liquor store, and lives several blocks from his mother. He's in excellent health. No allergies. Never has shown any signs of depression.

Meanwhile, in the crash room, Stockwell is beginning to regain consciousness. He blinks, then opens his eyes and looks around vacantly. A nurse tells him where he is and that the doctors are taking care of him; that everything will be all right. "Robert, do you remember what happened?" she asks, leaning close to his face to hear the answer. In a barely audible voice, he mumbles one word: "Fell."

Within half an hour, the X rays and the lab reports are back. Both show multiple-system involvement, and it's clear that additional expertise is necessary. Because of Stockwell's altered mental status, a neurologist has been called and is examining him. The general surgeon suspects internal bleeding from a possible ruptured spleen, because bones are broken in that area. The surgical residents have already put in a chest tube on the left side; with all those rib fractures, there's a good possibility that the lungs may be torn, even if it's not obvious on the chest X ray.

The orthopedists are in one corner of the room examining the X rays, which show evidence of fractures of the pelvis and several of the left leg. Stockwell drifts in and out of consciousness. Each time he opens his eyes, a different person is talking to him. With the nurses, doctors, technicians, attendants, and a medical student, there are ten people in the room.

During the hour and a half that Stockwell is being cared for in the crash room, it's business as usual in the rest of the ER. The waiting room, half empty only ninety minutes before, is filling up fast. The emergency room is equipped to treat a large number of people at once, and often does so in the case of a fire or a multivehicle accident on the George Washington Bridge.

Tonight, between 9:45 and 11:15, ten new patients are registered: a fifty-three-year-old construction worker with a severe back spasm; a twenty-two-year-old student who dropped a barbell on his toe; a toddler who fell down a stairwell; a twenty-year-old woman who had a baby four days ago and whose stitches pulled out prematurely; a secretary with a scratched cornea; a woman who thought she had a fish bone caught in her throat; a diabetic in insulin shock; an executive who suffered a heart attack (he subsequently died in the examining room); a woman whose boyfriend slashed her face with a razor; and a homeless man picked up from the streets after a drug overdose.

As the pace in the rest of the emergency room picks up, things in the crash room have begun to quiet down. Robert Stockwell is now considered stable enough to be taken to the operating room, where the general surgeons will locate and control the internal bleeding. After that, the orthopedic surgeons will attend to his broken bones. A plastic surgeon will reduce his broken nose and suture the gashes in Stockwell's face.

The nurse goes out to the waiting area to see Stockwell's mother, who clearly is afraid to see her son. "Just tell me he's gonna be okay," she says, her hands shaking. The nurse kneels down in front of her. "He's on his way to the operating room, Mrs. Stockwell. He'll probably be there well into the night, so you may want to go home and get some rest. The doctors say that if they can stop the internal bleeding, and they think they can, his chances of full recovery look pretty good." The old woman, weeping into the hem of her apron, gets up to leave, holding on to the arm of her son's friend. The surgical intern comes through the door, picks up a new chart from the desk, and calls "Raymond Velasquez . . ."

ALICE RUIZ

Receptionist, Area A

Her office is the waiting room of area A. Her desk is the long counter that separates the staff from the patients. Behind the counter, the quarters are cramped. Doctors are conferring, nurses lean across to talk with patients, a cop squeezes behind a clerk to answer a phone call, the triage nurse is interviewing a patient. The phones are ringing.

She's "salt-of-the-earth." The oldest of thirteen children, she dropped out of school and married at fifteen. She has four boys, ranging in age from twenty-four to five. The oldest works at Presbyterian. Many of the people walking through the emergency room seem to know her. One legless man, wheeling himself past her desk, waves. "Hiya, Ray," she calls, raising a hand that's holding a phone. "How ya doin', girlfriend?" he asks. "Hangin' in," she smiles. "What else can an old broad do, right?" She's in her early forties and has been at this for seventeen years.

The thing with me is, I always wanted to be a nurse. So when I was twenty-five, and my kids were in school, I decided to apply for a job here. I knew there wouldn't be much available because I only went as far as ninth grade. I couldn't even be a nurse's aide because I didn't have a high school diploma. Anyway, I said I'd do anything, just to be working in a hospital, so they sent me to Harkness Pavilion to be a waitress. The gentleman that interviewed me, though, said he didn't think I was the type. I was too young—I don't know what it was. So they sent me up to Group Clinic, where I learned how to read lab reports, how to abbreviate—ICU (intensive care unit), EKG (electrocardiogram), CBC (complete blood count), and so forth. Then one day the receptionist down here got into a fight with the registrar and she walked off the job. I was put in as a temporary and I've never left.

Right away I knew I loved it. I loved being with the people, the action. It was fantastic! Every so often I think about the early days. Especially the thing that happened when I was working here not even two, three weeks. I was young, and I really wanted to make a good impression; I'm working overtime one night and the phone by my desk rings. The guy on the other end says it's the Port Authority Police Department—there was an explosion on the George Washington Bridge. He said they had sent patients to three hospitals in New Jersey but they had thirty burn victims they were bringing in to us right away.

Now I knew I should have transferred a call like that to the unit manager. That's a disaster call, and the rule is you're supposed to alert him first. But, oh no, not Alice. I just tell them to hang on the phone and I go to the back and tell the nurses, "We've got a disaster on our hands!" Then I return to the phone and say, "Okay, bring 'em in."

Well, everybody got really crazy and we proceeded to call every available person in the hospital down here. Extra surgeons, residents. I mean, I had everybody plus their mother down here! Then we started running around pulling available stretchers from every place we could find them. And we were moving, because the bridge is only five minutes from here! Once we had a load of stretchers, we took them outside to the ER ramp and waited for the victims. We're all out there on the ramp, looking in the direction of the bridge. We're waiting. We're looking. Five minutes go by. Ten minutes. Nothing. There we all are, standing there like idiots and nothing's happening; nothing's coming! All of a sudden, I got this weird feeling and it dawned on me—the whole thing had to be a hoax.

I thought I would die! It was probably somebody in a phone booth standing across the street, saying "Ha, ha, ha! Look at that idiot!"

Two weeks I'm here and I had to make a complete ass of myself. There was no reason for me to doubt that it was legit, though. I mean, it *sounded* legitimate—background sounds and all that sort of stuff. Seventeen years and I've never lived that one down. I still have the residents saying, "Another disaster, Alice?"

They're talking about putting up a Plexiglas divider at the counter in the waiting room to protect us from some of the crazy people who wander in here. Everyone else is for it, but I'm not. It's impersonal enough for the patients just being in here. It's a rotten feeling sitting there waiting for five hours. And then having to talk through a little slot in the window? I don't like it at all. I guess they know what they're doing, though. Because crazy things do happen. Like the other day, there was an SSC [special services for children] case in here where they were going to take the child away from the mother because they felt she was abusing it. Well, the mother goes storming out of here with the child in her arms, and the doctors and nurses go running after them. They caught her and brought her back and they took the child. But that wasn't the end of it. Yesterday, the family calls up and threatens everybody. They're coming back, they said, and they're going to shoot everybody up. So I know we probably need the screen for our protection; somebody is always threatening us. But I still don't like the idea.

In this job you have to know how to handle people. I always try to treat them with respect, so I very rarely have trouble. Even some of the drug addicts are my best friends. They see me in the street—"Hi, Alice!" They're our neighbors, these people. The armory across the street is a human storehouse where the homeless sleep, and there's a methadone center on the corner, so there are some seamy characters around here. These guys can really give everybody a hard time. But they're usually fine with me.

I have my dependents here—I say I'm going to put them down at the end of the year as my dependents. They're the drunks and the bums that wander in for no reason that I end up giving a dollar to every day. Joey Rand is one. Everyone here knows Joey. He's very, very old—but there's nothing really the matter with him. Still, he always comes in and comes right to me complaining about something weird like next week he thinks he's going to have a "brain attack." And so I give him a dollar, and say "Okay, Joey, but why don't you go get coffee first?" So he takes the dollar and he leaves. And then I don't see him until the next time. Most of these guys come in here because they have no place else to go. And sometimes if the weather gets bad, they come in just to keep warm.

Most of the time this place is wall-to-wall people. It gets crazy in here. So many people. In the summer we get a lot of patients because it's nice weather, everybody's out drinking and then they decide to kill each other. Have a few drinks and do each other in. But as of the last couple of years, it's been all year round, mostly on the days when the welfare checks come in. We've doubled our ambulance cases, too. We went from something like fifty to sixty a month to two hundred a month.

After being here so long, your attitude can't help but change. Especially when you see somebody come in with a Medicaid card, dressed better than you'll ever be able to dress. Or when you see the way some people act

. . . or overreact. And that's putting it mildly. We had one patient who came in with abdominal pain. She laid down in front of my desk and started rolling. I'm not kidding! She rolled across the floor, bumping into the chairs. Knocking them down. "Ai-ai-ai." And everyone's trying to stop her. Or they come in with husbands or boyfriends and they think they're dying or they're passed out but I see them fluttering their eyes—so I put two ammonia capsules under their noses. *That* revives them—*real* fast!

Sometimes we get them where they won't talk. They're giving us the silent treatment, you know? So I say, "She won't talk, okay, she won't talk." I mean, if you don't want to say how you're feeling, how're we supposed to know what the problem is? She had a fight with her boyfriend or whatever and she has to play this role of dying. Some women are like that. They're always "dying." Nonsense. So you see things like that, your attitude can't help but change. You try not to, but you do.

You have to harden yourself to some of the things that go on in here. It aggravates me most when someone brings in a five-year-old kid who's been hit by a car, and no parent is with him. Then two hours later the mother shows up and she's hysterical because her child was hit. Why wasn't she with her five-year-old child? I can't stand the hypocrisy. I can't stand that nonsense of the devoted mother. Where the hell was the mother when it happened? When I see burns, when I hear about child abuse, sexual abuse, I'd knock them on their asses. I really would.

They had a thing here where a courtesy award was given to certain employees. Patients nominated the employees and the award was written up in the hospital magazine. I won the first one. I was nominated by a patient whom I had seen numerous times here and had never really gone out of my way for. I just did what I would do for anybody else, and he nominated me. I feel foolish about something like that. I get really uncomfortable. I don't know how to take a compliment at all. Insult me, I can handle it. But give me a compliment . . . No way.

It's a lot of work. As administrations change, policies change, and I can get in a lot of trouble for doing more than I'm supposed to do, which is basically what I get in trouble for all the time. Someone's always on my case. I can't change, though. I care for these people. I'm the mother, you know? I'm the eternal mother.

MAX SALAZAR
Registrar, Area A

He sits at one end of the reception counter in the waiting area. A short, stocky man, he was a boxer when he was growing up in Puerto Rico. "Twice I reached the finals of the Golden Gloves." He turned professional and fought for four more years. "Then, after seventeen fights, of which I won eleven, I took a terrible beating. So I left fighting, went to college, and got a job.

"I used to work in the investigations office of the city of New York—I was there under two different mayors. Then, in 1977, the job situation got real bad and I was out of work, so I applied here. The man who interviewed me recognized my name right away. "Hey," he says, "I hear your name at those Latin music concerts at the Garden. And I listen to you over the radio on Saturdays." I have a Spanish music program on WBAI and WKCR at Columbia University. So that sort of helped me get the job. That, and I passed the typing test."

A registrar is a person who marshals information from the patients who come in here for treatment. We do what they call up-front registration. After a person has been seen by the triage nurse, we ask them to fill out a form with their insurance; or if they have no insurance, just their personal information. Years ago we really took a beating financially when we took everybody's word about who they were and where they lived. So now I ask them for identification. It's easy for me to catch someone in a lie, because when I was an investigator for the city, I learned all the zip codes in the city of New York. So if someone gives me an address and they give me the wrong zip code, right away I know they don't live there. My experience as an investigator for the city of New York was like going to the Harvard School of Law and Criminology.

Most people are pretty straight with us, but not everyone. We ask them lots of questions: name, mother's and father's name, social security number. We ask to see any insurance cards. But they're very smart, some of the patients. They know how to get around that. They use other people's Medicare and Medicaid cards. And they get away with it!

Different people have different ways of trying to fool you. With Spanish-speaking people and people from the South American countries, the Canal Zone, the Caribbean, they use a name like John Rodriguez Rivera. Rodriguez is the father. Rivera is the mother. Sometimes it's Rivera Rodriguez. Being of Hispanic heritage, I understand all that. Look, we're not going to turn them away, but we don't like to get fooled, that's all.

There are so many patients here, there are times when I don't even look up from my desk for three hours—I just get one right behind the other. Yesterday, I saw forty-eight people. There are times I see sixty. Not all of them are here because they're ill, though. Some of them come in here just because they're so lonely, they just want to see other people, to hear some voices. They don't bother anybody. When I'm not busy, I ask one of them to come to the desk and I say, "Hello. How are you?" You'd be surprised what a difference that makes. That's all they want.

I guess one reason I feel for them is because I'm so grateful for my own good health. When I see people being moved in here on the stretcher with that pallid look and limp body, boy, it's a feeling that I'm so glad that I'm alive and I'm on this side of the counter. When I started working here, I learned about all the afflictions people have lupus, leukemia, kidney problems. I had no *idea* there was so much—all those illnesses I don't even know about. My mother, my family, we're free of that. I just feel so lucky.

One night here I'll never forget as long as I live. I was working the four-to-twelve shift so I went out to dinner about eight and I came back fifteen minutes early, so I sat down to read the newspaper. Suddenly I heard a scream. One of the nurses yelled, "It's Dr. Wood!" Everybody ran to the front as the ambulance attendants wheeled one of our young doctors into the emergency room. He had been shot in the chest and he was bleeding all over the place. It looked to me like he was already dead. He was a resident and he had been working in the emergency room and we all knew him. The poor man had just gone home for dinner. He was walking his dog on Riverside Drive, and apparently someone tried to hold him up. He was shot and killed. My God—we had just talked to him! It was terrible! Everybody was so shaken up. Especially the nurses who were close to him. It's hard, really hard, when you know the person. He was so young.

I sometimes wonder how these things can happen. The other day I came in and the nurses were talking about this man who took out a machine gun and shot another man to death on 172nd Street. It was an argument over a parking space. How does a man walk around with a machine gun and not be seen? We had a nurse come in a year ago at eleven-thirty in the morning. She was raped on the Eighth Avenue subway. How could she be raped? Where were the cops? Nobody saw anything? Eleven o'clock in the morning! Where were the cops, I said? They're never the same after that, you know? They're never the same.

When someone is brought in by ambulance, I still have to get his information. If they're at all conscious, I'll at least try to get the name of their next of kin. I can't stand it though if there's blood dripping from their fingertips, and they're lifeless—when you see them with the gash in the head or in the throat or something like that, or the bullet-riddled face, you know . . . And you have to ask them their name—or their next of kin. Sometimes that's not so easy. About two years ago the EMS came running through the doors with a man on a stretcher. He had been shot in the chest. The police were there, and a woman, and everyone was around him. As they were bringing him in I asked if he had a next of kin. And the policeman said, "Yeah, his wife," and he nods at the lady. And I look at her and I see she's holding his ankles, tugging, trying to remove his socks. And the cops are yelling at her, "Get away from there! Leave him alone!" And she says, "No! Give me his socks!" They wouldn't let her go into the crash unit, so she's pleading by the door, "Can I have his socks? Please, I need his socks!" I mean, here's a man, dying, with three bullet wounds in his chest, and his wife wants his socks! In the crash room, they pulled off his socks. He had something like five or six hundred dollars in there! He was a drug dealer—and it turns out he was carrying the bank. Here I'm wondering, what the heck is she worrying about his socks for?

Sometimes it falls to me to tell the next of kin about an accident. One time, though, there was a woman waiting here and I made the mistake of telling her that her baby had expired. Oh, my God! She went berserk! It was awful. I was told never to do that again. And I never did. Now, if there's a death, I refer them to the unit manager. If it's just an accident, and I'm asked to call a family member, I say, "This is the emergency officer." Then I warn them not to get excited about what I'm going to say. "Your son is here; your daughter's here—there was a car accident, but it's a superficial laceration. They wanted me to tell you that they're feeling fine and they'll be home as soon as they're discharged." I stop there all the time, because I still remember how I shocked that woman when I told her that the baby died.

This is not an easy job. There's a lot of stress involved, and some people just crawl underneath your skin. But here I feel like I make a difference. If I have to perform in a crisis, I know I'm gonna come through. If someone comes in and if I see them sweating, if I see that white, pallid look that you get when you're about to have a heart attack, right away I take them into the back myself. In fact, on three or four occasions during the last four or five years, I think I've saved their lives.

Time is of the essence in a place like this. You lose seconds, you could lose a life. What you need here is speed. And I can do things fast—you know, getting information, and other stuff. We're all that way down here. I'm just a spoke in the wheel. One spoke. Alice is another spoke; the surgeon is a spoke; the anesthesiologist is a spoke. The nurse. And if we all do our jobs, that wheel's going to spin, and we're going to save that patient's life.

TONY IRIZARRY

Security Officer, Area A

He is twenty-six. He's stationed in the waiting room, just outside of the double doors that lead to the treatment area. He wears a "hard blue" uniform and sports a dark, neatly trimmed mustache. He looks very much like a New York City cop.

Mostly I just try to keep peace in here. They try to take people in turn, but people who are sick or in pain and have to wait a long time to be seen start to get agitated. If somebody comes in and he's really bleeding a lot, and the person before him isn't, the "bleeder" will be taken first. Some people don't understand that, though, and that's where the fights begin. You might get a few gunshots in at one time, and you might have five people waiting with other wounds that need sewing up—and you only have three or four surgeons—so the people who are waiting an hour to be seen are now going to have to wait three hours. Or if you're waiting for something like gallstones and someone comes in with a cardiac arrest, that's going to pull three medical doctors and three nurses, plus you might already have twenty, twenty-five patients waiting.

Sometimes a mother will bring in a kid, say, two years old, with a head wound. Scalps bleed a lot because there's a lot of blood vessels there, but those wounds are generally not serious enough that the kid will lose consciousness. Still, the mother doesn't know that so she keeps getting up and coming to one of us and saying, "How long do I have to wait? How long do I have to wait?" And you keep explaining, and all of a sudden ten people side with her and they're going to attack you! You'd better be a pretty good peacemaker then. I can tell who's getting agitated just by looking, so I try to get to a person before they get out of their seats and start trouble. Most of the time, though, just seeing somebody in a uniform keeps them in line.

Some of the gunshots that are brought in on stretchers are talking like nothing happened. It's unbelievable! You see somebody with two shots in the head and he wants to get off the stretcher—he wants to leave. Crazy! Last week a triple gunshot came in. We called all the doctors down from the operating room—chief surgeons, and all that—and the guy doesn't want to stay! He has three gunshots in him and he gets off the stretcher!

You get used to working the ER. You're trained how to use your nightstick, but everything else is just common sense. I think the most important thing is not to turn your back on the room. You never know what's going to happen. Someone might come in with a drug overdose, or they're having family problems and you can never be sure what they're going to do. Sometimes we have to search people to make sure they don't have anything on them. We've taken knives off some real old people. Like this seventy-year-old man who was really out of it. You can't leave somebody like that alone. He was on the stretcher and we had tied a couple of straps around it so he wouldn't fall off. So he reached under his pants and he pulled out a knife, and he cut the ties off. We had to wrestle with him to get the knife away!

We get a lot of drug-related emergencies in here, because the hospital handles the area from 145th Street all the way up to 225th Street. We've got probably the biggest area in the city. The overdoses who are brought in unconscious are given a drug called Narcan to counteract whatever they have in their system—cocaine, heroin, whatever. The minute they get it, they want to jump right off the stretcher. The drug overdoses are a hassle. They do everything—they spit, they pee on you, they scratch you. And you don't want to be anywhere near them if you don't have to, what with AIDS and everything else.

Some people OD regularly. Like Rhoda. She's only about twenty-five but she comes in here every month, like clockwork. The first of the month, when she gets her welfare check, she's in with her overdose. Lately she's been getting seizures, which isn't a good sign. She either walks in here by herself, or EMS finds her in the street, or one of her other druggie friends sees her lying unconscious on the floor and they call an ambulance. Sometimes the police bring her in. And she's got a mouth on her! Forget it. She screams. She cusses at everyone—she's just awful.

The thing is, if the police or the EMS see anyone who's unconscious on the street, they have to try to revive them. If they can't revive them, they bring them into the hospital. So we constantly get these people who get their money, then get their bottle, and they empty it. They fall, they hit their head. They're unconscious. They end up in the emergency room. We see that they get something to eat, something to drink. They've got so much alcohol in them at that point, though, that you have to wait until the alcohol level is low enough that it's safe to let them leave. That could take eight, maybe ten hours. Some of these people have lice and other bugs. I don't delouse them, but I might have to help the nurses give them a bath. Sometimes, the nurse is in there trying to wash them and they start swinging at the nurse. So I help when I can.

Rhoda's one who always starts swinging. The minute the Narcan works, she starts screaming, she wants to get out. But she can't get out until the tox level is down. The Narcan counteracts the drugs, but it doesn't knock them out of the system. If you can't walk out on your own, we can't let you leave. So she might be here for two shifts, until her blood and urine levels are normal. And then within an hour you'll see her back on the street.

I know a lot more about people and medicine now than I did when I started. Sometimes you can tell how sick somebody is by how they look. I might see somebody sitting there waiting, and all of a sudden he doesn't look so good. So I'll get the nurse. "Look, this guy is anoxic, sweating, pale, holding his chest." That spells a possible heart attack to me. I know the symptoms just from being here. I mean, you can't hang out in the emergency room and not pick up something. You get three kids and right away you can pick out the one with a broken arm. How do you know it's a broken arm? We've had about ten in the last six months, and they all look alike.

It's interesting when we get the new security recruits. We just hired maybe eight guys in the last three weeks. We bring one through each day to show him the emergency room. You can usually tell right off who's going to work out and who's not. Yesterday, they brought in a guy who had been robbing a sixth-floor apartment somewhere, fell out the window. Six flights. Right on his back. The new recruit who was here looked at this messed up guy and—nothing. It didn't faze him. So he'll probably work out. On the other hand, we've lost maybe three people that worked emergency the first day. They just didn't know it was part of their job to go into the crash room. Even if a guy's bleeding all over the place, security still has to take his clothes, go through his pockets, see what his name is. If he's unconscious, we try to get any information that we can. If they're dead on arrival, usually you wait for the cops to tell the family. Or you can let the chaplain do it, or you can let one of the nurses or the doctors do it.

I like the action of this job. I can't stand it if nothing exciting happens all day. Like the day I don't go into the crash room. You just stand here all day. There's no fights, there's no quarrels, there's no fire alarms. Those things make the day go quickly. A gunshot will kill an hour like it was five minutes. The patient's unconscious. The police come in. The detectives come in. The family comes in. I gotta take the clothing. I gotta look through it, try to get an address. Most guys would probably prefer dealing with somebody with a stomachache or a headache. But I'm always saying, give me a gunshot or a stab wound any day.

MEG BARRY, R.N.

Clinical Nurse Instructor

Her prematurely gray hair is cut short in a no-nonsense bob. She has a serious air about her although every now and then a soft smile breaks across her face. Her job is to teach experienced nurses how to work in the emergency room. The course runs ten weeks, during which time the nurses learn to handle everything from acute asthma to rape.

The orientees are a little scared in the beginning. Every orientee has that "new kid on the block" look. And since some people who frequent the emergency room can be very manipulative, you try to teach your nurses how not to be taken in by every story that comes in. You'll get a family who will bring in a woman, and they're all hysterical. "She can't breathe! She can't breathe!" And yet this lady's yelling and screaming. So you say, "Look, if she couldn't breathe, she couldn't yell. She's *got* to be breathing." Then the whole waiting room stands up and everybody starts hollering, "She's dying! She's dying! You're not taking care of her!" But I know she's just hysterical. And maybe I have a couple of chest pains being evaluated and there are other people who are sicker than she is.

Things that happen here stay with you for a long time. Not too long ago a guy came running into the emergency room—barged in—he had cut his hand on glass, he said, and he was bleeding like crazy. I brought him in and I put him in one of the side rooms and the guy kept saying, "My hand! It's falling off! I'm going to lose my hand!" I was trying to quiet him down and see how extensively he had hurt himself, when I heard a lot of commotion in the hallway. I looked out, and we had a gunshot wound to the chest coming in on a stretcher. So I left this man for a minute and went to the crash room.

The victim was an elderly lady. I remember she was so small and I kept looking at her, thinking, "Who would shoot a little lady? Who would *do* such a thing?" Well, what had happened was she and her husband had gone down to the store that afternoon to get a loaf of bread, and while they were waiting to pay for it, a robber came in. He yelled at everybody to move out of the way, but the lady didn't understand English, so she must have just stood there. So he shot her.

Her husband rode down in the ambulance with her and he was waiting outside of the room while we tried frantically to save her. The doctors tried everything. We worked on her quite a while, but we just couldn't save her. When I realized it was hopeless, I left to go back to the guy with the cut hand. And just as I'm walking out of the crash room, the guy comes running out of the examining room looking for me—and the lady's husband spots him! This little old man sees this huge guy in the hallway, and starts to jump on him! Well, it turned out that the guy who cut his hand did it robbing a grocery store. And *he* was the guy who shot the lady.

He just made it down to the hospital before she did.

It's real frustrating. Here's this guy; I've given him attention, tried to get a doctor in there to take care of his hand, and he's just killed a person. You say to yourself, "I really don't care if he does lose his hand. Let him bleed to death!" You know? I mean, he just killed somebody's mother! This poor little lady. She just went down to the store to get a loaf of bread. Where's the justice?

There are always cases that will take you a couple of days to get out of your mind either because they're so horrid or they just touched you. You try very much not to take them home, you try very much to just keep the work here. I remember one that happened, I think it was just before Christmas, where a mother was giving a bath to her nine-month-old baby and had just gotten the four-year-old dressed. The mother said that she just turned her head for a minute to say something to the older child and when she turned back, her baby had drowned. The ambulance brought the baby in and we tried to save it, but we couldn't bring the baby back. She was a young parent—nineteen years old. They had just moved here from Greece so they were away from their family. She called her husband at work and he met her here. The police were involved because the police said that it might be murder. So their apartment became a crime scene, and the family wasn't going to be allowed to go back in. And the police were here in the back interrogating the mother, asking her exactly what happened. And you could see that the mother was totally grief stricken and the father was standing there saying, "No, no, no! She wouldn't do this, I know she wouldn't do this!" And it was right before Christmas, and the police were just doing their job. But you remember some stories.

Like "the machete lady." She was attacked while she was in bed in her apartment by a guy with a machete. The way we heard it, she knew the guy. We never really knew for sure what happened, but when he came at her she must have put her arms up to protect herself and he just hacked away. When she was brought in, both arms were laying on top of her, one just hanging on by a piece of skin. The bones and everything had been cut through. And yet, she was awake and alert! He had also cut the back of her head so that the skin flap was open enough that you could see her spinal column. It was unbelievable! Everyone was stunned by that one. We all stood there and looked at her for a minute, and I remember saying to one of the nurses, "Jeeze, I've gotta get a blood pressure! How am I gonna' get a blood pressure? I need an arm!"

We stabilized her down here, gave her tons of blood, and then they took her up to the operating room. Subsequently we heard that she was in surgical ICU. I don't know if they made any attempts to reattach both of her arms; I don't know if they were able to. But the most amazing part of it all is, we subsequently heard that she didn't even press charges against the guy! I'll never understand that one.

We get our share of rape victims. Unfortunately, rape victims run the gamut. Some women come in here because they were actually raped, and some come to use rape as a tool to get back at whoever raped them. For example, a girl comes in who went over to her former boyfriend's apartment to pick up her stuff, and he rapes her. You say to yourself, why did she go over there? Why did she place herself in that situation? You wonder if it was truly rape. But you can't be judgmental. The other end of the spectrum is where a lady was raped in the parking lot right below her building. The guy tells her that if she goes to the police about it—he knows that she has two children—he's going to "take care" of the children. She was raped on a Tuesday night and came in on Thursday to get medication in case the guy had any disease. So we said to her, "That's a crime of violence; you have to call the police." She said, "No! If you call the police, he's going to kill my children!" We said, "Listen, he's probably doing this to other women. You can help the police capture him. If the police come, if you don't want to talk to them, you don't have to, but maybe you can prevent this from happening again." She finally did talk to them, and we heard they caught the guy.

We have a rape protocol here, a rape program; we call a rape advocate to stay with the woman while she's here. And a social worker from GYN will call twenty-four to forty-eight hours later to make sure she's all right. If she thinks the victim is in any trouble, she'll usually refer her to the appropriate agency to help take care of the situation. Lots of times the husband is here; they're usually so upset you need to pull them aside and talk to them a little bit. It's a very hard situation for them sometimes.

One of the things you have to learn down here is to be able to remove yourself from the situation when you're no longer in control of yourself. You work very, very hard. You're physically and mentally toxic by the end of the day, and when people are cussing and swearing at you and accusing you, sometimes you lose your cool. I remember situations where Alice has stood between me and a patient, because she knew that I was losing control of myself—not that I was going to hit the patient, but I was starting to yell back, and that doesn't serve any purpose. You need to drop back from the situation and let somebody else deal with the people, because you just can't deal with it anymore—sometimes you've done as much as you can and you just know you've reached your limit.

BARBARA TANG

Housekeeper, Area A

She came to the United States from Jamaica fifteen years ago. She has never worked anywhere but Presbyterian Hospital. Three of her six children work here.

When I started working in Housekeeping, I really didn't know what part of the hospital I was going to be assigned to. Happily for me, they started me out in Babies' Hospital. I really wanted that. I just love kids. "Lord," I said, "if I should get this job I would prefer to work in Babies' Hospital." And that's where they put me.

I loved Babies', and I loved the children. I got to know lots of them real well, especially the ones who would come in, go home, come back. I was there for eleven years. They all knew me, those kids. Then, three years ago they transferred me to the emergency room.

At first I really didn't like coming down here. It wasn't the work. It was the environment. A lot of things go on in emergency. A lot of terrible things. And even though your job is to clean, you get involved in everything that goes on. As for the work, it's about the same as in Babies' Hospital. A little harder, maybe, because you know how adults can be. Usually they're worse than kids. They make more waste. Drop things on the floor on purpose. Especially in that asthma room. They take those things that they give them to spit in and they use them and drop them on the floor. They just leave it there. They're probably thinking the hospital has somebody to clean up so let *them* do it. So that's the thing. It's not the work. It's just the people that you have to deal with.

I'm never in a room when the patient is there. It's when they finish with the patient and take him upstairs that I go in the room and clean up. Oh, I've seen a lot of blood when they die. Some of them get bullets in the heart and the doctors open the chest and everything is just open right there. That stuff doesn't bother me. I don't know, blood never seemed to bother me. This place could be swimming in blood and it wouldn't bother me. You know what really bothers me? Smells. The smell of stool or shoes or vomit. If a patient vomits on the floor, I have to clean it up. Sometimes the stretchers are right by the sink and they do it in the sink and I have to clean it up from there. Well, I just hold my breath the best I can and I clean it. The smell is the thing that upsets me most, but blood really never bothers me.

The first time I saw an open chest was when a young guy had been stabbed five times. Five stabs! I think one was in the heart. They opened his chest right there in the room. People were running in and out and you could see a little from the hallway. I was surprised to see the chest opened and the doctor with his hand in there. But I wasn't scared or anything or nervous about it. I just looked.

We get so many teenagers who come in with gun shots and stab wounds; seventeen, eighteen, nineteen years old. Some of them are unconscious. Or they're dead. I watch as they wheel them in—and I look at them coming out. Sometimes I'm cleaning outside the door with them right in there, dead. Even that really doesn't bother me. Everybody is surprised to know that I do these things, and some of the other workers are scared stiff. People tell me I should be a nurse.

They had a class for us the other day, telling us about the different types of diseases there are and how you can get them. They told us what we're supposed to look for. For instance, when we have a patient with AIDS, there's supposed to be a sign on the door telling you to take extra precautions. But an AIDS patient's germs are not airborne. You don't get AIDS from the air so you don't have to put on a mask. But you do have to put on your gloves. Now if the patient should have meningitis, you have to be careful, or if the patient has TB. You can catch TB from the air. I'm always learning something, or I'm trying to. Just for myself. I listen to hear what the doctors ask for. The things that they use. Things like that. I could have been a nurse's aide long ago if I wanted to, but I like cleaning. They say it's in my nature. Even my horoscope would say I'm a good housekeeper.

TONY ROGERS

Senior Attendant, Area A

We're in his first-floor apartment across the street from the hospital. The living-room curtains are drawn for privacy and the windows are closed to drown out the noise from the street traffic. Still, the sounds of construction filter through, and twice our conversation is halted by the shrill of an ambulance's siren. It's a spacious living room, dimly lit, with an oversized stereo set resting in the corner and a large portrait of Martin Luther King hanging on the wall.

He pulls out a framed award and reads it: "Certificate of Appreciation Award to Anthony Rogers for outstanding and dedicated service in the Presbyterian Hospital." It's signed by the hospital president, Dr. Thomas Q. Morris.

We handle the disasters. The gunshots, stabbings, somebody falls out of a window, somebody gets their legs cut off, somebody's eye gets knocked out. These are the things that I deal with every day. When a case like that comes in, it's the job of the attendant to set up IVs and to assist the doctors and the nurses. We do whatever they need. Like running to the lab, running upstairs to the blood bank, rushing the patient to the OR. Things like that.

Plenty of this stuff gets to you. Like seeing someone brought in with their legs cut off. First time that happened to me was in 1977. This guy got run over by a train in the subway, and both of his legs were severed. The EMS called ahead, so we knew they were bringing him in. Now usually when a trauma case like that comes in, the first thing they do is draw his blood for type and cross match in case he needs a transfusion. They put the blood in vials and then I put the vials in a cup of ice and run it up to the lab. So when I heard they were bringing this guy up—I ran to get the ice. Within minutes, two of the EMTs came bursting into the crash room with the man on a stretcher, followed by a third who was holding the man's legs. The last guy handed the legs to one of the doctors, who immediately turned around and handed them to me. He said, "Here, put them in the ice!" Now, I'm standing there holding these two Styrofoam cups full of ice chips and I said, "Do what?" It took me a second to realize what he was talking about, but for a minute there, it was a real scene.

Until recently, part of my duty was taking dead bodies down to the morgue and putting them in the freezer. Now they have a morgue attendant come up and get the body. But sometimes if he needs assistance, he'll ask me to come down with him—especially if the person is large. One particular night he was busy and they asked me to take the body down by myself. They usually put the body in the room next to the utility room where the attendants make up the instrument trays for the doctors, so that's where I went to get the body. When I opened the door, though, I didn't see a body. So I looked in another room they call the ID room— that's the room where they clean up infections, and I see this body on the bed with a sheet covering it up. So I just went in and started wheeling the bed out. Well, the body sat up! It was one of the doctors and he was sleeping. I jumped and I ran to the nurses' station and said, "That body is not dead!" I could hear the doctor laughing from down the hall. See, I didn't even stay long enough to look at who it was. I was out of there! Boy, I mean that was . . . Everybody laughed all night. Every time they looked at me, they just laughed.

Part of my job is to see that everything is well stocked for the shift that I'm going into. I check everything: the rooms, the IV cart, the blood cart, and the general supplies. This way, when an emergency does come in, nobody will have to be calling me. "How come we don't have this and how come we don't have that?" Some people just go in and if it isn't stocked, well, so what?" But that's not how I do things.

I saved a life once. It happened one day when I was taking a patient through the tunnel to the Eye Institute. Just as we got on to the elevator and the doors closed behind us, his heart stopped. I noticed it immediately when he started turning a different color. I looked at his eyelids and right away started giving him CPR. When we got to the fourth floor, as soon as the door opened, I yelled that we had an arrest. So right away, everybody started going every which-a-way, getting everything they needed. I stayed with him until everybody got there. That was it, and then I left. Later his son came and told me that everything was fine. He thanked me and the nurses congratulated me and everything. It was no big deal. I just did the best thing I knew how to do.

I've delivered a couple of babies. They don't train us to do that but sometimes you have no choice. Once a lady pulled up in a cab. Someone came running to me from the emergency ramp, "Somebody needs help getting out of a cab!" They didn't say what's wrong with the person. So I didn't know until I got there. I leaned in to help her out and darned if she wasn't having a baby. She was on her way and so I just told her to push, push, push. Then I told the cab driver to go get a doctor. Any doctor. Or a nurse. Just as long as they got out there! Two nurses came out and one of the doctors and they took over. But I delivered that baby. I don't know how I did it, I was so nervous.

For eight years I've been trying to get a job in the dialysis unit. I hear only good things about it there. They say you learn something new every day. And you get a chance to move up. See, where I'm at now as a senior attendant, I'm not moving anywhere. I'm only going to be a senior attendant and that's all. You go to dialysis, they train you, you learn about those machines. Something like that would make me feel more important than I do in the emergency room.

I just want a chance to prove myself. My mother always told all of her children, "If you can't get to be what you want to be, try to be the best at whatever you do." She said, "You may not be able to be a doctor, you may not be able to be a lawyer, or whatever you wanted to be; but whatever it is, even if you aren't anything but a janitor, try to be the best janitor there is." That's the way she taught all of us. And that's been my motive. Just go to work, and try to be the best. And that's how I think I would feel if I was to go into dialysis. Now, a lot of my friends think dialysis will be boring for me after the ER. But I don't think so. Not really. It would be more or less, I think, for me . . . tranquillity.

In January 1987 Tony Rogers became a dialysis technician.

JAN CONNOLLY, R.N.

Nursing Director, Area A

We talk in a small room that is used for everything from consoling bereaved families to detaining suspected criminals. Our conversation is interrupted periodically by nurses keeping her informed of new arrivals. "In the beginning I wanted to be a teacher. My whole life, they told me I was going to be a teacher. And then when I got to college there were no teaching jobs. So nursing was the other alternative." She has been here for ten years. She has been nursing director for three.

There are two kinds of nurses who work the ER. Those who burn out within a year or two and those who stay for four, five, six years, or even longer. It's a tough place to be in for a long time. It's a very high-stress job. Yet there are times when it's incredibly exciting. You have emergencies where everything clicks and everybody becomes part of a team that works without any verbal communication and saves a life. Days like that, things just fall into place. But there are also times when it's a lot less glamorous than people think. People don't think of delousing patients when they think of an ER, but that's part of our job. People don't realize what someone looks like who lives in the street. When you're the first one to come in contact with them, it's not real glamorous.

The training is specialized. Not just any nurse can come in here and work right away. There's a high priority placed on your ability to assess a patient. The ER nurse is supposed to be able to tell whether a patient is sick or not and if so, how sick. That's a skill that takes a lot of time to develop. It's called triaging. It's a French term that means there are three categories you put people into: emergent, urgent, and nonurgent. Emergent means life threatening; they need to be seen right away. Urgent means they need care, but not within a few minutes. And nonurgent means they can wait. In area A we see, for the most part, emergent and urgent adult medical patients and all surgical and trauma patients regardless of age or severity.

There's a small desk out in the waiting room behind the clerical desk. After a patient signs in, the triage nurse will sit the patient down and take a history, vital signs, collect specimens, if necessary, and then decide where the patient will be seen and in what order. Then the patient either waits or gets brought into the treatment area right away.

The average number of patients we see in area A is a hundred seventy-five to two hundred a day. And that's just in area A. Area B sees mostly nonurgent medical patients. It's almost like a walk-in clinic, but it is part of the ER. A twenty-year-old with an upper respiratory infection would go to area B. Somebody with a painful urinary-tract infection, the patient who can wait to be seen, would go to area B.

For the most part, people show up first at area A. I remember working one night—this was when I was a staff nurse. It was a crazy night, extremely busy. Ambulances were rolling in, the place was off the wall, and this little old man comes in and I'm assessing him. He tells me he has abdominal pains, so I said to him, "Sir, how long have you had the pain?" He said, "Since 1953." And I said, "Sir, I was born in 1953." Then I said, "What made you come to the emergency room today?" And he looked at me, and he was serious, and he said, "Nurse, I just couldn't take the pain any more."

We have one or two security officers around area A at all times. Sometimes more, depending on what the needs of the area are. Security plays a role in traffic control. You have people in and out those automatic doors all the time, so there has to be someone monitoring who goes in and out. Also, people do get unruly, particularly in the waiting area, where they're concerned about relatives or someone not feeling well. They feel they're not being seen quickly enough. Things can get out of hand very fast, so you need someone to keep control of that.

Someone who is suicidal and has perhaps taken an overdose, needs to be cleared here medically first before he can be cleared psychiatrically. If someone has swallowed a bottle of Valium, we can't send him to the psychiatrist right away. What's a psychiatrist going to do? First we've got to take care of the fact that he's got too much Valium on board. Then the psychiatrist can worry about why he took it.

The people from the armory across the street, a few of the homeless, come in here for a free lunch occasionally. They know that we have sandwiches and things here for those patients who are here a long time. Depending on what their illness is, providing they can eat, we have to feed them. Some of our patients are here all day and all night, just for observation. You can't starve them to death. So these homeless guys know we have food here and they come in for a warm place to stay, and a meal. Some of them are truly sick. There are a lot of alcoholics who have seizures, and most of them do have chronic medical problems that can act up at any time. But a lot of times they just want a place to go. All they have to say is they need to see a physician, and legally we must see them. We must see every patient who comes in here. How are you to know that a patient isn't really sick? You can't pass judgment. We can't send them out until we've cleared them. So they say they have something or other wrong, say chest pain, and we have to write up the history, do the cardiogram, take the proper blood tests, and prove that, in fact, the chest pain is not something life threatening. And then this man ends up with a meal and a warm place to stay. He gets a shower and clean clothes.

Some of the street people who come in have to be cleaned up before the doctors examine them. A lot of them have lice and have to be deloused. Well, we can't clean them and put them back into filthy clothes, so we give them clothes we keep around for that purpose. We're not allowed to throw out anyone's things without asking them. So we ask them if it's okay if we get rid of their clothes. I love it when they say "No." That means you have to get a plastic bag for these bug-ridden clothes, and you have to give them back to them.

When we give them clean clothes, they usually get things that members of our nursing staff have brought in. We ask the staff, when they're cleaning out their closets, to bring in usable clothes so we have something to put on these people. Well, it wasn't too long ago that one of the nurses said to me, "You don't know how unnerving it is to be walking across the street to get a cup of coffee and to see this bum wearing my Jamaica T-shirt and my Jordache jeans!" Somehow you picture your clothes going to needy people who appreciate them, not the man who's sitting on the corner with a bottle of Thunderbird.

One time we got a call that someone had had a cardiac arrest downstairs in the subway. They brought the man into the ER, right back to the crash room. He was in full arrest. As soon as that happens, everyone's adrenaline starts flowing and the team just kicks in and starts to work. One of the first things you do whenever someone is brought to the crash room is you cut their clothes off. You literally take a pair of scissors and cut them right off so you can work on the patient. If somebody is in real trouble, you can't waste time trying to lift them up to pull their clothes off. And if they're injured, you don't want to move them. So with a big pair of scissors you just slash their clothes straight up the leg, straight up the arm, and everything comes off. Anyway, we went through the whole procedure, the man was in and out of cardiac arrest, we finally got him stable and shipped him off to the coronary unit.

No sooner was he rolled out of the ER and up to the floor than the transit cop comes running into the ER again and says, "You got another one down there! We're bringing up another one from the subway." Now everyone's pumped. Here we just finished with this big arrest and they roll another man in on the stretcher. He's not responsive at all. So while the doctors are attending to him, once again, out come the scissors and we start in on his clothing. Then, two seconds into this thing, someone says, "Wait a minute! Wait a minute! I have a pulse!" Well, his respirations were okay, and as it turned out, according to the doctors the man had just fainted. A little old Oriental man. Polite as could be. He was just so grateful to us for saving his life. He thanks us and says he doesn't know what he would have done if we hadn't gotten him from the subway. So he gets up to leave and he's walking out and here he is . . . one side of his clothing is in shreds. I mean, the man had a suit—a full three-piece suit, the raincoat, everything on. And now, one side of his clothing is completely intact and the other side, the left leg, the left arm, are sliced all the way up! He's walking out with one side of his clothing flapping in the wind, and he's saying, "Thank you, thank you, thank you," and bowing.

I guess the saddest things to me are families. I don't really think about anything during an arrest except what must be done to save the patient. It's when a patient dies and the family arrives that my emotions come forward. It's then that I feel so useless. A little old lady was brought in recently. She had arrested and she didn't make it. The only person with her was her husband, and he was in his eighties. He was alone. We had to bring him back to view her and after he viewed the body, he said "Well, I guess I'll be going home now." I was crying and saying, "Please, let me call someone. Please don't go home like this." But he said, "No, no, no, I don't want to call anyone. It's my granddaughter's first holy communion and I don't want to upset the family." I still cry when I think of that man. He left by himself and I thought, "Life is so cruel." To lose your spouse and then walk out alone and just go home alone. Something like that will stay with me for a long time.

Even though I'm the director now, I still pitch in if it's real busy, or if there's a big emergency and the staff can't handle it. They need an extra pair of hands? Most definitely I will step in and be there. I don't think I could work too far from an ER. Here, there's immediate gratification, immediate results. My patients are here, I take care of them, and there's a result. Either they get treated and go home, or they get admitted. Sometimes they die. But each day, I see the results of what we've done here.

KENNETH FINE, M.D.

Medical Director, Emergency Room

━━◞━━━━━━

There is a strong tradition of medicine in his family. His father is a general practitioner and two of his three brothers are doctors. "My father actually tried to talk all of us out of it when we expressed any kind of desire to go into medicine, probably to be sure that the decision was being made objectively and that his love for what he was doing hadn't biased us. He felt medicine was a difficult life, and one needed to be very dedicated if one was going to do it. In fact, he tried to convince us that if we were going to go in that direction, we should give very strong consideration to dentistry. But no one listened."

━━━━━━━━━

I don't think that people who work in emergency rooms consider saving a life an heroic act. It's what they're here to do; it's what they're trained to do; it's what is expected of them. When you save a life, it's usually because you've got a system in place and things are working well. I think the dramatic things in medicine, the great saves—and people in emergency medicine will probably have my head for this—involve things like transplanting a heart. That's medicine and technology at its superb best. Sure, somebody comes into the ER and they've had a heart attack, they have no pulse or blood pressure, they're in ventricular fibrillation and near death and you shock them and the heart rhythm comes back—in the eyes of a lot of people, that's high drama. But that's what people are supposed to do in the ER. If we don't do that, then we're not doing our jobs. And I'll bet dollars to doughnuts most people who work in an ER would agree with that. They would probably look wide-eyed at the fire-rescue guys who rappel down a building from the twelfth story to pluck somebody from a window and they'd say, "Now *that's* heroic!" It's all very relative. It really is.

To a large degree, emergency rooms that serve inner-city populations lose money. But the reimbursement issues are more than just one-dimensional. Certainly the money we get back is not adequate to pay for the care that's provided. Seventy-five dollars, which is our fee, is not enough for what we spend on the average patient coming through the door.

But there's still another issue, and that has to do with who's paying the bill. You have to take into account the patient population that you're serving. A hospital in a different location than ours, seeing sixty thousand patients, might very well have a booming business. Or if seventy-five percent or eighty percent of the problems seen in the emergency room were simple, straightforward, easily handled problems, it might not cost so much. But the sixty thousand patients we take care of include a fairly large percentage who are seriously ill or injured, so the initial cost of taking care of them is quite high and not covered at all by current reimbursement. If a patient is brought in to the ER in cardiac arrest and we resuscitate him in area A, the cost, considering all the people who respond to an arrest and all the equipment it takes, is probably upwards of a thousand dollars. And still, on the books, we are paid seventy-five dollars for that endeavor.

Another problem for us is that our patients don't always pay for their care. The emergency room door is always open. If somebody comes in, by law and by design, we cannot and will not turn them away. They must be seen by a physician. And once you've provided the physician evaluation, you might as well go all the way—it's sort of like giving somebody a kiss on the cheek and then . . . So, because we don't demand to be paid before service is rendered, we have to rely on the information the patient provides us for billing purposes. That information is a name and an address. Sometimes it's right; sometimes it's not. We depend on the patient to fulfill the obligation of that contract. It's difficult, though. There's no guarantee we'll get paid, especially as far as illegal aliens are concerned. We provide care to a sizable number of people from whom, for whatever reason, we never receive a penny.

I've just heard that a number of hospitals in Los Angeles have refused to treat victims of sexual assault—rape victims and the like. And the reason that they're refusing to do it is because the reimbursement is not adequate to pay for the service that's provided. That service now includes evidentiary kinds of things; you have to collect certain types of specimens from the patient and handle them as evidence; there are certain immediate support things that you need to do; and longer-term support things. These hospitals have found that they can't continue to provide these services because they cost much too much. Now, we're not talking about heart transplants, we're talking about a very basic emergency room kind of service that includes an examination by a physician and some support from other professional personnel in the area, both nursing and social service, and some follow-up. I don't think that would happen here because we have such a tremendous commitment to providing for the needs of this community. So we're in it for the duration, whether the financial perspective is going to get better over time or not.

We get a lot of complaints about the long periods of time people have to wait in the waiting room before they're seen by a doctor. There's no easy solution to that. The problem, of course, is volume. If we set a standard of everybody being seen and out of the system in an hour, we'd have to have ten times the personnel and therefore ten times the resources that we have. And we're already losing money. So in a way, it's a very simple issue. I think busy emergency rooms like ours have always had to triage. There are different gradations of illness and injury that come in, and you can't care for each person the minute he walks through the door. You have to understand the sicker people go before the less sick. The other issue is, what is meant by "a long time"? If you have a cold and you have a private doctor and you want to see him, how soon could your doctor see you? I would bet that a person with a private doctor would see that doctor the next day, or maybe even the day after. Somebody who walks through the door here with a cough or a cold will see the doctor anywhere from five minutes to maybe five or six hours after he gets here, which isn't bad for that kind of problem.

I'm not in any way saying that somebody should come into an emergency room and wait five or six hours. I'm the strongest advocate of getting people through as quickly as possible. But given the constraints that we function under, given the volume, given the resources, given the fact that a lot of people who come through the door don't really *have* to be in an emergency room, but because they're here, by legislative fiat we have to take care of them, my response is: We will do everything we can to get people through here as fast as we can, but chances are, on a moderate to heavy day we're going to fall short of somebody's expectations. We're sorry that that happens, but our job is to make sure that we've properly identified and provided care to people who have serious illness or injury in a reasonable time frame. For the people who don't fall into that category, we provide a good service—hopefully in a reasonable amount of time, but often not.

One of the things that makes this place so outstanding is the depth of expertise available to us—the fact that we're in such a large medical center allows us to bring in the best possible physicians any time we need them. We had a teenager just a few days ago who came in with what was initially thought to be an allergic reaction. She said she had eaten a banana, which is a common food to which people are allergic, and she had some itching of her eyes and scratchiness in her throat. So she was signed in as "allergic to bananas." On examination, we saw nothing of particular gravity in terms of an allergic reaction, so she was given some mild medication and we watched her for a while. Within a short time, she developed what appeared to be a movement disorder. So we called for a neurological consult, and in the course of a reasonably brief amount of time the world's expert on movement disorders evaluated this young girl from the neurologic perspective. Then, because there was some concern about her upper airway, the ear, nose, and throat people came to see her. In fact, somebody from that department has a particular interest in palatal myoclonus, an involuntary contraction of muscles in the mouth and the upper airway, which was the woman's preliminary diagnosis. We felt initially that there was some risk that her upper airway might go into spasm. So she was admitted from here to the hospital and, just to be sure, yet another level of expertise saw her—a psychiatrist. It turns out that what she was having was a hysterical reaction, which often manifests itself in a number of physical symptoms. So we were ultimately able to diagnose and treat her properly.

Emergency rooms take a terrible knock—not just this one, but most places that are busy. I'll be the first to admit that there are problems here, but when you scratch the surface a little bit, I don't think you'll ever find people who are more committed or dedicated than the people who work in these areas. Every person in the ER is here because he or she wants to be. On the other hand, we have to be careful not to look at ourselves as more holy than other people. There's a tendency to get a little missionary doing this stuff.

II
HEART TRANSPLANTS

Every Friday morning at seven the heart transplant team assembles in a conference room on Fourteen to discuss the status of preoperative and postoperative transplant patients. The meeting is generally free-form, the only structure—and even this is loosely followed—is the order in which patients are discussed: first, patients in the hospital, then patients who have been discharged but who have problems, and finally, patients who are at home waiting for a heart. Everyone at the meeting has an equal say and each person is expected to contribute his or her viewpoint. Even with differences of opinion, the working together of this group with a single goal—the welfare of the patient—demonstrates the strengths of the multidisciplinary team.

On this crisp December morning, with daylight still thirty minutes away, people begin drifting into the room, each one stopping to take coffee and a doughnut from a cart just inside the door. Around the oversized conference table, informal conversation ranges from skiing in Utah to a recent newspaper article about a pregnant woman carrying an anencephalic (without a brain) baby. Although the mother wanted to donate the child's organs, New York law did not allow it. "Seems a shame," says one of the surgeons, "when so many babies are so badly in need." The conversation drifts to the frustration of late lab reports, and a nurse recommends a movie, *The Fly*.

By seven o'clock, twenty-five people have taken seats around the table and the room quiets down. With no one calling the meeting to order, it begins. Dr. Ronald Drusin, a cardiologist, speaks first:

DR. DRUSIN: The following people are in the house. Mr. Rickman, a thirty-six-year-old stockbroker, is on Nine West. His surgery was two weeks ago today. His new heart is doing fine. In fact, he's doing quite well overall. The nurses report that his only concern is taking his mask off. He's afraid of being infected by his roommate. Richard Stone is a forty-six-year-old security guard from Philadelphia. He's ten days postop and developing new problems daily. He's had irregular heart beats, anorexia, and nausea, and we're concerned. I'm afraid we may have to retransplant him. Gertie Evans is also on Nine, waiting for a heart. She's a fifty-year-old lady from Brooklyn, five-one and one hundred fifty pounds. She had an infarct in 1986, with normal coronary arteries. Her disease is progressing and she has shortness of breath. She's on a ton of drugs and worsening. We're hoping to get a heart for her soon. I think she's going to need it fast.

LEE SUSZYCKI (social worker): She's a pleasant woman—with a pleasant husband. She has mixed feelings about having a transplant because she didn't grow up in an era of high-tech medicine and she's dazzled by it. But she's willing to go through with it if that's the only way she can live.

DR. PETER SHAPIRO (psychiatrist): I found her husband to be irritable and snappy. I think he's having a hard time coping with her illness. He says he just can't deal with her being sick.

LAURA SECHE (clinical nurse coordinator): She asked me how soon after the surgery she could go disco dancing, although she just didn't seem to be the type who goes for that sort of thing.

DR. DRUSIN: Mr. Belsky is on Four West. He had his transplant last year. He's hard to follow because of his personality. He's very lethargic. He called and I asked him to come in or let me know how he was doing. When a week went by and I didn't hear from him, I was annoyed. By the time he finally called, he'd had significant changes and hadn't bothered to report them. He had developed congestive heart failure, so we boosted his steroids without a biopsy. [Periodically after a heart transplant, under local anesthesia, a tiny piece of heart muscle is snipped off and examined under a microscope for signs of rejection.] We finally admitted him on Tuesday, and his biopsy shows minimal changes. No significant findings on echo. He's very anxious to be discharged. He owns his own candy store and he's worried about leaving it. I think, though, that we're obligated to continue treatment for rejection even though the biopsy showed only minimal changes.

DR. CRAIG SMITH (heart surgeon): I could find no clinical findings consistent with rejection, Ron.

DR. DRUSIN: There may not be any, but I'm still worried about him.

DR. DENNIS REISON (cardiologist): Mike Connor has been in the ICU awaiting a heart for six weeks. He's definitely a young man in chaos. He's had five dry runs. The potential donors just didn't pan out, not *one* out of all five was any good. Now when we tell him we may have a heart for him, he says, "Sure, Doc. Tell me another." And I can understand how he feels.

MS. SUSZYCKI: He's becoming resigned to all this. He says he thinks God will fix up his old heart eventually, so now he's resigned to whatever happens.

DR. REISON: Sara Sanders is a young woman in her late twenties. She used to be a competitive swimmer. She's here with an idiopathic cardiomyopathy [slow death of heart muscle due to unknown causes]. We're working her up now. She has normal pulmonary resistance but recurrent tachycardia [rapid heartbeat]. She's having trouble tolerating at least the last seven or eight drugs. She gets nauseated and vomits. We've tried tocainide, flecainide, and encainide. . . .

JOANN LAMB (clinical nurse coordinator): All the "ides," huh? Beware the Ides of December . . .

DR. REISON: She can't leave the hospital this way. She's too sick to wait for her heart at home.

MS. LAMB: I'm not so sure she *wants* a transplant. She's struggled a long time with the idea. We first saw her last month and her body language was incredible. When I went in with the doctor, she just turned in bed and faced the wall. I gave her a manual to read and she didn't read it. As far as I know she hasn't signed the consent forms yet.

RESIDENT: I think she *is* resigned to the transplant. Yesterday I saw her reading all the information, so maybe she just changed her mind.

MS. LAMB: We did a patient check the other day. We called all the patients on the list and found out that Bob Brown has died.

DR. DRUSIN: That's a shame.

MS. LAMB: It's always a shame when they die waiting.

DR. LINDA ADDONIZIO (pediatric cardiologist): Andrea Herbert, our fifteen-year-old, is still waiting. She's been waiting two months. Her family is holding up—but just barely. Before we moved her to the ICU, she was getting phony phone calls. A woman calling herself Lady Luck kept calling her and saying there was an accident, there's a heart for her. It's terrible. The woman must be a real case. The parents appealed to the media for a heart and I sure hope we get one soon. Also, I'd like to give a follow-up on John Yeager, whom I saw yesterday. He's the kid who has a heterotopic heart [a new heart is implanted piggyback style to the original, weakened heart, which remains in place]. His last X ray showed the two hearts together are barely bigger than one normal-sized heart. All goes well with him. The new left ventricle looks great. March will be one year with his new heart. He's getting ready to go back to school.

DR. REISON: That's a wonderful result. The two hearts have trained them-selves to co-pulsate, which is just what we hoped they would do.

DR. KEITH REEMTSMA (heart surgeon): What is the donor situation?

RICHARD GEMMING (physician's assistant): We've been getting a lot of seconds lately. Unadvertised specials.One donor coordinator at a hospital in Michigan told us the donor's CPK [an enzyme released into the blood-stream from muscle tissue. An elevated CPK can indicate possible heart muscle-damage] was 74. We went out for the heart and it turns out it's 1,074. In another the heart was too small, and in a third the patient was too ill for the heart to be good enough. It's really annoying, not to mention expensive, to take those trips for nothing.

Incidentally, for those of you who don't know this, we have a new ambulance service. The one we were using will no longer take us to get the local hearts *or* to the airports. Do any of you remember Paul, the driver? If you drove once with Paul—you'd remember him. Paul hit any-thing moving . . . and a lot that *wasn't* moving. He hit a police car, a few toll booths. Once he even hit our police escorts. I was petrified to ride with him. Anyway, the company went out of business.

RESIDENT: No wonder. Sounds like he may turn into a donor himself one day.

DR. DRUSIN: We finished the work-up on Mr. Granger. He's all cleared and waiting for a heart.

DR. LARRY SCHULMAN (pulmonary specialist): If he ever *does* get a heart, he should *never* be encouraged to talk to the media. He has a real barroom vocabulary, that guy.

MS. SECHE: Yeah. He told me whatever happens, he doesn't want a "fag-got" heart. I gave up trying to make a gentleman out of him. When I asked who would be bringing him in since he lives so far away, he became real demure and he said, "I'll get the little bride to do it." He's a real trip.

DR. REISON: Arnie Peck is on Four. He's two weeks post-transplant. Boy, if ever there was a candidate for before and after, he is it. The guy is a rose!

RESIDENT: Say, how about we do before and after videos of our patients?

DR. REISON: He was cathed this week, he's off all drips. He looks quite good, actually. His hematocrit is in the low twenties. Let's give him some blood prior to discharge next week.

On Nine is Mrs. Schwartz. She's the schoolteacher whom we talked about a couple of months ago. She was rejecting her new heart and we started looking for another one. She was just admitted in cardiogenic shock. She was scheduled to come to clinic Monday morning. Instead, she ended up in the ER Sunday night. We transferred her to the coronary care unit with no pressures. We put in a central venous pressure line in the cath lab. Her biopsy showed rejection is continuing. She's had a very rocky course. We continued the cyclosporine and now we're faced with kidney shutdown. Yesterday we dialyzed her and she responded well, until last night when she had a seizure.

DR. ERIC POWERS (cardiologist): It sounds like she's too sick to be transplanted again.

DR. REISON: Her husband called me Saturday night and I asked him to put her on the phone. She said she hadn't slept well and I told her to take her temperature every four hours. She had no fever. I asked her to come in on Sunday morning but she said no, she'd wait till Monday.

DR. SHAPIRO: Regardless of her problems, she reports little. She's denying her illness.

DR. REISON: I don't agree with that. She's called me maybe three times per week, sometimes three times a day in the past.

Mr. Kline was admitted Friday night. He's very difficult. He has a history of substance abuse prior to transplant. He had a temp of 103 and was complaining of sternal wound pain. We kept him in the hospital over the weekend and sent him home Monday. In clinic Thursday, Craig saw him and his wound was healed well.

DR. SHAPIRO: He told me he can't take a deep breath.

DR. SMITH: He can, though. I think we can sit on this one.

DR. SHAPIRO: His wife calls all the time. She feels he's playing it straight but everybody here feels he's not.

MS. LAMB: He's a very passive man. He's formed no relationships with the other patients or, for that matter, with anybody. He comes in, he's seen, and he leaves.

MR. GEMMING: The man has no team spirit!

DR. REISON: I think he's asking for Percocet.

DR. DRUSIN: Well, he's all better as far as we're concerned.

DR. REISON: If I see him on Monday and he's still in pain, I think Peter should see him again.

DR. SHAPIRO: I'll be glad to. I asked him to come in one month post-transplant and he was quite agreeable. Trouble was, he spent his time bemoaning his current problems and fears.

DR. DRUSIN: Lee, want to share the ongoing saga of Rhonda?

MS. SUSZYCKI: Sure. Rhonda is a teenage girl whom we transplanted who doesn't come in for appointments. She's irresponsible and impossible to keep track of. You can't contact her because she has no telephone. We don't know from one day to the next what's happening with her. I sent a telegram to where I thought she lived but we got no response. I called her aunt, who is her only New York relative, and she said Rhonda stays away for days on end. She's not sure she even takes her medication.

MS. LAMB: The girl will surface when she runs out of cyclosporine. Meanwhile, I think she's thriving on all the attention she's getting. I mean, just think about it. We send telegrams. Lee calls her aunt. I think this is teaching us something. I think in the future we should think twice before we accept somebody for transplant who doesn't have a telephone and won't get one.

MS. SUSZYCKI: I agree. It's difficult if not impossible to follow these people when there's no way to reach them but by telegram. And even then, you never know if they got it.

DR. DRUSIN: Look, we knew this would be a problem. We took a risk. The kid's alive. It's as simple as that. It's better, I think, to make a mistake this way than the other way.

DR. RITA WATSON (cardiologist): What's with Harvey Ramirez? He's starting to reject his new heart.

DR. DRUSIN: At what point do you start looking for another heart?

DR. DAVID ROTHMAN (professor): What do you all think about the fairness of retransplant? That is—should someone who got one heart get a second if they need it—before offering a first to a new patient?

DR. ERIC ROSE (heart surgeon): I think once you transplant someone, you have a commitment to help keep him alive. That's my feeling anyway.

DR. DRUSIN: On Harkness Seven is Mr. Simmons. He has meningitis. We've got him on triple drug therapy intravenously.

MR. GEMMING: He was sniffing around in our offices the other day.

DR. DRUSIN: What was he doing up there?

DR. SMITH: I don't know, but he was there with his IV poles and everything two or three days ago.

THERESA MORRONE (physical therapist): For me, he won't walk anywhere.

DR. DRUSIN: The last person is a new work-up. Jim Kelly. He's a retired manager of a country club on Long Island. He doesn't exactly fit our criteria. He's sixty-three and he's already had open heart surgery. And, he had a stroke prior to his surgery.

MS. SUSZYCKI: He's of Irish descent, second marriage, dabbles in painting. Despite doctors' orders and the fact that he has already had heart surgery, he continues to smoke. Also, he looks much older than sixty-three. At first he was scared to think about a transplant. Now, though, he wants it badly.

DR. DRUSIN: His blood type is AB. Not a lot of people can take an AB heart. In fact, there's no one on our waiting list who can use an AB heart. But even if one does come up, I'm still not sure he's a suitable candidate for transplant. He's above our age limit.

DR. ROSE: Age and blood type are no grounds not to transplant him. Policy about people should deal with people, not blood types.

RESIDENT: Aren't we under constant scrutiny here as to our survival rates? Aren't heart transplant programs approved on the basis of a minimal mortality rate based on some sort of average?

DR. MARK HARDY (kidney transplant surgeon): Those people should look at the type of patients you're taking, the last ditch efforts—the salvages. If they're looking at success rates, they need to account for how sick some of these people are beforehand.

DR. REEMTSMA: They should look. But they don't.

DR. REISON: This man is sixty-three, poststroke, post–open heart surgery. He's still smoking, so he's obviously noncompliant. I don't know if we should do it.

DR. ROSE: He can use an AB heart. If we get one, let's give it to him. There are so few people who can take an AB heart—actually only four percent of the population has blood type AB. I think, because so few people can use an AB heart, if one should become available, it doesn't qualify as a scarce resource.

DR. DRUSIN: If it was an O heart we'd need it for seven others first.

DR. ROSE: Yes, but an AB heart will go in the garbage for lack of someone to put it into! He's the only one on our list who can receive an AB heart.

MS. LAMB: Before you decide to do it, I think you should consider the cost-benefit ratio with a man like this. He's sure to be sick and lingering in the hospital post-transplant . . .

DR. HARDY: . . . as opposed to lying today in the ICU because his present heart is so bad.

DR. ROSE: The whole rationale for limiting heart transplants is the issue of not enough heart donors.

DR. DRUSIN: David, can you comment on the ethics of dealing with a sixty-three-year-old with all these other problems as a potential recipient?

DR. ROTHMAN: Sure. You guys have never played the numbers game. Why start doing that now? Why even consider survival rates? Now that you're a pace setter, they'll have to start taking their numbers from you.

DR. ROSE: A thirty percent chance of survival versus certain death when you're using a heart that is not a scarce resource is worth the gamble.

DR. ROTHMAN: Social issues. Compliance. Once you start using these, when do you stop?

DR. ROSE: The only reason to ration a heart is if it is a scarce resource. Should the fact that he's sixty-three, noncompliant, and had a stroke be punishable by death?

MS. LAMB: So then why do we screen them? Why don't we just take any AB that comes down?

DR. ROSE: Maybe we can learn something. Maybe this kind of patient will do okay.

MS. LAMB: His chances are lousy.

DR. ROSE: Yes, the outcome is predictably poor. But if he's willing to accept that, why not go ahead?

DR. HARDY: This is the issue of a death committee; who shall live and who shall die? It started in Seattle in the sixties with the kidney patients. Resources were scarce, and dialysis machines were limited. Only those patients who it was felt would function morally and physically during dialysis and afterwards were given the opportunity to use a kidney machine. The others were denied dialysis and eventually died. Are we now addressing the same thing?

DR. ROTHMAN: The question of social worth never entered into it before. You never decided on whether or not to transplant the parolee, but I can guess how that would have come out. A question of high morality and dismal outcome has never been a deciding factor before. My suggestion is to pay attention to what you've done in the past.

DR. DRUSIN: All three red flags are up. He's above our age limit, he's not compliant, and he's got a residual deficit from a stroke.

DR. ROSE: I vote for transplant.

MS. LAMB: We didn't finish his work-up yet.

MS. SUSZYCKI: Can I just say one thing? I think that the objective of this group is to help people if they want to be helped. If the surgeons think they can do that, they should do it.

DR. ROSE: The objective of this group is to keep all of the people who started the year with us alive, alive at the end of the year. That's what *I* think we're all here for.

Dr. Reemtsma looks up at the clock on the wall. It's ten after eight. He pushes his chair back quietly and stands up, and the rest follow suit. The meeting is over.

THOMAS HICKEY, P.A.

Physician's Assistant

We're in his office, which he shares with two other members of the transplant team. A trim, handsome, easy-going man, he looks much younger than his thirty-nine years. Pasted on the wall above his desk is a child's crayon drawing. It's a picture of a little boy drawn in stick figures, holding flowers and smiling. At the bottom, it says, "I love you. J.P." J.P. was the first child in the country to successfully receive a new heart.

"Heart transplants. Dr. Reemtsma says it's a goddamned miracle every time! And he's right—it's really a miracle how you can take a dead, limp heart that's been in an ice bucket for four hours, put it into someone's chest and it starts to beat—just like that! By itself! It's phenomenal! Or you look at this four-year-old kid who we just transplanted, a lovely little boy who couldn't do anything before his surgery. Before he left the hospital, he was riding a tricycle up and down the hall, smiling, having a great time! It brings tears to your eyes—it's just so wonderful to see the looks on his parents' faces. This kid was dead—his heart was failing—and we put a new heart in him and two weeks later he's riding his tricycle with a big grin on his face. You do it to a forty-year-old, and it's nice, it's good to see them do well. But you do it to a four-year-old . . . it really melts your heart."

I was a corpsman in the navy; that's where I learned about medicine. I had had no medical experience whatever until the navy threw me into it. I was pre-med in college—everyone goes into premed in college—so I had a lot of biology and chemistry, and because of that the navy immediately puts you in the medical field. You really have no choice. I wanted to be a sonar engineer but they would have nothing to do with that.

I thought about going to mcd school at one time, but given the sequence of events in my life, it wasn't possible—at least, I didn't think it was possible for me. Physicians lead difficult lives in terms of the hours they keep, and I thought I'd like a little better lifestyle—not working such long hours, but still be in medicine. So being a physician's assistant is a nice middle ground—you get to do a lot of what physicians do. As a matter of fact, in a family-practice setting, PAs can diagnose and treat about eighty percent of what comes in through the door—earaches, throats, that sort of stuff. The more difficult cases obviously go to the physicians, but you can do a lot.

We have four coordinators on our heart transplant team. Joann Lamb and Laura Seche are the recipient coordinators, which means they take care of things from this end. They're more involved with the patient who will get a new heart. Richard Gemming, another PA, and I work as donor recovery coordinators; we coordinate the evaluation, organization, and retrieval of the hearts from donors to use in our transplant recipients.

When we have a patient who needs a heart, there's a whole formal structure of procurement and coordination that we have to go through. Once a hospital has identified a donor and it looks like the donor is a good match for our patient, they call me or Richard; we evaluate the information on the donor, going over the patient's history, chest X rays, EKG, blood-pressure history, medications they're on. Essentially we're looking to see if they are a reasonable heart donor. If they are, their cardiologist will talk to our cardiologist.

In the meantime, if we think it's going to be good, we'll start to organize the recovery. We get the residents that are working with us in the lab, and we call the airport to get a Lear jet ready, or if it's local, we'll get an ambulance. The cost depends on how far you go, but the jet costs from two thousand to seven thousand dollars. To go to Dallas, it's around six or seven thousand dollars. Third-party insurers will sometimes pay for organ recovery. Other than that, the hospital has been absorbing those recovery costs. So we get the transportation organized, and we fly to whatever hospital we're going to.

Occasionally when we get someplace, what we're seeing is not what we've been told. That happens rarely, but the point is that we have to go and make sure that the person who is going to donate the heart is actually a good heart donor. In the time that we're flying, any number of things can happen. There could be a drop in his blood pressure, anything. We have actually gotten to a place, looked at the donor, decided it would not be a good heart for our patient, and turned around and come back.

When we arrive at the designated hospital, we evaluate the potential donor and then I and one of the residents remove the heart. In the meantime, another person who has come with us is making phone calls home, telling them we have a good heart and they can start things moving with our patient.

Once we take the donor heart out, we put it in an ice chest, and we head back to the plane. On the ride back, we take what's called lifeline. That is, the shortest, most direct route from wherever we are to Teterboro Airport in New Jersey. We don't have to go through landing patterns and waiting patterns, so there's no delay. And while we're in the air, our patient at home is being put to sleep in the operating room and the surgeons will begin opening his chest.

The idea is to coordinate the recovery so when we're arriving with the heart, the patient's heart is coming out. Joann usually stands at the window of the operating room and when she sees the lights and sirens coming across the bridge, she can turn around and tell the surgeons that we've come back safely, nothing has happened to us en route. When they hear that, they begin to remove our patient's heart. And just about the time we get upstairs, they're ready to take the donor heart and sew it in.

Most of the patients we've transplanted at Presbyterian know who I am. They know I went for the heart, so they try to pry information out of me. "What was my donor like? How old was he? Where did he come from?" You really try to remove yourself from that. Mostly we tell them the age and the sex and that's all. And sometimes we tell them where the person was from. But nothing more.

We've had instances where the donor family has gotten in touch with the recipient family; sometimes that's good and sometimes that's bad. Mostly we think it's bad. Donor families think that when they donate something, certainly the heart—the loved one lives on in some way. But a donation is a gift. When you give somebody a gift, you don't ask them, "How's my chess set that I gave you? How's the basketball I gave you?" The same is true with organs. We don't want people saying, "How's Johnny's heart? Are you taking good care of it?" Some people feel that just because you have their brother's heart in you, they have some influence over your life. And we don't like to foster that feeling at all. We like to keep them very removed from each other.

We've had donor families call up recipients. Finding them isn't hard if you're a good investigator. For a while we publicized that we were doing heart transplants, mostly to make people more aware that donation's a good thing, that you're saving a life. So we gave the information to the paper about the transplant recipient. But the donor's family knows that "Johnny" died in New Jersey. And they read in the paper that a heart was recovered from northern New Jersey and put into this transplant recipient. It's not hard to put them together. Now we try to keep that down. But once the press has that information, they'll do what's good for the paper, not what's good for either us or the recipient. It's a problem.

And even in this hospital, we pull up in an ambulance, we come barging through the doors; security's getting people out of the way, we're racing through the halls with a heart. It's obvious what's going on, and it's not hard for other staff members to know what's happening. Word gets around. No matter what you do, when you're doing a transplant, even though it's four o'clock in the morning, the next morning people know. It's really very difficult to keep something like that quiet. If it was just up to the immediate team, that wouldn't be a problem, but it's not an isolated incident in a hospital setting.

It's hard for me not to get emotionally involved with our patients. These are people who before the transplant are in such failure that they sometimes can't talk. And you put a heart in them, and four days later they're different people; they're walking around. It's wonderful to see how well they do. When they die or do poorly, though, it really affects the whole team. It takes all of us a long time to get over it. The way we look at it, our patients belong to us—they are ours, and we are theirs. Forever.

JOANN LAMB, R.N.
Clinical Coordinator

She's Canadian by birth. She was head nurse in the surgical intensive care unit and joined the transplant team in 1980. A blonde with short hair and deep blue eyes, her face and hands come alive with earnest expression as she talks about her patients.

"We've done well over two hundred patients and I remember almost every one. People are amazed, because there have been so many. But you remember them, especially the first ones, because the early years were so painful and so stressful in trying to pull these patients along. Even now, every rejection is memorable, every infection a knife in the heart. These people are not easy to forget."

Most of our patients are referred to us from other hospitals, so we send out forms that tell them what this is all about. What we do and what they must do. The first discusses who is a candidate, what the work-up entails, and what a patient's obligations are. Patients who are waiting for a heart but aren't sick enough to stay in the hospital are required to live nearby. Those at the top of the list are told to stay within range of the phone number we have for them, so if a heart comes up we can reach them immediately. We give them beepers just in case they leave home for an hour. We insist that our post-transplant patients live in the New York area for six to eight months after their surgery so we can keep a close eye on them and ward off any impending problems. The farther they get from the day of transplant, the less the chance of problems with the new heart.

We also tell them right up front about cyclosporine—that's the anti-rejection drug they have to take—what it does and how expensive it is. It's about a hundred sixty dollars a bottle, and a bottle lasts anywhere from a few days to a couple of weeks. Some people use a bottle every five days. So cyclosporine becomes a very big financial obligation on the part of the patient and we think it's important that they understand that.

When they return the forms, they're given to one of our cardiologists to review. If the patient appears to be a reasonable candidate, we ask him—or her—to come into the hospital for four or five days for a pre-transplant evaluation. After that, we put them on the waiting list. If they're well enough, we send them home to wait for a call saying we have a heart. If not, they stay here. The waiting list is organized by classes—how sick a patient is determines the class he's in. Class nine, for example, is the sickest, and they'll always get the first crack at an available heart. Other than that, within a class it runs on a first-come, first-served basis. If someone on the list suddenly gets much worse, we'll transplant that person ahead of the others. The patients all know that that's a possibility, and that's okay. They like to know that if that happened to them, they'd be next. They're also divided by blood type, by size, by weight or height, if they are particularly tall or short. The size of the patient is important, because you don't want to put in a heart that's too big or too small for them. If you've got a seventy-pound child, you're not going to give him the heart of a two-hundred-pound person. Conversely, a two-hundred-ten-pound recipient probably won't be helped by a heart from a seventy-pound person. We usually go about twenty percent in weight above and below.

I usually go right to the OR with the patient, stay with him while they stick needles in his arms, and hold his hand 'til he falls asleep. Once the chest is open, it only takes about an hour to put a heart into a patient and get it started up in a good rhythm. Then it'll take another couple of hours to stabilize the patient and close the chest. Of course, a lot of things can go wrong. Every once in a while the new heart just doesn't work. The heart doesn't start up or it starts and then it just stops. When that happens, most of the time there's not a thing anyone can do. It's tragic. There's almost never time to get another heart—although we managed to do it once. We had one patient where we put the heart in, and we started looking for another donor while he was still on the table. We managed to squeak him through the first two days posttransplant with the donor heart, although it was not good. We were lucky enough to get another heart and retransplant the patient, but he died shortly after the second surgery.

It's wrenching when a patient dies, so I try not to get too personally involved with them. I know that there are people who, if their patient dies, will go the funeral or the wake, or they'll keep in touch with the family. But I can't do that. I guess it's self-protection. I don't know, I just can't do it. Now, sometimes you might have a patient who became a particular friend, or you got to know his family for some other reason. But by and large I've always kept my distance from them. I don't have enough emotional reserve to do otherwise. I'd be crying in the living room all day long.

In one of Eric's interviews he said something which I thought was terrifically descriptive. He said, "Every surgeon has a graveyard he walks through by himself," meaning the patients he's taken care of who have died. I guess nurses feel the same thing in a certain sense. They may not feel so directly responsible if someone doesn't survive as a physician might, but they're still our patients, too, and we do feel a sense of loss. I think you have to develop a mechanism to protect yourself from that.

ROBERT MCMANUS, M.D.

Chief Resident, Cardiac Surgery

He's thirty-six, of average height, slightly stocky, with thick, sandy-blond hair that sports a cowlick he continually pushes off his forehead. In two weeks, he and his family will leave New York for a hospital in Minnesota where he has accepted the position of chief of the heart transplant team—a notable achievement for someone just starting out in practice, and a statement also about the physicians who trained him.

I came to Presbyterian Hospital for one month in December of 1978. At the time, I was a fourth-year medical student at Boston University. Fourth year you could choose one-month electives at any hospital and since I had just gotten married and my wife had a job with a New York law firm, I chose all my electives in New York. My elective here was in cardiothoracic surgery. It was a busy month. I was in the operating room all day long, just fascinated by every heart operation I saw. Heart transplantation was just beginning here at the time. I saw my first one—it was the fourth they had done here—on December 25th, Christmas Day, 1978. Because it was Christmas Day, there was only a skeleton crew. Kathy McNichols and Dr. Reemtsma, the chief of Surgery, went off to get the donor heart, and the resident who was on call that night was in the open heart recovery room acting as sort of a communications link between the hospital where the donor was and our operating room. That left me and the surgeon who was going to do the implantation here. I assisted him as he put the patient on bypass and got him ready for the transplant. When Reemtsma came back with the heart, I moved down to the foot of the table. I was so incredibly impressed by this operation. Here was a patient who was dying, they clamped his aorta, took out his old, beat-up heart, sewed a brand new one in, opened the clamp, and as soon as the blood flowed into the new heart it started beating!

I followed his progress daily after that and one week to the day, New Year's Day, which was the last day of my rotation at Presbyterian, I went in to see him for the last time. There he was, sitting up in bed, watching the football games, feeling fine. We had to take an EKG on him, which was what we used in those days to determine if the new heart was okay or if it was being rejected by the patient's body. At that time they didn't have the biopsy system they have now. The EKG gave you a rough estimate, but it was all we had. The object was to measure very carefully, and if you saw the blip on the EKG getting smaller or if it changed, that was your clue that the patient might be rejecting his new heart.

Well, here's the patient, sitting up watching TV, looking great, but his EKG shows the spike was definitely smaller than it should have been. Certainly it was cause for concern. I didn't say anything to him, but I was really worried, so I picked up the phone—as a fourth-year medical student, that in itself was a really big leap—and I called Dr. Reemtsma at home.

He got here in no time flat. First he looked at the EKG and he said, "Damn! Looks like this patient's rejecting." And then he looked at the EKG machine, and there's a little switch that determines the calibration, and that had apparently been turned down by somebody. So he said, "Is this the machine you used?" And I said, "Yes," and he just turned the switch up and sure enough, the guy's EKG was normal. Boy, did I feel stupid! But he was very nice about it. He said, "Well, Bob, I guess I fixed this man's rejection right up." He said, "I'll just go ahead and walk back home now. I think I'll go on down to the Hudson River and walk on water, I fixed this problem up so well." He's really a tremendous man. In fact, he was one of the main reasons I decided to come here.

I interviewed for my residency at a lot of hospitals in New York. When you're a fourth-year student, you start interviewing early in that year for the places you want to eventually do your training. A surgical residency is not easy to come by at the really good hospitals, especially in New York. So while I was doing my fourth-year electives, I was also doing interviews for the next year. I interviewed first at a few different hospitals in New York and I walked around these places and everything was very nice and very beautiful, but the attitudes of the house staff and some of the attending surgeons made me very uncomfortable. There was not a lot of camaraderie there. There was a lot of tooth-and-nail kind of stuff. I'd ask the residents, "Do you get together with any of these people here?" And they'd say, "You kidding? Soon as I get out of here, I'm gone." It wasn't like that here, so I decided to try for a residency at Presbyterian.

The problem was, in December, when you're supposed to get your interviews done, I wasn't able to break away for ten minutes. Once you become a part of the team, you are really a *part* of the team, and you are utilized, even as a student. Everybody has to help and everybody is necessary. So I was needed every single day from six in the morning until ten at night. I was here, and in the operating room, or doing things that needed to be done. There's always something going on somewhere; there's an emergency developing, there's a patient who's in trouble here, there's a patient with chest pain. So although I had interviewed at every other place in the city, I'd missed all the opportunities to have an interview for the surgical program here. I'd made it to the other ones because I'd done those before, but I figured, well, December, since I'm there, I'll be able to go down to the general surgical office any time during the month and have my interview. I didn't realize the extent to which you can get embroiled in these things. So although I had decided that I really wanted to come here, I could see I was never going to get time to have an interview.

I remember vividly the last day of the month, December 31st, I was sitting in the open heart recovery room. I had been assisting in surgery all day—this was New Year's Eve—the last day for possible interviews, and they had already given me extensions and extensions and extensions, and reassigned me to different dates and times, and I had canceled out on every one of them. I was always in the operating room. So there I was, in this little cubbyhole which is the doctors' area in the old open heart recovery room, and I called the secretary in general surgery, and she said, "I'm sorry, Mr. McManus, you missed all of your opportunities and there won't be any more." I hung up and I felt awful. I was just sitting there, staring at the telephone, and Dr. Bowman walked in. He's the second-in-command here, in heart surgery. We had just finished working together—this was probably five-thirty, six in the evening, and he said, "What's wrong?" And I said, "I think I missed my last opportunity for an interview here in general surgery." And he said, "You applied here?" And I said, "Yes, I did all the paperwork but I missed my interview." So he just looked at me and he said, "Bob, I've got what I need. Consider yourself interviewed."

I started my training here in July of 1979. The way it works is, the internship in general surgery is the first year of your general surgical residency. There're five years of general surgical residency in total. Then you do two more at least in cardiothoracic surgery if you want to be a heart surgeon. So the total time of training, after you graduate from medical school, is at least seven years. I did some work in the lab, some research, so I've been here for almost eight years.

Internship is probably the hardest year anyone ever goes through. I remember a time when there were sixty-eight patients on the service. They had to be seen every day, and generally cared for. Notes had to be written on every one of them. I would be here twenty-four hours a day. There'd be twelve or thirteen patients who would be admitted every day. And you'd have to sit down and talk to them. To do a history and physical takes at least a half hour, forty-five minutes. And to do that on twelve to thirteen patients a day, plus see all your patients, plus make sure all of the lab values are taken care of, plus there was no blood-drawing team in those days, so we would do all of that—I was literally here in this hospital twenty-four hours a day, seven days a week.

The only time I read a newspaper was if I was waiting for the elevator. I'd sorta squat down and look in the vending machine—I got a lot of reading of current events done that way. In fact half the time that was the only way I knew what day it was. You tend to lose touch with what's going on in the outside world for a year. You do get to go home occasionally, but then you turn on the TV and you fall asleep.

The worst thing about internship is what it can do to your family life. It was very hard on my wife. Everything was fine when I was in medical school and we were living in New York, but once I hit the internship and all of these hours, things were different. We'd bought a co-op apartment in Hoboken, and she was working on Wall Street and making a lot of money, while I was making very little, comparatively, as an intern. As a first-year lawyer on Wall Street, she was making around forty-five thousand dollars a year. As an intern, I was making about eighteen thousand.

But that wasn't the problem. I think the problem was, she was a lawyer, and she really didn't understand what medical internship involved. If I didn't come home when I said I would, if plans had to be canceled, it was just because there were things going on which, if I didn't take care of, would not be taken care of. My jobs had a direct bearing on the health and well-being of people. There was nobody else around who could do them, or would do them, or knew how to do them. And so I would continually break appointments and not be home. For someone who is not in the medical profession, its hard to understand that. It was sort of like being married but not being married. She had all the disadvantages of being married—she couldn't go out with other people and have a good time, and none of the advantages of being married, because she never saw her husband. I knew that things were falling apart, but the time it takes to sit down and work things out just wasn't available.

Around the end of December, around Christmas time, I came home one day and she wasn't there. And neither were any of her things. She had simply decided that enough was enough. And so, after eighteen months of marriage—six of which were during my internship—she decided to move out.

For a few months I sort of wallowed in self-pity. Then I started to date again. This time I started dating nurses. Not too long after that I met my present wife, Mary, who at the time was a nurse working here on the tenth floor. She understood, and continues to understand, that when I'm not at home, I'm doing something I can't avoid, I can't get out of, nor do I really wish to.

We've had some good times here. In the past the residents would gather together on a nightly basis, if they possibly could, to eat dinner. I remember one night, it was in the summertime. It was a very slow night. Nothing was going on and all of the patients had been taken care of, and we decided we would try to get together and eat on the hospital roof. Everybody was assigned to do something. Bring tables, chairs. We ordered a couple of hundred dollars' worth of Chinese food and we sent a medical student down to Chinatown to pick it up. It got to be one of those ornate affairs. To get to the roof, you take the elevator to the twenty-second floor, and you walk through the door and it's right there. There are no signs that say you're not allowed up there, so we went. We got the tables and somebody got some bed sheets for tablecloths, and somebody else brought a couple of lamps from the on-call rooms. There's a telephone right up there so every time you got beeped you could walk over and answer your page. So we ended up having this terrific banquet on the roof. Most of the house staff in the entire hospital, and some of the nurses who could get away, and medical students—we were all up on the roof at this big, long table spread out with Chinese food. For some reason, our chief resident—this was when I was on the general surgery service—came back to the hospital, and it was around nine-thirty and he met one of the attending surgeons and they went to see a patient. They were walking around and they didn't see any of us. Then, as they were waiting for the elevator, they heard the nurses saying, "Let's go, let's go." So they got on the same elevator and followed the nurses up to the roof, and suddenly they walk onto the roof and there's this huge feast going on, and people milling around—there were probably thirty or forty of us. And they just sat down and picked up a pair of chopsticks. That's the kind of thing that would happen from time to time.

There's a camaraderie that forms among friends you meet during your residency; a lasting bond. We lost one of those friends a couple of years ago. John Wood was shot here when I was a second-year resident. We were interns together, and we were very close friends. I was on call with him that night. He wanted to go home and check on his wife, who was pregnant. They lived right down on Riverside Drive. She had called him and said that she had been vomiting all day and thought she might need to go into the hospital; she couldn't keep anything down and she was feeling dizzy. So John asked me if I would cover for him and carry his arrest beeper—a certain number of house staff carry one at all times—it's a beeper that goes off every time there's a cardiac arrest anywhere in the house, and you have to respond to it. So I carried the arrest beeper for him while he went home to see his wife. On the way back he cut through the park that's behind the parking lot and he was accosted by some young boys and shot in the chest. I was waiting for him to come back because I wanted to go to McDonald's and get some dinner, but since I had the arrest beeper, I couldn't leave the hospital. So I was waiting in the emergency room for him to come back. Suddenly, I heard a commotion and a rush of people and I saw him being carried in on a stretcher by the EMT.

The bullet had gone right through his heart. I was right there. I had to do the surgery to open his chest. To do that on a friend . . . Someone you just saw an hour ago. Well, as soon as I opened his chest I saw that the bullet had gone through his coronary artery. The minute he was brought in, we had the secretary call Dr. Bowman at home and he made it to the emergency room in seven minutes. But there was nothing he or any of us could do. Even though we got his heartbeat back temporarily, there was no hope for it to be repaired, ever. It was the main artery to his heart. So he died, literally, in my hands. The chief resident who was on call with me that night was Paul Demartini. He was also a very good friend of John's. We all worked on him for two or three hours in the crash room, but finally we said, that's enough. So Paul and I went out to tell his wife. It was terrible . . .

One hard thing about that was, when it was over we couldn't just drop everything and leave. Paul and I had to do an emergency appendectomy an hour after we finished. A man had an appendix that was ready to rupture, so we had to operate on him less than an hour after John died. Then for the rest of the night we had to keep going; there were people who needed operations.

Mornings for me are the quietest time of day. I get up about four-thirty A.M., and tiptoe around trying not to wake up my wife, my daughter, or my son. My son always hears me, though, and he gets up and we go into the kitchen and I make myself some coffee and he patters around after me. He's decided that this is the best time of the day to see his father, because he's almost never still awake when I get home. He's now almost four years old, but I always remember a very telling experience that happened just about a year and a half ago when he was two. I was scheduled to spend six months in the open heart recovery room, where you're on every other night. What that means is, in addition to working all day, you work all night every other night. That meant that out of a hundred sixty-eight hours in any given week, which is how many hours there are in a week, you will be away from this hospital for maybe eighteen to twenty hours, total. The rest of the time, you're just here working or trying to sleep in a little cubicle across the hallway that you live in. Your "room" has nothing more in it than a bed, a night table, and a small desk with a telephone. But that's okay because you don't stay in there very much, you have to be in the open heart recovery room more often than not.

So it was early one Sunday morning, we had been up all night the night before, and I was half asleep in my room, in my bed. It was Father's Day and I hadn't seen my son for what seemed like ages. My wife got the idea it would be nice for me and for my son if she surprised me at the hospital and so she decided to bring him in to see me. He was about two years old at that time, just a toddler. She found out from the other resident where I was and she and my son came to my room. She opened the door and she saw me in bed, and with one eye open I watched her as she bent down and whispered to my son, "Go say 'hello' to Daddy." Then she let go of his hand. Well, this little toddler came running into the room, and he stopped, and he looked at me and then he looked around, and then he ran over to the desk, picked up the phone, put it to his ear—a big smile on his face—and he said, "Hello, Daddy?"

RONALD DRUSIN, M.D.
Cardiologist

He is well over six feet tall and reed thin. A soft-spoken, gentle man with an ingratiating smile. We are in his office. As we talk, his eyes shoot toward the telephone every time it rings. He is awaiting the birth of his first child "any minute now."

In the ten years since I started here, I've seen some major changes in heart transplantation. The most exciting has been what has happened since the introduction of cyclosporine, a drug that suppresses the body's natural tendency to fight off any foreign body, in this case the new heart. In the precyclosporine era, we gave patients huge amounts of drugs to prevent the body from rejecting the new heart—a body will automatically attack anything foreign that it senses—but by doing that the drugs prevented attack on other foreign bodies as well, so people were developing massive infections, from which many died. Their new heart was working fine and they would die of infection.

In those early years, rejection was a very dramatic thing. The patients were admitted to the hospital and many were desperately ill, and occasionally you would lose them. Most of the rejection we're seeing since cyclosporine is unsuspected, and most patients have no symptoms that one can pinpoint. We find out by the surveillance biopsies. We take a microscopic snip of heart tissue and examine it under a microscope. The cells give us the answer. These biopsies are initially done weekly, and the longer one gets from the transplant the less likely that rejection is going to take place, so the interval, between biopsies is widened until the longest interval, which is now either three or four months.

As for what we're looking at in the future, I think finding ways of getting more donor hearts is one of the most important things. There are a number of potential solutions that everyone in the field is talking about at this point—how to manage end-stage problems in patients who are going to die unless they get a heart immediately. If there's no heart for the person who desperately needs it, what do you do? If you think a heart is coming but need to carry a patient over, even for a few critical hours until it arrives, what do you do? There's a lot of talk now about using mechanical devices as a bridging gap until a heart becomes available. And there have been some suggestions about extending the age of donors who are acceptable— right now we won't use the heart of anyone older than fifty—and using them occasionally as bridging devices until a more normal heart is available. And there has been some talk within our own center about using non-human hearts as bridging devices or ultimately as the heart used for transplant. So there's a lot on the horizon as far as new research.

Of all the patients I've come to know over these years, the most memorable for me is Bruce, our longest surviving heart transplant patient. He was transplanted in the beginning of December in 1980. He was twenty-four years old at the time and had just spent two months in an intensive care unit at another hospital on experimental drugs, just trying to keep his heart pumping.

When Bruce first arrived in the intensive care unit, I went up to meet him. Immediately he started to set up ground rules. "I make telephone calls, I use the bathroom, I don't use a commode." He just spouted off a whole list of things that were important to him. I mean, here was this man, twenty-four years old, who was clearly dying, who'd been in an intensive care unit for two months, and the one thing he wanted to do when he arrived was to lay out his territory. I thought that was very impressive. And I let him do those things.

As the days passed, Bruce was doing worse and worse, and we were desperately trying to find a heart for him. We spent two weeks beating the bushes and couldn't find a suitable donor and he just got weaker and weaker, and we kept going up higher and higher on the medicines to keep his heart pumping adequately. It was a desperate situation, and we were losing ground day by day.

Finally we located a heart of his blood group type available in Richmond, Virginia. So I canceled my office hours, got somebody to cover my practice, and Henry Spotnitz and I took a plane to Richmond that afternoon. By that night, Bruce had a new heart. He had a few problems at first, and we were worried about him for a while, but eventually he was stabilized and he has done well ever since.

He's a very independent, scrappy kind of survivor who's been a pleasure to take care of. I wouldn't let him go back to the job that he used to do—he used to be involved with garbage processing in a sewage plant in Hempstead. Instead he got himself into a rehabilitation and training program and he took a nine-month course in learning to be an electronics technician and then he went out into the job market.

He got a good job repairing computers, but he didn't tell his boss about his heart transplant, because he thought it would be such a negative thing in terms of whether he would be a risk to employ. Well, maybe six or eight months after he started working at this place, it was time for him to be admitted to the hospital for his annual cardiac catheterization, which tells us how his heart is doing and which requires that he spend two nights here. So one afternoon he went to his boss and he said that he needed two days off because he had to go into the hospital, and his boss asked, "Well, what's wrong?" And Bruce said something about a heart transplant. His boss was shocked. "You don't need a heart transplant! You're perfectly healthy!" And Bruce said, "No, no, no. Not *need* one. *Had* one! And I need to go back for a checkup." Of course the man didn't believe him. He ended up having to bare his chest and show his scars. He loves to tell that story.

It's always hard on a doctor when on of his patients dies. We work so long with these people, and we become very close to all of them. Part of being able to take care of somebody so desperately ill is helping them get back to being themselves after they receive a new heart. To be able to do that, you have to understand what their lives are about. They become fairly dependent on our group. They spend a lot of time here after the transplant, and we get to be friends. I think we, as a transplant group, are a little more mother-hennish about our patients than other transplant centers. We maintain a closer relationship with them and see them more often than some of the other programs do. You can't be *too* protective, though. You have to help them deal with the problems that come up, but your job is also to get them back to being independent.

Of course each of us has feelings, each of us has a couple of patients that we are terribly attached to. If something were to happen we'd feel absolutely dreadful—more so than the others. I think we're talking about human interactions. It's normal to become more intimately involved with some people than others. Any physician has patients in his practice who will become friends. Real friends.

One of the younger patients has almost adopted me as an auxiliary parent, and it's been kind of nice. He's twenty-two or twenty-three, comes from upstate New York. He was a sophomore or a junior at an upstate school when he was referred to us with end-stage heart failure. He was a terrific kid with a wonderful family, but he was very dependent on his mother. Like other patients, he had to stay around the New York area for a while after his transplant, so for the first three months he and his mother took an apartment in one of the New Jersey suburbs. That worked very well for both of them, but then as the spring wore on she had things she had to do at home—she had to think about going back. She felt torn in terms of what to do about him. I thought it would be good for him to gain some independence, even to see New York on his own, so I encouraged her to go back home, and I offered to help find him a place to live. I arranged for him to sublet a room in a medical student's apartment—and agreed to assume some responsibility for being there if he needed someone. And so overnight I became a parent.

We had dinner maybe one night a week. That's the kind of thing that I'm talking about. You can develop friendships with patients in the transplant program or out of the transplant program, where it goes a bit beyond what is expected of a physician and patient relationship. And that's how it was with us. I mean, the kid sent me a Father's Day card.

DAVID ROTHMAN, PH.D.

Director, Center for the Study
of Society and Medicine

He is a professor of history at Columbia University, and the author of
numerous books about the medical and hospital world. A dapper man—
short gray hair, tweed jacket with elbow patches—he looks every bit the
college professor.

I came to the medical center to see if, and how, the humanities and the
social sciences could be made relevant to the practice of medicine. My first
task was to learn the language, learn the players. I spent a good part of my
first year here—at least the mornings—going on rounds. It was quite an
experience, being a chaired professor with a certain amount of gray hair,
standing next to two twenty-five-year-olds who talked to each other for five
minutes and I didn't understand a word they were saying. It was very
humbling.

There is extraordinary energy at a medical center compared to a college
of arts and sciences. The hours are long. The physical survival over a course
of a day that can start at six A.M. and end at seven P.M. is quite extraordinary. And there is exceptional intelligence, no question about that. Yet
with it all comes a tunnel vision, an extraordinary unawareness of much
that is going on outside the medical universe. In all sorts of ways I began

to discover that physicians are strangers to the outside world and, indeed, the outside world is strange to them.

The trick in my position is not to lose sight of what this place looks like from the outside. So, how can you be an "insider" without giving up some of the qualities of being an "outsider"? That's the tension that someone who gets to sit in a setting of this sort experiences; where you know the world from within a medical center—and yet you're not a physician. I determined very early on not to confuse what I was here for. I was asked at various points whether I wanted to put on a white coat for going on rounds, and I always said no. My feeling is that as soon as I put on a white coat, I become another insider, and a medical center doesn't need one more insider. What it does need is people who can cross the line between the inside and the outside.

There's a certain suspicion in medicine about those who come wearing tweed jackets. I think that's because the first intrusion of bioethics into the medical establishment often caused a lot of ill will between physician and bio-ethicist. In some ways, as I look back on it, the ethicists were all elbows and the physicians were all toes. They were constantly misinterpreting each other. There was a conflict in which the physicians saw the bioethicists as trying to capture medical decision-making, and bioethicists saw physicians as unwilling to allow external values to influence medical decision-making.

Back in the 1970s, a group of philosophers began to take an interest in clinical encounters between doctors and patients. Part of it had to do with human experimentation: How was it that scientific researchers infected the retarded at Willowbrook with hepatitis in order to study them? Some of it had to do with the basic issue of truth-telling. Why was it that physicians appear reluctant to tell patients a grim diagnosis? Some of it also had to do with problems already clear in the seventies: definitions of death, termination of treatment. Some of it, too, had to do with basic questions of allocation of scarce resources, the classic case here being the dialysis machines and the creation of the so-called right-to-life committees. These questions were clearly questions involving values, not clinical skills, and a group of philosophers began to take an interest in how those decisions were being made.

Physicians often resisted some of this thinking, insisting that bioethicists were "armchair" doctors who never faced a patient. Certainly, the first fruits of bringing the discipline of philosophy into medicine was to make physicians quite wary of those who didn't wear white coats. Later they became quite wary, not of those who came carrying Immanuel Kant, but of those who came carrying account books. But in the seventies, the people carrying account books hadn't yet arrived. The philosophers had arrived, and with them a series of disaster stories about the clash between the two.

The bioethicists were interested in questions of ethics as they affected doctor-patient relationships. They used rules that would hold physicians to a uniform quality of behavior. Take the basic example—the one that was originally fought out—truth-telling. How can a patient begin to make decisions that express his individual values, unless he knows what the nature of his ailment is? How can he decide whether or not he wants treatment if he's not told the diagnosis? Rule: Doctors should tell patients their diagnosis. The physicians' initial response was to come up with a case in which truth-telling would seem to them to do harm, to force the patient to confront something that the patient didn't want to confront. Physicians kept repeating, "Don't bind us to rules! You've got to understand medicine is a case-by-case profession! Every patient is different!"

In certain ways the bioethicists of the seventies were the first outside group to really try to exert an impact on medical decision-making. This profession, certainly for the past fifty years, had been relatively free of external influences on its decision-making. All this means is that when I came up here I was greeted with open arms by some and suspicion by others: "Are you one more philosopher who is going to tell us how to practice medicine?"

What I began to do was to frame alternatives for them, to give them a sense of options, not simply to supply answers but to explore alternatives. I found myself very much attracted to the heart transplant team. Keith Reemtsma, Eric Rose, Ron Drusin, and the others find the sort of questions that I put to them interesting.

The question of allocation of scarce resources—we're talking now about human hearts—is terribly complicated. I think that group is supersensitive to the use of social criteria as a means of allocating a heart. When one makes a decision about who gets the next heart, obviously the first and most relevant criteria are of a purely medical sort: Does the patient have the sort of disease that will be cured through a new heart? Is the patient a medically appropriate candidate for a new heart? Those issues involve a description of the particular patient's health status, and in the discussions physicians need no one else.

But problems quickly arise because of the scarcity of hearts. Should other considerations beyond the medical ones affect the decision-making? For example, ought the fact that the recipient is unemployed go in the column against him, when that same week a well-employed, and indeed, quite wealthy individual also needs a heart? Does that count? Does intellectual contribution count for a patient, a criminal record against? In the original experience with dialysis machines in Seattle, when machines were limited and there were more needy patients than available machines, criteria were set up to determine who took priority over whom. The Seattle group actually tried to use social criteria and it turned out to be a disaster. The best line I ever heard was: "Henry David Thoreau ought never to have bad kidneys in the Northwest." That's because the committee selected middle-class, suburban, boy-scout types. Here, I'm pleased to say, the team doesn't discriminate. In fact, they reject social criteria.

But that doesn't end the problem, because there is another consideration that is very important to their minds, one that sounds medical, but actually may become a bridge into social. And that is, a good candidate for a heart has to be able to (a) go through the procedure successfully psychologically, and (b) and even more important, must be someone who can comply with a somewhat complicated medical regimen after transplant. By complying with a medical regimen they mean not doing things which would clearly be injurious to the heart: smoking, heavy drinking, drug use. So in the first instance, as you begin to move to compliance, it may sound as though you're still on medical grounds, but you may be leaving it. What do you do, for example, with someone who has in the past had a drinking problem, but now tells you, "I'm cured." Or what do you do with the fact that a black raised in a ghetto community will confess to you that in his youth he was a regular user of marijuana but he is no more. Sometimes the questions of psychiatry come into it. Is this off-beat patient one who will in fact have deep psychiatric problems such that he will not turn out to be a compliant patient? Are we talking about a social odd-ball? At what point does a substance-abuse criterion or a psychiatric criterion begin to fade into a social criterion? Here the lines blur and the questions get complicated.

If I have done anything at those Friday morning meetings, it's been to make them altogether aware of the blurred line. The people who sit around that table are perfectly capable of making these judgments without my presence. But my presence does help make certain that this type of issue will not be overlooked or lost. By labeling a particular patient compliant, are we really ducking the harder question as to whether or not, at this juncture, we're allowing social criteria to make the decision?

Other issues also surface. Should the gravely ill "bump" other patients on the list? Such bumping is in purest accord with standard medical criteria of triage: We serve the sickest whom we can do well by. On the other hand it certainly introduces a level of unfairness in the sense that the team is not following the principle of first come, first served. Giving preference to the most gravely ill introduces possible levels of unfairness to those who have been waiting on the list who have been ill, but not gravely ill, and keep getting bounced back.

Another issue I've raised is the fairness of transplanting patients twice. There's a long waiting list of people who have not had one heart. Does that common family rule hold—everybody gets one dessert before anybody gets two? Again the medical orientation is clear; once we're committed to you, we're committed to you. We gave you that first heart and if you're rejecting it or in need of another heart, we feel if anything a greater obligation to you because you're now someone to whom we're devoted. Yet, on the other hand, what about the unfairness of two hearts to somebody before someone else gets so much as one?

By a series of strange and unanticipated events, I have been given a key to a door which most people who are not medically trained don't receive: I have access to the world of a medical center in which clinical decision-making takes place. I'm aware of all the pressures which are exerted upon a medical center, whether it's from bioethicists, or economists, or legislators. My question is: What happens to those external pressures which come through the medical center? It's commonsensical to know that those pressures are not going to simply travel through and emerge at the other end unchanged. Medical centers are going to accept some ideas, block others, distort still others. And properly so. Physicians are not simply going to take their marching orders from outside all the time. Sometimes they will, sometimes they won't. It's the interaction of these pressures on medical decision-making that is presently at the heart of our agenda.

THERESA MORRONE, R.P.T.
Physical Therapist

She is in her twenties. Soft, brown hair frames her round face. She smiles as she talks, using her hands to emphasize her words. She has just come back from an exercise class where she puts the posttransplant patients "through their paces."

I see every patient who comes in to the hospital for a pre transplant work-up. I get a general idea of what they're physically capable of, how strong and how flexible they are. Then I give them all sorts of tips on how to make it through the day while they're waiting for their new heart, using the least amount of energy possible. For instance, if you take a shower and the water is hot, it's going to be more stressful for your heart than if the water's cooler. I say, "You don't have to stand in the shower, you can take a kitchen chair and put it in there and then sit and wash yourself." Eating smaller meals with softer food is sometimes helpful to patients who are too short of breath to eat. We're trying to help them save as much heart muscle as they have left.

Another thing I tell them is what to expect right after their surgery. I say, "You're going to have this crazy woman—me—who is going to come in a few days after your transplant and tell you to start exercising, and you're going to say, 'Look lady, you don't understand. I just had a heart transplant!' and I'm going to say, 'I don't care *what* you had. Get out of bed!' "

If the transplant surgery goes well, within a day or two, I do just as I promised. I'll go up to the patient's room and start exercising him in bed. A few days later we walk up and down the hall. I devise all these stupid ways of walking to make it harder. Pick your arm up and your leg, walk like a drum majorette. Some of them I think I'm a little crazy because I get them going so soon. But the patients are *afraid*. They're afraid the new heart is going to disconnect. They're afraid that if they do too much their heart is going to fall off. Some of them think it's only held in there by little pieces of string. I had a patient who used to call me "the colonel." Another patient told me that working with me was like being on the rack! He'd say, "The rack! The rack is here!" It's really funny. I've had such nicknames.

I went to my first Friday morning transplant conference with great apprehension—these guys had all been together so long and I was like the new kid on the block. But anybody new walks in that first day and Dr. Reemtsma is so nice to you. He gets you a cup of coffee. He sits right next to you, too. I guess because he probably figures it's scary to be there. After the first few meetings, I started talking up because I had things to say. And in fact they started listening to me. Now I've reached a point where they ask me if a patient is ready to go home as far as walking and stairs go. So it's nice. It's nice to know other people recognize that what you do is important.

One thing that gripes me is the way the media gives so much attention to the people who perform the transplant and so little to the patient. The media plays up getting the heart, bringing it down, putting it in. And I agree, there's a lot of drama with that. It's miraculous that you can remove an organ that was beating in one person, put it into somebody else, and have it work. But nobody knows how much work the *patients* do afterwards, how much time they have to spend getting back to what they were. The exercise that it takes. The fear that they have to overcome. The sensationalism is always brought out about the operation, but for the patients, after the surgery the work has just begun. It's true. For example, people are out of breath before a heart transplant because their hearts don't work. I'm forcing them back into that same state because I'm consciously working their hearts. That's scary. They panic that they're breathless just like before their heart transplant! But I tell them it's different. I say, "Trust me. Just let me exercise you to the point of breathlessness and then sit there and you'll feel better in a few minutes." It's a hard concept to grasp. You have to establish a bond between the patient and you.

When patients are about ready to go home, I explain to them that they're going to have to come and see me as an outpatient. They also have to come to clinic twice a week. I tell them it's not like having a gall bladder taken out. You don't say, "Gee, thanks a lot, doc. I'll see you later." Our patients are sort of stuck with coming back and forth. There are a lot of strings attached to having a heart transplant in that respect. I tell them, "Look, it's wonderful to have us. It's wonderful to have people who, seven days a week, twenty-four hours a day, know you or something about you, and can care for you. But at the same time, those same people are going to tell you a lot of things you can and can't do. Like if you have *any* physical problems, not just with your heart—you have to check in first with us. It's like a two-way street, you know? If your mother gives you everything, you have to go visit her on Sunday.

ERIC ROSE, M.D.

Director, Heart Transplantation Service

"I come from a family of musicians. In fact, I'm the only nonprofessional musician in my family at this point. My father leads a band that does weddings and bar mitzvahs and all that kind of stuff. When I was growing up, he taught me how to play club dates—I play the piano—and all through college I worked weekends for him and for other band leaders. It was fun, actually, and I made enough money to put myself through college and medical school."

He is thirty-five, boyishly handsome despite his prematurely gray hair. His wife is an anesthesiologist who works in the hospital.

He talks about the "old days."

Doing a heart surgery residency here is a lot like being in the army. The hours are incredible. You're on call every other night. You're always running to do one thing or another. We used to sleep in a little room back behind the regular recovery room where the open heart patients were put fresh out of the operating room. Since there was no place even remotely near it for residents to sleep, we'd sleep right along with the patients on the beds with the rubber sheets and the rubber pillows. And in the morning, we'd strip our beds to make it look like the recovery room again. It was really something, listening to their ventilators all night, and the cardiac monitors. You'd rarely sleep the whole night up there, anyway. There was enough to do in the unit that you were usually up for a few hours, and back to sleep for an hour or two. We did that every other night for two years.

Sometimes you wonder how you'll get up the next morning and operate, but you do. The energy is there and certainly the stimulation is there to do it. There's no question there are times where you're wiped out. And certainly it's tough on your personal life, but you do it. We always used to say the mental state of a resident was: Too tired to eat, too hungry to sleep.

Toward the end of my six years of training, I was kind of hoping they'd offer me a position in heart surgery here. I liked the hospital, I was attracted to an academic career. I liked New York, and being here seemed to have it all for me in terms of that. I didn't know what Keith Reemtsma's agenda was at that time—he is generally about twenty-five years ahead of all of us in terms of where he's pushing us. At the same time I was finishing my residency and thinking about jobs, he decided he was going to have a substantial heart transplant service here. Well, up until that time, my only exposure to heart transplantation was reading through the literature. A couple of heart transplants had been done here when I was a general surgical resident, but only one of them was done when I was a heart surgery resident. To me heart surgery was bypass, valves, and children's congenital defects. Transplantation was something that some eccentric, immunologically oriented people got interested in doing.

Anyway, there I was, hoping to be asked to go on staff here, and there was Keith, looking for someone to bring into the hospital who'd be interested in heart transplantation. One of the most painful evenings of my life was when he invited me to a dinner for a surgeon that he was trying to recruit. I just had to sit there and say good things about this place and encourage him to take the job I wanted. We had dinner down at the Century Club, and we smoked lots of cigars, and ate a lot of rack of lamb, all kinds of stuff like that. This guy was a superb heart surgeon. By the end of the evening, I had given up on the notion of their offering me a job to stay here. But fortunately for me, the surgeon decided to go elsewhere. Not too long after that Keith called me into his office and said to me, "Eric, I want you to come on staff as an attending, but I want you to do heart transplantation." Then he added, "I want you to go to Stanford, soak up the knowledge you need to do this well, and I want you to make a heart transplant program that in five years' time will be one of the best in the country." That was what he said five years ago. And I think we've done just that.

I did my first transplant here in April of '82. It was a twenty-year-old man who had been in the hospital here for several months with an ideopathic cardiomyopathy [the heart muscle begins to deteriorate for some unknown reason.] He lived for about two and a half years after the transplant, and then died from an infection. The second one that I did was a remarkable man, Robert Andrews, who lived up in Albany. We had tried for a long time to find a donor for him and finally we got lucky. As soon as we heard we called him up and we said, "Come on down; we've got your heart!" We sent the team out to Detroit on the jet and we had organized things at this end, and so there we were, sitting around, waiting, and no Bob. The guy suddenly got cold feet about doing this. He really had second thoughts! And while we were getting everything going, he was driving half-way around the state of Connecticut deciding if he should go for it.

We were going crazy! You know? "Where the hell is this guy?" The donor crunch was not as great then as it is now, but you do feel a tremendous obligation to have at least *somebody* to put the heart into when it comes back. He finally walked in the door and said, "Okay, I'll do it." He did beautifully. And he's still fine. It's going to be four years in April.

People often ask me how the decision is made, when a heart becomes available. That's one of the things we do in our Friday morning meetings. We have a large team, now, and we all meet together and confront the issues as to who is a candidate and who is not. The decisions are made in a quasi-public forum. One of the reasons we don't agonize over these decisions is that we've not had too many social contraindications to transplantation. We don't look for somebody who can afford the hundred-thousand-dollar hospital bill. We're not making decisions about transplanting somebody because he's got a fat wallet, or he's a relative of mine or Ron's, or he's Dr. Reemtsma's college buddy. By and large, we've been able to stick to medical criteria for making a decision. The only social issue I'd say that's really come up, and it came up just at our conference last week, was the issue of substance abuse.

Our policy has been if somebody has a history of alcohol or drug abuse, that we'd like to see them drug-free for a period of six months before considering them for transplantation. Just to elicit the type of commitment that we think that they have to make to keeping appointments for checkups, for taking medications, that kind of thing. So if we know in advance that they're substance abusers, we hold off temporarily. We've got a couple of people who were substance abusers who didn't let us know about it before they were transplanted, and they're doing fine. People now point that out and say, Mr. Jones used to take cocaine and he is now two years after the transplant and looks great and he hasn't taken any cocaine since. So is cocaine abuse an absolute contraindication to transplant? Who can answer that?

For me, the most exhilarating experience was transplanting a four-year-old little boy that we did two and a half years ago. We hadn't done any small children before that. And I don't think anybody else had either. His name was J.P. He was from Denver, four years old, just twenty pounds. He had congenital heart disease and had had his previous surgery here. His parents are phenomenal people. Very involved. Essentially they said, "We don't want our son to die." They were told in Denver that the only thing that would save him at this point would be a heart transplant. So they brought him here. He was evaluated by a pediatric cardiologist, Welton Gersony, and we told the parents this had not been done before. They said they wanted us to try it anyway. I think they had a lot more confidence at that point than we did.

The surgery was extremely complicated. It always is when a person's chest has already been opened. Fred Bowman, who had done his previous surgery, was there to make sure we understood what we were looking at, which was a big help. We got a donor in our own hospital. It was a real tragedy—a kid had fallen out of a window on a hot summer night—but it was a blessing to J.P. He's six now. A wonderful little boy whose picture I keep on my desk just to remind me what courage can do.

We have research going on in our labs that points toward what I think is the future of transplantation. I think in the not-too-distant future we're going to be putting animal hearts into people to take over function. There's no question about it in my mind. And it's not a question of whether, it's only a question of when. The animal rights people notwithstanding, we slaughter hundreds of thousands of cattle per year to keep us eating, and I don't think people are going to complain about the use of animals as a source for human cardiac replacement.

We have animals going now as long as two hundred days with hearts from another genus. It's called cross species. A cynomologus monkey is alive and well in our laboratory with the heart of a baboon. They're both primates and the genetic disparity we think is the equivalent of about a chimp to a man. In view of the scarcity of human hearts, this research is of tremendous importance.

A heart transplant is an easy thing to do. The bigger, the more emotionally wrenching phenomenon we face is seeing people who we think are perfectly appropriate candidates for it die, waiting. That's the pits. We've got a twelve-year-old girl downstairs right now who I think would do beautifully if we could find a heart for her. If we can't, I'm not sure she'll be here by the end of the week.

LINDA ADDONIZIO, M.D.
Pediatric Cardiologist

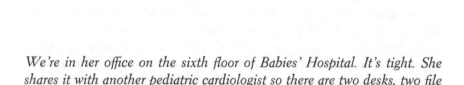

We're in her office on the sixth floor of Babies' Hospital. It's tight. She shares it with another pediatric cardiologist so there are two desks, two file cabinets, two of everything. Pictures of children are everywhere. Outside, it's a bleak, rainy day but that does not diminish her ebullience as she speaks of her patients.

Our conversation is interrupted once by a young teenage boy—one of her post-transplant patients—who bursts through the door to ask her a question. When he leaves, she says to me, "See that kid? Last year at this time that kid was dead."

Children who need heart transplants have either been born with defective hearts for which there is no known surgical cure, or they've had their hearts unsuccessfully repaired. Some get a virus that attacks the heart and slowly destroys it, and some have what we call idiopathic cardiomyopathy, which means we just don't know why their heart has started to fail.

It's terrible to think how many of these children have died waiting for a heart to become available. Recently, one little girl died while they were actually flying to get her new heart. We just couldn't get her to survive any longer. It's tragic when you come that close. I think we could save a lot of these children if we got them earlier in their illness. But some members of the medical profession still aren't familiar with the success rates of heart transplantation and so they don't always think of it as a viable therapy. They hang on to their patients, hoping that maybe they'll improve, and, as a result, the child doesn't get seen until he or she is so sick we have a very short period of time left to help them. I think that's why I have so many gray hairs.

Before they come here to see us, I insist that the referring physicians tell the parents *and* the child that a transplant might be a therapeutic option, if, of course, the child is old enough to understand, and I consider even a nine-year-old, old enough. A lot of these kids are pretty savvy anyway. They've been hospitalized for a long time and they really know a lot. You have to be straight with them. I do a lot of explaining and drawing pictures and talking about things, but one of the best things is just have them meet some of the other kids who've been through it. That allays more fears than any other way. Generally, though, a child in need of a new heart usually feels so sick, he doesn't care what you have to do. One child recently said, "I'll do anything to feel better, anything you want. Just do it, please. And soon."

I always go into the operating room with the kids. I stay with them during the operation and afterwards, until they're stable. And I'm here for the parents because, in part, we're treating them, too. They need a familiar face to come down and talk to them in the middle of the operation, someone to say, "Things are going well." They need that continuity.

Being part of a transplant team can definitely interfere with your family life. My husband is a doctor, but he leads a very different life than I do. He's a psychiatrist, so he has much more regular hours. And I have a sixteen-year-old son. They're both used to my working long hours, but what they object to is the unpredictability of those hours, the fact that I may get a call at any time. If someone from the hospital calls and says they've found a donor, that means there might be a heart that's right for one of my kids. And *that* means that all plans are off. I'm committed to being in the hospital from then on. Everything gets dropped from that point, and that's what my family objects to. For example, I had planned to take Christmas week off the year before last, and two days before Christmas we transplanted one of my kids. Then New Year's Day we transplanted another one. So it's hard. It's strange, it seems that all of the kids have been operated on around holidays. That probably has to do with donor supply being more prevalent around holidays, but every holiday you can think of, I've had a transplant.

We lost two wonderful children very recently, and it's always very wrenching. I keep telling myself these children would have been dead if we hadn't tried this. I think the fact that I'm basically an optimist is what sustains me. That, and the great success stories. Angela Roberts is one. She's a special girl. She'd had a cardiomyopathy for about four years and was followed by an adult cardiologist in her home town. She was ten when we transplanted her; she's now twelve. The parents came to see Dr. Reemtsma and he sent them to me. I interviewed both her and her parents. It was very clear when she walked in the office that she belonged in the hospital on IV medication. She was very sick and had been ill so long. Her nails were always done, her hair was always in place. She's very meticulous. A very bright, straight A student. Very engaging. And yet, here was a kid who never owned a pair of sneakers. Imagine that—in this day and age. But that's because she couldn't do any exercise or anything.

When I interviewed her, she was very scared and didn't want to have anything to do with the whole process. She didn't realize how sick she was because she'd been getting there so gradually. So I did something which I haven't done before. I showed her her chest X ray. I said, "You see this? This is your heart." She was a small girl and even she could see a heart in her chest the size of a football, and she said, "Oh, my God!" She had never really realized that she was that sick. She agreed to be admitted to the hospital that day. She was transplanted at the end of August, on my husband's birthday.

Another success story was the little boy who was just running down the corridor—Josh. He was one of the sickest patients we've ever transplanted. We thought we found him a heart one time and then we couldn't operate for some reason and he had to go home. He was one of these kids who was at home and doing fairly well, but as time went on and we had no heart, he got sicker and sicker. Finally he had to be admitted to the hospital. He continued to deteriorate and we still couldn't find a heart. He was in the ICU; he was almost comatose with such low blood pressure and heart failure, and finally on Easter Sunday—another holiday transplant— we found a heart for him. We took him to the operating room and just as he got to the room and we were about to transfer him from the stretcher to the operating table, he went into cardiac arrest—his heart just stopped. We did an unbelievably fast resuscitation. Fortunately, I had shock trousers on him, and they kept on pumping up, rotating, pumping . . . We were improvising, anything to keep him alive. It took us a while to get him going again, and we got him on the heart-lung machine, and the big question on our minds was, "What's going to happen to this child's brain afterwards?" We had no idea if we were able to get enough perfusion to his brain during the arrest. It was a pretty scary few days. It took three days before he woke up, but when he did, he was fine. Perfectly fine. Now he's this big, active kid who continually wants to play football, and do all the things I don't want him to do. But those are the experiences that take their toll.

I try to leave this place behind when I go home at night. That's one of the therapeutic things about having a long drive home. If I needed only five minutes to get home, I might spend a good deal more time thinking about things. You have to try to have some life other than here. You do the best you can not to always be thinking about these children. And yet you remember them—all of them—at one time or another. For me, it's hardest to forget one little girl who died. I drive past her town every day, and every day I think about her. So you see, you never get rid of the memories of these kids. You just don't.

BONNIE ARCHER, R.N.

Assistant Head Nurse,
Surgical Cardiac Intensive Coronary Care Unit

We're in a conference room next door to the coronary unit where the open heart and transplant patients are taken directly after surgery. Ten minutes into our conversation, a nurse appears at the door and beckons her to the unit. A patient is just coming down from the operating room.

The patient, a gray-haired man who appears to be about fifty, is wheeled into a room filled with high-tech equipment. A closed-circuit television camera perched in the corner of the room transmits a picture of the patient to the nurses' station at all times. An electrocardiogram machine is next to the bed, as are a respirator and a cart holding the equipment necessary to care for this patient. We stand in a corner of the room watching the feverish activity as the sleeping patient is hooked up to the many mechanical-assist devices and monitors. In less than twenty minutes, the hookup is complete. The patient is still sleeping soundly as his assigned nurse takes over. We return to the conference room.

The heart surgery unit is run by nurses. When a nurse comes to work here, he or she has to forget about being task oriented. Nurses here have to gear their thinking to clinically managing a patient. Here you must think like a doctor. You have to. A patient has a crisis, there's not always time for you to go get a doctor. They'll die.

Our standards are extremely high. The hospital runs a core course which you have to pass before you can be a critical care nurse. They weed out people who can't make it. I run the clinical orientation course, which is a six-week training course for nurses who want to work in this unit. My last group, in September, started with eight nurses, and only four made it through the core course. It's a waste of time and money to bump someone out of the program, but the alternative is they could injure a patient. So if they're not up to our standards, out they go.

It's hard to turn down a nurse. We need every one we can get. This unit is going through a *horrible* crisis. There are just not enough nurses. Actually, there's a massive shortage of nurses everywhere. They are not graduating as many—people aren't going into it like they used to. Critical care units, open heart, and ER are hardest hit. We have a three-hundred-dollar bounty here. If one of us recruits another RN, we get paid three hundred bucks. And still, no one has recruited anybody. Not one nurse. No kidding.

Most of the pre-transplant patients are at home waiting for a heart to become available. When we get a heart, the patient it's for is called and told to come directly up to us. When they arrive, when they see this place, they just stand there, dazed. They can't believe it! The unit looks to them like something from outer space. The first thing we do is put them in a room and preop them. We draw blood, shave them, do all the usual preop things. It can take about two hours. And then we wait.

The worst thing that can happen preoperatively is that the donor heart is no good. You don't know that for sure until the team has gone to see it, but you can't hold off bringing the patient in, because time is so important. If the heart is no good, the team won't take it. We've had patients go upstairs and be put to sleep, and then the surgery is canceled. The patient knows that can happen—some have had three or four false alarms. Even our children say, "Maybe I'll get it this time, maybe I won't." Sometimes when they see someone else getting a heart they'll say, "You know I've waited three times?" But we try to assure them—"You'll get yours, you'll get it. Don't worry."

Once I went to Michigan with Dr. Reemtsma to pick up a donor heart. I remember him reading a horror book the whole way there—a horror story! He's a lot of fun. He's just the way anybody else is, you know? Even with his position, he's always the same. He and a chest resident were scheduled to go and no one else was available, so they asked me if I wanted go. I said, "Me?" I thought they were kidding. "Sure, you," they said. "But we want you to work, not just go along for the ride."

We took an ambulance to Teterboro Airport and took a Lear jet to a suburb outside of Detroit. The donor was at a six-hundred-bed hospital. The people there were really excited about our coming. I think it was their first donor. All we knew in advance was, this family was giving away their son's heart. Usually you see the patient for the first time in the operating room, but this particular family wanted to meet the heart team while the boy was still alive. When we walked into the room, the grieving family was surrounding his bed, which is unusual.

So we went to the bedside like they wanted and, of course, who does Reemtsma push in front of the family? Me! I'll never forget it. About six family members were on or around the bed, crying. The patient was seventeen years old, nine days brain dead from a motorcycle accident. He had been hit by a tractor trailer. So I peeked through the curtain and saw them all crying and grieving over this body that was only alive because of all these machines. The mother came out of the room and she asked me who the heart was going to. I told her the recipient was a young woman with two small children. Well, that made the whole family so happy. They were almost relieved. For them the continuation of life had begun. The grieving was over.

In less than fifteen minutes the boy was in the operating room. In addition to his heart, the family had decided to donate his liver and pancreas. That meant we had to wait until the end to get the heart, because taking it earlier would discontinue circulation; we would literally kill the patient. It was incredible. They had me directing the OR staff, people I'd never seen before. "Anything Miss Archer tells you to do, do it," they said, and I think if I told them to jump off the roof, they would have jumped!

The other procurement teams had all this technology, this fancy kidney pump machine and fancy pancreas conserver. They thought we were much too calm. We only had this Igloo picnic ice-chest. But that's all we need, because the heart is just put into a bag with a special solution that preserves it for the trip, and the bag goes directly into a Styrofoam ice-chest. They see us being really calm, and Reemtsma is so easy going.

When we got ready to take the heart the anesthesiologist looked at me for direction in everything. When the other teams got what they wanted we opened the chest. Greg, who was the chest resident, clamped the aorta and I was supposed to flush this special solution on the heart and assist the anesthesiologist. I'll never forget that moment. The blood pressure was 120 over 70; then they clamped the boy's aorta, removed his heart, and the pressure dropped to zero. There was no blood. I held the bag and they dropped the heart into it and I put it in the ice chest. Everyone was standing around saying, "Oh, my goodness. Is that all there is?" It really looks so simple. An amazing organ, the heart.

We left the hospital as soon as we finished. We were rushing like crazy, because our patient at home was *very* sick. We were going to be lucky if we could make it back in time. I mean, *minutes* were important! The plan was, when we were in the air coming back I was to radio in to Eric Rose, who was standing by in the Presbyterian OR with the patient asleep. He needed the estimated time of arrival so he could put her on bypass and remove her heart. Timing was everything. This woman was dying. When we were up in the air, I radioed in and said we'd be arriving at Teterboro almost on the dot of two in the morning. That was the signal to Eric to begin removing her heart. After I hung up the phone, the pilot said to me, "Miss Archer, what's the nearest airport?" I said, "What do you mean, what's the nearest airport?" He told us there was a storm coming up and we were going to have to land elsewhere. I said, "We can't! We can't land anywhere else! They've cut her heart out! They already put the woman on bypass!"

So, with our fingers crossed, we landed at Teterboro. It had taken us an hour and a half to fly to Detroit and we made it back in forty-five minutes. The storm practically carried the plane. It was just me, Reemtsma, the chest resident, and the two pilots. We had flown out of the storm. When we got to Jersey, the ambulance rushed us across the bridge and we met the state troopers from New York. We got to the ER platform, ran into the hospital, went right up to the operating room, gave them the heart, and they put it into the patient. Just in time. Believe me, *just* in time.

KEITH REEMTSMA, M.D.

Chairman, Department of Surgery

⟋⟍

Almost everyone calls him K.R., or "Chief." He's well over six feet tall and reed-thin. He has white hair and steel-blue eyes that peer at the world through wire-rimmed glasses. In fact, he looks so much like the prototypical surgeon, some say he descended upon the hospital directly from central casting. (Rumors also abound that it was he upon whom the M*A*S*H character Hawkeye was based.)

He has been chief for fourteen years. He's sixty-two.

I grew up on a Navajo Indian reservation in Fort Defiance, Arizona, where my father was a Presbyterian missionary. Fort Defiance was where Kit Carson brought his troops to round up the Navajo Indians after the Civil War. When I grew up it was a town of about six hundred people, all of whom were Indians except my family and the postmaster and the guy that owned the trading post. I thought it was a wonderful place.

I went to school in a two-room log cabin, where one teacher covered both rooms. There were three people in my class and I was the second smartest. The Indian girl did better than I did.

After the eighth grade, there was no place for white children so I was sent to a Presbyterian boarding school in the middle of Utah. A fascinating school. Very small. My favorite teacher taught typing, so I became an excellent typist. In fact, the summer following my junior year in high school, I hitchhiked to New York and got a job as a teletype operator at a place called Transradio Press. From there I was promoted rapidly, probably because it was the Second World War and no one else was around. So by default I become the editor of the foreign desk at the age of sixteen.

I became so absorbed in journalism that I applied to Columbia and I got accepted, and even got a scholarship to the School of Journalism. I was very proud of myself! Then, when I went back to Utah, I heard that if you joined the Navy they would pay for your education and you could go wherever you wanted. And I believed them! So I enlisted one day in Salt Lake City and they sent me to the nearest V-12 school, which was in Pocatello, Idaho. So I ended up going to college at Idaho State.

The way I got into medicine is kind of interesting. When I joined the Navy they gave me an application for officer training and there were six choices, as I recall. I could be a preengineer, or a predeck officer, or a predental, or a premedical, or a prewhatever. But it turned out that you had to have mechanical drawing for four of them and I had flunked mechanical drawing in high school—I was never very good at drawing pictures of hinges on screen doors. Well, what you didn't need it for was premedical and prechaplain. Now, I didn't know anything about being a doctor but I sure as hell knew about being a preacher, so I checked the box that said premedical.

When it came time to pick a medical school, I didn't even know where to start. Hell, I didn't know *anything* about it. I only knew one doctor and he worked on the Indian reservation down in Fort Defiance, so I called and asked him where he had gone and he said he had gone to the University of Pennsylvania, so I wrote down the University of Pennsylvania and that's where I went.

The first two years at med school I was thinking I'd end up in psychiatry or something, but in my third year I had an experience that changed my mind. For my surgical rotation I was assigned to a hospital in the heart of Philadelphia. There was a woman in my class whom I knew fairly well and she had been assigned to Children's Hospital, which in those days was in a rather scruffy section of town. She asked if I would mind trading with her since she didn't want to go down there at night and so forth. Well, I wasn't interested in surgery anyway. So it didn't matter to me where I did it.

It so happened that at that time the chief of surgery at Children's was a young surgeon named C. Everett Koop, who is now surgeon general of the United States. When I showed up, "Chick" Koop came out to meet me. He knew my name, which amazed me. It was the first time anybody had ever called me by my name in medical school. Before that, it seemed my name was, "Hey, you! Where are the X rays?" So Chick comes out and shakes my hand and says "Reemtsma, this is a *great* opportunity for you. There's a room that you can live in and you can have free meals. All you have to do is stay here and work twenty-four hours a day and do everything I tell you to do." "Dr. Koop," I said, "you've got a deal." Nobody had ever offered me free board and room before, and I just thought that was marvelous. By the time I finished there, I knew I was going to become a surgeon. When it came time to look for a residency, I asked Dr. Koop where he thought I should go for my training. He suggested Cornell, because he had graduated from there, and he wrote me this fancy letter.

Well, I went up to the Cornell affiliate, which is New York Hospital, and I went in, somewhat nervously, to be interviewed by Dr. S. William Moore. I walked into the room, shook his hand, and sat down. "Boy," he said, "what did your daddy do?" I told him what my daddy did, and we talked for a few minutes and then he said, "Boy, I don't think you'd be very happy here. This is a very competitive institution. These people are really tough and mean to each other and you don't look to me like you're very tough and mean." He said, "I don't think you would fit in here." So I said, "Well, Dr. Moore, I've taken a day off and I've come to New York, so do you have any suggestions where else I might apply?" So he said, "You could go up to Columbia-Presbyterian. They might have a slot." I'd never heard of it at that time, but I got on the A train, came up here, knocked on the door, and wound up in a residency program.

In 1952, early in my residency, I was recalled into the Navy. When I was in the Second World War, I was an enlisted man. Now they called me back as a doctor.

As a doctor during the Korean War, I was on a Navy surgical team, assigned to several different units in Korea, including the Marine Corps. It was during the period after the Marines had evacuated on the eastern coast. We were at the front near Panmunjom. It was a remarkable experience. When I first saw the movie *M*A*S*H*, I thought it was a documentary of my life! I looked at that and I was sure my entire stint in Korea had been recreated on film. From the minute those helicopters spun down and landed and people ran up to take the casualties off the helicopters, throughout the whole thing, I sat back and I couldn't believe what I saw! The football game in Tokyo, operating on the little baby in Japan. All of that was what I had done.

I left Korea sometime around 1953 and I resumed my residency here. I finished in 1957 and then I had to decide what I was going to do with my life. I'd originally planned to return to New Mexico. I was going to practice in Santa Fe. But doing new and different things appealed to me and one thing led to another and I was offered a job at Tulane University in New Orleans and I took it.

They had just appointed a new chief named Oscar Creech, the finest person, most outstanding surgeon and thinker I had ever met. I don't know why he picked me to give a job to because I certainly didn't have anything that outstanding in my credentials. But I've always thought maybe it was because he was a minister's son, too. The job paid six thousand dollars a year. It was a fantastic nine years. Creech let me develop in the two areas that were brand new, cardiac surgery and transplantation.

In those days there was no clinical activity in heart transplantation. Zero. Very little in kidney transplants, and open heart surgery was just getting started. So in 1960 I set up the kidney transplant program and started doing the only operation that was available in those days—related-donor transplants.

By 1963, an interesting opportunity arose. It was before dialysis had become widely available and it was before cadaver kidney transplants had been used—the only kidneys were from living related donors, so there was a bleak outlook for people with kidney disease. Under those circumstances I decided to explore the use of nonhumans as a source of organs. I picked a chimpanzee because it was the highest of the apes related to humans that was available. This was all highly controversial. The consequence was that it changed our view toward nonhuman sources. It took a lot of research and a lot of work on the part of a lot of people, but eventually we were ready to attempt the first transplant of a chimpanzee kidney into a human.

The patient was a very fine young man named Jefferson Davis. He was a thoughtful, intelligent stevedore who worked on the docks in New Orleans. He knew exactly what his risks were and he knew what his chances of survival were without any treatment. There was no dialysis available to him, we had no cadaver organs. He had nothing. I offered him this as an experiment. I told him that it had never been done before, and that the chances of success were unpredictable, and that it might not work at all. Still, he decided to go ahead with it and the results were really fantastic!

There was a tremendous outburst of criticism initially because at that time, in 1963, I was an unknown and I was working in an institution which had not been noted for its transplantation work. At first people thought this was some sort of an adventure. Later, it became apparent that we had done it in a way that was scientifically sound. We had outstanding immunologists working with us. We had a very, very good group. So by the time all of the evidence came out people understood that this was incredible scientific work.

There's a phrase we use, "the thrill of discovery." That's probably a little overstated, but there is something about taking an idea, especially one that is controversial, and being able to develop it in a way that is scientifically sound and ethically appropriate, and going ahead with it. The patient did remarkably well and we ended up doing a number of those procedures, as did other surgeons who had come to watch us. The reason we discontinued it is because we were able by 1965 to do human cadaver grafts, and I didn't think it was justified to continue subjecting patients to those risks. But that was a moment of discovery which was so marvelous.

In 1966, I was offered the job of chief of surgery at the University of Utah. I felt it was an outstanding opportunity, although most people warned me against Utah. They said that it was a small school and it had never had a successful department of surgery—which generally was true. But I went out there and it seemed to me that it had everything to offer. They had a brand-new hospital, a first-rate medical school, a remarkable community. The first thing I did was to start building a new team. I was most successful recruiting Mormons and skiers who were also surgeons.

I had been there about a week and the dean walked into my office one afternoon and said, "Keith, how are things going?" And I said, "Dean, they're just going great. I'm very happy here." And he said to me, "Keith, what are you going to do with Building 512?" Now, I hadn't been a chairman very long, but I had been around long enough *not* to say, "What's Building 512?" So I said, "Dr. Castleton, I've got some great plans on developing Building 512, and I'll get right back to you on them."

After he left I turned to my secretary and I said, "Marge, what the *hell* is Building 512?" And she said, "Oh God, I forgot to tell you. Out there behind the medical school, there's an old barracks. Your predecessor used to do genetics out there and he kept a bunch of mason jars with fruit flies or something in them. That building is part of the department of surgery."

Well, I went out and looked at it and I wondered what I was going to do with it. There I was, standing in the mud in November of 1966 and looking down the hill at this huge building, just a seven-iron shot away from what turned out to be the College of Engineering. So there was the College of Engineering, and here was the College of Medicine, and right in between was this big, empty building. So I said, "I know what I'll do. I'll make myself the world's greatest bioengineering institute."

Well, I didn't know anything about bioengineering, but I figured I'd go for the best guy I could find to head it up and I thought of Willem Kolff, the guy who invented the artificial kidney and who was working on the artificial heart. I didn't know Kolff well. He's a fellow Dutchman and I'd met him, but we weren't close friends or anything. So, I called him up and introduced myself and he said, "Oh, yeah, I know who you are. I read about that crazy stuff you did on that nutty chimpanzee." He said, "You should have been thrown out of the country for that!" "Pim," I said (Pim is the diminutive for Willem), "I want you and your wife to come to Salt Lake." At the time, he was at the Cleveland Clinic. So he said, "Where in the world is Salt Lake?" And I said, "Don't give me any of that stuff. Call your travel agent, bring your wife out, and spend three days here."

When he came out, I put him and his wife up in the bridal suite at the top of Hotel Utah, looking out over Temple Square, with fruit, food, wine, and flowers. And I arranged for him to have breakfast with the governor. We had lunch with the president of the university, Jim Fletcher, who is now the director of NASA. Then I introduced him to all the engineering people and all the computer people and all the surgeons and medical people.

At the end of his visit I took him out and showed him Building 512. I said, "Pim, we have a fantastic opportunity here. There's the College of Engineering. There's the College of Medicine. I can make you a professor of surgery. I can give you all the stationery you need. I can't pay you a god damn nickel, because I don't have any money. But I *can* give you all of Building 512!"

He said, "I'll take it." Just like that.

He came out there and we set up this thing, which is still going on. It's still the foremost biomedical system in the country. And that's due to him.

At that time Bill DeVries was my medical student, and he came to me one day and he wanted to know what he could do in the summer. I said, "Why don't you go over and work with Pim Kolff on the artificial heart? You have a Dutch name. He'll like you, I guess." So he went over there and he introduced himself and Kolff asked him his name and he said "DeVries," and Kolff said, "You're hired. Your job will be to lift sheep from the floor up onto the operating table." So Bill DeVries—the fellow who would later implant the world's first artificial heart—spent a summer lifting up sheep.

My areas of interest then were in diabetes, islet-cell transplant, and heart transplant, and I wanted a different, bigger canvas. So I left Utah in 1971. I felt that I had done my job. I had been there five years and I had built a very strong department and gotten good people and good programs and I started thinking of other things I wanted to do, things that required a larger institution with a different environment. I was offered the chairmanship here, as the director of surgery, and I took it.

Even though this is one of the world's largest and most prestigious institutions, when I arrived in 1971, they were nowhere in the field of transplantation. They didn't even have a dialysis unit. It was 1971! As far as I was concerned, every hospital—even Fort Defiance, Arizona—had a dialysis machine. But it's indicative of the fact that this institution, despite its prominence in some areas, had lagged in others. So we got a dialysis unit going, then we got the renal transplant program going under Dr. Mark Hardy, who did an excellent job. After I had been here four years, I was able to think about going into heart transplants.

Heart transplants had had a meteoric rise around the globe, and then an equally sudden decline. It rose in the late sixties and early seventies because of the promising work being done. All around the world, I think there were something like seventy teams. By 1973, there was one team left. Essentially, Stanford carried the candle through the years of darkness, which is a tribute to Norman Shumway. He was the father of this field; his work has been the gold standard. Shumway appreciated, as many others did not, that in order to take care of heart transplant patients, you have to do more than just heart surgery. You've got to take care of your patients forever.

By 1975, there was no one in this part of the country who was doing heart transplants, so I decided to do them here, and I began planning. I did the first heart transplant here in 1976.

Ron Drusin took care of our first patient. After that, I was able to persuade him to take on the medical side of the program and gradually we got other cardiologists, so we are very, very strong. In the surgical area, we're very fortunate that we have two outstanding cardiac surgeons. One of them is Eric Rose, who trained here, and the other is Craig Smith, who trained at Case Western Reserve, the University of Rochester, and here. Those two guys are just absolutely superb. And we have key people in immunology, psychiatry, neurology, social work, infectious disease, pediatrics. Across the board.

We've now done well over a hundred and fifty patients, and the results are really quite striking. We're discharging a patient today who had his heart transplant done eight days ago. He's going home. He came out of the operating room and never required any kind of support other than immune suppression. Eight days and he is going home! My God, you just think about the results! Something like eighty percent of our patients will be alive in a year, and as far as we know they will continue to live after that, and a hundred percent of our patients in their second year are fully rehabilitated. Every one of them is doing something. Working full time, teaching, going to school.

To see how well these patients do gives me an enormous sense of pride and satisfaction. Not in my work, but in the group of people who are here. If someone asked me, I'd say that my greatest contribution has been developing such an outstanding group of young people.

At our Friday morning meeting I often look around the table at this group. To see a group of people so committed tells you something. The reason that we're successful is not just because we have cyclosporine, or because we know how to do the operation, it's because we've got this group of people here to take on the care of these patients for the rest of their lives. Our patients know—it doesn't matter where they are or what time it is—if they get a cold or anything else, they are supposed to pick up the phone and call us.

It's interesting how you develop a group like this. I'm sure that I do it differently than some other surgeons do. Other surgeons are probably more autocratic than I am. One of the people that I've learned a little bit from is Tom Landry, the coach of the Dallas Cowboys. If you ever notice him on the sidelines, he's always well dressed and he's calm. If anything goes wrong, you never see him kicking helmets or slugging players or berating someone. Somebody asked him once, "Why are you so calm and all these other guys are behaving like a bunch of madmen?" He answered, "Well, I always make the assumption that the people out there on the field are trying to do a good job. If you make that assumption, and if something goes wrong, the first question you ask is, 'Why haven't I been able to communicate my plans to these people?' You don't start off with, 'Why did that dope drop the ball?' "

In research, I take a similar approach with people in the lab, with the young scientists, who are asking questions. One of the big problems is to try to help them without being intrusive. I don't want to tell them what to do, but at the same time, I want to give them some guidance so they don't waste a lot of time on what I consider to be irrelevant. The problem is that I'm not always right. I've told people in my department, "Don't follow that idea. That's the dumbest thing I ever heard of." And a year later they come back with a pretty significant observation. So you've got to be careful with guidance. How do you nurture a good idea? When do you cut bait? When do you discard something?

One research project I'm currently involved in is the use of nonhuman islet cells from the pancreas to treat diabetes. What I'm doing right now is to take islet cells, which make insulin and other hormones, get them out of the pancreas of healthy animals, and then transplant them into diabetic animals in hopes that they will make insulin as needed.

The idea is to transplant the machinery that makes the insulin rather than injecting insulin. Transplanting the islet cells would be like providing a factory for the manufacture of insulin, which would be responsive to their blood-sugar level. There are two main problems involved in this. One is getting the islet cells—the other is keeping them from being destroyed after they're transplanted.

I got interested in this back in 1957 when I was at Tulane. I was taking care of people with vascular disease, many of whom had diabetes. I decided

I'd like to learn something about the relationship of diabetes to vascular disease.

I began to look at this with various animal models, and a medical student came by one day and said that he was able to show that by transplanting the pancreas of a healthy rat into a diabetic one, he could reverse diabetes. So that led me to try to isolate the part of the pancreas that made the insulin. There was no point in transplanting the entire pancreas if you could transplant just the part that makes insulin.

Then one evening I came upon an article on insulin by a physiologist named McLeod. On the last page of that article, he said he'd found a species of fish that had anatomically separated islet cells. So he took these things out of the fish, ground them up, and injected them into a rabbit, and the blood sugar promptly went way down. He showed that the fish insulin was active in the rabbit. So I figured, what the hell, why not figure out a way to transplant the islet cells of a fish? So I started fishing.

I went out on the Gulf of Mexico and I caught more goddamn fish. And then I learned something that everybody who had ever looked at this already knew: that only certain species of fish had these particular isolated cells. And none of the ones I caught had them.

When I got to Utah I was still curious about it. I was sitting in the cafeteria with the residents one night, talking about my fishing trip with a young surgeon named Hugh Hogle. He said, "Listen, Doc, I know how to get those fish. All we need is permission. Just get out your best stationery and write my uncle—he's the director of Fish and Game in Utah—and tell him we need to electrocute these fish." So we got the permission, and he said, "Okay, Doc. Meet me at the emergency room Saturday morning, eight o'clock, and wear your waders. He came driving up in this Pontiac station wagon with a ten-thousand-watt generator and a barrel of water in the back, and we went to a stream up in the mountains and cranked up the generator. He went upstream with a cathode and I was downstream with the anode and a net. What happens is that you shock everything between the cathode and the anode; it puts the fish into ventricular fibrillation. You pick them up and you throw 'em in the barrel and they start swimming around.

It was called the Utah sucker; a little two-pounder, ugliest fish you ever saw! So I took this barrel full of fish back to the medical school and went to work. I took out the islets and I transplanted them into diabetic rats, and the blood sugars came right down to normal. I thought, "My God, Reemtsma, you're going to be *rich* beyond your fondest dreams!" Problem was, in about forty-eight hours the blood sugar went right back up. I tried putting them in capsules. I put them in chambers. I did everything, but

I could never achieve any prolonged function. But it was the first example of transplanted islet cells and it showed that it worked temporarily.

About that time, a young intern named Colin Weber came into my office. It was one of those accidents that turns out to be providential. He was a very good scientist and he happened to be interested in islet transplant.

One day Colin came to me and said, "You know, these animals that we've transplanted islet cells into are eating a lot more but they're not gaining weight." One of the things about diabetes is that animals eat more. And I started to say, "Colin, I don't care a hoot whether those animals are eating more or not." But I started to think we might be onto something here! Maybe we could get that thing worked out and open up a boutique outside Zabar's for fat people—give 'em an injection of "Dr. Reemtsma's Magical Islet Cell." You can eat anything you want! *Now* you're talking rich and famous!

That's an example of the fact that he saw something I would have missed. Even if I had picked up on it, I probably would have ignored it. But he didn't. Colin is superb in that sense. He said, "I'd like to track it down." I had enough sense to say, "Go ahead." So he found out that these animals are hyperinsulinemic, that is, they make too much insulin. Their blood sugars were normal, but they were making too much insulin and were eating more in order to counteract it.

I've been working on this for twenty-five years. It's so tantalizing. I keep thinking, I'm almost there. I can *taste* it, I'm so close.

There are a lot of thrills in this business. One of them is taking care of people; another is helping to educate the next generation that comes along. But if I had to pick one thing that gives me a personal sense of gratification, it would be discovery. I don't know much that everybody else doesn't know. But there are a couple of things. It's not that I'm going to keep it that way for long, though. I'm going to share anything good I learn. In fact, that's one of the nice things about medicine, compared with, say, General Motors—they want to hide their cars so Ford doesn't find out what they're doing. Well, hell, in medicine you can't *wait* to tell your buddies what you've learned!

III
MEDICINE

Friday morning. Nine forty-five. Team Four is assembling in the ninth-floor staff lounge for attending rounds, a formal two-hour teaching session where attending physicians, house staff, and students discuss the diagnoses and management of hospitalized patients whose diseases are thought to be interesting for teaching and learning purposes. The house staff and students have already arrived and are seated around a table littered with used Styrofoam cups, crumpled napkins, and a grease-stained pizza box, evidence of last night's shift.

There are six teams on the medical service. Team Four, like the others, has one senior resident, two interns, and three medical students. Each team is officially headed by two attendings, physicians who have already completed their training and who generally devote two months of service each year to bedside teaching and the care of clinic and ward patients. The attendings this morning are Dr. Robert Glickman, director of the medical service, a specialist in gastroenterology, and Dr. Dorothy Estes, a specialist in rheumatology. The resident and team leader is Dr. Jackie Brown, an easy-going young woman with a bright smile, who is now in her third year of postgraduate training.

Dave Greenwald and Bill Berger are the interns on the team. This is their first year as doctors. Dave Greenwald, a dark-haired man who speaks in clipped tones as if to get things moving fast, is "post call." He has been on duty now for thirty hours and has six more hours at the hospital before he can go home. As last night's intern on call, he was responsible, at six-thirty this morning, to report last night's events to the rest of the team. (Somewhere between then and now he has managed to shower and shave so that he is no longer identifiable as the one who has been up all night.) Two of the three medical students, Joe Lopez and Lisa Rubin, have been here since six for pre-rounds. The third student, Jim Johnston, was here all night with Dave Greenwald. Jim Johnston spent his free minutes yesterday and last night reading up on the possible causes of gastroenteritis in order to be prepared for his presentation this morning.

At precisely ten o'clock, Dr. Glickman materializes at the door.

"Okay," he says, taking a seat at the already overcrowded table, "who's up first?"

Jim Johnston begins his presentation. "Mr. Rosen is a twenty-nine-year-old white diabetic male who came into the ER two days ago with severe nausea, vomiting, and stomach pain that he suspects was caused by rancid tuna fish he had eaten that noon at a local diner." The student continues, citing the patient's past medical history, social history—he is married, a father of two—occupation, and recent travel experience. He says the patient denies drinking, smoking, and intravenous drug use. He reports on the history and physical examination that was done upon admission, his overall appearance (a well-developed male who appears his stated age), and gives specifics of his temperature, respiration, blood pressure and pulse rate, and rectal exam. He reports the results of the laboratory work, blood, X rays, and urine, and remarks that the patient has responded well to antibiotics. "In summary," he says, "we have a twenty-nine-year-old diabetic with an infection of undetermined cause who was treated with antibotics and is improving." Jackie Brown adds, "We plan to discharge him tomorrow."

"How do we know it was the tuna fish that caused the infection?" asks Dr. Glickman. The student replies that there were no other indications of infection and the timing and history were consistent with a diagnosis of food poisoning. Dr. Glickman asks which GI infections respond to antibiotics. Another of the students answers. Dr. Glickman continues grilling the group, "What were you treating when you gave him antibiotics? Could it have been salmonella?" Dr. Brown, running her fingers through her hair, tells why it could not have been salmonella.

Suddenly, over the hospital paging system an urgent female voice says, "ARREST. STAT. Harkness Pavilion, ninth floor. ARREST. STAT. Harkness Pavilion, ninth floor. ARREST . . ." Although the sound has filled the room, no one seems to hear it except Dr. Berger, who leaps out of his chair and dashes out the door.

The next patient presented is a sixty-six-year-old man from the Dominican Republic with severe abdominal pain. After some discussion, it is decided that he probably has an abdominal tumor, cholecystitis (inflamed gall bladder), or a bile duct obstruction. Because gastroenterology is Dr. Glickman's specialty, he gives a brief but detailed review of various causes of gastrointestinal pain. Finally he asks, "So, what are you going to do for this man? Remember, before you answer," he says, smiling, "in this hospital we like the diagnosis and the thereapy to be related wherever possible."

A third patient is presented by Dr. Greenwald. A woman with panhypothyroidism who was admitted with fever, sore throat, and vomiting, a serious symptom in her case because she could not retain vital medications.

"Her mental status is confused," says Dr. Greenwald, "and she has a strange affect. When I asked her the year, she answered, '1979.' Several minutes later I asked her again and she said the same thing. When I was ready to leave, I asked her the date again and she practically yelled, '1979! 1979! How many times do I have to say it?' "

Dr. Estes asks what has been done for the patient so far. "We cultured her throat and put her on steroids, and she felt a lot better very fast."

"Why do you think she got well so fast?" she asks. "You always feel better quickly after taking steroids," shoots back the student, "but they eventually depress the immune system and leave you more open to infection."

"Right," says Dr. Glickman. "So in effect we're talking here about a double-edged sword." With that, he glances at his watch, pushes back his chair, and stands up. The second hour of rounds will be taken up seeing the patients who were just discussed. The rest of the group follows Dr. Glickman, who is now out the door and headed for the first patient's room.

On "walk rounds" there is an unspoken formation that corresponds to the hospital hierarchy. The attending is always in the lead, followed by the resident, the interns, and finally the students, and this is precisely the order in which Team Four files into room 909 to see the patient with the possible abdominal tumor. He is a large man with huge calloused hands that suggest a lifetime of manual labor. As he looks at the group, his face reflects pain.

Dr. Glickman steps to the man's left and the rest of the team assembles in picket-fence order around the bed. Two of the students at the periphery are forced to stand on tiptoe and glance over the shoulder of the resident. Dr. Glickman introduces himself to the patient and then gently raises the man's hospital gown to reveal a distended belly with a large scar from a past operation. He presses lightly with flat fingers. "Does this hurt?" he asks. "Here? Here?"

"Breathe in," he says. The patient does not understand. "He speaks only Spanish, perhaps," says the student. "Well, tell him in Spanish then." "Respire profundo," says Joe Lopez. The patient takes a breath and holds it. Dr. Glickman keeps his hand in place, eyes almost closed as if to aid his sense of touch, listening past the silence. He looks up at his interpreter, "You'd better tell him he can exhale, Joe. I think he's taking it all too literally." He turns to the other students. "You people will want to feel this." The students take turns examining the abdominal mass under Dr. Glickman's careful eye.

In the hallway outside the patient's room, there is further discussion and it is decided that the patient will need further tests before a final diagnosis can be made.

Next, the group sees the diabetic patient with suspected food poisoning.

David Rosen, a free-lance writer, is a slightly built man in his late twenties. Dr. Estes asks him several questions related to his present symptoms. A general discussion of diabetes follows, and at one point Dr. Glickman asks the patient, "Do you know why an increase in sugar in the blood is bad for diabetics?" The patient answers that he has a ball-park idea. Glickman puts the question differently. "What has your doctor told you about the connection between diabetes and sugar?" Rosen replies he doesn't really know for sure. Dr. Glickman explains. A student takes notes. Rosen appears to understand. Then Dr. Estes reminds him to come to the clinic or to be checked somewhere else at regular intervals. Rosen agrees.

Next the group heads for Five East to the room of Mrs. Jackson, the woman with panhypothyroidism. As the white coats stream through the door, the patient sits up and begins preening a bit. It is clear this is not the first time she has been presented at teaching rounds. Dr. Estes examines her, slowly, methodically, as the group watches in silence. The intern who left earlier for the STAT call has slipped into the room. No one asks him what happened or even acknowledges his return, so routine are these sudden departures.

It is decided that Mrs. Jackson is well enough to be discharged the next day. "We're going to keep an eye on you," says Dr. Estes, "and if you continue to do well, we'll let you go home tomorrow." "Oh, Lord," says the patient, casting her eyes up at the ceiling. "Thank you, Lord." Dr. Greenwald, at the foot of the bed, leans over and whispers to Jim Johnston, "Go on. Ask her what year it is," and slips out the door.

"Mrs. Jackson, what year is it?" the student asks. "It's 1987," she answers, flashing a smile that reveals a gold tooth. "That other one has some *learning* to do, honey," she says, laughing. "This morning? I was just having some fun with him."

In the hallway, Dr. Greenwald waits for the rest of the team. It's eleven forty-five and he asks the resident if there is time to see one more patient. "I'm off this weekend and I want to present Mrs. Vella. She may die before I get back and there are some things we should talk about."

The group walks to the end of the hall and assembles near the patient's room. The door is closed. A nurse who is about to go in puts on a paper cap, mask, and gown. A sign on the door says REVERSE ISOLATION. The entourage circles around Greenwald, who is leaning heavily against the wall, showing signs of having been awake for thirty-two hours. With the patient's chart tucked under his arm, he begins his story. "Mrs. Vella is a seventy-year-old Hispanic woman with a history of asthma. Four weeks ago, at ten in the morning, she arrived in the emergency room with a fever of 103, having become ill around midnight the night before. The ER resident, noting her fever and lack of other acute symptoms, asked her if anyone else in the family had been ill recently. She said that her four-year-old grandson had been brought to this hospital with a fever of 105 earlier the same night.

"The child had been brought to the pediatric emergency room by his mother—Mrs. Vella's daughter—who became concerned when his fever jumped to 104. Soon after, he developed skin spots suggestive of meningo-coccal meningitis. Hearing that, the resident examining Mrs. Vella immediately called the pediatric ICU and was told the child was gravely ill and was now on a respirator. He was being treated with antibiotics for meningitis.

"At that point, the decision was made not to wait for culture results but to start the grandmother on intravenous antibiotics immediately and to admit her to the intensive care unit. By eleven o'clock, exactly one hour after she arrived in the ER, the woman was on her way to the ICU. It was there that I first met her."

Shifting his weight from one leg to the other, Dr. Greenwald continues. "We told her we thought she had meningitis like her grandson, and that she would probably feel very sick over the next twelve hours. The family was understandably overwrought, especially the daughter who now had her mother and her son six floors apart, both fighting for their lives. I told the daughter that this disease carries a very high mortality and that we were all quite concerned.

"Within twenty-four hours, Mrs. Vella's grandson showed a noticeable improvement, but Mrs. Vella's condition got worse. Her infection continued to spread rapidly and she was put on a respirator. By evening she required dialysis for kidney failure. We also noted a distinct change in her mental status."

Dr. Greenwald now begins reading from the patient's chart, describing an erratic course of events in which the patient showed improvement, regression, slight improvement, and then began a rapid deterioration of her physical and mental status as a series of complications developed. The most recent and serious was respiratory arrest followed by general convulsions. She was resuscitated and reintubated, but subsequently, probably due to a lack of oxygen to the brain during the arrest, developed signs of brain damage. "At this point, a neurologist was called in. He reported that an EEG showed no brain activity, and he gave her a hopeless prognosis. Additional consultations confirmed the neurologist's prognosis, and the family was summoned. After consulting with the physicians, and realizing that she would not recover, the family decided it was best if from then on the patient would receive supportive care only."

Dr. Greenwald begins winding down his presentation. "As of yesterday, in keeping with the family's wishes, we have discontinued her antibiotics.

Her IV will not be replaced and we have discontinued any blood tests, or dialysis. As of six this morning, she does not respond to painful stimuli. We are keeping her as comfortable as possible and are satisfied that she is in no pain."

Dr. Estes asks if anyone else in the family has come down with the disease. Greenwald says that a large number of people live in the house and the decision was made to put all of the family members on medication as a precaution. Because the cost was $284, and the family could not afford to pay for it, the hospital donated the medicine. "But there's more," he adds. "I hear they all just spent a week visiting another family."

Dr. Glickman, who has been listening, arms crossed, head down, through the whole presentation, now looks up and smiles. "Sure," he says, "and they all live in some beautiful resort town in the Caribbean and you need to go down there to treat them. Right, David?"

Everyone laughs, breaking the tension of two solid hours of teaching, learning, and problem solving. The laughter quickly diminishes, though, as Team Four turns serious again. Each person methodically dons isolation garb: gown, mask, cap. Then, silently, the group follows Dr. Glickman into Mrs. Vella's room.

ROBERT GLICKMAN, M.D.
Chairman, Department of Medicine

He went to Harvard Medical School—"Tuition was nine hundred dollars a year," and trained at Boston City Hospital. "An intern earned eight hundred dollars a year." In 1977, he came to Columbia-Presbyterian as head of the department of gastroenterology. In 1982, he was named director of medicine, the largest service in the hospital, with fifteen divisions, a house staff of 113, and two to three hundred physicians associated with it. He is currently the president of the American Association of Gastroenterologists, editor of the Journal of Clinical Investigation, *the most prestigous medical research journal in the country, and president of the hospital medical board.*

As director of medicine, I'm paid half by the hospital and half by the university. I have responsibilities in both areas. On the hospital side I'm responsible for the care of every patient on the medical service. On the university side, I'm responsible for all of the academic research activity that makes up the medical department—all of the department renovations, all of the recruiting, all of the finances. The department of medicine has total revenues of thirty-three million dollars and I'm responsible for every penny. There are fifteen million dollars in research grants alone.

We have all different kinds of financial setups for our physicians. Some physicians who are on contract, they're employees of the university but they earn their own income, they pay their own expenses, and then we tithe ten percent of their gross income to help pay for the academic programs here. If you're in an academic medical center and if everyone just takes out all the money for personal gain, then there's no money to grow anything, so this is an attempt to divert a piece of earnings for program development. Then, we have people who are in practice whom we don't pay and they don't pay us. The people who practice and keep their earnings give a lot of time to teaching; a lot of free time. So the system originally was kind of a Robin Hood system. You practiced and you gave of your time away teaching *pro bono*. And the return was you were left alone and you could earn a very good living. That's becoming less common. And some of our physicians get a straight salary and they either do or don't practice. Those who do research primarily, get their salary from their research grants. We usually have to add to their salaries. We try to spread the money around because there are haves and have nots. Contrary to popular belief, not everyone who practices medicine earns a lot of money.

There has been a lot of talk lately about the justification and rationale of interns and other house staff working thirty-six hours straight. I personally don't think it's unreasonable to require intensive training. Continuity of care is a big part of it, from two perspectives: the patient's and the person's who is in training. Somebody has to provide the patient with care in a continuous fashion. Discontinuity is the worst thing for the patient. And it's not much better for the intern.

If you work from eight to five and then you go home, you never really see the whole process of a disease. Diseases don't keep track of the clock. As many things happen in the nighttime as happen in the daytime. So the question is: How does a physician-in-training get the continuity of seeing how an illness evolves and all the problems that occur when someone is sick and he takes a turn for the worse, if he's not around a decent part of that time? How does he get the feel of it? How does he learn what that illness is capable of?

Medicine is an apprenticeship craft, and the more you do of it the better you are at it. You have to get a certain amount of experience and you have to get it at some point. How safe is it to take some two-thirds trained person who is well rested and say, "Okay, he's a licensed doctor"? Should he learn on the first patient? If you're going to be a violinist you're supposed to practice violin a lot of hours of the day. You practice all day and you practice in the evening. If you want to be a professional anything you've *got* to spend the hours. Now the issue is: How do you train people?

Maybe we should require half the amount of hours and then take twice the time to train them. I don't know. I just don't think intensive training is unreasonable.

There's an economic side to this, too. There's a lot of salary money paid out to the house staff by the hospital. But hospitals are under regulation and they're losing money, especially in a place like this that takes care of a lot of poor people. So, if we cut the house staff's hours in half, who would care for the patients? Could the hospital even *afford* to double its house staff? If this system of long hours was so terrible, they'd change it—cost or no cost they'd have to take the money from someplace else. I'm just not convinced it's terrible. These interns are young people, and they are certainly well backed up. In this system, we don't leave an intern out there to make major decisions. There are two or three levels of people behind him. As he tires, can he make as good a decision as if he's totally rested? Probably not. But two people converging on a problem are probably better than a single doctor coming in. Besides, someone has to provide the continuity of care. If the doctor's at home sleeping, who is watching the patient?

I don't think the field of medicine polices itself very well, although it tries. I think the most important way to assure quality control is a nonformal system. Like any large medical center, this place is a fishbowl. It's very hard to do something here without a lot of people knowing about it. There are residents and students and fellows around constantly watching and questioning. Every patient in the place is open to view. And medical students and house staff are not constrained from asking questions.

On top of that, there are formal rounds every week, when every death is reviewed. Some of them are kind of one liners—someone had advanced cancer, came in, and died. But others are real issues of management— judgment issues. And they are reviewed and discussed at length. A group of people get together in a conference, maybe fifty or sixty people, and we really examine these deaths closely.

Most places have mortality conferences. But there are mortality conferences and *mortality* conferences. You can just pat each other on the back and say, "Boy, that's life, you know? God just took her and there's not much we can do about that." It's not easy, though, to do the opposite. People are sometimes shy about criticizing their colleagues. The form our conference has taken is that we usually don't identify people's names. We don't think it's that important. We just discuss the case and then if there's an issue involved of a given physician doing something marginal or incorrect, I deal with that afterwards. In other words, we don't say, "Okay, Joe. You did a bad thing here." We'll say a bad thing was done. We won't necessarily identify who the doctor was because this is not the forum for that. That's a very inhibitory kind of a thing—to publicly criticize some-body. The main thing is to get the medical aspects of it out and discussed critically and not have to worry about stigmatizing somebody.

This is one of the best medical training programs in the country. We get two thousand applications a year here, for thirty-three intern spots. A lot of those can be weeded out early for one reason or another. So that cuts the number down to a thousand. Then we go through those applications and we invite maybe two hundred people to be interviewed. They come in groups throughout the whole fall. We show them around and two people interview each one. Then we rank them on a big list which is eventually fed into a computer along with the applicant's rank of the programs they want in the order they want them, and then on March 15 or so they match for the residency.

The qualities we look for in the people we take are stability and reliabil-ity. Everyone is on a certain level academically. They all do well in medical school. They are all very bright. It's really the personal qualities that matter. If somebody is brilliant but is a very brittle person, he or she won't survive this kind of training simply because it's very frustrating. It's diffi-cult to deal with people who are ill and dying. This is a difficult internship because it's high quality and the work keeps coming and coming.

We spend a lot of time selecting our interns, and our choices are usually excellent, although we did discharge an intern once. Not because she wasn't good—with the screening process we have, everyone we pick has got to be all right. You can't be intellectually incompetent and survive our screening process. But some people have character disorders that you may not have picked up in your interviews. Some people are very good at interviewing and they just fake you out. And occasionally you have some-one whose letters of recommendation are not accurate.

The intern we let go was from an Ivy League school and a top medical school. She graduated with high honors—just a brilliant woman. But her personal affairs were a total mess. The first index that something was wrong was she didn't show up on July first—she had some kind of personal problems. When she finally showed up in September, she had no arrange-ments for living quarters and she wound up living in an on-call room for a couple of months. Worst of all, you couldn't trust what she said. The residents would say, "You've got to do this," and she'd say, "Fine," and then they'd come back an hour later and they'd say, "Did you do that?" and she'd say, "Yeah, I did it," and they'd check and she wouldn't have done it. This just kept going on and on, so we finally said, "That's enough." And we let her go.

If someone is slow catching on but his attitude is good, then that's our problem and our responsibility to help him out. We recognize that and we do it. We have a person like that now. Lovely guy. Works hard; he's here till ten at night every night. He just can't get it, though. He doesn't know how to come up to a sick person and figure out what's going on. You can ask him anything—he knows everything. You can say, "Tell me about such and such," and he spends a half hour telling you about whatever you want. But he just can't get it. So we've got to work with him until he can. We picked him, and we'll get him through this. But then the issue is, is he so bad that we can't certify him? Hopefully that's not the case. It's a matter of trying to get him better.

But this other intern—she wasn't safe. Another program picked her up, but we told them up front what to expect. We told them specifically what her problems were. Maybe they'll be better at dealing with her than we were. I hope so.

I only see patients in small numbers now. I see a couple of private patients a week, but that's all I have time for. I do a lot of teaching. Every morning, from nine to ten, I do morning report, where all of the admissions from the night before are presented to me by the house staff. Then I do a month of attending, which I'm doing this month. That's kind of hard to do because it takes four hours out of a day that doesn't have four hours to give up. It's important, though. It lets me see what's happening in the hospital and what the frustration toll is for people who are trying to take care of patients. I really enjoy diagnosing, especially tough cases, the harder the better. I find that very relaxing; it's kind of a break from all of the administrative work I do.

A couple of years ago my picture was on the cover of *New York* magazine. I was one of the people selected for an article on the best physicians in New York City. After that article appeared, I got hundreds of calls, but the best one was from my mother, who saw the magazine in Miami Beach and called me up and said, "Look, *now* you can go into private practice! With that kind of publicity, you could have as many patients as you want!"

For fun I build eighteenth-century antique furniture. Okay, eighteenth-century reproductions. And I go canoeing in the wilderness—Ontario, Minnesota—to get away from all this craziness. I love it. I sleep on the ground. Get bitten by bugs. Catch fish. Quiet. No one bothers me. It's wonderful.

THOMAS FRIEDEN, M.D.

Intern

We're in his on-call room on the ninth floor of the hospital, a room he uses when he sleeps here overnight. There's hardly space for more than one person. A small dresser. A desk. A bed shoved against the wall, under the window. Every gust of March wind sets the window rattling. Two heaters plugged into the wall try to warm the room, but they cannot keep up with the frigid air blowing through.

He sits crosslegged on his rumpled bed, a small man in wire-rimmed glasses, wearing the intern's uniform of white pants, short white jacket, shirt, and tie. A stethoscope is draped around his neck.

There's a certain passion in his voice as he recounts a day in the life of an intern

For an intern, there's never a typical day, but there *are* typical hours—long. Very long. I wake up around five-thirty. I get in about six-thirty and I immediately begin looking after anywhere from eight to fifteen patients who are my responsibility. These are patients I have admitted and taken care of since they arrived in the hospital. I try to see them all before eight o'clock in the morning.

Each patient takes time. I walk into their room; I ask them how they feel. They tell me. If they're in for stomach pain, we talk about that; if they're in for pneumonia, I ask them about their breathing and coughing; if they're in for chest pain, it's a different set of questions. Then I examine them. I listen to the heart, the lungs, the belly. I feel their legs and make sure they don't have a clot from lying in bed too much. I see what their needs are for the day. Maybe they need to get out of bed. Maybe they need to see the social worker about their Medicare. If a patient has a weak heart and is in for congestive failure, I have to find out his weight. So I end up weighing all my own patients in the morning, which means finding a scale, wheeling it over to the bed, then spending five minutes to get the patient out of bed and onto the scale because he has an IV in, or oxygen. Then I write a note saying how he feels and what the plan is for the day; I specify any orders that the nurses should pick up—blood tests, any special diagnostic studies that they should get. And then I go on to the next patient.

If I'm fast, I can write the notes on them all. If I'm not, I'm going to have to take time out from all the other things I have to do to write those notes later on in the day. If I get the notes written early I'm in good shape; if I don't, I'm in trouble. I've had as many as eighteen, nineteen patients at a time. Then, no matter how early I get in, I'm not going to be able to write notes on each of them before eight o'clock in the morning. I'm lucky if I can *see* everyone before eight o'clock in the morning.

Ideally, all medical patients are on floors eight and eleven, East and West. But when the hospital is full, which frequently happens, or when the medical service is full, we have patients everywhere: Harkness Two, Harkness Eight, Harkness Seven, Presbyterian Fifteen, Presbyterian Fourteen, Presbyterian Five, Presbyterian Seven. So you can imagine what that does to me between six-thirty and eight o'clock in the morning.

From eight o'clock to nine o'clock we meet with the resident, who is second or third year, and go over the patients. We either walk around and see the patients or just sit down and talk about them, deciding what needs to be done over the next day or two. Should we change their antibiotics? Should we order a different test? Should we discharge them from the hospital? Should we get social service in so we can discharge them tomorrow? It's kind of a strategic planning session.

Between nine and ten is the prime time for scheduling tests and calling consults. My strategy is to find a telephone and not let anyone else get near it. I pick it up and call the page operator and say, "Page Neurology, Urology, GYN, and Psychiatry to this number." Click. Then I start calling the different diagnostic areas and I schedule echocardiograms, CAT scans, noninvasive flow studies of the legs.

If I have a patient who I think is not moving normally, or his speech is slightly slurred, I call a neurology consult. If my patient has an infection, the infectious diseases fellows come by. They're wonderful. They see the patients and they recommend antibiotics, tests. The GI service will do procedures, the pulmonary service will do procedures. The renal service will be helpful. An intern can call any of them and bring them in on a case. We may not always agree with the things they say, but at least we have their knowledge and know-how. So that's from nine to ten, and that's a prime time. You can't waste that time or else you'll be here forever.

The bottom line of internship is getting out early. The first two months I seldom left here before nine-thirty at night. I was on call every fourth night and when I wasn't I was frequently here till ten or eleven. As my internship has progressed, though, it's gotten better. I've learned to write my notes before eight o'clock in the morning. I've learned that you have to schedule tests and call consults between nine and ten in the morning because if you forget and call the neurologist at one-thirty in the afternoon, they're not going to see the patient until four, and you're going to be here at seven-thirty at night taking the patient through the emergency procedure, instead of doing it at one o'clock in the afternoon.

Now it sounds very self-serving, to want to get home early—that being your only goal in life. But in fact, internship is a tremendously stressful time. It's horrible for your personal life. It's horrible for your intellectual growth. It's horrible for your attitude towards patients. The less it ruins your life the better you're going to be with patients. By "early" I don't mean three o'clock in the afternoon. I don't want to go out and play golf. I want to get home in time to eat dinner with the woman I live with, or in time to read a little bit before I go to sleep. I want to go to sleep by ten o'clock so that I'm not exhausted when I wake up at five-thirty the next morning. Now obviously, I'm not going to leave if someone is sick. I'll stay here as long as they need me. But in order to do that effectively, I have to go home, too.

On one of my first clinical rotations as a medical student, a very wonderful neurology resident said to me, "At some point in your training you're going to start thinking that patients come to the hospital in order to hurt you. Your goal is to keep in mind that people come to the hospital because they have pain. In some way they hurt and they want to get better." He meant that at some point I might come to feel that the patient is the enemy. And that can happen at times. Listen to how we speak: We don't say, "A patient has a fever." We say, "She spiked a fever. She did this to me, just because I'm about to go home! Now I've got to do blood cultures and check her lab tests and send her for an X ray and get urine or start her on antibiotics, and check her chest X ray. I'll be here another two and a half hours!" And that's part of your attitude. The patient with an ulcer didn't begin bleeding again, he dropped his crit. Maliciously! He dropped his crit so I would have to go running up to the blood bank, get blood, start another IV on him, start pouring blood in, do a rectal exam, call the GI consultant, maybe transfer him to the unit. He didn't start bleeding again. He "dropped his crit." It's an active expression.

Attending rounds are from ten to twelve. That's when we present the patients to the attendings. They provide feedback and are very helpful in suggesting what might be wrong with the patient, how we might help him, what lab tests we need to get or don't need to get, and how we should approach things. They have twenty, thirty years' experience—many of them—and are tremendously helpful.

For a medical student, presenting a patient at attending rounds is a hairy experience. For an intern, though, it's an art form. It's telling a story. It's trying to keep someone's interest and painting a picture of what you think is going on. People don't come in with diagnoses on their chests. People come in with pain somewhere or a problem and we have to figure out what's going on. That's the fun of medicine—making a diagnosis and trying to treat someone and make them better. So giving a history is very tied up in how well you understand what's going on; how well you've examined the patient, talked to the patient. Have you asked the right questions?

We have a scheduled talk every day from twelve to one, about some aspect of medical care. They serve lunch at this talk, so if I have the energy, if I'm really hungry, if I don't have a lot of really sick patients, I go to the talk and I fall asleep, frequently. Otherwise I go about my work.

Around one, one-thirty, the lab tests come back. So in the middle of seeing patients I find a computer and plunk myself down and plug in my patients' names and numbers and get the results of their lab tests. It takes a half hour at least to go over all the labs of all the patients. Then I've got to write orders pending those results. If someone's hematocrit is low, I've got to go up to the blood bank and get blood. The rest of the afternoon is spent seeing patients again, doing small procedures, and making rounds, and that takes me well up to six o'clock.

If I'm not on call that night, before I leave I find my fellow intern, the one who *is* on call, and give him a list of all the patients; name, unit number, how old they are, what floor they're on, if they're a private patient, who the private doctor is, whether they're DNR [do not resuscitate] or not, NAP [no arrest page] or not. If I'm the one on call that night, instead of signing out at six o'clock, I just keep going.

When you're on call, you're on from eight A.M. one morning until six P.M. the next day—thirty-four hours. You take all the admissions for that day from eight A.M. on. On the medical service there are three interns on call each night so the three of us rotate admissions all that day and evening. We admit in sequence—one, two, three; one, two, three; one, two, three.

You're up first or second or third. Now that leads to a tremendous persecution complex because generally you each get an average of three to four admissions a night; usually an average of four. So whoever's up first gets the most. They counted up who had the most admissions this year, and I did. You can get five admissions. Suppose it was five, four, four, and you were up first. That hurts. That's an extra two and a half hours of work that I have to do that no one else has to do. If I'm up second, it goes five, five, four; and if I'm up third, it goes five, five, five. Everyone gets a persecution complex. Anyway, it evens out in the end. It really does.

There's a lot of talk these days about how good an intern's judgment is if he or she has been up and working for twenty-four or thirty-six hours straight. In terms of making decisions after being up twenty-four hours or so, very few decisions need to be made. Most of the decisions are made when you admit the patient. But if something goes sour—if someone gets a fever or chest pain, or palpitations, or low blood pressure, or high blood pressure, you reevaluate them, but always in conjunction with other higher ranking people.

The worst experience I ever had working thirty-six hours straight was with a patient who had come into the emergency room with a bowel problem. He had an IV placed and was doing okay, and I admitted him to the floor. I was up all that night—it was very busy and I didn't get any sleep. At five o'clock the next afternoon I went by to see this man to make sure he was still okay. And in fact, he was doing fine. But I thought I saw a little bit of redness at the site of his IV. Now IVs should be changed every two to three days or else they can get infected. And they have to be watched very carefully because if they look bad, they probably should be changed after twelve hours or twenty-four hours. So I figured I should change his just to be on the safe side. I remember it was one of the last things I had to do that evening before I went home. So I went in to his room to take care of it. He was a very cantankerous, unpleasant man who cursed at me every time I touched him. I was very tired—I'd been up thirty-six hours—and when I tried to put in the IV, I missed. I tried again. I missed again. My hands weren't working well, and he was cursing at me and screaming and moving every time I tried to put the IV in. I missed it four times. Then I said to myself, his IV has been in for less than twenty-four hours, the likelihood of his getting infected from it is nil. I'll change it tomorrow first thing in the morning when I get here. Now what I could have done at that point is called my resident and said, "Look, I can't do it. Would you please do it?" and he would have done it, of course. The residents understand and they come and do it. But I didn't call.

The next morning when I got in I went to see him and he had a fever. He had copious diarrhea from his bowel problem and he had smeared it on his IV. So immediately I changed the IV and started treating him for an infection. But he got septic anyway. He became hypotensive and was transferred to the Intensive Care Unit. His blood was cultured and what grew out of his blood was an organism that could have been from an infected IV. He got better from that event. But then he got worse from his bowel disease, had a million medical problems going on, and refused medical care. At that point he was declared by psychiatry to be competent to refuse medical care. He said he was eighty-five years old, he wanted to die. He was bleeding out from his bowel, refused blood transfusions, and died.

It was probably unrelated but I just keep thinking, if I had changed the IV that afternoon maybe he wouldn't have gotten septic and maybe he wouldn't have died. Maybe this was just one more in a series of complications that ultimately led to his refusing medical care and dying.

So I blame myself. I felt horrible. I couldn't sleep at night. Nevertheless, certainly, if I wanted to rationalize, I'd say IVs should be changed every forty-eight hours. I changed his IV in less than thirty-six hours, but the fact is that maybe I should have changed it sooner. Certainly if anything like that ever happens, you're going to blame yourself and it's going to bother you for a long time. There are lots of things that have kept me up for weeks. I do make mistakes. Mistakes are human.

ROSLYN HAWKINS
Secretary and Receptionist

_____

She is a short woman with dark curly hair and an accent that confirms her Georgia upbringing. She's wearing a flowered print dress, glasses hang from a cord around her neck. Her left hand sports a silver ring on each finger and at least twenty silver bangle-bracelets practically obliterate her right wrist. She exudes a certain energy as she speaks, continually using her hands to make a point.

Her desk is in the eighth floor "stem"—the wide corridor that houses departmental administrative offices and connects the medical-school building and the Presbyterian Hospital building.

She's been at this job for twelve years, including the period of time when Dr. Morris, now president of the hospital, was chairman of the department of medicine. "My daughter Margaret works in the hospital and is helping to teach him Spanish. Dr. Morris feels that in this neighborhood, which is now predominantly Spanish, the people need to be given some recognition of their language and their background. He speaks it beautifully, too."

_____

I look on myself as the accommodation desk for the Department of Medicine. I dispense information within the department, between the different doctors and the house staff and the medical personnel. Things like, who did this? Where do I go to see about this? Who do I return this to? I feel like I work at Macy's. In addition, I do all the jobs nobody else wants to do. I've been offered jobs behind the scenes in nice quiet offices with hanging baskets and stuff, but I'm a people watcher. I like the action to swirl around me.

I can't even say who comes to me for what. It would be much easier to say who *doesn't* come to me for what. For example, I might be called upon for a small thing like, if the switchboard operator has a word or term that she doesn't know or a name of a doctor that she is not familiar with, her best chance to find out about it is to call the Department of Medicine, because we're the biggest department in the hospital. Also, any physician from outside who calls in for a referral to the doctors in internal medicine or the medical subspecialties gets referred to me. I also get the public calling in asking for a doctor to treat a certain disease. Say you had a problem and wanted a doctor of internal medicine. You'd get me on the phone and you'd describe your symptoms and so forth and so on and I'd suggest the names of several of our physicians.

Most of our doctors are so busy that they would prefer I didn't give their names at all. Especially the cardiologists. Some of them have to refuse to accept patients who are not referred by another doctor because they want to be sure that they're dealing with an established cardiology problem. And that's just because they're so busy. It's not that they aren't interested, but it's not easy. Too many people wait until they're desperately ill, then they want the best. They call and ask for the chairman of the department all the time. They want the *best* and they want it *right now.*

On occasion I get involved in a phone conversation where I wonder what happened to the person afterwards, especially when I get a weird one. And there's at least one weird one a day. I get calls for information on sex changes. That always tickles me. Sometimes I'll get a call from a husband trying to make his wife come to the hospital because he's worried about her and she doesn't want to come and so he puts her on, or I get both the husband and wife on the phone. Things like that. I've had a few people who called just because they felt like they needed to be listened to. They've found an outlet to talk about their physical problems. And I have two or three who are regulars. I recognize their voices even if they identify themselves by different names. They just need to have somebody listen to them. So I do, if I can. People need to be listened to.

Over the years I've been at this desk, I've seen a big change in the intern applicants. A few years ago, the kids came in for interviews in suspenders and jeans and Afros, and I mean *way* out. Now they're all in three-piece pinstripes. It's the most incredible difference.

I think internship has gotten easier in the last several years. You wouldn't get an intern to admit that, though. It's a terrible year. It's a stressful year. If we're going to have somebody break down or have an illness or something, that's the year. It's tough. But it used to be tougher. They used to be on every other night. Now they're on every fourth night. To be perfectly honest, I've got a tough side. I hate to see the internship made easier. I think the tougher it is the more it separates those who are really dedicated to medicine and those in it only because it is a very lucrative profession. Maybe I shouldn't feel that way, and maybe if I went one turn on the ward, I wouldn't. But I think a certain amount of toughness and requirements are good.

We just posted our intern list for next year. It's amazing. The moment that list goes up, the interns we have now start thinking that the end of their "indentured servitude" is near—other people are soon coming in to take their places and next year they'll be one step higher and can give it to them. You notice the difference—both in the interns, who know that their time is coming to an end, and in the third-year residents, who know when that list is posted that either they're going to stay here and go into subspecialty training or go into fellowship in other hospitals. The ones who are leaving start to leave in their minds. The list is posted March 15th, and I've noticed that from March until July they start a little bit of a grieving process. They start separating themselves from the medical center.

From where I sit, I watch the interns become second-, then third-year residents. It makes me feel very old. They get younger all the time. It's funny. Some of the interns hang out on the Stem and I get to know them right away. And with others, it's their third year before I really get to place a name.

I thrive on the people and the constant noise and swirl that goes on around my desk. Since we're always short of space, sometimes I have a group of doctors and students sitting to the left of me in little clusters of chairs, and another group of kids and their preceptors sitting to the right in those Shoe-Town chairs, all ganged together. And both are going at it at the top of their lungs, talking about medical problems. That kind of activity makes people in the nearby offices very nervous and they get up and shut the doors. But me, I love it.

GEORGE PETROSIAN, M.D.

Chief Resident, Department of Medicine

His father was born in Teheran and his mother in Russia. One of his grandfathers was a physician. The other started a caviar business in Europe many years ago. That family remained in Europe while the physician brought his family to America.

"Education was very important to my parents when my sisters and I were growing up. Although my father is in business, he made it quite clear to us that we were expected to become professionals in some field." He's tall, lean, and darkly handsome. He's married and has a young son.

This is a fourth year for me. Being chief is the equivalent of an extra year of residency. It's the job of the chief—there are two of us—to administrate the house staff [the interns and the second- and third-year medical residents]. Medicine is the largest service in the hospital. We have thirty-three interns, twenty-six second-year residents, and twenty-three third-year residents. The chief resident has to set up schedules for all of them. Everybody on the house staff does different things during the course of the year. For example, an intern can spend a month on the ward service with two weeks in the emergency room and two weeks in the medical ICU, and then a month on the private service, with two weeks more in the emergency room, two weeks in the medical ICU, two weeks vacation, and so on throughout the course of the year. It's great exposure and gives you a good opportunity to see if you want to subspecialize.

The chief resident is also responsible for a large part of the training program for the house staff. That requires planning teaching conferences, rounds, and meetings. We have noon conferences on the average of three or four days a week, where we ask various members of the attending staff to give small lectures. And, each week we review all the deaths that occurred on the medical service and select three or four patients who either present an interesting disease, a difficult management issue, or a case where perhaps there was an error in management. So there are a lot of different things going on all the time.

We deal a lot with AIDS patients on the medical service. I have a concern, and in fact I think a lot of people I work with have concerns about catching the disease. Our fears are not of being in the same room or touching the patients or examining them. We're more concerned with the risk of cutting ourselves or getting stuck with a contaminated needle. The literature would suggest that that risk is small—I think only one or two people have become positive for the virus, and certainly there are a lot more people who have stuck themselves with an AIDS-contaminated needle—but it's still probably the highest risk exposure as far as the physician is concerned.

There are a number of other AIDS-related problems the residents and interns face though. One concerns the emotional strain of dealing with people who have a terminal illness. I'm generalizing from my own experience, but it seems to me that a lot of times we detach ourselves from the patients we take care of. Many are much older than we are and you kind of have a feeling that these diseases won't strike you for a very long time. But with AIDS patients, the majority of people dying are young. They're our ages. And I think that's a lot harder to deal with. It's a constant reminder of your own mortality. It's the same as when you have a young patient who is admitted with leukemia. You feel different emotionally treating that patient than you do treating a seventy-five-year-old with the same disease. One person has lived his life and one hasn't. You care about both patients, but is one a greater tragedy than the other? I think it is.

The time it takes to care for a patient with AIDS is enormous. Although the patient may come in with one failing organ system, a lot of them tend to develop multiple system problems. They have profound diarrhea, kidney dysfunction, skin abnormalities. Multiple things go wrong. Because they have very little in the way of host defenses, it takes a tremendous amount of time to care for them. For somebody like an intern, who is already overworked, it really is a stress when you have three, four, or five AIDS patients on your service.

Then you have to consider the nature of the patient population that we're dealing with. Although a lot of us are altruistic, we're also human beings, and the nature of our population is such that many of our AIDS patients are IV drug abusers. Some have problems that have gotten them into this situation, and they are combative and argumentative. They don't comply with our medical directions, they fight their physicians every step of the way. And that, superimposed on everything else, makes it difficult to take care of them.

Finally, there's the fact that AIDS patients, for the most part, do not survive. For me, it's much harder to go in to see a patient who is dying— any patient, not just those with AIDS—for whom we have nothing left to offer, than to deal with a patient who, for example, has come in with uncontrolled diabetes. In two days the diabetic is ready to go home. With her, you feel that you've at least accomplished something. But a doctor may behave differently when he knows that his patient is terminally ill. And patients feel that. I'm sure they do. It's not so much that the doctor doesn't come back to see them—I always come back—but it's a matter of not knowing what to say or not being as reassuring as you'd like to be.

I met my wife after my first year of medical school. She's a special education teacher who works with handicapped kids. While I was in medical school, I'm sure I was very selfish at times; I needed to be, to be able to survive and perform and get through what I had to get through, and if I got wrapped up in myself, she seemed to understand. We got engaged when I started my internship. I didn't want to get married until I got through that year because I knew it was going to be tough and the thought of starting a marriage at the same time was more than I thought I could deal with. Internship is unlike anything else you ever experience. One of the hardest things for me that year was the feeling of always being under pressure. As a student, in college or med school, I was used to doing things a hundred percent. As an intern, the demands placed on you are such that you simply can't. You can't be perfect at everything and you can't complete everything all the time and often you feel like you're failing. Eventually, you learn to set priorities, you learn how to plug a hole and come back to it. You do what is essential to keep people alive.

Now that I'll be going into practice at the end of this year, I have other concerns. I think a lot about what the future will hold for all of us just starting out. Who knows where we'll be ten years from now. Medicine is changing in so many ways. HMOs have exploded on the market in the last two years. That alone is creating a big question mark in the minds of young doctors like me in terms of what opportunities there are going to be for us. Are all physicians going to be employed by large corporations? We all talk about it. Most of our friends in other professions know the ultrastructure of their professions, so they know what's out there and where they'd like to go or what they'd like to go after. But medicine is evolving in such a way that no one knows for sure what's coming.

Superimposed on that uncertainty is the uncertainty of the system. The autonomy of the physician is eroding tremendously. There is increasing involvement of the government in how the private practitioner is reimbursed. In addition, malpractice insurance is just astronomical. It creates tremendous pressures on a group of people who, I believe, care about delivering a service that will extend people's lives, but who also want to make a living and be comfortable.

I made twenty-six thousand dollars my first year and twenty-eight thousand my second. I worked between eighty and a hundred hours a week. During my third year, I earned thirty thousand and I'll make thirty-two this year. In a city that's probably one of the most expensive cities in the world, that's not a whole lot of money when you're trying to support a family. Even though my wife is working, it's difficult to make ends meet on that kind of salary. In view of all of this, I still think medicine is the greatest profession in the world. Even with the uncertainty. That's not to say that the uncertainty doesn't bother me or that I'm not scared about not knowing where I'm going to be ten years from now or what options are going to be out there. I wish I knew. But if I had to pick a profession now, knowing what I already know, I most certainly would do this again.

MOLLY MCCOY, M.D.

Director,
Medical Intensive Care Unit

An apparent favorite of the medical students, she was named Teacher of the Year twice in her career, a very unusual honor. "The thing that struck me was the amount of time between the first and second awards, the class of '76 and class of '85. Almost ten years apart. When I won the award the first time, a person who had won it several years before said, 'You must be feeling very sad now that you've finally won this.' I said, 'Of all the emotions that I'm feeling at this time, sadness is definitely not one of them.' 'But now it's over,' he said. 'You'll never win it again.' I told this story to a colleague and his comment was, 'Should the person who wins a Nobel Prize be sad because she's never going to win it again?' And so nine years later when this happened again, I thought, this is incredible! It's like winning the Nobel Prize twice!"

She is a tall, thin, gentle woman. She wears her brown hair pulled back from her face in a ponytail. Wire-rimmed half glasses perch on the bridge of her nose.

I went to medical school here in the sixties. There were a hundred twenty students in our class, of whom ten were women. It was still part of the old "chivalry days," so the men treated us extremely well. But I think they were uncomfortable with so many women in the class. For example, on

St. Valentine's Day they sent us all roses. They didn't quite know what to do with us, actually. Many of my classmates are still here. Over the years, as we talk about medical school, I've been able to put together a little picture of what they thought of me. Apparently, I was a very serious little person who was always taking notes.

I wear three hats here. I see patients with infectious diseases, I direct the medical intensive care unit, and I run the third-year Medicine clerkship for the medical students. Infectious disease is an umbrella for a large number of problems that include illness caused by microbes—living creatures—things that are not normally part of us. It includes tropical medicine, like the treatment of malaria and it includes diagnosis and treatment of patients who are immunologically deficient and who are at risk of certain kinds of infections, like AIDS patients or even transplant patients who, because of anti-rejection drugs, can get certain kinds of infections.

The sickest patients in the hospital go to the intensive care unit. They require constant care and intensive nursing. We have fourteen beds up there and the ratio of nurses to patients is either one to one or two to one. One of the biggest problems we face in the ICU is recognizing when reversibility has passed; in other words, when the point is reached where it's clear the patient will not get better. In these cases it's important to teach the house staff to recognize and understand our limitations; to recognize just what we can and cannot do. Everybody brings his own bias to a situation like this. But I think trying to set standard criteria for when to discontinue life support is foolish. You're never going to do that.

Sometimes a patient is brought in to the ER by ambulance. He's unconscious, he has no doctor, nobody knows who he is. He has no family that they know of; nobody knows his wishes about having heroic measures taken for him. And he's dying. The first thing that will happen is the staff will begin lifesaving measures. He's put on a respirator. Tubes are inserted. Blood pressure is supported. After he's stabilized, he's brought up to the intensive care unit. Some of these patients get better, but some of them have had a major stroke and will never wake up. At that point, working out what we're going to do and what purpose we can serve is probably the hardest thing.

There are lots of stories along these lines. One has to do with a derelict, a kind of "street person," a man who lived in the armory across the street. He arrived with a very, very low body temperature—sixty or seventy degrees. The chances of surviving that are very low. It was wintertime and he came into the emergency room and was admitted from there to our intensive care unit. We had to mechanically breathe for him. His kidneys didn't work so we had to dialyze him. We had to support his body functions with all kinds of machines. But there was something about this man . . . his head was always with him. We figured he was somewhere between forty-five and sixty years old—it was very hard to tell. He was in the ICU for probably two months, where he received one-on-one nursing—the works. Eventually he got off the ventilator, his kidney function came back, he started eating, and he was transferred out of the ICU. He was a totally engaging character who had probably never had three squares a day in his life. But there he was, gaining weight and doing well. He taught us an important lesson. They all teach you something, but here was a situation where the low body temperature and all those other medical problems told us that the likelihood of his surviving was probably less than ten percent. But there he was. And someone said, "So, big deal. What did you achieve? Now he's a placement problem. He still doesn't have a home." I said, "Talk to him. Here's this person. He's back in the world. He thinks it's great. He's sorry he's a placement problem." Do we let someone die because he's going to be a social-service problem? Maybe in the future that's what doctors are going to be asked to do. I don't know.

The other day I was discussing these issues with a group of students and one of them asked, "When you have a patient whom you really feel cannot get back to any useful or pleasant quality of life, a patient who's comatose but not brain dead, his kidneys don't work so he needs to be dialyzed, he needs all kinds of specialized attention—what do you do?" I said, "You start to work with the family." He said, "What happens if the family believes in miracles and wants everything possible done indefinitely for this patient?" My answer was, "You keep working with the family until we live in a society that has a better solution." There just aren't any rules of the road for this. Sooner or later, when the family sees no change, they'll realize what's happening and they'll begin to accept it.

When we've done as much as we can for the patient, we have to start taking care of the family. We have to prepare them for the inevitable. Part of doctoring the critically ill patient is to involve the family. We understand what's happening, but they may not. They may not be ready to acknowledge it. There's always a lot of guilt.

Here's another issue: If a patient is comatose for a long time, though not formally brain dead, and is being assisted in his breathing by a mechanical ventilator, do you at some point take them off the ventilator? What do you do? When do you do it? These questions are always floating around. Sometimes the patient's family will say, let nature take its course, and then the physicians will determine what they think nature taking its course is. It's all so hair-raising.

Costs are another issue that you can't escape. We had one patient, a wonderful woman in generally good health who had a history of arthritis; about seventy-three years old; happily married; wonderful husband. She came in with a bleeding problem, she had acquired immunity to clotted blood—a very interesting case and very bad. She needed a special blood preparation, a lot of fancy care, and a lot of expensive special medicines. One morning on rounds, we were discussing this patient, and one of the residents said, "Well, I think today's the day that I'm going to speak to Mrs. So-and-so's husband." I said, "To say what?" And he said, "Well, I'm going to give him the choice." I said, "Give him the choice of what?" And he said, "Does he want to be left financially destitute or should we just stop?" I said, "You're saying to this man, 'Do you want us to let your wife die or do you want us to continue?' " I said, "Never! I will *never* let you speak to him! Where is your brain?" Then I said, "Look, since money seems to be on your mind, call hospital administration and you'll find out that there's a way of calling this a catastrophic illness and the hospital will find a way to help out."

What is *our* role? We're the doctors. The system's wrong, maybe, to make it so costly, but that doesn't mean we should deprive the patient of care. I don't usually say things that way, but I was livid. And apparently they can tell when I'm really angry because I get very quiet and my eyebrows go up.

Our first AIDS patient, I'll call him Alex, came in late in '78 or '79. He was a very talented and fairly successful artist; a handsome man. AIDS was in its infancy at that time. I'd heard of it only because I had a former student working down in infectious disease at the CDC [Center for Disease Control] in Atlanta. One day we were gossiping on the phone, and he said, "Molly, there's something so strange going on here," and he started telling me about AIDS and the symptoms and how a person's body could lose its ability to fight infection; how they have weight loss; the whole thing. So when Alex was admitted, something about his weight loss and his other symptoms rang a bell. Here was an otherwise healthy man who came in with a cough and pneumonia. When we took a history he said he had recently lost weight, had some fever and some diarrhea. But his major problem was a pneumonia that resisted the usual treatment. The diagnosis of AIDS is based on the presence of an unusual infection. We didn't know what or how to tell him. For some reason, though, he seemed to know that this was not going to be good. He had a wonderful group of well-educated friends who were already becoming familiar with AIDS and what was happening, and they were very supportive of him—right to the very end.

Some of these patients have such wonderful courage and determination, especially in the face of such a terrible disease. A young gay man, a writer named Rob, came in around this time last year. He had pneumocystis pneumonia; a very bad case of it. He was in our unit for at least three months and then he went to the floor for another month and a half. His family was from Iowa and they didn't have the first idea, one, that he was gay, and two, that he was even sick. Eventually he had to tell them because he was in the hospital so long and never at home and they were beginning to wonder about him. I think at first he was scared to death of his father's reaction, but he knew if he didn't tell him he might never get to see his family again. So he wrote them a letter. They flew in the day they received it and came to his bedside straight from the airport. His father sat on his bed and he held his son and he cried and his son cried and in no time at all they were telling each other they loved each other. Rob told them he wanted to come home. That was all he cared about at that point. Just going home. He said, "If I can just get home to a hospital there I wouldn't care what happened. I want to go back home to Iowa." Well, he got home to Iowa, and in fact he got out of the hospital and has written a letter to the nurses in the unit. When he was here he had said that his sister was pregnant and what he wanted most was to live long enough for her to have her child. The letter started out by saying that his sister had had the baby and that he'd seen her and that she is very pretty. And that he was now out of the hospital. We talk about him occasionally, and we all remember how hard everybody in the ICU worked to keep this man going. He was so sick and for so long. But when he left here to go back to Iowa, we knew what we had been working so hard for—so this man could get home and see his niece get born and have this wonderful sense of achievement.

There are so many things that are peculiar about AIDS, but one thing we don't know enough about is its transmission. There is no question that it will move increasingly into the heterosexual population. One, because of the number of bisexual men there are in this country—a new surprise—two, because of intravenous drug use, and three, because there was a lot of contaminated blood given before we knew what to look for. Sexual transmission will probably remain the major route, though. Dr. Koop, the surgeon general, says the future of this disease may astonish all of us. Certainly he started a lot of people thinking about the enormous possibilities of risk when he said: "When you go to bed with somebody, you are essentially going to bed with every other person they have ever gone to bed with."

IV
LABOR AND DELIVERY

In 1986, nearly forty-five hundred babies entered this world via one of the rooms on the ninth floor of Babies' Hospital. The labor and delivery suite is one of the most active areas in Presbyterian Hospital. It runs fully staffed around the clock. At any given time an attending, a resident, a midwife, from eight to ten nurses, and a nursing attendant are on hand. During the day, the unit staff also includes a nursing supervisor, unit clerk, and one or two laboratory technicians. It's a rare day that the unit is not pulsing with activity. On average, twelve babies a day, every day of the year, are born here.

On this particular morning, the beds in all twelve labor rooms are occupied and both delivery rooms are in use. It's 8:30, but Ira Reimer, the chief resident, is already delivering his third baby of the day. At a table behind the central nurses' station, Eileen Tuohy, the midwife on duty, and Laurie Solomon, a second-year OB-GYN resident, are drinking cold coffee and going over charts from last night. They both look up as one of the nurses starts writing on a blackboard hanging on the wall directly across from the nurses' station. "The board," as it is called, is central to the unit. It lists, by room, every woman on the floor, along with essential information about her including how many weeks pregnant she is and the number of children she has. It also charts the progress of her labor since she arrived at the hospital.

In LR (labor room) 1 is Mrs. Alvarez, a forty-year-old woman from the neighborhood. This is her second pregnancy, and the baby is already two weeks late. Her doctor has prescribed Pitocin, a drug given intravenously to induce labor. A woman on Pitocin has a nurse with her at all times. If the nurse must leave, even for five minutes, she gets someone to cover for her. Labor nurses are responsible for their patients up to and through delivery. Although they are not expected to deliver a baby, all of them can and often they do, if a baby arrives fast and unexpectedly. For the most part, though, the labor nurse's job is to monitor and comfort her patient—to instruct, to guide, and to teach her. A bond develops more quickly between a laboring woman and her nurse than between any two other people short of a mother and her newborn. Mrs. Alvarez's nurse is Amy, a young woman who speaks Spanish and can converse with Mrs. Alvarez, who speaks no English. Mr. Alvarez, who is quite a bit older than his wife, is nervously pacing up and down the hallway outside his wife's door. He has not set foot inside his wife's room since he brought her here at seven o'clock last night.

In LR 2 is Mrs. Moscow. Her baby is in breech position and will probably have to be delivered by Cesarean section, but her contractions are not yet strong enough to require attention.

In LR 3 is Mrs. Luis. She arrived at 3:10 this morning after she began to bleed heavily at home. She is apparently having a placenta previa where the placenta, which normally follows the baby in delivery, in some cases separates from the uterus before delivery. Mrs. Luis's doctor has monitored her for five hours in the hope that she might deliver the baby, her third, on her own. But labor is not progressing and eventually the oxygen supply to the baby will run out. Mrs. Luis will be delivered by cesarean section. The doctors are waiting for blood from the blood bank before beginning her operation.

Mrs. Weissman, an overweight Orthodox Jew in mild labor with her fourth baby is in LR 4. Because she is overdue, she is being induced with Pitocin. She is shuffling along the corridors in a flowered housedress, a scarf on her head, pulling her IV stand along, and talking with her husband.

LR 5 has Mrs. Olesky, who has waited ten years for this first pregnancy. Her strong labor pains don't seem to faze her. Her husband is at her bedside, taking home movies and coaching his wife in breathing techniques. The baby, which they know will be a girl, is to be named Sarah, after its maternal grandmother.

In LR 6, Mrs. Gross is in the very early stages of labor with her first child. Her private physician has stopped in twice since she arrived at 6:30 A.M., but that doesn't satisfy her husband, who is demanding a nurse full time. Assured that there is no need for constant scrutiny, he nonetheless warns the clerk behind the desk that his brother is a lawyer.

LR 7. Laney Binik, sixteen years old and in early labor, has just left her room and is walking the floors in a hospital gown and black knee-high socks. She is chatting with the nurses and the expectant fathers in the hallway, and appears to be watching, like an uninvolved observer, all of the activity surrounding her.

HR (High Risk) 1 has Mrs. James, whose contractions are coming close together. She clutches a pillow and bites her lip with each one. Rubber disks on her abdomen are attached by wire to a machine that continually monitors her baby's heartbeat. Her nurse concentrates on the tracing being spit out by the monitor, which shows the baby's heart rate is slow and getting slower. The nurse is concerned. The baby's head is low enough in the birth canal so that the doctor can take a tiny sample of blood from the baby's scalp, which he does with a tiny glass pipette. The sample is taken immediately to the laboratory down the hall for analysis.

In HR 2, Mrs. Kingsley, only thirty weeks pregnant, is in premature labor with twins. Her doctor is giving her medication to try to temporarily stop the labor because the babies are not sufficiently developed yet and might not survive.

In the recovery room, often used for women in labor, the four beds are full. In bed A is Jenny Fox, an eighteen-year-old who was born with fetal alcohol syndrome—a condition sometimes passed on to a child when the pregnant mother is an alcoholic, which Jenny's mother was. Jenny is four feet ten inches tall, with distinctive facial features resembling those of people with Down's syndrome, although she does not have Down's. Like her mother, Jenny is an alcoholic. The doctors are fearful that her baby will be born with fetal alcohol syndrome.

In bed B, Sandra DeMaio is doing the breathing exercises she learned in the Lamaze classes given in the hospital. As a contraction starts, she squeezes her husband's hand. He says, "Breathe slowly, Sandy. Now . . . blow out! Blow out! Blow out . . . ," In bed C, Julia Robbins is nursing her just-born daughter Melissa. The baby's proud father is passing out pencils lettered in gold saying, "It's a Girl—Melissa Robbins." "How did you get them so fast?" asks Mr. DeMaio. "Ever hear of amniocentesis?" answers Melissa's father. "It's this test that tells you what you're going to have. We've known it's a girl for months." In bed D is Mrs. Lewis, who has just been admitted from the clinic. This is her fourth baby. Her husband stands by her bed and a suitcase full of camera equipment rests on the floor.

Two women are in the triage room, a small, two-bed room at the front of the suite where women are evaluated to see if they should remain in the hospital or be sent home. Mrs. Roberto is from Queens, where she has been receiving her prenatal care at a local hospital, but these past two days she has been in Washington Heights visiting her brother. She will be charted as "unregistered" and be allowed to have her baby here if her labor is too active for her to be transferred. Twenty percent of all women who deliver at Presbyterian Hospital are unregistered—meaning the first time they are seen here is when they come in to have their babies. Many unregistered mothers-to-be have never seen a physician throughout nine months of pregnancy. Many have no insurance coverage. In keeping with the policy of Presbyterian Hospital of never turning anyone away, if Mrs. Roberto is in active labor, she will be allowed to stay.

Also in the triage room, for the second time this week, is Mrs. Greenberg. The first time was a false alarm. Now the midwife examines her. Active labor has started and her private physician is called.

9:00: The lab results on the James baby show it's in distress; its oxygen supply is slowly diminishing. Dr. Reimer calls an emergency cesarean and goes immediately to the sink to scrub. Within minutes, two nurses are wheeling Mrs. James down the hall to the operating room. Already in the room are the anesthesiologist, the anesthesia resident, a scrub nurse, a circulating nurse, an OB-GYN second-year resident, and Dr. Claudia Holland, the attending on duty today. (Attendings are physicians who have completed their residency training.) The rule is that an attending must be present at all deliveries to supervise the residents. OB attendings rotate duty in Labor and Delivery and are usually on two days a month. They belong to the Sloane Obstetrical Group and are known on the floor as SOGs.

9:04: Three nurses transfer Mrs. James from her bed to the operating table, and within ten seconds the anesthesiologist has started an intravenous and is getting ready to put a mask over her face to put her to sleep. By 9:06, the mother-to-be is fully anesthetized. Everyone in the room recognizes that every extra minute means a minute more the baby's brain may be deprived of oxygen. "Okay," says Dr. Reimer, "let's go!" Everyone watches as he makes the incision, low on the woman's belly. Within seconds, a baby's head is in view. Reimer lifts the infant and dislodges it from the umbilical cord, which is wrapped around its neck. The baby is blue. Suddenly, with no coaxing, the child, a boy, begins to wail.

The doctor hands him immediately to the pediatric resident. There is a pediatric resident in attendance at every high-risk delivery and every C-section. Because the pediatric neonatal intensive care unit is across the hall from L & D, a pediatrician is never more than a minute away. He carries the infant to a small cart with warming lights in the corner of the room and begins to tap the child gently on his chest with the flat half of a rubber suction bulb. "Turn pink!" he commands. He taps it again. "Come on! Come on!" says the pediatrician, as he suctions the baby's nostrils and throat. He turns the baby over and pats his chest again. Slowly, the infant takes on a pink color. The pediatrician rubs the baby's back softly and smiles down at him. "There you go, young man." The nurse assisting him clutches her chest and lets out a sigh of relief. Another nurse sticks her head into the room. "Dr. Reimer," she says, "they need you for an emergency breech next door!"

"I'm on my way," Dr. Reimer answers, as he completes one last stitch. He snaps off his rubber gloves, leaving Mrs. James to be bandaged by the junior resident.

The circulating nurse records the time of birth at 9:10 A.M., four minutes after the incision, seven minutes from the time the patient was wheeled into the room.

Dr. Reimer heads for the sink outside Delivery Room 2. He steps up to scrub next to a junior resident. "I just returned yesterday from two weeks in the Carribean," Dr. Reimer says, wistfully. "It seems like years ago."

Dr. Reimer backs into the operating room, arms dripping. He's gowned and gloved by the scrub nurse. Dr. Holland has entered the room and has stepped up to the table. Mrs. Moscow is already asleep. The room is quiet. This time the second-year resident makes the incision. "Slow and careful," Reimer instructs, his eyes intently watching the resident's hands. The baby's back and buttocks come into view. "Now, gently slide your hand under the belly and lift the baby." It's a perfect delivery. Mrs. Moscow has a beautiful baby girl.

11:40: Mrs. Lewis's water has broken. Eileen Touhey, the midwife, is with her, listening through her stethoscope to the baby's heartbeat. "If you want to push, push," she says, placing a clean sheet over Mrs. Lewis, who is now gripping the sides of the bed. Mr. Lewis leaves the room to get a hospital gown. While he's gone, his wife lets out a yell. "Let's go have a baby!" says Eileen Touhy, pushing the bed out the door.

Four babies are born between noon and three P.M. Mrs. Olesky, Mrs. Luis, and Mrs. Binik have had little girls. This is the fourth daughter for Mrs. Binik, who has vowed to keep going until she gets the boy her husband wants. Jenny Fox, the young girl with fetal alcohol syndrome, has given birth to a son. The baby has been taken to the transitional nursery for observation. He is placed in an isolette next to Mrs. Luis's daughter. Four new patients have been admitted to the floor.

At 3:20, an eerie silence descends on the floor. A few of the nurses join the attendings in the lounge for what remains of lunch—cold pizza and warm soda. Eileen Touhey uses the time to write notes on the morning's patients. As she writes, she nibbles a piece of leftover chocolate Easter bunny that has been in her locker for two weeks. "Want some lunch?" she asks Claudia Holland. "My mother sent me this. She's still sending me chocolate bunnies at Easter. Can you believe it?" Laurie Solomon, the resident, collapses, exhausted, into a wheelchair parked in a corner and closes her eyes. Dr. Reimer, the back of his head resting heavily on the wall, is talking on the telephone and jotting notes on a three-by-five card.

A nurse announces that Anna Alvarez is finally ready to go. Dr. Solomon heads for the delivery room. Three nurses roll the bed down the hall. As Mrs. Alvarez is moved to the delivery table, Amy, the nurse who has been with her for eight hours, places her arm under her patient's neck. "*Está bien,*" she says into Mrs. Alvarez's ear. "It's okay." The patient is covered with perspiration. "Okay, Anna, you gotta help us here," Dr. Solomon says from the foot of the table. Within seconds, the baby's dark, wet scalp comes into view.

"Push!" says Amy in Spanish. "Here it comes! Here it comes! Here it comes!" she yells, sounding like a cheerleader at a football game.

"Anesthesia," Mrs. Alvarez whimpers. "No time," says Dr. Solomon, glancing up at her patient. "Here comes the baby!" Mrs. Alvarez lets out a single yell. The baby's head emerges, face down. Seconds elapse before the baby's shoulders emerge. The resident uses those seconds to suction the baby's nose and mouth, making its first breath easier. Mrs. Alvarez wails again and the baby is out. Laurie Solomon beams at the baby as she hands it to the waiting pediatrician. "You have a beautiful baby girl, Mrs. Alvarez."

The baby is placed on a table under warming lights while the pediatrician examines her. Her hair is thick and wet. The little girl is pronounced "perfect," swaddled in a blanket, and laid on her mother's belly. "*Mamasita,*" says Mrs. Alvarez, exhausted but smiling. She looks at her nurse, Amy. "*Gracias,*" she says. As her lips brush across the baby's head, a tear falls down her cheek.

Four o'clock signals the end of the shift for some of the nurses. The board is still full, but most of the names from this morning have been replaced by new ones. Mrs. Gross is still in room 3, her contractions coming closer together now. Mrs. Greenberg has gone to LR 4. Mrs. Weissman is in the delivery room. Mrs. DeMaio has a new daughter, five minutes old. Her husband, a professional photographer, tried to take pictures but ended up leaving the delivery room after the going got rough. It has been decided that Mrs. Roberto is not in labor so she has been sent home to her brother's to wait for contractions to start. Mrs. Greenberg and her baby are on their way to the maternity floor. Terri, one of the nurses, is saying goodbye as she leaves for two weeks' vacation. Mr. Gross is on the hall phone reporting his wife's progress to his mother-in-law. The Fox baby and the Luis baby are in isolettes in the hallway in front of the nurses' station, waiting to be transported to the neonatal intensive care unit. The Luis baby will be observed for respiratory distress. Jenny Fox's son, like his mother, has fetal alcohol syndrome.

W. DUANE TODD, M.D.

Obstetrician and Gynecologist

⟳————————

We're in his office on Sixteen East. It is not a very large space, but it is well appointed, with several pieces of antique furniture. He points out his favorite: "This particular desk was the desk of the first chairman of the department of obstetrics and gynecology after Sloane Hospital moved from 59th Street up to Presbyterian in 1929. It has been the desk of all of the department chairmen—Benjamin Watson, Howard Taylor, George Moore—ever since. It even served for part of Raymond Vande Wiele's tenure. Raymond was a more modern individual though, and he decided to have all modern furniture in his office. Well, when I heard that, I said, 'For heaven's sakes, don't let anything ever happen to this desk. It's got too much history tied up in it.' And that's when I inherited it. It's truly a wonderful desk."

He came to Presbyterian Hospital as a resident in 1948. He and his wife lived in a building across the street that has since been torn down and replaced by the Hammer Health Sciences Building.

——————

I have no idea how many children I've delivered—probably well over five thousand over the years. I'd love to say I remember each of them, but after a certain number of deliveries, you get to the point where you deliver a child and then you come back an hour or so later to write the doctor's notes and you can't remember if the baby was a boy or a girl. Or, a child will be delivered and the relatives will say, "This child is the spitting image of So-and-so of the family." I usually say, "It certainly is," but I've never been able to see anything. I mean, babies to me have always looked very, very much the same.

One of the most monumental changes to come about over the years in our field is the abortion law. Before abortion was legalized in 1973, we used to have a therapeutic abortion committee that included a member of the department of obstetrics and gynecology, a member of the department of medicine, and usually a psychiatrist. The obstetrician who was going to do the abortion would present the case to the abortion committee along with the physician who was going to support this abortion. If the woman had a medical problem indicating that she should not carry this pregnancy, then the internist would also come along. The committee then had to approve the abortion unanimously.

The problem was that certain abortions were being done for psychiatric reasons; and there you get into a very difficult never-never land. For instance, let's say a woman is in a panic because she's been exposed to German measles. She doesn't want to take the chance of carrying this pregnancy. Well, there was no abortion committee that would accept that as a reason for doing an abortion, so she sees a psychiatrist who says that she's distraught enough about this to pose a major psychiatric problem. So you get into a very difficult area. Although abortion committees took their responsibility very, very seriously, there were difficult situations whereby you couldn't in good conscience turn a woman down.

During that era, there were a lot of women who had abortions that didn't fall under the heading of therapeutic. We called them "criminal abortions." They were done by abortionists on the outside. That was a terrible era. A terrible era. We had a unit on this floor at the far end of this corridor which had about a half a dozen cubicles. It was referred to on the service as "the septic tank." And it was filled, day in, day out, with women who had had criminal abortions and who were septic. Infections were rampant, and any number of them died from their complications. At that time, there really was very little you could do, unless you happened to get them early enough and all the right decisions were made. But many of them, by the time they came in, were in irreversible shock from their infections.

Once, when I was a resident, a sixteen-year-old girl was brought in by her mother. She was about sixteen or eighteen weeks pregnant and they claimed she was having problems related to the pregnancy and that she had miscarried. She was infected. There wasn't any question about it. But there were other problems that suggested that she had a phlebitis of her leg, all sorts of things. She denied having had an abortion. Now the policy at that time was that any woman who came in who had had an abortion and who had a fever—you essentially never had fever related to an uninter-fered-with miscarriage—had to be reported to the police. Then the police would usually send somebody up to interview the patient. But in the case of this girl no information at all related to any kind of abortion. Yet she was becoming more and more ill, and I felt certain that she had some problem related to, perhaps, a perforation of her uterus. One morning when I was making rounds and trying to come to some decision about what we should do for this girl, I told her she was only harming herself if she didn't tell all of us what had occurred, *if* anything had occurred. I was essentially certain that something had. I told her that the consequences of withholding information could actually be very threatening to her own life.

I left that area and about an hour a later I had a call from her through the nurse, and I went back to her floor. At that time she told me that she had had an abortion done and that they had used, she thought, a coat hanger. The problem was that she didn't abort after the abortionist did it the first time, so she went back a second time. Her mother had taken her to the abortionist both times. It then became apparent what the problem was, and we went ahead and treated her. She had a totally destroyed uterus. She had to be given a hysterectomy at the age of sixteen.

That evening, the father came in to the hospital. When he discovered what his wife and daughter had done, I thought he was literally going to destroy his wife.

The police were able to identify the abortionist and the woman was ultimately arrested. The police officer who was involved later told me how he had made the arrest. He said they had gone to the woman's apartment. It was very sparsely furnished. As they were going through everything they found an unbent coat hanger in the closet, and they asked the woman what she did with this coat hanger. She said, "I pick up pieces of paper off the floor." She was that callous. Well, the woman was charged with infanti-cide, because in those days if a termination of pregnancy was done after sixteen weeks, theoretically you had a live fetus. You could hear a heartbeat at eighteen weeks of pregnancy. So this fell into the grounds of infanticide rather than just an induced abortion. The woman eventually pleaded guilty to something like assault and was given a one-month sentence. That was the end of it.

All of us became very, very familiar with these things. You'd go down to the emergency room and see somebody who was bleeding; they were pregnant and they were febrile and they would invariably tell a story of how they fell down the stairs. There were standard stories. Then you'd go to examine the patient and when you put a speculum in the vagina, you'd find a rubber catheter coming out of the cervix. One of the techniques they used was, they'd put a rubber catheter over the tip of a coat hanger and then introduce it into the uterus. They'd remove the coat hanger, but leave the rubber tip there, which eventually the uterus would try to expel, and along with it, they hoped, would come the baby.

Now if you went to somebody who was a medical abortionist but doing it illegally, they would do a scraping, but they usually would do it under sterile techniques, and with relative safety to the patient.

I was so relieved when the abortion law was changed. Not that I'm that happy about abortions, but it did away with a terrible era and under no circumstances would I ever want to see that kind of an era coming back. If abortions were ever again made illegal, there isn't any question that that's the kind of thing that we would eventually get back into. And it isn't worth it.

Now in all honesty, in the course of my career I did do some therapeutic abortions—and I did a few induced abortions after the law was changed. But I always felt very uncomfortable doing it. I didn't like to do it. There are enough people who will do abortions, who it doesn't seem to bother that much, so that I eventually developed a policy within my own practice, that when patients of mine requested a termination of pregnancy, I would refer them to one of my colleagues who I knew it didn't particularly bother. Even though it's legal, it bothers me on a moral basis.

I'm sixty-three . . . and a half. In this institution, there's a retirement age of sixty-five; however, you're permitted to continue to practice until the age of seventy. Every physician here has two appointments. One is an academic, the other is a hospital appointment. My appointment from the university is clinical professor of obstetrics and gynecology. My appointment from the hospital is attending obstetrician and gynecologist. At age sixty-five you can continue to teach if you want to, although most clinicians who reach that age drop their university obligations because they aren't obligated to teach medical students any longer. They can lead committees related to the college if they want to, though. The university will continue their academic rank and the hospital will let them continue to practice as long as they remain qualified.

When you get to the age of seventy then you have to be reviewed every year. You're reviewed within your own department, particularly by your chairman, to ensure that you're still mentally, physically, and emotionally sound. Now there is a point—I think it's when you reach the age of seventy—whereby the hospital will no longer give you office privileges here in the hospital. And that's understandable. That's a policy to ensure that there is room for the younger people who are coming up. If everybody stayed until they were eighty-five, there wouldn't be any room left in this place for patients. So some people may be approved to continue, but they're going to have to find an office outside the institution.

I remember when I was first going into practice, I thought everything in this field was so great. I could hardly wait to get started. But I can remember also some of the older obstetricians talking then about what it was like twenty years before. Maybe it's a natural phenomenon that occurs, that those of us who are around today think things were that much better twenty years ago, while those who were around twenty years ago were in the same position, thinking it was better twenty years before that. It's part of youth, in fact, that you don't pay attention to what's in the past as much as what's in the future. And maybe that's how it should be.

YVONNE GOMEZ-CARRION, M.D.

Chief Resident,
Obstetrics and Gynecology

She walks into the lounge pushing an empty bassinet, a sleeping infant draped over her shoulder. She's wearing a green scrub suit, the shirt stretched tightly across her six-months-pregnant belly. She transfers the sleeping baby to the crook of her arm and settles herself into an armchair. She places her finger in the palm of the baby's open hand. In his sleep, his fingers close around hers.

Ever since I was an intern, one of the things that soothed me whenever I got very frustrated or tired was to go to the nursery and feed a couple of babies. Just rocking in the chair a little bit is sometimes better for me than sleep. It sort of rejuvenates me, and heaven knows these babies need to be held. With the boarder babies it can be pretty depressing. You go to the nursery and you see the same babies there every day, sometimes for months. So the OB-GYN residents tend to take these kids around with them whenever they have a chance. If it's a quiet day, you take them in the bassinet up to the labor and delivery suite, and they're stimulated by different noises and different faces. At least they're not just lying in a nursery. These babies need to be stimulated. If they were home, they'd have that with family and friends. We try to create that kind of environment here in the hospital.

I came to medical school here from Princeton. There were three black students, including me, and between twenty-five and thirty women in my med school class of around a hundred and fifty. Being in the minority in both areas didn't really bother me, though. In fact, I think the experience strengthened me—not only dealing with being a woman, but also being black. I'd never use any of that stuff as a crutch. I was always made to feel it doesn't matter what you look like. I knew I was as good if not better than most of the people around me. You just have to have confidence in yourself. To tell you the truth, in med school I felt more highly scrutinized because I was a woman than because I was black.

The National Health Service paid for my whole four years of medical school. I'd say it was worth a good eighty thousand dollars. The deal is that for every year they pay for you, you have to give back a year of service. You usually get assigned to a clinic in a physician shortage area—the only way they can get a doctor there. I'm being sent to the Roxbury Comprehensive Health Center in Boston as director of the OB-GYN department.

I've always wanted to practice medicine in a ghetto setting. I grew up in an area that bordered on a real ghetto, right above Bedford Stuyvesant in Brooklyn. From the time I was small, I thought just because these people can't afford good medical care is no reason for them not to have it. When I heard about the National Health Service, I thought that was wonderful. They'll pay for me to become a doctor and I'll get to do what I've always wanted to do.

This is my *eighth* year at this place. As a first-year intern, you do scut work. Second year, you have a lot more responsibility. I think that was my most difficult year here. I did a lot of obstetrics. The second-year resident runs the board in the labor and delivery room, which means you have to know all the patients on the service, whether they're private or ward patients. The second-year residents also do the initial evaluations on all pregnant patients who come in.

Third year is more concentrated on gynecology. As a third-year resident, you're available for consultation to anyone in this entire institution. I remember on July first—my first day as a third-year resident—my beeper went off. It was a private attending calling. He said, "I have a seventy-odd-year-old woman in the house. I just did a pelvic exam and I think she has an adnexal mass. I'd like you to come by and evaluate her." I said, "Excuse me?" I mean, this was July first. I had just become a third-year resident *that* day. It's very scary to have that kind of responsibility at first. But you go. You do your exam, you present an evaluation, and you write a coherent note. The good thing is, if you're ever not sure what's going on, there's always someone around to consult with. But it's nice because you're seen as the expert, as a third-year resident. And it really matures you.

Also, as a third-year resident, you and your chief—under the supervision of an attending—basically do all the surgery on ward cases. A ward case is any patient who comes in through clinic, whether she has insurance or not. These women are taken care of by the residents. Anyone who comes in through the emergency room who has a life-threatening situation—like a ruptured ectopic, for instance [the fertilized egg stays in the fallopian tube rather than traveling to the uterus. As it matures, it eventually bursts the tube]—comes in as a ward case. We have a mixture of ward and private patients on our service, and they all get equal treatment. You wouldn't know walking into a room whether it's a ward patient or a private patient.

Fourth year you feel a little more pressure, especially being administrative chief. Every little problem comes to the chief resident, but I like it. When you're on GYN you decide who goes to the operating room; on OB you decide if and when the patient needs a cesarean section. You're always right there in the middle of things, always making decisions.

In this specialty you really get attached to some of your ladies, especially when you go through labor with them. Even though it's a short time, you develop a very special bond. There are six babies out in this world named after me that I know of. Four Yvonnes and two Ivans. And that was just because we had such a nice experience together through labor and delivery—these are women I'd never seen before. You just try to make their labor as comfortable as possible. You hand them a beautiful baby and they look up at you and they say, "Thank you, doctor—and by the way, what's your name?" In GYN when you have a patient who comes to the ER who is incredibly ill, you take her onto your service. You treat her. A couple of days later she feels great. It's that "thank you"—that smile—that's got to be why I went into medicine. Not that I want people thanking me all the time, but it's an incredibly good feeling to know that you've helped in some way to ease someone else's pain.

For the entire eight years I've been here, I've been involved with a clinic called the Young Adult Clinic, for young women from the ages of maybe eleven to twenty-one. You look around here, you read the papers, and you see how many teenage pregnancies there are. So I attend the clinic and explain contraception to these young women. But I think there's more to it. I think it's just as important to sit down and listen to them and talk to them about what they are going to do with their lives. Some of these are young girls of fourteen who already have two kids. I explain that they might think their life is over but it's not. I do this for a number of reasons. I love the women, but also, I'm just trying to give back a little that was given to me. So I share my life with them. I tell them about the people in my life who told me I would never make it. "How dare you think you could be a doctor? Your parents don't have the money. What role models do you have in your family?" Just thinking about how I had to buck those people and how I made it to where I am now, makes me want to tell these young women, "You can do it too. You can be anything you want to be." I've been involved with the teenagers the whole eight years I've been here. Some have come back to visit me. Some are in college. It feels good that I've been able to touch some lives. I'm sure that sometimes I just talk and talk and nothing gets through, but those few that you make a difference with are so worth it.

This field has its challenges, not only in the diseases, but also in the psychology of taking care of people. You can meet someone you've never seen before in your life and within minutes you're telling them some disastrous news they don't want to hear or can't understand. I had a patient last week, a ruptured ectopic pregnancy. She was in real trouble. I was explaining to her that we really needed to go to the OR right away because she was bleeding internally. She looked up at me and said, "I want a second opinion." I said, "You don't understand. I can get another doctor from here to explain what's going on, but we don't have time to send you to another hospital or to find you another physician outside of this institution." She had heard so many bad things about the medical care system, she was petrified. Then she said, "Have you done many of these procedures before?" I guess she was just doubting who I was and what I wanted to do. But after I talked to her for a while, I gained her confidence and we went to the OR. That's frightening, though, when you meet someone who could die any minute and they say, "I'm not going to allow you to operate on me."

When you become a doctor, you tend to view death differently from the way you did before. The first time I had to deal with death was when I was a young girl and my stepfather died. I loved him very much and it was a great shock. I was furious! Why had he left me? Now I'm dealing with the oncology patients and helping them go through the stages of the Kübler-Ross concept of dealing with death. I watch an OB patient lose a baby or a father lose his wife during childbearing, and I've learned to respect death. I understand it a lot better. Watching these women, particularly those who know they're dying, and seeing how they accept it and what arrangements they make, has a permanent effect on you. I think about it myself at times, especially now that I'm having a baby. Sometimes I wonder, "Well, how many years will I actually spend with my child?"

I'm one who advocates going with dignity. I've considered how far I would go to stay alive if I were to get, say, a terrible form of cancer. There are some tough people who just keep holding on, and it's hard for them and hard for their family, and they suffer. But they want to hang in there, pain and all, no matter what. And I respect that. After all, you never know.

Maybe a new cure will come through while you're waiting. I think if I were in an advanced stage of some terminal disease I'd probably want to go home and just have my Häagen-Dazs ice cream and prepare my family and say, "I love you all, and goodbye." I don't think I'd want the tubes in.

It appears that women are taking over this field. And I think that's fabulous! All of the interns we accepted for this year are women. We have two men in my year, there are two men in third year. There are none in second and none in first. We'll see what happens next year. Of course, there are still very good men who are going into the field. In fact, I think we're getting better men because of the pressure. I mean, if a man goes ito OB-GYN now, he *has* to be good.

EILEEN TUOHY, R.N.

Midwife

———

We're talking at a small desk in examining room B in the obstetrical clinic. A young girl walks in and tentatively approaches the midwife. "I'm sorry! I forgot to come. Am I too late?" She's young—seventeen, perhaps younger—with a soft, childlike face. The midwife is in her thirties, blue eyes, with a wide, toothy smile. She is wearing navy slacks and a blue blouse under her lab coat. A stethoscope hangs from the jacket pocket.

"It's never too late," she says, helping the girl onto the examining table. She lifts the girl's shirt and places a stethoscope on her belly. She listens intently, her head bent forward. Then she hands the instrument to the girl and lets her listen. A grin spreads across the girl's face as she hears her baby's rapid heartbeat. "Hey," she says, "it sounds like Belmont in there!"

"You had a sonogram. What did it show?" asks the midwife.

"They think it's a girl. If it is, I'm naming her after you. I'm calling her Eileen."

———

In this hospital, the midwives take care of clinic patients. Not all of them of course. Some are cared for by obstetrical residents. Because we're midwives, not doctors, we care for only those women who are having normal, problem-free pregnancies. If a woman comes into the clinic, she may be assigned to me. Then she remains my patient throughout her pregnancy or as long as no problems arise. If she shows any signs of trouble, she's immediately referred to one of the physicians and I no longer continue to manage her. All of us follow our own patients for the duration of their pregnancies. We see them for all of their prenatal visits, we deliver their babies, and we do the postpartum follow-ups.

The traditional view of the midwife is somebody who sits with the woman throughout her labor. We don't always have the time to do that here, but if we can do it, we do. I think that extra attention may be one reason some women prefer to go to a midwife. Another may be that they just prefer to have another woman with them during their delivery. If you have a midwife, the chances are ninety-nine out of a hundred that a woman will deliver your baby. The chances are not quite so high if you have a doctor, but that's changing. Today, more and more obstetricians are women. In the residency here, for example, I think there are twenty residents and only three of them are male.

Another reason for using a midwife is that midwives are noninterventionist. That means we don't use forceps or instruments in the delivery. Not that all doctors do—they don't—but there's a certainty about it when a midwife delivers your baby.

When I say I'm a midwife people always assume that I deliver babies at home. That's not the case. I work only here in the hospital. The distinction between a certified nurse midwife [CNM], which is what I am, and a lay midwife, is that CNMs have to be registered nurses first. You have to go to an accredited midwifery program like the one here at Columbia. This is a master's program—it goes for twelve full months. We have to take boards to be certified, and then we can work in a hospital. A lay midwife will never practice in a hospital. Certainly not in New York State, anyway.

I work two, twelve-hour shifts in the labor room every week—from seven-thirty to seven-thirty. Yesterday I delivered six babies in a twelve-hour period. I think in that time there were twelve deliveries altogether, two or three of which were cesarean sections and two of which were private deliveries. The rest of them were clinic patients. There's always a resident in labor and delivery, so we sort of split the work between us, with me focusing on the normal deliveries and her focusing on the high risk.

At the end of the day, I generally go down to the floors and see the patients I've delivered, just to see how they're doing. It's interesting. You'd think that they'd feel a personal closeness to the person who delivered their baby, but you can get a patient who delivers when you're on call in Labor and Delivery, and you've never seen the woman prior to her delivery. Well, she probably won't remember you afterwards. Especially if she delivers quickly. So it can happen that I'll go to see a woman the day after I've delivered her baby and I'll walk in the room and she'll sort of look at me funny—who are you?—and then after a minute, she'll remember. It's like the time and the situation brought us together for one of the most important events in her life and then . . . that's it. See you later. It took me a while to get used to that, but now I expect it. It's okay.

It's a great profession, but it has its stresses. I think about my patients a lot. I worry about when a patient's going to deliver. I get nervous if she goes too long after her due date because it's easier then for complications to occur. Is the baby getting too big? Is she going to need a C-section? Is she going to come in when she's supposed to? That kind of thing. And then, every time you go into a delivery you get that little bit of nervous energy that puts you right on your toes. It doesn't matter at all how many times you've done it before. You never know for sure what's going to happen in that delivery room.

Yesterday was one of those normally abnormal experiences you can get in here. One of our patients, a Turkish woman in her twenties, was in labor with her second baby. She didn't speak a word of English and she was here by herself, so nobody could speak to her—except we did find somebody who knew how to say "push" in Turkish. She had been registered in the clinic but she always had an interpreter with her when she came for checkups. So she came in and we took her into one of the labor rooms and we indicated the bed and change your clothes and she did all that. Then the labor pains started and with the first really strong one, she just went wild! She kept pointing to her back so we'd give her anesthesia. It seems she had had her first baby in Turkey and she must have had epidural [spinal] anesthesia with that one. At first we weren't quite sure *what* she was doing because she was very uncontrolled and thrashing about and yelling things in Turkish and nobody could understand what she was saying. Finally, by the time we figured out what she wanted, she was almost ready to deliver. So we did our best to explain to her that it was too late for an epidural. But she didn't want to hear that. She was mad. And she was determined not to help us with this delivery at all. There were three other nurses and a doctor in the room by then and we were all having a terrible time, but we managed to calm her enough for the baby to be delivered. It was a struggle, though. Well, no sooner was the baby out—it was a very big baby—than the woman sat up on the table and right away started talking to us in *English:* "Excuse me, is the baby a boy or a girl?" This was a woman who five minutes before didn't speak a word of English!

Nobody gets put under anesthesia to have a baby anymore. Everyone is awake and with us and pushing her baby out. Some people have epidural anesthesia so they don't feel that much pain. And some people have Demerol during their labor, but that doesn't put them out; it just takes the edge off the pain. Some people respond to it a little more strongly than others, so they may go to sleep, but as soon as they have a contraction, they wake up. Most women love to see their babies being born. I frequently hand the baby to the mother before I even cut the cord—the baby comes out, you see the baby's all right, and you lay it right on the mother's belly, soaking wet. It's a wonderful sight. It's really beautiful.

Fewer people are going into midwifery now. It had quite a resurgence for a while, the last fifteen, twenty years, say. But now fewer people are going into nursing to begin with, and the applications to the midwifery programs are down. Possibly that's because of the malpractice situation, possibly because there are so many more opportunities for women. For a long time nursing was a decent-paying job that women could go into and be respected and have their own career. It was nursing and teaching and that was it. Now there's everything available to us. So now, why not be an obstetrician? You know? Why think small?

EDWARD BOWE, M.D.

Obstetrician and Gynecologist

———

He's a big bear of a man, well over six feet tall, with thick graying hair and a broad, warm smile. His eyes light up when he talks about his work: "There's nothing in this world like delivering a baby. It's a magic time, an inspiring thing. No matter how the world is and where we're going—nuclear disarmament, no nuclear disarmament, whatever—I still get such a bang just seeing a baby come out."

He has five children of his own.

———

As soon as I got out of high school, I went to work playing the jazz tenor saxophone and clarinet. I worked with some name bands, too. Louis Prima and others like him. Then the Korean War came along and I was drafted into the army. By the end of my service I decided to take advantage of the GI bill. And so I started at Columbia University. I was going to major in public relations.

By mistake, I took a zoology course that was for premed students, and I just went crazy! I adored it! Looking through microscopes and dissecting dogfish and things like that really turned me on. The people in the course were all premeds and it didn't sound too hard, so I changed my goals in the middle of my undergraduate education, and I became a "premed." I was in that part of Columbia that was known as General Studies. It was populated by "old" people; people who were working at a job during the day or at night and were educating themselves. I was twenty-four when I started, six years behind where I might have been, so I fit right in.

I had scholarships practically all the way through P and S. They had a terrific endowment then; a lot of money. I had enough from the GI bill to pay for the first year, but then I had to go on scholarship because I had no resources at all, except my saxophone, and I sold that to buy an engagement ring for the woman I eventually married.

I did most of my residency here. When I finished, I didn't go into private practice right away. I stayed on as an instructor in the medical school and I did research in fetal monitoring and fetal blood sampling. In the fifties, there was lots of grant money. You could always get the NIH to support a research project if you had the right people doing it and had a question or a clinical problem you wanted to solve. Then in the sixties, the well went dry for all of medicine and science, but it was especially hard on clinical research. Since then, they've been looking mostly at heart disease, stroke, cancer—diseases of old age and aging. There isn't much money available for the very beginning of life. That's always struck me as very shortsighted, but legislators are old men and old women, so research for problems of the aging is what they're interested in.

Anyway, research money became harder to come by and I had to support myself and my family by seeing patients. I had five kids. I had to do more private practice to earn a living, and as I saw more and more patients, I had less and less time to do my research. There were still so many problems to solve—monitoring the fetus, the mysteries of the placenta. There just weren't enough hours in the day to do it all.

In the late sixties I started a peri-natal clinic here to take care of high-risk obstetrical patients. Before that all of our prenatal patients were lumped together. Vince Freda, the physician who was instrumental in developing the vaccine against Rh disease, set a precedent. He started a special clinic to take care of women who were Rh negative. Our clinic identifies high-risk babies before they're born and conducts various tests, like ultrasonography and cultures for various organisms.

Because of my work in this area, I became increasingly known as a high-risk obstetrician. I used to see Rh-affected mothers, the ones Vince Freda couldn't see because he was too busy, and then I began to get referrals from other obstetricians of patients who had other problems. That's the sort of flavor of my private obstetrical practice now—a lot of women who are, for various reasons, at high risk of having problems with their pregnancy. We see patients above the age of thirty-five, diabetics, hypertensives, Rh-affected, poor obstetrical histories, history of prematurity, history of multiple pregnancy losses, things like that. There is a group of us now who see such patients, but I was more or less in the vanguard here in that area.

The issue of malpractice has led a lot of physicians to question whether or not to deliver babies at all. Everybody seems to be litigation-minded and liability-minded. It isn't just obstetrics and gynecology; all physicians are in trouble. I'm not accusing the lawyers or the insurance companies or the doctors themselves—I mean, there are bad docs and there are bad outcomes—it's just unfortunate that people in general expect every baby will be perfect. That's unrealistic. It's impossible, in fact. People think that if a baby is born and it's not perfect, the doctor is responsible. We're not super docs who can guarantee you a good baby regardless. It seems a shame that doctors who are trying their damnedest and using all their skills are being accused of negligence or malpractice. The great majority are innocent. The definition of malpractice is nebulous anyway; it has no precise definition.

As a result of all these lawsuits, the insurance rates are knocking a lot of obstetricians out of the field. They're doing straight GYN, or going into research. It's so disheartening when you do exactly what you've always done, and you do it exactly right, and yet you get a bad outcome, and you get a lawsuit.

My malpractice insurance was about eight thousand dollars in 1967, when I started. It's now over sixty-two thousand dollars and I'm getting off easy because I'm under a program that the university runs. Some of my colleagues who are in practice out in Long Island pay almost a hundred thousand dollars a year. If I were a young doctor and I had to pick a specialty, I would shy away from this one. What astounds me is that they don't. We're now interviewing next year's resident candidates for this department. We have over two hundred applications for five openings. There are a lot of either really naive or really optimistic people out there. And when I talk to these students about the issue of lawsuits—we bring it up sometimes to try to get an idea of how well they're motivated—they say, "Oh, that won't apply to me," or "I don't plan to go out into private practice. I'm going to be in a medical center."

This influences the way you practice medicine. I think it has helped a lot of us to clean up our acts in terms of documentation, writing notes. I never used to write a note when I made a phone call to a patient. Now I write meticulously in the chart every time I speak to somebody, and I make about twenty to thirty phone calls a day—the bane of my existence.

I still play music when time permits. When I sold my saxophone, I took up the oboe. I play classical music with some other amateur musicians. We used to have a quintet of doctors here, a woodwind quintet, and we'd play for small audiences. It was a wonderful group. But it broke up several years ago, and that's a sad story. One of the members, John Wood, was murdered. John was a resident in the surgical department at the time. His goal was to become a pediatric surgeon. He had already done his pediatric residency, and he was in the middle of the second year of his surgical residency with Dr. Reemtsma when he was killed. I knew him from the time he started medical school here. He had everything going for him. He was bright. He was musically gifted. He played French horn of professional quality. He also composed music, and I have some of his compositions that have never been published. We played them. While John was here we gave a number of concerts at Bard Hall for the medical students and the staff of the medical center. After he died the rest of us gave one more concert, a memorial concert, and some members of the philharmonic performed with us. John Wood was just a magnificent human being. He was a wonderful friend. He's still a very important part of my life.

DEBORAH MUÑIZ, R.N.

Baby Nurse, Eight East

She works the twelve-to-twelve shift so that she can take her daughter to school, and have breakfast with her two-and-a-half year-old son. "The morning is absolutely ours. We watch TV together for a little while, then I take him down to my aunt, who babysits for him, and then I can come to work. When my husband gets home from work he picks up my son. They get dinner, and he puts them to sleep, so when I get home I have a little time for myself if I want. It works out real well."

I love this floor. Six and Eight are the postpartum floors, where mothers and their newborns come straight from the delivery room. We have both private and ward patients on these floors, but I must admit I'm most attracted to the ward patients. They're the ones who are seen here for their prenatal care in the clinic or the ones who come in unregistered, never having been seen here before. We have a lot of new mommies on this floor who haven't had any prenatal care and have no idea how to handle a new baby. They call me. "What's going on with my baby? Why is he doing this, that, or the other thing?" I have to teach many of my new mothers to burp or diaper their babies. Sometimes they say they want to breast feed, so I sit with them for an hour, and after I'm sitting there for an hour and they've got the baby on breast, the next thing they want a bottle. Some-times you want to pull your hair out of your head. I don't really mind, though. Don't get me wrong. These are just young women who have had a baby for the first time and they're just not experienced.

This floor has room for thirty-three mothers and the nursery down the hall holds thirty-three babies. But we also accommodate some boarder babies. That's a baby who remains here after its mother has left the hospital. Absolutely all care of this baby is dependent on us—the feeding, the changing, the cleaning, the clothing. Everything. Some of these babies are here because they were sick and the doctors want to observe them for a little while longer. Some, though, are here because the mommies just left them here. These babies stay here in the nursery waiting for foster place-ment or adoption. We have mommies who come and visit constantly. And we have mommies who forget that they ever had a child. I don't know how they can do that, but they do. We have one baby now whose mother used to come the first couple of weeks and then has never been heard from again. It's heartbreaking.

If a mother doesn't come back, the Department of Special Services for Children goes out to look for her. If they find her, they investigate the home to see if it's suitable for the baby. Often, though, they don't find her. Right now maybe three or four of our boarder babies are abandoned. The others are partially abandoned; the mother will show up once, twice a week.

Some boarder babies are here because their urine samples were positive for cocaine and the mothers were told that until their homes were investi-gated, the babies would not be released. But we tell the mothers they have visiting rights. They can come at any time, call at any time. We *want* them to come see their babies.

One mother absolutely struck me. She came in, unregistered, and deliv-ered her baby. She was so anxious to get out of here; she wanted to go home the first day postpartum. We told her she couldn't because the doctors want to make sure everything is okay; that she isn't bleeding, that she's not anemic. "Oh, no," she said, "I have to go. I have to do things. I'll sign myself out if I have to and I'll come back for my baby tomorrow." And so she left by herself. There was no way we would discharge a newborn who was just twenty-four hours old. But she never came back. She never ever, ever came back for her baby. The baby was put in foster care within a week. But that mother just never, ever came back. The address she gave was phony. No one could find her after that. I don't know what her story was, but I was so shocked because she just didn't seem the type who would do that.

I make a special point to hold these babies. At least I try to. They need the contact and the stimulation. They absolutely need it. What I do is, while I'm feeding a new-born I pull the cribs of the boarder babies around me and I talk to them. Just hearing my voice kind of quiets them and they look up and they're content just to see a face they know.

ELYNNE MARGULIS, M.D.

Medical Director,
In Vitro Fertilization Program

~~~~~~~~~~

She came to our meeting directly from the delivery room, still in her white
scrub suit. A white, paper OR cap covered her hair. She had arrived at the
hospital at one-thirty in the morning to deliver a baby that took nine hours
to make its way into the world.

"It's a marvelous experience, delivering a baby. Not just to see life
brought into the world, but to see the extreme effort and agony one second
and the supreme joy the next. Being able to participate in this, to be there
and see it happen, is really just such a privilege."

Originally, in vitro fertilization [IVF]—or what some people still refer to
as "test-tube babies"—was designed for women who had no functioning
fallopian tubes, and therefore a zero possibility of getting pregnant. This
procedure allows us to reopen the doors to these women and to offer them
the possibility of a child. The concept is for the egg and the sperm to be
united outside of the body.

The technical steps of IVF are easy. We stimulate a woman's ovaries
with fertility drugs so that she produces several eggs at one time, rather
than just the one normally produced. When testing tells us that the eggs
are mature and ready to be released by the ovaries, we go in with a

laparoscope, which is a fiber-optic telescope we place through the belly button. We can see the ovaries and so we place a needle directly into the developing egg sacs, and suck out the eggs. The important thing is to grab the eggs within two hours of when the ovary will expel them. If we wait until they've been expelled, it's too late. Timing, in this procedure, is everything.

We want to get as many eggs as possible because not every egg will fertilize or divide successfully for transfer. At the same time we're doing egg retrieval on a woman, her husband provides us with a sperm specimen through masturbation. In the lab we put the sperm in direct contact with the eggs in a culture dish. And then we wait. Once we know that the eggs have been fertilized, we transfer them into another medium which promotes the growth of the embryo. Within forty-eight hours, we have however-many, usually four to eight, cell embryos. Then the woman returns to the hospital and, under controlled conditions, the embryos are placed directly into her uterus, through the vagina. With luck, an embryo will attach to the uterus wall and we will have the start of a new life.

It's a very time-consuming process for everyone involved. A woman is seen every single day once she starts the drug—a period of two and a half weeks. She's seen for ultrasound, she's seen for a physical exam, she's seen for hormonal monitoring of the blood. She's spoken to every afternoon with the results of that day's laboratory work, and she's told what to do that night.

The husband only has to be here the day of the egg retrieval to provide us with sperm, but we encourage him to be here the day the fertilized embryo is transferred back to his wife, because if pregnancy has occurred, it occurs at precisely that moment, and we think that's a time the husbands and wives should be together. We also have the husbands give the women the evening injections of the drugs. We teach them how to do it because we feel that this is something intimate between the two of them.

After the transfer of the embryos, the woman rests for about six hours just to let everything calm down so she doesn't expel them. The husbands are always there for that period. We have a little bedroom set up in the back and we encourage them to bring a record player or a little TV, cards and books. It's just a relaxing time and an intimate time and then we let them go home.

IVF is a physically, economically, and emotionally stressful protocol. That's because all the eggs are in one basket, if you will. And all of this is geared for just one cycle. It either works or it doesn't and if they're not pregnant that cycle they've got to go through the whole thing all over again. We do it on the average of four times before we call a halt. Success the first time around is probably no better than twelve percent. The statistics suggest that if someone goes through it four times they'll have better than a fifty percent chance of bringing home a baby.

It's a very expensive process. Right now the expense to most patients averages about five thousand dollars per cycle. There are programs that charge as high as seven. Unfortunately, insurance does not yet cover it. That's because originally IVF was caught in a catch-22 situation. Back in the late seventies the Department of Health, Education, and Welfare decided that in vitro fertilization was a worthwhile endeavor, that it needed to be further investigated, and that because it dealt with such sensitive ethical and moral issues, it required an overseeing governing board. That meant any work pertaining to research with human embryos or with IVF would be funneled through the NIH via an ethics advisory review board. Well, the NIH then turned around and disbanded the ethics review board, so they wouldn't have to deal with issues dealing with human embryo research. So a de facto moratorium has existed since the late seventies on any work with human embryos.

One of the main issues is: When you retrieve and fertilize a number of eggs, who decides what goes back and what doesn't. Is it enough for me to say to a patient, "You only want a girl and you don't want a boy so I'm only going to transfer the girls back and throw out the boys?" Who knows? Maybe it is. Maybe people feel sex selection is a reasonable thing to utilize technology for. We don't know. But think of the benefits that can be derived. What about patients who carry genetic diseases, where fifty percent of their offspring may be affected, or even twenty-five percent. If a woman carries the gene for Duchenne's muscular dystrophy, each of her male offspring has a fifty percent chance of having muscular dystrophy. Well, if I could separate the male embryos from the females and only put back the females, I would unquestionably protect that patient from having a child with muscular dystrophy.

But where are we headed? Are we moving toward the perfect society where anything less than perfect will not be tolerated? Is it wrong to allow a baby to be born with muscular dystrophy if you could diagnose it before? What's the answer? I don't have it. I don't know who does. What we do clinically with IVF is just the tip of the iceberg of what can be done, but because of these very sticky issues, people don't want to get involved, including the governing bodies that direct research dollars. And that's why there's been no funding forthcoming.

IVF is terribly expensive because of the quality control. Remember, we're working with human embryos, sperm and egg, outside of the body. To maintain a laboratory that is absolutely clean, sterile, free of any contamination on a twenty-four-hour-a-day, seven-day-a-week basis, is expensive. To maintain personnel on seven-day-a-week, twenty-four-hour-a-day notice, is expensive. We can't time when an egg is ready. If it's Saturday, it's Saturday. If it's Monday, it's Monday. We can't plan these things. So we have to have doctors, nurses, OR techs, anesthesiologists, laboratory technicians, ultrasound technicians, hormonal lab technicians, plus a lot more who have to be primed and ready to function seven days a week. Also, the drugs are very expensive. The drug bill alone is going to be between five hundred and seven hundred and fifty dollars just to get through one month of the procedure.

We optimally like to transfer four embryos. The likelihood that all of them will successfully fertilize and divide is small. I try to retrieve the number of eggs that I want to put back. I look at each egg as I go and I stop when I hear that there are four good eggs. There are some programs where they take as many eggs as they can because any extra embryos are just frozen, stored, and transferred in a later cycle.

We're not doing freezing here yet for two reasons. Part of it is just the expense of setting it up. But more important is the legal aspect. Two years ago there was an interesting case that was splattered all over the news headlines, of a couple who were flying in the Andes. Their plane crashed and they were killed. They had gone through an in vitro cycle in Australia where two of their embryos were transferred and two were frozen. She did not conceive with the first two, and when she died, she still had these two embryos in storage. Now we have these two embryos and the parents, the potential parents I should say, are deceased—and to make matters more complicated, they're multimillionaires and there's not just an ethical question on whether these embryos need to still be transferred or considered life, but also whether they are a part of the estate in terms of the disposition of the assets of the estate.

They've been wrestling with this for years. There have been multiple commissions convened to decide what to do with these two embryos. The bottom line is that after so many years the likelihood that they would ever take in anyone's uterus is extremely small. But you don't have to go into craziness like multimillionaires and airplanes in the Andes. What happens to a couple who come to you and say, "I want a baby," and you take out four eggs, and you fertilize and transfer two or three and you freeze the other one. Say she gets pregnant with the first transfer. She's happily pregnant, she came to you for that baby, and she doesn't want any more. Now I've got two more sitting in the lab. What do I do with them? Is it incumbent upon me to find a surrogate uterus? Is surrogacy something that is to be fostered where the mother has no genetic continuity? It's hard enough with Baby M where it's clear that Mary Whitehead is the mother and Stern is the father, and it's still a question of whose child she is. But can you imagine when the embryo has no genetic link to the mother, when she really is a womb for rent? What potential legal hassles this could unfold. And even more complicated, let's say we take a couple where the wife has no uterus, so someone else carries the pregnancy for nine months but has no genetic link. Who is the mother? Is the nine months of pregnancy and the labor and the giving birth what makes someone a mother, or is it the genetic DNA that's imprinted that makes someone the mother? Talk about Solomon's decision.

There are major legal implications that have yet to be ironed out with these frozen embryos. What happens to spare embryos that are not needed or wanted that are left in storage? What is your legal responsibility? What if something happens to your storage tank and the freezing system goes off? Are you culpable for potential multiple manslaughter suits, because these are potential lives that have been killed in your incubator? It all goes back to: What is the status of the embryo outside the body?

Now, as an individual, I have a very clear concept of that. To me, while the embryo is surely more than just an egg and a sperm individually, without the vector of a human body, there is no life. There is a potential life, but it's not a *true* life. I don't have any problems with the concept of not transferring back everything that I have in hand. But there are a lot of patients who do. And more important, there are a lot of legislators who do and there are a lot of religious people who do.

V
MAIN STREET, U.S.A.

On the main path leading from the park, you pass the Pauline Hartford Chapel, a cafeteria, a full-service bank, a gift shop, Joe's Barber Shop, Thelma's Beauty Salon, a fast-food take-out, and a Barnes & Noble book shop. Along the way you might see a group of young children and their teacher walking toward the nursery school, a team of hard-hatted construction workers congregating on a coffee break, a priest in a long frock coat waiting patiently on line at a money machine, and a guard stopping to give directions to a young couple pushing a baby in a stroller. This isn't Main Street—it's the main floor of Presbyterian Hospital. But in many ways the trappings are so alike it seems to be the artery of a small town.

The similarity isn't just physical. In fact, a hospital has in many ways been described as a perfect microcosm of society. Nearly every social institution found outside its walls is replicated inside them: medicine, of course, and science, but also education and religion and business. Presbyterian Hospital's chief executive officer, Dr. Thomas Morris, is a physician, but as president of the hospital, he works with a board of trustees who conduct and are responsible for the business aspects of this institution. They are, in effect, the mayor and selectmen. They deal, every day, not only with medical issues but also with social, political, and economic problems that go along with running any sizable institution, through which twenty-five thousand people pass each day.

The people who work in this hospital are an equally representative cross section of society. There are old people and young, black and white, educated and uneducated, single, married, and divorced, with occupations running the gamut from artist to baker, rabbi to laundress, librarian to computer expert. For all their diversity, what they have in common is that most of them could do their jobs on any Main Street. And while they don't participate in the drama played out daily in the operating room and they are generally not the ones who get the glory—some never even see a patient—they are the backbones of the hospital, the ones who hold it together, the mortar.

There are any number of reasons why they are here. For some, it is the implicit satisfaction of service, of making a difference. Others had an interest in medicine and for some reason could not enter the profession. Whatever their reasons, these are the people who, along with the medical staff, make up the social structure of this hospital, the people who reflect the society outside Presbyterian's walls. And although they are a heterogeneous group, taken together they're as fine a gallery of the American scene as can be found anywhere.

MARY MUCKLER
Laundry Worker

"I guess everybody has dreams. When I was a little girl, I thought I would like to be a nurse, but being from a poor family, it just didn't work out for me. At least I'm working in a hospital. I don't think I'd want my kids or my grandchildren to do this job, though. Working in the laundry. I mean, I like it a lot, but I think I'd want something better for them." She's been at this job for over twenty years.

My job is to process clean sheets. All I do all day is feed sheets into a machine. There are four of us who work at one machine. It's called a mangler and it takes the sheets and finishes and presses them. It takes four people to feed just one sheet. Two guys and two girls. The other girl and I stand in front of the mangler and the men stand behind us. The sheets are in a cart behind the men. First they take a damp, clean sheet from the cart, each one takes a corner, they shake it out, and they each hand a corner to each of us. Then we feed it into the mangler. When it comes out on the other side, it's pressed, folded, and stacked.

While the other girl and I are feeding one sheet, the men are already shaking out another one. So that's how it goes, just one behind the other. As the finished sheets come out on the other side, another guy takes the stacks of sheets and puts them into a cart. He delivers them to a woman who counts them, puts them on a delivery truck, and they're taken through the tunnel to each of the different floors. The mangler is very easy to learn. You just take two ends of the sheet, you feed it in and that's it. But you have to be fast. That's why not just anybody can do it. You have to be fast.

I have to be at work at seven-thirty and I get off at a quarter to four. I get forty-five minutes for lunch and two coffee breaks, one in the morning and one at a quarter to three. Also, each hour we're on the sheet machine we get a five-minute break in case we have to go to the bathroom or something like that. But somebody will relieve us so the machine can keep going. No matter what, they don't stop the machine.

Years ago we used to sit down and do it, but now everything is different. Now we stand at the machine. I'm on my feet all day, and by the end of the day, my feet always hurt me. But I like what I do. Nobody bothers me, it's nice work.

I guess you can do six thousand sheets in a day. Five thousand if the machine isn't working as good as it should be. One time our team did a thousand sheets in one hour. We broke a record! You know, sometimes you get carried away. You start going fast, you feel good, you go, you go, you go. We knew how many we did because they have a clicker that counts the sheets automatically as they come through. A *thousand* sheets in under an hour! We did it three times! Everyone congratulated us. The bosses came around. Even Dr. Morris came. And they took our picture and put it in the hospital magazine. A thousand sheets in one hour. You don't do that all the time, you know.

They put our names up on the wall, mine and the other girl and the two men. They made a gold plaque for us. Across the top it says, Presbyterian Hospital Laundry Department Flatwork Production Hall of Fame. It's hanging right up there on the wall in the laundry. It's really something to be proud of. For me anyway. Because when I'm dead and gone, I know that plaque will still be there. And when the next people come, they'll see it and they'll know that I did something really special on this earth.

FRANK VACARELLI

Grounds Supervisor

―*ᴸ*―――――

*We're in a small, overcrowded, eight-by-eight-foot shed that houses garden-
ing tools and also serves as his office. Four yellow lawn sprinklers hang from
a pipe running across the ceiling. He calls them "my four chickens." Among
the bags of dirt and the tools is a desk covered with papers, a telephone,
and several half-filled coffee containers. He offers me the unbroken chair,
turns a broken one around, straddles it, and rests his arms across the back.*

*He was a kid from the ghetto. Growing up in the Bronx right underneath
the elevated subway, he didn't see a tree until he was fourteen years old. But
he always loved beautiful things. In his twenties he tried life in Greenwich
Village as a struggling artist. Today, he lives in two different worlds. While
his weekdays are spent in the hospital gardens, his weekends are spent in
Daly's Gym or in Madison Square Garden, where he is trainer and manager
of two New Jersey prizefighters. He is forty-six years old.*

━━━━━━━

It's wonderful just to watch a flower grow. From nothing, you see the
plant. It's born. It lives. And then after the season, it dies. A whole living
process. That's why I love to work in the greenhouse. You can watch all
that happen.

I started here in May 1961. Originally I worked in the pharmacy for a
couple of months. Then I saw there was an opening in the grounds

department, so I took it. At that time I was young, but I saw the future. Here I was twenty-five years old and everybody I worked with was approaching sixty. I figured, sooner or later . . . And sure enough, in 1973 or '74 I became foreman. Then gradually all of the crew I started with either died off or retired.

It was all Irishmen working here when I started, and Dominick Redo, the foreman, kind of took me under his wing. He put me to work in the greenhouse, and that's where I remained for a while. At that time, where the Atchley Building is now, we had a huge greenhouse—at least seventy feet long. That's where we planted the seeds and watched them propagate. Then we'd transplant them outside. The new Babies' Hospital building wasn't there yet and there were a lot more gardens than there are now. There were tennis courts where the service building is now. The whole area was full of flowers and big giant vases and lavish gardens, gardens in front of Maxwell Hall and Harkness Hall, which were nurses' residences. It was beautiful! We had seven people just to tend the gardens.

Through the years, my crew got gradually whittled down to three men. It seems the first one to go is always the gardener. "What do we need a gardener for?" You know, "We can keep a plumber or an electrician, but what's a gardener?" That has changed things. I can't do a lot of what I would like to do. First of all, I can't plant certain flowers because I don't think they would get the care that they need. When I had six or seven men, I could have perennials. I mean it was beautiful. Azaleas. It was beautiful, it was a knockout! Now I have to more or less concentrate on just this side of the street because this is where the patients are.

With three men it's tough. There's always somebody on vacation, it seems. One person has to clean the sidewalk in the morning so that leaves me with two men. And now with the union, since I'm management, I'm not allowed to do anything. So that's actually another man cut off. The only time I can do anything now is in an emergency, like if it snows.

Sometimes I'll sneak up to work at the greenhouse. But it's not like being a plumber or electrician. A gardener likes to get soil underneath his fingernails. Once I got turned in for watering the flowers! I was standing out here with a hose and watering the flowers, and someone turned me in. They said I was taking a man's job away. It is so frustrating.

We had a strike in the midseventies and everyone who was nonunion had to do different jobs. I had the worst job in the whole hospital. I had to work in the incinerator. The first day I went there was one of the most depressing days of my life. One room was piled to the ceiling with bags of garbage. And there were more in the hall. I'm not used to dragging a bag and blood coming out of the bottom. I'm used to flowers.

The strike ran through July and August. During that period, once or twice a day I would come outside and check things out. I would run out and put the sprinklers on. I did that for seven weeks. In the flower bed by the front gate I had "PH" written in blue and white petunias. But I couldn't care for them. Now, when the contract years come up, I won't put in any flowers that take a lot of care. I'll put, say, geraniums, where all you have to do is cut the flower head off.

The time I love it here the most is in late June when everything is at the height of bloom. You can sit back and see everything. The grass is green, not yet burnt from the summer sun. The flowers are at their height. I think the garden brings a little cheerfulness into patients' lives, given the situations that they're in when they're here. I'm sure they look out the windows and see the flowers and the gardens. And in the afternoon when the people come down in their wheelchairs, they'll sit outside and get the sun and enjoy the flowers. I mean, it has to cheer you up.

There's another side to me, too. I'm the trainer and manager for a couple of professional prizefighters, which is, I suppose, one extreme to another—flowers, and then violence.

I got interested in fighting when I was a kid. You grow up in the Bronx, you got to know how to fight. My father was a fighter and we always went down to the gym, we always went to fights together. I even went into the amateurs for a little while. I had a tremendous punch; but I also had a glass chin.

About six years ago I was working out in the Middletown Gym in New Jersey and I got to talking with this young fighter. He wasn't a city boy, and he had no contacts or managers. He had no way of getting started, so I took him in to New York. My friend and I put him in the ring and he was fantastic! So we started to expose him to Madison Square Garden and places like that and he's doing very well.

You get all your aggressions out when you watch one of your fighters in the ring. When you win, you get a real high. You almost feel like you fought the fight yourself, because as the fight is going on you're sitting at the end of the ring and you're taking every blow, you're ducking every punch. You don't realize you're doing it, but you're doing everything the fighter is doing.

It's not as strange as it may seem, going from flowers to fighters. With the flowers you have to be tender, and you'd think you always have to be tough with the fighters. But that's not always the case. Sure, when they're losing the fight you have to be tough, you have to tell them to move their butt, you have to be rough with them. But when the fight's over and he loses a close decision or he gets hurt, then you have to have compassion.

I would never give up my job here to go into fighters full time. Not unless one of my fighters becomes champion or something and gets like a million-dollar purse. But that's something different. Right now it's more or less a hobby. Every once in a while I make a little money, but its more or less a hobby.

I consider myself very fortunate to be the grounds supervisor. There's a certain freedom to it. In all the twenty-five years I'm here, nobody ever, ever, ever told us what to plant. It was just up to the gardeners. We made the decision what flowers to put around, what shrubs. And working in the greenhouse—that's like going to Florida every day! Best job in the hospital, without a doubt.

MARY THIEL
Resident, Department of Pastoral Care

———

Presbyterian Hospital runs a clinical pastoral education training program for pastoral care residents. They're often ordained clergy who have been out of seminary for a while and come back wanting further training in how to work in an institution such as a hospital. Or they may be young people just starting out.

We're in a small room just down the hall from the Pauline Hartford Chapel, a magnificent stone structure with beautifully designed stained-glass windows and an altar that can be changed to accommodate Catholic, Protestant, or Jewish services. She's a Protestant minister who was ordained a year ago to work as a chaplain trainee in this hospital. She's in her mid-twenties.

———

My original plan was to be a physician. I went to seminary to get theological and ethical training that I thought would help me to be the kind of physician I wanted to be, and I knew that I wouldn't get to seminary unless I did it *before* I went to medical school. I discovered while I was there that I loved the ministry. I also decided I had had enough schooling and really wanted to just get going with my life—so that was it for medicine.

I'm assigned to the orthopedic service in this hospital, which means that I'm there for staff, patients, and families on the orthopedic floors. But our department is responsible for twenty-four-hour emergency care all over the hospital every day of the year, so someone is always on call for the whole hospital. There are six resident chaplains, and we all share the responsibility of being on call. We carry arrest beepers so if any patient goes into cardiac arrest, we can respond immediately. And quite often we get called to the emergency room, or to the family of a patient in trouble.

Our normal day starts at eight-thirty in the morning, when all the members of the pastoral care department come together to hear a report from the person who was on call the night before—what kind of emergencies are going on in the hospital, what else may have happened, who is in crisis and really needs somebody to talk to. After report we have worship— the whole department—for half an hour. We all rotate the responsibility to lead it. There's a pretty good mixture of denominations among us so the worship is nondenominational. Last year we had a bunch of Protestants and a Jew, so Chapel became a very creative time. All of us gained a whole lot more respect for our own tradition and for other traditions.

One of the joys and frustrations of being a hospital chaplain is that we have no previous history with the people who we meet, and that can give somebody great freedom to unload a lot of stuff that they don't want people out there to know about. For example, there may be something in their past that they feel extraordinarily guilty about and they're afraid of dying without getting rid of it. So in that sense, the anonymity can be helpful.

I think the way a person experiences a crisis situation is eased by the presence of someone who's not there to judge, or to tell them that everything's going to be all right when it may not be, but rather is someone who understands why the situation is awful and who can be with them during that time.

We're often called to the emergency room to help a family deal with a trauma death. That kind of death is always a shock. I remember a situation a year or so ago with a fourteen-month-old baby who was brought in brain-dead. The mother—a very young woman—was just hysterical. As I listened to her frustrations about what was going on, it became clear that the child had died from curious causes, which helped explain the panic and the fear and the disbelief and the horror of this young woman and her boyfriend. I spent quite a bit of time with them. Then they were asked by Special Services for Children—a city agency—to go home and bring in their other child. That child was examined for marks of child abuse and was found to be okay, but it was going to be taken away from them anyway. We're there to be a presence and to support the family in situations like that, when they need us.

People ask how I can want to make a person feel better after they have committed a terrible act. It's not that I'm trying to make a person feel better. Chances are good that that person is going to feel about as awful as he or she has ever felt. I'm there to be as open as I can be; to listen, not to judge; to let them feel what they feel. They've got enough internal problems, and they've got a whole legal system starting to come after them. Certainly I feel great rage too, and that part of my job I've found very difficult. I'm sure nurses and doctors feel the same way.

We're a part of so many life passages. Especially death. Helping a person in the face of death can be really very rewarding if that person has enough time to get ready. If someone is elderly and they've lived a normal life span, there's an internal process whereby they start letting go of things. For them, death is not the obscenity it is for younger people. I had a woman last year with whom I established a close relationship. She was an old woman, alone, dying of lung cancer. Her doctors had told me she would live several weeks. I thought she felt readier to die than that. She had been refusing to eat and was being a noncompliant patient. One evening I walked into her room. She put out her arms, and she said, "Mary, kiss me and say goodbye." And I held her and I kissed her and I said goodbye. She died the next day. So a lot of them know. They know.

I was on duty Monday night and they woke me up at five in the morning to tell me about a fourteen-year-old boy who had had a heart transplant during the night. A very rare thing had happened. When they put the new heart in, one side of the heart beat but the other side wouldn't. The surgeons tried everything they could do to make the new heart work, but it was to no avail. When it was clear the child was going to die, I was called to be with his family. It was a quarter of six. I stayed with them for several hours, doctors and nurses were constantly coming in and out through the morning. Everyone was weeping, sobbing, crying, yelling, screaming, praying. After he died, they went to see the body. Then they had to decide whether they wanted to donate any of his organs, and they finally did decide to do that. These were all difficult decisions that had to be made at a time of crisis. It's a beautiful family. They were Roman Catholic. They had waited a long time for this heart. What is there to say?

This is a great place to train because of the diversity in the situations you see. Old and young, rich and poor, tragedies, emergencies. If you can learn to deal with the situations here, you can go someplace else and you're going to be in pretty good shape. On occasion, I go back to Ohio to visit my parents. I love how green it looks to me after living in New York City. I'll probably leave here for good at some point. I've lived here for six years—and have been glad to be here for that time. But my soul just does better where it's greener.

TOM DORRIAN
Investigations Officer

———

He's sixty-five years old, a stocky man with thick gray hair and a strong face; an ex-cop from the Manhattan South homicide squad. He has been at the hospital for twelve years and is planning to retire in a few months. He has eleven children, none of whom are in police work. Three of his daughters are nurses.

———

My main job is to investigate the different crimes that occur in the hospital—theft, assault, anything at all of a criminal nature. When I started here, security was treated like a stepchild. Today we're a good-sized department. Besides investigation officers, we have access-control people who stand at the entrances and make sure whoever comes in here, belongs here. We have crime-prevention officers who go up on the floors and explain to the people that they should secure their valuables. And we have plainclothesmen—undercover guys stationed all over the hospital. We put them in different types of uniforms, like housekeeping coveralls, or a doctor's white coat and stethoscope. Some look like hippies, others like visitors.

The majority of arrests we make here are for theft of hospital property, and I guess a large percentage of that is drug-related stuff—hypodermic needles, syringes. We also have thefts of linens and things like that. You've got to keep on your toes in a large complex like this, there are so many ways to get in and out. We have an access-control desk at every entrance. A visitor is supposed to give the name of the patient he's visiting. Then our officer looks at the patient list to see if there is such a patient in the house, and he gives the visitor a pass. But many of the people in this area have animal cunning; they know the hospital better than I do. They've figured out all kinds of ways to get by the access system, and once they do that, they're entitled to get on the elevators. They know the premises, and they know the different floors where there might be a lot of hypodermic syringes, things like that. So they just go in and take what they want. Most of the time our fellows can pick up on a person who looks like he doesn't belong on the floor. When that happens they just follow him or her around. If the trespasser goes somewhere he doesn't belong, we grab him.

We made an arrest here recently of a young man who I think truly had an interest in medicine. He was well educated—I think he probably wanted to be a doctor. He used to go to all the major hospitals in the city. He'd wear a white lab coat and would actually get into conversations with doctors. Then he'd accompany them into the locker rooms, and when they left, he'd steal their wallets or whatever he could. He was stealing just unbelievable amounts of stuff! And not just at this hospital, but all the major hospitals in the city! He was so sincere in the way he approached the other doctors that they thought he was a student. It took us a long time, but we finally arrested him. We had a very good description and we beefed up our plainclothes. One of our guys saw him come in and followed him right to the second floor where the doctors have their lockers. He watched him go into the locker room. When he came out, the officer grabbed him. Sure enough, he had several wallets and wristwatches, things like that.

We get a lot of SSC [Special Services for Children] cases here. Sometimes kids, even babies, are brought into the emergency room messed up and battered. We treat the kid and then the parent wants to take him back home. I'll never forget one father. The kid was so messed up. A little baby. After we treated him, the father said he wanted to take him home. Under the circumstances, the child had been put under the supervision of the SSC and it was our responsibility not to let him out until there was an adjudication made. But this guy somehow found the baby and was taking him out of the hospital. I was there that night so I got the call from the floor for help. When I arrived, the father was holding the baby and as I approached him he said, "If you don't step back I'm going to smash it on the floor!" A city police officer who had been called in yelled from the doorway, "Don't drop the baby! That won't help anything!" But the guy didn't care what we said. We backed off and he took the baby and ran. Three hours later the cops went to his house and arrested him, and we retrieved the child. I couldn't get over it. He actually threatened to smash his baby!

We've got employee theft down pretty well now. If there's an area where we know there's been some thievery, we might plant a wallet which we have dusted with a powder that can only been seen under a certain light. If the powder gets on your fingers, it takes days to wash it off. Then we go up on the floor and we ask the people to cooperate and we put the ultraviolet light on their hands.

This happened not too long ago. We were watching one of the employees who worked on a nursing floor and who was going into places where he didn't belong. We followed him for a while and, sure enough, he went for the planted wallet. When we thought we had him, we went to the floor and asked everybody to submit to the test. They were all willing to do it, even the thief, because he didn't even know that he was suspected. Also, we had the bills recorded prior to the light test, and it turned out the guy had the money on his person. In fact, we photostated the money ahead of time so we could show that the person had this exact money in his pocket. You know, "You have this dye on your hands. And these are the serial numbers that we have photostated. So we've got you." It's really hard when you have to arrest an employee. It's no fun, believe me.

A couple of years ago there was a murder just a few blocks from here. It was terrible! One of our doctors was murdered—Dr. Wood from the emergency room. He was young—I think in his thirties. He lived in the area here, and I think he had gone home for his supper. He was on his way back to the hospital when he was accosted. They must have asked him for his wallet and whatever; he must have refused, and I guess the young men or whoever did it got scared and killed him.

The case was immediately turned over to the New York Police Department. This hospital is probably the most important institution within this precinct—the Thirty-Fourth—and they devoted every effort and resource to try to apprehend the killers. Up to now, there've been no results. But they still come in here from time to time, following up on new information. That'll never end. Someday they'll pick somebody up who might be able to give them just the right information and maybe someday they'll make an arrest.

That incident caused everyone to be more security-conscious. The security department became more important. The hospital administration gave us more money and we added more officers to the force. And we have vehicles now that transport people to different areas. It's a regular pickup and dropoff system. It's a whole lot safer here now than it's ever been. It's a shame, though, that it took a murder to do it.

SUSAN ALICEA

Librarian

We're sitting on well-worn leather chairs at the rear of the Milbank Library, which is on the twentieth floor of the hospital. Every so often, the sounds of construction filter through the windows. Other than that, only two oscillating floor fans humming steadily in the corners break the silence.

"Most people think the librarian's going to have her hair in a bun and wear lace-up shoes and you have to walk around and be quiet, and "Shh, shh," and all that. But that's not really true. I only wear these shoes because they're comfortable. I have to be on my feet a lot." She's twenty-eight.

The first thing a stranger might notice when he walks into our library is people sleeping. A lot of people come in on their lunch hour, sit in a comfortable chair, and immediately fall asleep. You'll see pharmacists who sleep up here. You'll see people from medical records, people from the blood bank. This is the only area, aside from the cafeteria, where they can come and relax, where they can sit and not be hassled by anybody. In the beginning, I didn't know how to accept it, but then I realized that this is the only time during the day that these people get to relax and I'm not going to deprive them of that.

People always wonder why someone would want to be a librarian. I guess it's a combination of the love of books and the love of wanting to know more. You have to satisfy something that's inside you; you want to grow and you want to learn. Being a librarian attracts anybody who has that love of knowledge and of serving others.

Originally, when I was in school, I thought I would work in a law library, maybe on Wall Street. Actually, I think I wanted to marry a lawyer and to be in a glamorous field—Wall Street or Fifth Avenue—wherever the lawyers were. In my wildest dreams I never thought I'd be working in a major hospital in the northeast section of the United States. I never thought I would wind up here.

One reason I was so interested in the library is because I'm attracted to museums and the preservation of things. Everything has to have a time and a place, and it can't all be on computers. There has to be a continuity, a tradition that has to be passed on so young children can enjoy it, can understand it. That's what libraries do. Libraries pass on the knowledge; they preserve the books; they preserve the history.

This library is for everyone. For patients who can't come up here, we have a book cart which the volunteers take to the patient floors. It holds all kinds of books and all the current periodicals in Spanish and English. It's like a cornucopia of things. The patient chooses a book or whatever he wants, and can keep it as long as he's here. When he leaves, he puts it in a book drop which is on every floor. These special services have to be preserved. Some New York hospitals have cut back or abolished the hospital library. They look at the bottom line, and the library is not a money maker, so they phase it out. Thank God we have a strong auxiliary that protects us.

When staff people use the library, they pay to borrow books—a minimal charge of five or ten cents a day for two weeks, depending on the kind of book. The money goes into a special fund to buy new books. On file, I have at least a third of the employees in this hospital who have at some time or other taken books out. That's two thousand people.

I'm busy from the time I get here until I leave at five o'clock. You finish one project, you go to the next. We check books in, check them out. Shelve the ones the patients drop off in the book box on the floors. We order new materials every day, stamp and catalogue them, get rid of the old and add the new ones. And that's just books. There are about two hundred magazines here. Things that are outdated or that we can't use anymore we send down to the clinics, and maybe, hopefully, somebody will pick up a magazine and read. We get donations from time to time, and with the money we buy new books. I get other books from publishers who have printed too many. I go to the Bronx with the hospital van, and with a couple of other departments, we pick up all sorts of other books. And then I order best sellers.

I work a full day, but I can't say it's just a job—I don't want to make it sound like I come in and it's a factory kind of thing, nine to five, and that's it. I love it here. I love being with books. I love being with people. I want to feel that I contribute something to the service of others, and I think I do.

JACK ROTHSTEIN
The Baker

He calls it the "bake shop." It's a large space, gleaming with steel machinery and ovens, located in the basement, in the rear of the hospital kitchen. Machines hum and whir loudly in the background. At a large steel table, his assistant, whistling a John Philip Sousa march, casually slathers icing on five dozen coffee rings. Another assistant keeps close watch on a machine more than half his size as it mixes batter for tomorrow's chocolate-chip cookies.

He is wearing a white uniform with a white apron and a chef's hat, which sets off his full head of white hair. Flour dusts his arms as he squeezes cookies from a pastry tube—one by one—onto an oversized cookie sheet that looks as if it might have been in use since the kitchen was first built.

He talks as he works. "I have a large collection of baking books at home. I started to buy them when I was sixteen years old and, as of today, I have three hundred books on baking alone. When I retire, I want to write my own. I want to put all the knowledge and formulas I have into a book for the industry. That's always been my dream."

People think there's no glamour in the baking business. When I started here in 1963, there were eleven of us in the bake shop. The problem was when people retired or left, for whatever reasons, we couldn't get replacements of the same caliber. The American public just doesn't go into baking as a trade. I wouldn't say baking itself is dying, but the hand skills are dying. I would say that ninety percent of all the baked items sold in the United States are machine-made as opposed to handmade, so there's no need for bakers who are skilled anymore. If a big baking company needs help, it doesn't matter if the person they hire has any prior skills as a baker. They can assign them to a machine and in an hour or two hours they can be as proficient as the machine allows them to be. So, sure, the hospital would be glad to have an expanded bake shop, but the help is just not there.

I won't hire someone if they're not up to my standards because it'll be detrimental to all of us. You have to remember you're always under a lot of time pressure here. The patient must eat at "X" hours, three times a day. If you don't have proficient help and for some reason they can't produce a standard product at that particular time, you have a problem. If a patient's sick and he orders food, it must come up on time, come hell or high water. It's not like calling a maintenance man to say that your lightbulb burns out, or your faucet leaks. They don't come today, they can come tomorrow. You can't do that in the baking business—especially in a hospital.

You never see the ultimate customer here, in this case the patient. So you don't get personally involved enough to hear someone say, "Hey, that was a fabulous Danish!" It's not like a retail store where you talk to the customer. Here, you're removed from the people who are eating your food. Once in a while, though, you'll get a letter from a patient or someone, and that gives you a nice feeling.

We have two categories of baked goods; some get sold in the cafeteria and others go to the patients. You have to separate them. What the patients get is marked on a worksheet so we know exactly how much to make. The dieticians record whatever the patient orders and they send it down to the main office and it's all tabulated so you get the total. If we bake over the patient count we can always divert that to the cafeteria. Eventually, though, you'll reach a point where you can't push an item, especially a perishable item like a custard or something.

You have to face reality. Things do go bad. After a while you get to know the items that sell. Like they love bread pudding. They love layer cakes. They love some cookies as opposed to other cookies. You get to know what a good sell is and the more you're accurate at these figures, the less there is to get stale. It's all a question of experience.

I've made lots of cookies in my day. How many? Well, I never make less than a thousand every day. I usually bake them four or five times a week, so you can figure about four thousand cookies a week on a five-day basis. Four thousand times four, that's sixteen thousand, give or take, in a month. Sixteen thousand times twelve equals a hundred ninety-two thousand a year. Times twenty-four years, that's about *four million* cookies I've baked at Presbyterian Hospital. And it's probably higher because sometimes we have parties that have large numbers of people. So then, instead of the average four thousand a week, it may go up to eight thousand.

Last week the main dietician, Miss Brooks, came down and said, "A patient, a man eighty-six years old, with cancer, is getting married. Can you make a wedding cake?" This was eleven o'clock and he was getting married, at his bedside, at one. So I had two hours. Well, I always keep backup cakes in the freezer, so what I did was take two fifteen-inch layers, build them up high and make a wedding cake. That wasn't the first wedding cake I'd made for a patient, but it was the first I'd made on two hours' notice. It was pretty, the sides were embellished and I decorated it real fancy. I got a thank you from Miss Brooks, but not from the patient. But I didn't expect anything. You know, a patient is eighty-six, you're just glad that you can accommodate them.

We had a strike here in July of 1984. I'm the only nonunion person in the bake shop so I was all alone. The hospital had a strike plan and I was given help. Even people from administration worked here. None of them had prior experience, but they were very cooperative. Before the strike I really didn't know a whole lot of people in this place. I would come right into the basement from Fort Washington Avenue. I come in, I do my work, and I leave the same way. Twenty-three years and I never missed a day. But during the strike, I got to meet people, and people got to know me. They used to send me people from the fourteenth floor, which was the top administration floor, people from X ray. I met so many nice people, and we got to like each other, so after the strike was over we became very friendly and they'd come down to see me and they still do.

A lot of us slept here, because we worked twelve hours a day and going home seemed kind of foolish. Especially for me. I live thirty miles away. The hospital assigned us rooms in Maxwell Hall, the building that has been torn down to make way for the new hospital. Downstairs in the basement of that building, they had what we called a club. We used to get together there every night. Everyone came down. First of all, you had nothing to do in your room, which was just a couple of cots and a radio or a TV. So every night I would go down and have a beer and talk to the other people. There was wonderful camaraderie.

Now I'm back to the old ways; I just come in and I go home. Every once in a while, though, I'll get invited to a party by people I met during the strike. Recently I went to the fourteenth floor in Atchley Pavilion, which is the administrative floor. Beautiful offices. They had a nice party for somebody who was leaving the hospital. I was honored to be invited.

RABBI HAROLD GROSS
Rabbi

For eleven years he had a dual career: principal of an elementary school in Washington Heights, and rabbi of a synagogue in the same neighborhood. Two years ago, he retired from the school system and because "I had some time on my hands," he joined the staff as a part-time Jewish chaplain here at the hospital.

There are currently three part-time rabbis here. We divide the hospitals. I take care of Presbyterian and Babies' Hospital, Rabbi Mann takes care of Neurological, and Rabbi Hartstein the Harkness Pavilion. Since I live in the neighborhood I'm on call twenty-four hours and handle all emergencies. For example, we had a patient who arrested on Friday afternoon. They revived him and took him to intensive care. He and his wife are Orthodox. Since she doesn't answer the phone on the sabbath, and she couldn't sleep here, she was terribly concerned about what if something happened to him on Friday night or Saturday. How would they be able to reach her? Well, I was able to put her mind at ease. I don't answer the phone on the sabbath either, but I have an answering machine with a loudspeaker on it, so the hospital knows if there's an emergency, they can call me. They talk on the phone and I hear it. If they feel that I should come to the hospital they say, "It would be good, Rabbi Gross, if you would come over." So I come over. I can't drive on the sabbath so I walk. Twelve blocks. Rain, snow, sleet, hail . . . that shall not keep thee from making thy appointed rounds . . .

They know the times I conduct services at my synagogue. So if I'm there the caretaker is instructed to inform me or one of the ushers that there's an emergency at the hospital.

We have Orthodox patients who come here from all over. Israel. Out of state. Everywhere. Their families will not travel on the sabbath, so they need somewhere in the neighborhood to stay. We have a Society of Visitation of the Sick here in Washington Heights that makes provision to put up any family that likes to stay here over the sabbath. All you have to do is ask. They can stay in my house. And we have here a Mrs. Rothchild who is noted for her great hospitality and maintains an apartment one block away from the hospital. Everyone knows her and she knows she's needed by people and families who have to stay here.

We also have Jewish volunteers who visit the hospital every single day of the week. The college girls come in on Thursday night to see which patients need visitation on the sabbath. Then on Saturday, when Orthodox patients cannot get a telephone call, cannot get company, these college kids, who also won't use the elevator, walk up—some of them walk up to the fifteenth floor—and visit with patients.

Before I start my daily rounds I have to get a list of who's here. The hospital has three computerized lists of the patients. One lists the religions of those patients who chose to put it on the admission form. We run about two hundred, two hundred and fifty Jewish patients at a given time. I check the entire list and look into my box to see if there are any messages and then I map out a strategy of whom I'm going to visit. If someone was in surgery, I see them after the operation. Certainly I will visit all the intensive care units. I start always with the seventeenth floor, which is the heart transplant or open heart surgery floor, and see those patients there. And if there are Orthodox patients in Labor and Delivery, I go there too.

I have a set of *tefillin*, which Orthodox males wrap around their body before they pray. I keep it on hand because I have found sometimes patients come into the hospital in an emergency, and they will have no tefillin. So they call me and I supply that to them. And of course, if a patient is unable to put on the tefillin, I'll put it on for him.

I don't only visit Orthodox Jewish patients. I visit all Jewish patients and there's a broad spectrum of service from one to another. Sometimes patients will say, "Rabbi, I'm not observant." And I say, "I don't know what that means. I only know of two kinds of Jews, ones who are observant and ones who are not *yet* observant."

Often times, people who are sick in the hospital tend to make bargains with God. "God, I'll be good to you, you be good to me." That's under-standable. Or they make bargains with me. "You know, Rabbi, ever since I came here, I decided I'm going to eat kosher food." Sometimes a woman patient will say to me, "You know, I really don't light candles on the sabbath, but I saw here in the hospital that you supply electric candles for the sabbath. Is it possible that I could get some?" And I always say, "Certainly. Any patient who requests it will receive it."

Basically my day is spent visiting patients; counseling, if necessary; dealing with family, patients, sometimes with the doctors. Even doctors now will say, "You know, it's important, Rabbi; go to visit that patient. That patient's very nervous; try and calm him down." So we'll do that, and we'll answer some of their religious questions, see that their diet is properly taken care of, assure the family that everything is being done.

We have an association called Caring and Sharing. That's a Jewish-based organization that was organized about five years ago by a mother who lost a child to cancer. She felt that since she lost this child, she would like to be a support to other parents who may be in a similar situation. At that time she thought she was the only mother who had lost a child, the only mother who had a four- or five-year-old child with cancer. But as she started this Caring and Sharing organization, she suddenly found out that she had a lot of friends. She formed an organization to act as buddies and to give support to parents.

A woman came in recently. Her little girl had cancer and she was terribly distraught. I immediately contacted them and it didn't take twenty-four hours. They put this mother with a buddy who became the support to this mother. What a difference! This mother suddenly began to realize that she was not the only one, and it's possible the child can have a tumor and the child will live. The mother from the organization said her child went through this and is alive today. "Don't get scared at all these medical terms," she said. "They're only trying to help you." Here was not a rabbi talking or a doctor talking, but a real living mother with a living child. I can just scratch the surface of what this means to a parent.

Next week is Rosh Hashanah, where the *shofar* is blown. The shofar is the ram's horn. It's blown as a call of repentance and to remember the fact of the total devotion of our father Abraham who was called to sacrifice his son at the altar and the voice of God came and said, "Do not sacrifice your son." He sacrificed a ram instead. So we blow the ram's horn to remember the total dedication of our father Abraham and inspire us to be totally dedicated to the ways of God. Now, last year there wasn't a single Jewish patient that requested blowing of the shofar who did not receive it. I have a crew of ten groups of young boys who come from the community. They'll climb up the steps—sometimes to the fifteenth floor—they reach every building, be it Neurological, Harkness, Presbyterian, and they will blow the shofar at the bedside.

The best part of being a rabbi in this hospital is being with people. Working with people, that's the greatest. Here people really need you. Even though sometimes the visit may be just a short "Hello," I really don't know the seeds that I'm planting. Sometimes months later I will meet someone in the street, "You know, Rabbi, you visited my brother, he was there." The whole visit may have lasted maybe two minutes, but the fact that someone who symbolizes God, a religious person, was there, came, and extended him a blessing or a wish meant a lot to him.

Sometimes when I walk through the halls I wonder, what am I really doing, how much am I accomplishing? But see, like with that man's brother, you never know what you've left with people.

LENORE IGLESIAS
Volunteer Translator

—————

She's a small woman, white haired, very soft spoken, very serious. As we talk, she sits with her hands folded in her lap or pushed into the pockets of her pink smock. She is one of two hundred hospital volunteers.

She has been a volunteer for seven years. She came to New York from Puerto Rico at the age of twenty-one. "This was an English-speaking neighborhood, so when my kids played with the other kids in the neighborhood, they all spoke English. So I had to try to speak English to my kids so the other kids understood what I was telling mine." She's sixty-nine.

=====

It was my idea to be a translator here. I decided that myself. I'm here almost every day. On Mondays and every other Tuesday I work in the diabetic classes. The nurse gets up in front of the group and I get up beside her. She teaches in English and I translate what she says into Spanish because there are so many Spanish-speaking patients. When they have questions, they ask them in Spanish and I ask the nurse in English and then she answers and I translate it into Spanish for the patient. Sometimes it goes on for two hours.

On Wednesdays I do the same thing in the amniocentesis classes. I translate the lecture into Spanish. I explain why they have it and what it's all about. Everything. I've been doing it for five years, and I know it already by heart.

I only work on Thursday or Friday if they need me for speech and hearing or something special. In those cases, I go to the Harkness Pavilion or Atchley or the Eye Institute. At all these places I help a patient who doesn't know how to talk to the doctor in English. The head of volunteers tells me when I'm needed in another place and I just go.

I'm constantly doing something around here. The minute I walk in people start to ask me, "Where do I see this doctor? Where do I go to? Could you bring me there because I don't know the way?" Once we had a heart-transplant patient. A Spanish-speaking girl. Before her operation, the social worker called me to come and translate for her. The girl was near death, I remember. We spent a long time together, just talking. She looked so sick. I can still picture her. When she finally had the operation, I went right after to the recovery room. You had to cover yourself, gloves, shoes, hat, and a gown. She was full of wires, tubes. Everything. But when she saw me, oh, she was so happy! Her eyes lit up. I was happy, too, to see her. What a difference!

After that she had to come here once a week to have a biopsy and I used to go with her. Today, she is fine. She's even working as a beautician, part-time. I still keep in touch with her.

I don't usually spend so much time with one patient. I see them maybe a couple of times and that's it. There are so many that I often forget who they are. Sometimes I'm walking by and someone will stop me and say, "Oh, Mrs. Iglesias, I am so grateful to you. I won't ever forget you." And I don't know who the person is! I say to myself, "Where have I seen her? Where did I help her?" I can't remember everybody—I've been doing this for seven years.

Once a week I work in the GYN clinic. Some of these women come from the Dominican Republic or South America and they don't know a word of English. Not a word! My translating means a lot to them because sometimes the doctor knows only a little Spanish, or they can't understand him. They get confused. They say, "The doctor told me something, but I cannot understand it. Could you please come?" So I say, "Doctor, I know you told her in Spanish, but she wants me to tell her myself." They're such young mothers.

One day a girl came to me, desperate. She said, "I don't know, but I think the doctor told me that I have cancer." I said, "Yes? Come with me and we'll ask him again." So I went with her and I asked the doctor, "Is this true? Does this woman have cancer?" He said, "No! What I told her is that I want her to *cancel* this appointment!" It seems silly, but it wasn't to her. You know what I mean?

JOSÉ "PEPE" MAYORCA
The Chef

——————

It's a tiny, overcrowded office, just inside the doorway into the kitchen. The wall of windows overlooks a huge room brought to life by the flurry of busy people in white uniforms. Two chef's hats sit in the corner of the office. A bulletin board on the wall is papered with computer printouts, schedules, and menus. As we talk, people periodically stick their heads in the door to ask him questions. "Tomorrow's fish. What kind will we have?" "Did the new icemaker arrive?" "When does the vegetable truck come?"

He's a short, pleasant man. He comes from Peru. He's been head chef for eight years, the youngest chef the hospital ever had. He's forty-two. "I live with an uncle now. We spend our weekends on a busman's holiday, trying out restaurants all over town. What I found is, my food here is just as good as any good restaurant in New York. And that's the truth."

——————

The kitchen opens officially at three in the morning when my breakfast cooks arrive. They do all the breakfasts for the patients *and* the cafeteria, which opens at six-thirty for breakfast. They do breakfast for two thousand people or more. I used to do that before I became chef. I used to come in at one in the morning. You had to start cracking eggs then. One case of eggs contains thirty dozen eggs, and I got so good at it, I could crack eight cases in less than an hour. That's, let me see . . . two thousand eight hundred eighty eggs, or forty-eight eggs a minute. We broke them into this huge vat and then we'd beat them, strain them, and cook them. We used big paddles to stir the scrambled eggs. I used to make cereal, too. Fifty gallons of oatmeal, which you boil in huge vats. The vats, which are electrically heated, have spigots at the top, which let water in, and drains at the bottom. You fill them with water, cook in them, drain the food when you've finished, wash them, without ever moving them from their spot. You couldn't move them anyway because they're at least four feet high. When we do bacon or sausage for breakfast, you're talking about cooking one hundred pounds of bacon and sixty pounds of sausages.

As head chef, I'm responsible for ordering all the food for both the patients and the cafeteria. Eight thousand meals a day—special diets, kosher meals, you name it. When I get in, the first thing I look at is the census of the patients and see how many are in the house—this hospital can have nearly thirteen hundred patients when it's full. So we calculate the patient menus, and see what's going to be served in the cafeteria, and then I order exactly what I need. Sometimes you go a little bit over, but never under. It would cause a lot of problems to be under.

The key to being a chef, no matter where you work, is to like your trade. To like what you're doing. And, I suppose of equal importance is to produce good food. But there are many other things that either make or break it for you. A good chef knows how to motivate his people. If you don't motivate them, you don't get anywhere. I repeat this over and over: Work with your people. My job is supposed to be sitting in this office, managing my staff, and doing paper work. And I do that. But I also go out and work with my staff, usually every day. I work with them, talk to them, understand their problems. I don't just want to be called a chef and wear this tall white thing on my head.

My day is long, but varied and interesting. If I'm not cooking with my staff, I sit down with my butcher and see all the cuts of meat that we need, and the amounts we have to order. I have to discuss the groceries with my steward and storeroom manager. I have to deal with my pot washers regarding sanitation and things like that. The baker is independent. The only time he works with me is when we have a special party.

The chief dieticians propose the menus to the food service director. I get called when those menus are accepted, and then comes my part. I sit down with the new menus and I make all the calculations about how much I'm going to need. The meat is first. We have a meeting with the director and food production manager, the chief dietician, and my head butcher, and I decide how much I'm going to use, the kinds of cuts that I want to use. After I finish with the meats, I have to cover the vegetables. Say they have for lunch fillet of flounder. We produce five hundred seventy-six orders. In order to produce that amount—each portion is about six ounces of flounder—what I order is two hundred fifty pounds of fillet of flounder. The fish comes in ice and water, so you have to order more. Then you have eggplant Parmesan on the menu, too. We use about sixty pounds of eggplant cutlets. Brisket of beef? I order six hundred pounds for one meal. Mashed potatoes—I use about two hundred forty pounds of peeled potatoes.

Cooking is my life. I always make time to cook. I like Italian food, but *real* Italian food. And I like Oriental food. I've thought about opening my own restaurant. I think this is what every chef looks for. But first of all I would have to find the right place. The way that the rents are now, it's very hard. Also, you don't meet too many good cooks anymore. A lot of people get involved in the food business because of the salary and they have free meals, but not because they like it. I have a lot of friends who own restaurants. I visit them. We talk. I walk into the kitchen, and I tell you, it's not what I want.

Working in a hospital is different from working in another large institution. Here you feel you're helping people to recuperate from their illness, or whatever. A lot of people, when they hear you cook for a hospital say, "Oh, that doesn't mean anything. Anybody can cook for a hospital." But that's not true. Especially if you are a proud cook and you like what you're doing. I have a big responsibility here. I run the whole kitchen. If I don't produce, nobody eats.

ANNMARIE FECI
Page Operator

She has worked in the phone room for twelve years. It's a small room, adequate for five operators, located on the fourth floor of the service building. "They've given us the name 'Telecommunications.' Real fancy. To us, though, it's still the Phone Room."

The main number of this hospital is 305-2500. That's what people calling Presbyterian Hospital dial to reach us. During the day there are six girls here at one time. Three or four girls on the switchboard, plus one girl on page and one girl on patient information. On evenings and nights we have less.

They all do different things. The patient information girl tells the caller if a person is here, what room he's in, and the status of the patient. We're very careful about what information we give out, though. You'll get lots and lots of nosy neighbors who call and ask, "Can you tell me what the patient died of? Did he have AIDS? Did he have this? Did he have that?" They want to know things which are not anybody's business except the patient's immediate family. You have to be careful what you say and who you're saying it to because you really never know who's on the other end. And at all times you have to hold your patience, which often is not easy to do, sitting there all day, listening to some of these people.

I don't get ruffled easily . . . my personality runs basically the same all the time. To really get me riled somebody on the other end has to be so obnoxious that I can't deal with them. People get really annoyed when it takes too long to get through to the hospital. I understand that. Say a call comes in to 2500, the main number, and the caller asks to be connected to a patient named Smith. We transfer her to patient information to get Mr. Smith's room number. Those girls have a rack of index cards with patients' room numbers on them. Well, if they haven't gotten the information from admitting yet, they don't know where the patient is. So we have to transfer the call to admitting. So the caller has now waited to get through to 2500, they've gotten transfered to 3101—patient information—now we're connecting them down to 2536—admitting. In the interim they've gotten disconnected so you'll get them back on 2500 and now they're *really* riled. But we're doing our best. Really we are.

Sometimes we get calls from non–English-speaking people. You try and understand their broken English, if they even *speak* English. If the caller is speaking a language other than English or Spanish, we'll connect the call to Patient Relations. If they think it's something that's really important, they get an interpreter to come to the phone and try and speak to the person. Patient Relations is able to find people who speak languages I never heard of. I guess maybe when you come in to be interviewed for a job they ask if you speak a second language. That way they're able to keep track of people who speak various languages. If someone calls and asks for a person who we know has died, we tell them to get in contact with the family. If they get too upset or say they don't know the family—we connect them to our AOD [administrator on duty].

There are times when every one of our console positions is covered, and people are still waiting to get through to the hospital. We probably spend twenty seconds on an average call, assuming of course that it's not an old lady whose hearing aid isn't working, or somebody who doesn't speak English. Those are some of the things that hold you up. But barring unforeseen circumstances, we can easily handle three or four calls a minute. Then you have to figure if there are four girls sitting on four consoles, you've answered maybe twelve calls in a minute, at least, and that's not saying how many people are waiting during that time also to get in.

People say, "Telephone operator, eh? What an easy job." But it's a lot of work. Patient information girls have all those cards to file. They have all the ICUs to check to see how patients are. In the morning they have to get admissions from the emergency room from the night before. They write up all those cards from all those midnight people that have come in and file them, plus they're answering the calls that they're getting in on 3101, Patient Information.

The paging girl does the overhead paging that's heard throughout the hospital. Most of the doctors are on beepers now, though. They have a computerized system where you dial a number in the hospital and a computerized woman's voice speaks to you—everybody calls her "Patti Page"—but there are still reasons to use the overhead, like arrest calls and calls to staff without beepers.

A lot of things can happen just sitting up here in the service building. But I think the most devastating experience I ever had was the night that John Wood died. What happened was, we got a call from EMS that they were bringing in a gunshot. If it's a gunshot or a stabbing, EMS usually calls from the road—and you connect them to the emergency room. The next thing we get a call from the nurse in the ER to put Dr. John Wood on page. See, he was the resident on call that night in the ER, and he was on arrest duty too, so he was carrying the arrest beeper. But he wanted to go home to see his wife, who wasn't feeling well. So before he left, he gave the beeper to another doctor. We didn't know that at the time, though. So there we are paging "Dr. John Wood. Dr. John Wood." No answer. Next thing, maybe a minute later, the ER nurse calls back again and she says to us, "My God, my God," she says, "John Wood is the *patient!*"

We were all crying. He was special to everyone who knew him. To me, he was the pediatrician who took care of my kids and now all of a sudden you're paging an arrest for somebody only to find out that it's somebody who's probably the nicest person that God ever put on the face of the earth. I mean, he was an absolute sweetheart.

When you're on Patient Information, you begin to get familiar with names of people who come in for lots of admissions. Just the names. You have the patient information index so you're filing the cards and you say, "Oh, my God, that poor child, he's back in again." A lot of times you really don't know what's wrong with the child but you see that ticket and you know that child is in. Then all of a sudden you get notified of an expiration and it's him. And your heart drops; you never met the child, didn't know his mother or father, but yet you feel just as bad. Probably because it was a kid. Or even sometimes adults who come in that we know are oncology patients because they're on Harkness One. You never met the person but you say, "Oh, my God, So-and-so, they died." It's like one of the family passed away. You never met them but you feel awful about it.

I was raised on 169th Street. My mother worked in Presbyterian for thirty years. She retired in 1980. She worked in accounting. I feel like I have been raised in this place. When I graduated from high school I couldn't wait to work at Presbyterian. It was taken for granted; if you lived in the neighborhood, you had to work at Presbyterian. You weren't one of the "in" crowd if you didn't work here. But I put nine thousand applications in and never, never got hired. I was downstairs in personnel every time they turned around, trying to get a job. Nothing. Finally I came in one day and the fella down in personnel said, "Listen, I've got a job in the phone room." We weren't called telecommunications then. I said, "I can answer phones. That I can do."

In thirteen years, I've really seen this place grow. I've seen Babies' add the addition on and Eye add its addition and Atchley Pavilion go up. I watched them tear Maxwell Hall down. I watched them tear down Harkness Hall. My bridal shower was in Harkness Hall. Yes, that was a nice place. It was a shame that they tore it down. But that's what modernization is. You've got to keep moving.

Telecommunications is the main access point of this hospital. We're the central unit. When people call up for conditions on patients, that comes through us. When doctors need to be paged, that comes through us. When they need to put an arrest on, that's through us. When there's a fire, we put the fire brigade on. Those beepers are through us also. So we're touching kind of all bases: medical, maintenance . . . you name it.

Think about it. We're saving lives! You figure EMS calls us, they need to get the ER to let Alice know that they've got a gunshot coming in. If somebody is calling Dr. Rose because they have a heart in another state, we get the call. We give it to Dr. Rose. He gets the heart. But it came through us first. So, we're it! We're really where it starts from. The central unit that makes this place go. I'm telling you. People might not think of us that way, but it's true. We're the heart of this hospital.

VI
THE SPECIALISTS

The trend toward specialization coincided with the dawn of the golden age of modern medicine, around the time of World War I. As a result of improvements in communication combined with a flowering of medical and scientific research, doctors, whose knowledge had until then been limited to their own patients' diseases, were exposed to an infinitely greater range of information. It soon became clear though, that one person could not master all of this data. Physicians were impelled to narrow their turf, and the specialist was born.

By the 1930s, research scientists were penetrating ever more deeply into increasingly narrow areas, producing new surgical techniques, wonder drugs, and technologies like the X ray and the electrocardiograph. The horse-and-buggy doctor—the general practitioner—began to fade away as a growing number of doctors limited their practices. Some chose patients of a particular age group (pediatrics, geriatrics). Others focused on a single organ or body part (eye, kidney, heart), and still others became expert in various functions or systems (internal medicine, orthopedics, neurology).

Training programs were modified and residencies defined; specialty board certification became a measure of qualification. General practitioners no longer performed operations they had done for years, such as hernia repairs, tonsillectomies, and setting broken bones. Eventually, specialists acquired hospital "services" of their own, along with the most respect and the greatest income.

The sixties and seventies brought a new phenomenon—the subspecialist. It was no longer enough to be a surgeon. One became an oncology (cancer) surgeon, a vascular (blood vessels) surgeon, a thoracic (chest) surgeon, or a heart surgeon. A general surgeon no longer could treat a patient with an abscess in the chest—that was the domain of a thoracic surgeon; or repair a broken cheek bone—that would be done by an oral or head and neck surgeon. Compartmentalization took over the organ systems—pediatric urology, pediatric neurology, neonatal cardiology.

Presbyterian Hospital is a prime example of a large, medical school–affiliated tertiary-care hospital that provides a perfect setting for the superspecialists. Dr. Kenneth Forde, who was interviewed for this book, is a general surgeon who now subspecializes in surgical endoscopy and subsubspecializes in surgical endoscopy with a laser. Dr. John Driscoll is a pediatrician who subspecializes in the care of the newborn, and sub-subspecializes in intensive care of the premature and critically ill newborn (a neonatal intensivist). Dr. Linda Addonizio is a pediatric cardiologist sub-subspecializing in the care of children who require or have had heart transplants.

Today, more than a thousand of the nation's seventy-five hundred hospitals offer training programs in the twenty-four specialties recognized by the American Board of Medical Specialties. Like Presbyterian, most of these hospitals have affiliations with medical schools. Each specialty has its own regimen. Internal medicine requires three years of post–medical-school training; the general surgeon needs five years. Internists subspecializing in fields such as oncology, nephrology, and cardiology become fellows for an additional one, two, or three years. Time commitments like these mean that doctors will not enter practice on their own until they are at least thirty-two years old.

Why does a doctor pick a particular specialty? The reasons are as varied as the doctors who make the choices. Someone looking for reasonable hours might select ophthalmology, dermatology, or today's most popular specialty, emergency medicine, where physicians work shifts and are never "on call." A person who dislikes dealing with patients directly might choose anesthesiology or radiology. Dr. Herbert Pardes chose psychiatry because of the vastness of the field. Dr. Jay Lefkowitch picked pathology for its intellectual stimulation, and he has narrowed his field, specializing in the pathology of the liver.

Time and money are major factors when it comes to making a choice, although some young doctors do not like to admit that. Most students leave medical school in debt. Some owe over fifty thousand dollars or more and look ahead to years of paying it off. The range of remuneration in the different specialties is vast. Dermatology pays better than pediatrics. Surgeons earn more than psychiatrists. Time was important to Tom Bartlett, a third-year student at P & S, who began medical school at twenty-seven and will be in his mid-thirties when he finishes training. Although he found surgery tempting, he is opting for oncology because it has a shorter training period.

As we head into the nineties, the trend is toward ever narrowing specialization. Supporters point to the remarkable achievements of the superspecialist, from transplanting hearts in infants, for one example, to the better care a patient receives.

Critics, however, believe that the pendulum has swung too far, that superspecialization leads to depersonalization and the deterioration of the doctor-patient relationship. If no single physician assumes total responsibility for a patient, problems are sure to arise, especially in the elderly patient with arthritis, arteriosclerosis, and diabetes and no single physician with whom to talk about his troubles.

Some of the answer may lie in the newest specialist, the family practitioner. First recognized in 1960 and growing in stature every year, the specialty is almost as popular as the leading specialty, internal medicine. The horse and buggy has been gone for decades, but the physician trained to care for the whole patient seems to be making a return.

LEWIS ROWLAND, M.D.
Chairman, Department of Neurology

At sixty-two, he's at the top of his career. He has been department chairman since 1973. For the past ten years, he has been the editor-in-chief of Neurology, *a highly prestigious medical journal. Recently he was elected president of the American Academy of Neurology, the largest neurological organization in the world.*

We're in his office on the tenth floor of the Neurological Institute. I ask how he got into medicine. "When I was five years old, I was out walking with my mother and somebody we met asked me what I was going to be when I grew up. I said, 'A doctor,' my mother said, 'That's right!' and ever since then I never, ever wanted to do anything else.

"My childhood hero was Louis Pasteur. When I was eight or nine, I read about him in a book called Microbe Hunters. *Then I searched out all the other books I could find on him, and I saw a movie called* The Story of Louis Pasteur, *which starred Paul Muni. That did it. I knew after that that one day I would grow up to be either Louis Pasteur . . . or Paul Muni."*

The Neurological Institute was the first neurological hospital and became the center of training in neurology in this country. It's still considered one of the greatest departments of neurology in history. The best barometer of a department is the number of people trained there who go out to become department chairmen at other academic institutions. There are now over thirty chairmen of American neurology departments who were trained here, and we have at least half a dozen people here now who could or should be chairmen.

The medical students don't like neurology; they think it's more depressing than anything except oncology. And that's true, to a degree. There are lots of sad things in neurology, but tremendously challenging things too. There are well over six hundred described neurological diseases. The biggest challenge we face today, though, is not in the diagnosis or management of these diseases; I mean, either you've got a disease you can treat or you don't. Our challenge is to deal with the diseases where treatment is unsatisfactory. There are still so many of them. Alzheimer's is one; stroke; Parkinson's disease. ALS [amyotrophic lateral sclerosis, also known as Lou Gehrig's disease] is ours. Cerebral palsy. Epilepsy treatment is not terrific. We have a lot of bad diseases.

As a result of research efforts within the last several decades there has been a continuous outflow of new information about every one of our diseases. The organization of the Neurological Institute reflects this. In 1973 we set up divisions but we're all in one building and we communicate with each other all the time. We have a neuromuscular group, a movement disorder group, a stroke group, a dementia group for Alzheimer's disease, and an epilepsy group. We have pediatric neurology and neurosurgery. A multiple sclerosis clinic. Our neurologists are superspecialized to the degree that they ought to know as much or more than anybody else in the world about a particular disease. A general neurologist, like a general physician, can be good and can cover a lot of areas—but to be a world leader, you've really got to focus down.

Research is supposed to be central to the life of a department chairman. In fact, the chairmen in all the good medical schools are selected on the basis of their research achievements. And yet, you come to a big medical school like this, and it's tacitly understood that you're not going to be able to do research yourself anymore. You can't do it; there are just too many other commitments. So either you work through somebody else—fellows, assistant professors—or you stop. I tried working through other people for a while, but sooner or later these people grow up and they get minds of their own and it doesn't work.

I had a laboratory and I had some young people in it, and they didn't like my ideas and I didn't like their ideas, and so I ended up giving away the lab. But you want the chairman to have at least a *feel* for research to understand what it's all about. Because in a place like this, we're not just teaching medical students and house officers and we're not just taking care of patients. We are supposed to be—I hate this phrase—on the cutting edge of new knowledge. We're supposed to be *developing* new knowledge. We're supposed to be providing the scientific basis for medical care and to be improving it. That's what our job is, and that's what research is about.

I don't have much of a practice. I only see patients whose diseases have something to do with my research interest. ALS, muscular dystrophy, myasthenia gravis. It's very hard for me to get involved in continuing care; I tell patients at the beginning that I'd like to follow them, but if they want a doctor to talk to and call up all the time, I can't do that because of my administrative duties and because I travel a lot.

I was just in India. I gave a paper on neurology as it will be in the year 2000. I tried to go over the changes that I've seen in my lifetime. The point is that the rate of change has gotten faster and faster and faster. This stuff on molecular genetics is a wonderful example of that. Take Duchenne's muscular dystrophy, the kind that occurs in young boys. The notion that (a) we would locate the gene in three years after we started looking for it and (b) that we would have the gene product a month after we found the gene is phenomenal. Nobody would have believed that two years ago. Nobody, including me. *Especially* me. Then I tried to pick a couple of areas that I thought would be most likely to have an impact now that will last for the next fifteen years. I talked about one, just to say that it was impossible, and that was brain transplant.

It was interesting how it came out in the newspapers afterwards. There were two English language newspapers in Madras. One of them headlined: "American expert says, 'Brain transplants impossible.' " The other paper said, "American expert says, 'Brain cell transplants in progress!' " And they were both right, because you *can't* do a brain transplant, which is what I said, but people *are* taking cells and putting them into the brain. They take nerve cells from one part of the body and put them somewhere else. Now, whether that will have a lasting impact or not, I don't know. That's the kind of thing which is sort of science fiction, and it may or may not have an important impact. The one that's been done was for Parkinsonism—the cells in the Parkinson brain that make a particular chemical are missing or they've degenerated, so if you can get them from another part of the body, like the adrenal glands, and put those adrenal cells in the brain, you don't have to worry about immunological rejection. The question is whether you can get them to grow and do what they're supposed to do.

One afternoon a week I have a clinic here, and I also see private patients one afternoon a week. I see private patients for a couple of reasons. One is that I'm sort of the senior person in neuromuscular disease now. People get a fatal diagnosis, I'm the standard second opinion. Secondly, patients are important for our teaching and research programs. So I do it.

My patients are all memorable to me for one reason or another. We have a twenty-four-year-old woman here now who is going to die in a year and we can't do anything about it. That drives me crazy. Recently we had two men—both so outstanding in their fields. One, a top executive of a huge corporation, an absolutely sensational person, had a peripheral muscular disease—like Guillain-Barré but not quite that. He spent a horrible couple of months in the ICU before he died. And the other was a noted academician, an absolutely great guy, who had a cerebral hemorrhage and died, just like that.

One time, this was in the mid-fifties, I treated a woman in her thirties who was supposed to have a form of muscular dystrophy, which is an untreatable and progressively disabling disease. For a variety of reasons, though, I thought she might have a condition called myasthenia gravis. So we presented her at a conference to discuss the case. She came in, barely able to walk and using a cane, and she took a seat at the front of the room. I described her condition and then we gave her an injection of some medicine that works in myasthenia gravis and not in muscular dystrophy. Well, she threw away her cane and she went marching down the aisle. It was like Lourdes! When something is that dramatic, you worry that the patient is hysterical or that it's a psychogenic disorder or something like that. But she walked! There were other significant things that were more objective than her walking down the aisle, but she threw away her cane, and she *walked*. She was a rather flamboyant woman herself. She's still alive now. She's in her sixties.

We hear a lot about the changing face of medicine and frankly I find it a very distressing subject. I'm concerned about the fact that this country is the only industrialized country in the world, other than South Africa, that does not have a national health program. I don't know how many people realize that, but we're the only advanced country in the world that has no plan. It's truly the most chaotic health care system in the world and it's probably the most callous in terms of dealing with poor people. Now we're in a situation where everybody's concerned about the costs of health care, and they want to cut back.

Everybody thinks there's a lot of fat in the system and a lot of inefficiency and they talk about cutting costs. But nobody's talking about making the system better. Nobody's talking about better treatment of patients. I don't mean medical treatment, I mean more human treatment in hospitals. Nobody's talking about better medical care, and nobody's talking about improving the science. Nobody's talking about improving *anything*. They're just talking about spending less money. And I think that sooner or later people are going to realize, you spend less money, you're going to get less.

It's hard enough now to keep these places going. By the time they cut back, it will just get harder to do things. You flirt with the limits of tolerance. You cut down nurses' positions, and it makes it harder for the nurses who remain. And then they quit coming altogether and then you get yourself into a real crisis.

A lot of people think doctors make too much money and maybe some of them do. I've never understood why people who have an interesting job that's socially useful and intellectually stimulating wind up being treated like priests. I've never understood why they also have to be paid better. I don't know why doctors have to be in the upper half of one percent of the country in income. And yet, if you crack down on income, which seems to be the case now, and if you build up an antipathy towards physicians, which seems to be going on now, it discourages people from going into the profession. A lot of the smart young people don't want medicine anymore, which probably means that there's going to be lower quality physicians. So somehow you've got to balance these things out.

I'm distressed by the commercialization of medicine. All this business of advertising and competing for patients just doesn't make sense to me. I'm known for being a little odd this way, but I think a hospital is supposed to be a socially useful institution. What's happened is it has become a business.

I don't know what the solution is. Nobody talks about national health insurance anymore. It's not on the national agenda—it hasn't been since Truman. Medicare was a piece of it, but nobody ever went beyond Medicare. Now they're talking about catastrophic insurance. It may come back again. I don't know whether it's right. I mean, I can see that it could lead to all kinds of bureaucracies and so on, but it's the motivation that makes the difference. If you say we want to have a national health program, of course you're concerned about bureaucracies, you're concerned about inefficiencies; but at least you start out by saying we want to make health care accessible to everybody, and we want to do the best for everybody we can. You don't come out and say we want to save money. People ought to talk about these things.

There may be twenty great hospitals in this country. They take polls periodically of the ten best and this medical center is always on the list, right up there, among the first five; often among the first three. Johns Hopkins is also. I mention Hopkins for a specific reason. I graduated from high school in 1942 and one of the colleges I applied to was Johns Hopkins. I applied there because I thought I might want to go to medical school there. And I was told—I remember vividly—that it would be a bad idea to go to Johns Hopkins undergraduate school because the medical school was going downhill. So it's now forty-five years that I've been looking closely at Johns Hopkins for signs of going downhill. It's still one of the great university medical schools in the world, and still a great hospital. Hospitals don't slide down. They go through periods of ups and downs; but the ones with a tradition don't slide down. There's a self-perpetuating excellence that goes on. You put smart people in a place, and dedicated people, and they just make sure it goes on.

One thing that's special about this place is tradition. It was the first medical center in the country; the notion of the school and hospital working together—they didn't work together so well for a long time, but they're doing very well now. The location was important. Harkness was really a genius. Picking this location was good for the long haul, because the medical center had growing room. This was countryside in 1928. It's hard to believe, but it was. The neighborhood has gone through some tough changes, but everybody believes that sooner or later we'll pick up the gap. I've watched this neighborhood change. It's not terrific, but the dangers and the hazards and the unpleasantness are exaggerated, I think. You can have gunshots in the emergency room but you still know you can walk up to the corner and buy some flowers.

We don't have much trouble getting patients to come up here. I think they come because they know that the medical care here is top-notch. But our academic excellence depends on them coming—particularly those with tough problems. And if we're going to continue to get them, we have to offer more than a community hospital does. The only way we can offer more is to have the amenities. That's one of the reasons why it was crucial to build the new hospital. And we've got to be clinically better than anybody else. That's why, in neurology, we have to have stroke groups, movement disorder groups, epilepsy groups. We have to be the ones who are pushing forward, who have new treatments, the ones with new under-standing of diseases. That's always been the history of this medical center and that's its future too, I think.

CAROL MOSKOWITZ, R.N.

Dystonia Research Nurse

One of the world's finest movement disorder services is at the Neurological Institute, under the direction of Dr. Stanley Fahn. Patients, such as Muhammad Ali, come here from all over the world for diagnosis and treatment of problems involving the motor control system.

We're sitting in the corner of one of the laboratories connected with the movement-disorder group. People come and go and there is a lot of activity throughout our meeting but she continues as though we are alone. A bright and cheerful woman, she speaks excitedly about her job. She's forty-seven.

Most people have never even heard of dystonia. It's a movement disorder that manifests itself in twisted movements and postures of the entire body or only one part. We think it's inherited, but it can occur in people whose families have no history and sometimes it occurs after some kind of trauma. We just don't know for sure what causes it.

You can get dystonia just of the eyelids. That's called blepharospasm, involuntary eyelid closure. It's not just increased blinking, the eyelids clamp shut and the person is functionally blind. He can't see unless he holds his lids open with his fingers. It's bizarre. You can have involvement of the jaw, where the jaw opens forcibly and you can't close it. You can have an involvement of the neck, where the head turns to the left or the right, or maybe bends backwards. Some people wake up one morning and their head is turned slightly and as the day goes on it pulls to one side and is painful to move. It can stay that way permanently or it can resolve itself after a time.

It's especially sad when it happens to kids because the early symptoms are so confusing. A kid can have intermittent leg problems, for example. And the parents call the pediatrician and say, "Hey, what's going on here? How come he can play baseball, basketball, soccer, run all over the place, but he can't walk up to the second floor to his French class?" Stair walking produces painful spasms. The pediatrician says, "He'll outgrow it." Then, when he doesn't, he says, "Maybe he should go to a psychiatrist." So the kid goes to a psychiatrist, and he doesn't know what it is, either.

That's what happens to most people with dystonia, because it's rare and people don't recognize the symptoms. They start with their family doctor and end up with a psychiatrist. People think they have emotional problems because the symptoms vary so much. How come it's there one time, and not another? In the early stages, dystonia isn't present all the time.

I can explain dystonia like this: Normally, when you go to do something, one bunch of muscles relaxes and an opposing bunch contracts. In dystonia, all the muscles contract together so you have a tightening up of the entire limb, say, or the hand. Normally, you tell your muscles what to do, and you do it. With dystonia, all the muscles fire at the same time, so you have no control. Your body just is not under your command.

We don't cure dystonia. We suppress the symptoms with medicine. Sometimes patients develop their own little tricks to help themselves. Putting a finger on the top of a wrist helps block spasms in writing for some people. Other people learn that they can't write sitting down, but if they stand up and stiffen their elbow, they can write anything. One guy says, "I can always sign my checks at the bank, but I can't sign them at a desk." In severe cases, though, none of the tricks works.

The case that stands out most in my mind started quite a while ago. There was a young man, Steve, who had gone through medical school and was just about to start his internship when he began to have symptoms in his feet. He was only twenty-three at the time. It was typical childhood-onset dystonia which eventually progressed over his whole body. It got so bad he couldn't do anything. Not go to work. Nothing. Over the years it got worse. He was immobilized and in so much pain. Nothing worked for him. Every time you saw him, you'd just die a little. He was on everything, sleeping pills, pain medication, an unbelievable load. He had a computerized watch that would say, "Time for medication two." He was wheelchair confined for the most part. He could walk five steps, but he would fall at the end because he had severe leg spasms.

Like a lot of other patients, this man came here because of Dr. Fahn, but try as we might, we had never been able to help him. Then, one day, a research paper crossed my desk. A physician from London had written a manuscript—not yet published—and sent it to Dr. Fahn. It certainly wasn't a polished article yet. In fact, it looked like he took it right off the typewriter and sent it to us. It documented something that he had done with a twelve-year-old boy with severe dystonia in the ICU of a London hospital. The boy had reached a point where he was having difficulty breathing. In a desperate last-minute attempt to do something, the boy's doctor put together a combination of three specific drugs and gave them to the child. There was positively no logic to this, but it worked for this child. Here was a physician who cared and who was committed to what was going on with this boy, and he took a risk and it paid off.

Well, I read the manuscript, and then I reread it, and then I went tearing next door and I banged on Susan Bressman's door and I said, "You've gotta read this!" I said, "Look at this! How about this for Steve?" We all—doctors, nurses—gave it a lot of thought and we decided it was worth a try. We started him on this unlikely combination of medications. We took a chance.

Now I've been in this medical center for eleven years so I knew him from the time I had just gotten out of nursing school. This twisted person, who had a very strong personality, and was very demanding. But he was always one of my favorites. There would always be chaos on the floor because he was always pushing on his button, trying to get somebody to come in because he needed something. "Would you do this, would you do that?" That was his personality.

After three or four months, the drugs began to work. Slowly, he started getting better. I went away on vacation for a while, and on my first day back, I was heading down the hall when I approached a man pushing an empty wheelchair. I had no idea who he was. He smiled, and I looked at him. It was Steve! I had never seen him standing up—I had never seen his face level with mine. I burst into tears. What else do you do? I mean, after fifteen years of agony, it was just terrific. And *he's* terrific, but he's always been a terrific personality, a strong personality. You always knew he was in there.

Today, he's a pain researcher. For good reason. He was in pain for such a long time. He'd been the recipient of it and been released; he's able to work now, part-time, in a research center in his hometown. He walks and he talks and he hugs. It's wonderful.

Two years ago we began research on eyelid spasms. The research required us to inject the skin on the outside of the eyelids and by the nose with tiny amounts of a very, very dilute toxin which prevents the nerve from releasing a chemical which makes the muscles contract and the eyelids slam shut. This seemed to be a possible alternative to facial surgery. The body gets rid of the poison over about three months. It eventually wears off, but for months it can allow somebody's eyes to stay open and to blink normally. They can see again! Then, when we need to reinject them, we do.

Dr. Fahn wrote the protocol for this research about two years ago. Before we could take any steps with patients, it had to be approved by the Columbia-Presbyterian Institutional Review Board [IRB]. That's a group of scientific people and clinicians from the staff who review every research protocol before they let you begin a study. These people are tough. You don't do things irresponsibly here. You have to have your data and all your protective measures. Here was this great idea, we had patients with the problem waiting for treatment, I had set up a mini-ICU in case we had any problems at all. But it was hard to get it through. The board heard the word "toxin" and they had exactly the same reaction as I did. Why would you put toxins into someone electively?

But you have to try new treatments. Patients present the problems, you have to find the solutions. Until you find a cure, you have to do something. Patients first, research second. Anyway, we were finally approved and what we found was that this particular treatment, it turns out, works in sixty-five to seventy percent of the people with eyelid spasms and a hundred percent of the people who have hemifacial spasms, where the whole side of the face scrinches up.

When something like this works, the impact is huge. We recently had a patient, eighty-three years old. He only wanted to be in the park in the sunshine, but his eyes were slammed shut all the time. We started him on the injections and one day I called him up and I said, "So, how're you doing?" and he said, "Oh, terrific!" I said, "What do you mean?" He said, "I mean I can walk across the street without anybody with me." He hated being a baby. He was eighty-three years old, he wanted to be independent. He was a big, chubby, Greek guy with loving, doting daughters. It was, "Oh, poppa, let me take you across the street, let me do things for you," and he hated it. He wanted to go out by himself, damn it! There was nothing wrong with him except his eyelids were closed. He said, "I went over to the park and I sat in the sun for an hour and a half and I watched things!" I asked him how long it lasted. It only lasted an hour and a half, he said, but he didn't care, that was a hundred percent to him. I said, "You know, that's not really a hundred percent, Mr. G. That's an hour and a half." And he said, "Yeah, yeah, but it was such a great hour and a half!"

So here's this guy who's so happy because he sat in the sunlight with his eyes open. And we hope perhaps he'll eventually do better than that. See, the thing is, with disorders like this you can't hang around and wait for the cure. You have to take care of *people*.

HERBERT PARDES, M.D.

Chairman, Department of Psychiatry

—

His office is on the fourteenth floor of the Psychiatric Institute. It's a large corner room with picture windows that offer an astonishing view of the Hudson River and uptown Manhattan. It's late afternoon and the sun is beginning to set behind the Palisades. He is in his early fifties. Short graying hair, wire-rimmed glasses, suede-patch elbows on his tweed jacket. He's a pleasant man, understated, with boyish good looks. Before coming to Presbyterian, he spent six years as the director of the National Institute of Mental Health in Washington, D.C.

It has been an exciting day. The discovery of a gene that is associated with manic depressive behavior has just been announced. Although the discovery was not made at Columbia-Presbyterian, he is being called for comment. The New York Times and NBC News have already interviewed him and he has just finished filming a segment for CBS News. "They came in with the whole crew, set everything up—cameras, mikes, the whole number. Then they filmed for twenty minutes. I'll be lucky if the whole shot is four seconds. But this is a very exciting day for psychiatry."

The New York State Psychiatric Institute [PI] is probably one of the premier, if not *the* premier, research institutes and psychiatric facilities in the world. It's certainly the oldest institute doing research on psychiatric disorders. Since the affiliation with the medical center, the director of the institute has also been the chairman of the department of psychiatry at Columbia and the director of the psychiatric service at Presbyterian Hospital. That pulls together a distinguished hospital service, a major medical-school department, and a state research institute. The research institute is a marvel; something that is as much a jewel in the crown for New York State as Lincoln Center is in terms of music and culture.

We have a clinical service at PI which renders care for patients. The overwhelming number are research patients. That's necessary because there's no other way you can do clinical research. If you want to study anorexia, bulemia, the various treatments—you've got to have patients. You've got to watch them as you give them various trials or tests or treatments and see how they work. For some people, it's advantageous to come into a research program because they get super attention and they don't pay anything. We occasionally look for people who have a disorder or complex of factors that we're interested in, but in the majority of cases, patients come to us. We let it be known that we have such programs. One reason they come here is that they know they're going to be treated by some of the best physicians there are.

Psychiatry is a booming department. We have almost four hundred research projects going on. Everything from violence to sex offenders to childhood phobias. We have fourteen different projects on child psychiatric disorders alone. We have projects on the elderly; projects on Alzheimer's, schizophrenia, depression, anxiety, the epidemiology of brain disorders. The list is endless.

We're training young doctors, but we're also responding to the community with outreach programs for older patients; programs for children in school; we've developed an expanded Hispanic ambulatory program; a crisis intervention program; we've got a new program going in the shelter across the street for the homeless. We've got all that and at the same time we've got other people who are looking at neurons and molecular genetics. An academic health center can weave together those two dramatically different functions: community responsiveness and a research bent. In one room you can find a woman whose job it is to respond when an elderly person in a nursing home has a depression, and right next to her is a fellow who is taking two sides of a nerve synapse and studying it to figure out how people learn.

I have some of my own notions about what kind of people go into medicine. One type tries to gain control over a set of stresses that he finds overwhelming. It's not unusual to find people in medicine who had serious medical problems as children, or who worry so much about their health that becoming a doctor seems a magical way of protecting themselves. But

I suppose every doctor has his or her own reason. I loved it from the beginning. I remember when I was an intern and I would get called at three o'clock in the morning to admit a new patient. I worked in an enormous city hospital; we slept in a little building about a ten-minute walk from the medical office. I would get my bag and walk to the main building through halls with generators, the garbage plant, the morgue, on an internal street of a big city hospital . . . the place empty. As I walked I would think about the fact that the entire city was asleep, and that I was going to meet with another person who was waiting for me, and that person was in trouble, perhaps facing death, and I was going there to try to help him. In a sense it made me feel like a guardian, and I liked that.

There are different types of people who go into different specialties. Some want certain things that psychiatry offers. For example, I think psychiatrists like the fact that psychiatry relates to so many other fields; the arts, the sciences, religion. If you're a plastic surgeon, you have a certain technical skill, but it doesn't have much of an interactive character. You can go into psychiatry and in the middle of your training you can decide to become an expert in law and psychiatry, in literature and psychiatry. You can become a hard-line biological researcher, an epidemiologist. You can go any *number* of ways. Psychiatry also tends to involve a certain inclination to self-exploration or self-awareness. While that's not true of all psychiatrists, for the most part they are interested in understanding themselves. Third, I think psychiatrists tend to be somewhat more liberal than physicians in other medical fields. If you check the political orientation of specialists, I think you'll find most doctors are Republican, but a large proportion of psychiatrists are probably Democratic.

Now, which comes first, being liberal or being a psychiatrist? Probably the political orientation is there first. It's one of the things that intrigues me. People who are conservative, organized, orderly, tend to be in surgical specialties. Psychiatry wants to open things up. Take, for example, the kind of interview you might do with a patient. I'm stereotyping this, but a surgical interview might be relatively cut and dried. "Where is your pain? Is it in the left quadrant, the right quadrant? How long have you had it?" A psychiatrist might come in and say, "Tell me about yourself. Let me be a blank slate that you paint on."

JEFFERY ROSECAN, M.D.

Psychiatrist
Director, Cocaine Program

Patients participating in the cocaine clinic meet on the second floor of a hospital-affiliated office building on 61st Street. On this damp July afternoon, nine young adults in their late teens and early twenties, casually dressed, are sitting around the anteroom waiting for their group session to begin. Smoke sits heavily in the room; almost everyone is smoking. The repartee and personal tone of the conversation among these people gives the impression that they have known each other for quite some time.

At three o'clock, two young men appear in the doorway. The group follows one of them into a conference room. The other, a nattily-dressed, sandy-haired man in his thirties, smiles and extends his hand to me. "I'm Dr. Rosecan."

Because my father is a doctor, my earliest memories of growing up in St. Louis were of hospitals. Permanently imprinted on my brain is the smell of the hospital, the disinfectant, circa 1955. Medicine really wasn't dinner-table discussion at our house, but the topic came up when it came time to bring our parents into our third-grade class. You know, "What does *your* daddy do?" My father was a specialist in endocrinology—hormones—and I remember he would show us slides of the endocrine abnormalities of the Alton, Illinois, giant, who was nine feet tall. Then he showed pictures of midgets and fat people and thin people. The kids were fascinated. And so was I. By the time I was eight or nine, I was reading his medical journals and medical textbooks. While my friends were putting together model airplanes I was putting together the Visible Woman and the Visible Man.

It was a set of serendipitous events which got me started in what was to become my specialty, cocaine. When I started my psychiatry residency, I got interested in heart research. I started looking at type A behavior—hard-driving, aggressive behavior a lot of executives have, which many cardiologists now think is a risk factor for heart attacks. Quite naturally, a lot of the patients I was interviewing were executives in their thirties, forties, and fifties.

One of them—I'll call him Mike—had a terrible cocaine problem. That had nothing to do with why he was coming to see me though. I was trying to measure his type A behavior and to help him to change it to protect against his risk for heart attack. He had been referred to the study by one of his cardiologists who was concerned about him. He had all the classic risk factors. What Mike confided to me, which he didn't tell his internist, was that he also had a very heavy cocaine habit. I didn't know what to make of it. He didn't look like the drug addicts we had seen in internship or medical school. For one thing, he was wearing a three-piece Brooks Brothers' suit. I remember wondering how he could be addicted to cocaine because all of our professors in medical school had said that cocaine is not really addictive, that it's psychologically addictive but not physically addictive, and that people tend not to get into trouble with it.

Over the next few months I continued to treat him, but we didn't discuss his using cocaine. Frankly, I didn't know what to do with it. I'd seen junkies come into the emergency room with heroin overdoses, but I'd never seen a cocaine addict. Certainly, I'd never seen anyone like Mike before.

He gradually developed a pretty serious depression, which may or may not have been related to his cocaine use, but at the time we didn't know. So I decided to put him on antidepressant medication, which is nothing astounding. That's what psychiatrists often do when someone's depressed. Three weeks later he came back for a visit and told me two very interesting things. One was that he was starting to feel better and pull out of his depression. That was expected; he was on imipramine, a commonly prescribed antidepressant. The second thing he said was that he had lost his taste for cocaine. I didn't know what that meant. "I'm not getting high from it anymore," was what he said. I didn't say this to him, but my first thought was, talk to your drug dealer. I'm your psychiatrist; I don't know what he's giving you. I was finishing my residency and to tell the truth,

I didn't think much about the whole thing. Eventually, Mike gave up cocaine because he didn't like it anymore. He lost his taste for it. He didn't crave it, and when he did try it, he didn't get high.

A month or two later another patient came in to the cardiac stress clinic, also with type A behavior, also using a lot of cocaine. I said, okay, if this one gets depressed I'm going to put him on the medicine also. This time I'm going to ask him whether or not he's getting high from cocaine and how he feels about it. And, over the next few months, he also became quite depressed—at the time I wasn't aware of the association between cocaine addiction and depression which is now being established—so I put this second patient on imipramine. This time I questioned him quite carefully about the cocaine, how much he was using and whether or not he got high and, bingo! He also had stopped using cocaine. He didn't get high from it anymore.

I thought I was onto something. I talked to a couple of psychiatry professors about it. They had never heard of it before, but it certainly made sense if you look at the actions of cocaine and the actions of imipramine on the brain. They act very similarly so maybe the imipramine is blocking the cocaine. I went to the library and did a search of the literature and it seemed that it really did make sense. The more I looked into it the more the pieces seemed to fall into place. Word got around the medical center that I was treating cocaine addicts and within a few weeks, people started referring lots of these guys to me. My first twenty or thirty patients were all men. We set up a program for them at 61st Street because the numbers were just overwhelming. This was in the fall of 1982. I was still a fellow, still ostensibly doing type A research. I was picking and choosing among the type As that came in and getting the ones who used cocaine. I would ask them and they always told me. After I got the first fifteen, and most of them did quite well, I went back to my professor and showed him my results. He suggested I present them at a medical conference.

I ended up presenting my data several months later in Vienna, in July of 1983, at the World Congress of Psychiatry. It was very controversial. At that time most people didn't think cocaine was physically addicting. They felt it was a psychological addiction. What are you doing treating a psychological addiction with medication? It just didn't make sense to them. So in addition to presenting the treatment results, what I was trying to do was to convince a very skeptical audience about a new paradigm of cocaine addiction. I was trying to reconceptualize cocaine in biological and hormonal terms.

While I was doing my work here, there were two other scientists, one from Yale and one from UCLA, doing very similar work with a medication very closely related to imipramine. We heard about each other's work and compared notes, and we were all getting the same results. All of a sudden people started to take my work seriously, although I was the most junior person doing this work.

Usually, in the history of medicine, it takes a long time to change paradigms. I've seen a very rapid change in the past three years. Most people will now agree that cocaine creates a physiological as well as a psychological addiction, and that you might be able to correct this abnormal physiology with medications. It's been a minor revolution in its own right.

We see a lot of cocaine abusers who are successful men in their thirties and forties. Any number of them turned to cocaine after the breakup of a relationship, or what to them may have been an insolvable problem. The reason I think that men do it so much more than women is that culturally men are not allowed to go next door and have a good cry over coffee when they've been jilted, whereas women can do that.

No one really starts out to become a cocaine addict. All of the people I've treated started using cocaine for a variety of reasons; whether it was to numb emotional pain, or just to have fun—feeling that, well, it's not supposed to be addicting; let's have fun with it on Saturday night.

One of the hallmarks of cocaine addiction is denial. Even as their lives are falling apart, most addicts will deny that there is a problem. It's a real distortion of reality. They usually decide to stop because a spouse or a partner or a good friend or an employer will say "You better stop or else". Usually the first few times they come to the program, they're doing it for someone else. You hope that something happens after the first few times to convince them that they have a problem. Plenty of people in the group initially felt the same way. They were so stoned on cocaine they didn't even realize they had a problem. It's something the recovering cocaine addicts in the groups can tell these people that the doctors can't. The recovering cocaine addicts have experienced it firsthand.

Once someone enters our program, we ask them to commit themselves to discontinue the use of cocaine. We use urine tests to tell whether or not someone is living up to that commitment. You want to trust people, but we test their urine, just to make sure, just to keep them honest. We do it on a random basis. Usually if they've used cocaine and they can't face me they'll call in with a flimsy excuse and cancel the appointment. We use a very sensitive test which will pick up cocaine for up to a week in the urine. We keep people honest. When we tell people at the beginning of treatment, look, you're going to be subject to a random test for cocaine when we feel like it, they tend to be more honest, I think. It's tragic because a lot of these people are basically normal, stable, honest people who, once they're caught up in the cocaine cycle, start to deceive the people they care about the most because they can't face them. Dishonesty breeds dishonesty. Little lies breed big lies. They get into a vicious cycle. I sit them down and say, "Look, I want you to be completely honest with me." They'll nod and say, "Yes, I wouldn't be here if I didn't mean it." Still, I know that even though they want to be honest, I have to test their urine.

I'll say to the group, "Today is urine test day," and then just do everybody so no one gets singled out. If the test is positive on one person, the group gives him hell! Even though these people are strangers, there's a very powerful group process that develops over several weeks. When you start to rebuild honesty in the group, you can start to do it with the people who really matter—your family, your spouse, your friends.

About two hundred fifty people have come through the program over the past three years. Our success rate is about seventy-five percent. But we're seeing a select group of patients. Patients who come here are people with family support, with resources, with advanced degrees. Most of the patients we see in the cocaine clinic are like Mike. Most of them work in midtown. We see them individually and in groups. Some of them get imipramine and some of them don't. We're still continuing to use it. We're still getting excellent results.

I have another practice for treating general psychiatry patients, but this is my love. It's given me a tremendous education as to what cocaine is and why people use it, but the most gratifying thing about it is that not only are these people treatable, they're eminently treatable. They quickly get much better. People can be in psychoanalysis four times a week for six years, and they may be a little bit happier at the end of that time. When I first see the cocaine users, their lives are often in shambles. Once they stop using cocaine they're able to piece their lives back together—it usually happens within months, not years.

I can't give a cure rate. We hesitate to use the word cure when talking about an addiction, because these people are always prone to a relapse. They can't go back to a small amount of cocaine again. They will relapse. We don't want them to get the notion that they can be cured of it the way you can be cured of pneumonia. It's a lifelong struggle for many of them.

JACK GORMAN, M.D.
Psychiatrist

His subspecialty is "panic attacks." He's director of the Biological Studies Unit at Psychiatric Institute. His wife was his classmate in medical school. They both went to P&S. They're both psychiatrists. He's a playwright by avocation. His plays have been performed in workshops in Greenwich Village.

I got interested in panic attacks in the first year of my psychiatric residency. There was a woman admitted to the hospital with a condition called agoraphobia—sudden, episodic outbursts of anxiety where your heart pounds, you hyperventilate, you feel like you're going to die. These attacks come on for no good reason; they're spontaneous, out of the blue. They last twenty to thirty minutes and then they go away. People who experience these attacks become afraid to go anywhere where they might get one, where they can't get help right away. They start restricting their travel, and in the worst cases they become homebound.

This particular woman was so phobic of traveling that she couldn't come back and forth to the clinic for her visits, so we had to hospitalize her. Dr. Abby Thayer, who was an attending at that time, asked me to get an echocardiogram on this patient so we could evaluate her heart. She was looking at this woman's heart function because there were reports in the

literature that patients with agoraphobia have mitral valve prolapse
[MVP]—a benign heart condition—more often than normal people. So
I did the echocardiogram and to my surprise, this condition showed up.
At that time, like now, residents were encouraged to get involved in a
research project, so I went to Donald Klein, the director of research, who
years ago originally identified the panic disorder syndrome and how it
relates to agoraphobia. I told him about what I'd found, and I asked if I
could get echocardiograms on some of the other patients to see if the
correlation between the panic disorder and mitral valve prolapse really
existed. He agreed, and what I found was that fifty percent of people with
panic disorder did indeed have mitral valve prolapse.

The next question was: What the hell is MVP doing there? Why should
agoraphobics have it? What is it? Soon afterwards, I met a cardiologist at
the University of Texas named Andrew Gaffney who had published a lot
of papers on mitral valve prolapse. He said it was a disorder of the auto-
nomic nervous system. Those patients who had it had a lot of extra
epinephral adrenaline in their blood. So I thought perhaps that was the
link; maybe the prolapse causes outpouring of adrenaline, and that makes
these people anxious. And so that's how it started for me. I've always been
grateful to Abby. She was the one who said, "Get that echocardiogram!"
and she was very helpful in getting me to work it out.

We are now able to show that some of the psychiatric disorders are
genetic. We're starting to look for the genes for some of these conditions,
the way the gene for Huntington's disease was discovered at Harvard.
Abby Thayer and I have actually just started a collaboration with Jim
Cazell at Harvard to try to find the gene for panic disorder. I think it's
likely there is one. There are people who will insist that it's not a genetic
disease, that it's an environmental disease or a psychological one. But
there's substantial evidence that makes me think differently. Then again,
my whole shtick in psychiatry is to try to get away from these turf issues
and do my best to see where the data leads me. Maybe we'll show that
it's *not* a genetic disease. That would be very interesting, too. Any resolu-
tion for any given condition is a tremendous contribution that will help
people treat these things.

Panic disorders affect all sorts of everyday people. An example is one
man who came to see me several years ago—a successful businessman who
had a classic case of panic disorder and agoraphobia which restricted his
ability to travel. At the end of the interview I said to him, "It seems like
you have a condition which we can treat. My nurse will take you up to the
tenth floor where you'll get your blood drawn and your electrocardiogram
and the internist will examine you just to make sure that you're medically
healthy." He asked, "Are there any windows on the tenth floor?" I said,

"Of course there are windows." "I can't go up there, then." "Why not?" "Well, when I have one of my panic attacks I get gripped with a fear that I'm going to jump out the window." I said, "Do you want to jump out a window?" Of course he said no. But people made that mistake. On two occasions this guy had been admitted to hospitals because he said he was afraid he was going to jump out of a window and they thought he wanted to kill himself. In fact, he had this irrational fear that he was going to lose control of himself during a panic attack and might jump. So he had not gone above the second floor of any building for five years. Eventually, we cured him, and now he can go up to the ninety-ninth floor if he wants to.

Anxiety disorders, in general, are the most common psychiatric illnesses in the United States. There are three types of phobias: agoraphobia, social phobia, and simple phobia. Agoraphobia is certainly the most serious, and is probably the most common. Agoraphobia is more common than social phobia. How common simple phobia is, is a little tough to determine because people don't come to doctors with that. Simple phobias are the things that lay people think of as phobias, like fear of snakes or fear of heights. Things like that. Those people usually just deal with it. We don't usually see them so we may underestimate substantially the number of people that actually have it.

The strangest simple phobia I've dealt with was a bee phobia. Our patient had never been stung by a bee or anything, and yet he stayed in his house from May until October because he was so petrified of them. People tend to think these things are funny, but these phobias can be extremely debilitating. The man would not leave the house, other than once in a rare while, and then he would go out with a can of Raid in his hand. This was a very intelligent person.

We have absolutely no idea why something like that comes on. Freud had a theory of how phobias develop based on the case of little Hans. Little Hans was a boy who was afraid of the horses in Vienna. Freud actually never saw him; he saw the boy's father and told the father how to help him. Freud's theory was that horses were a symbol of the father in the boy's unconscious and the boy was afraid the father was going to castrate him because of the boy's Oedipal complex. He displaced fear of the father and castration anxiety onto horses. So the boy wouldn't go out of the house. Freud himself had a simple phobia, actually, of the trolley system. He'd have to go around the block whenever the trolley cars came. The behaviorists think that somehow or other people learn, like the Pavlovian theory, that if you have a bad situation with a bad stimulus you avoid it. I disagree though, because it's rare that people with simple phobias actually experienced this feared situation. With someone who's afraid of bees, but has never been stung, Pavlovian theory can't help you figure out exactly where the phobia started. Biological psychiatrists have no theory how these things develop. With the panic attacks, we think some of them develop with some abnormalities in neurochemistry, but with simple phobias we really have no theory at all.

JAY LEFKOWITCH, M.D.

Pathologist

His office-laboratory is on the fifth floor of the Physicians and Surgeons Building. It takes several minutes to get used to the pungent odor of chemicals in this large room, which is littered with test tubes, beakers, and slides. His desk is piled high with papers and journals. The centerpiece is a large, well-used microscope.

He's thirty-five years old, slightly built, very animated, and clearly very much at home in his laboratory. In 1983, he was named Distinguished Teacher of the Year by the medical school graduating class.

I love looking through a microscope, and I love the concept of pathology— you have to know diseases better than any of your colleagues because in a sense you're the final arbiter. You see biopsies and have to make an intelligent diagnosis based on tissue analysis combined with clinical information given to you by your colleagues. And you see autopsies, so you see the end stage of disease. Pathology is a completely different area of medicine. You have no patient contact as in a normal practice—no office practice, but it doesn't really bother me, because I am excited way out of expectation about dealing with scientific information.

Maybe one percent of a graduating class goes into pathology. In fact, many people couldn't tell you what we do. They think we're always in some room working with test tubes, or they know Quincy from television and they think we participate in extremely interesting murder cases. That's fine. But only forensic pathologists do that. Pathology is the study of disease. We look not only at the anatomic consequences—what happens to tissue as disease happens—but also at the setting and the epidemiology in which it happens; statistical things, such as what populations have certain diseases and what plays a role in causing disease.

We're called upon to make a definitive diagnosis of cancer, for instance. Say a patient has a lump in her breast. A piece of questionable tissue is removed—a biopsy—and a diagnosis of the disease and a plan for how to proceed is made. Should the surgeon do further excision? Should he do a so-called definitive procedure, which means either curative or irrevocable? If you make a diagnosis of breast cancer, a mastectomy is irrevocable—a definitive procedure. If you're not sure that it's a malignancy, it's always in the patient's best interest to stop with the biopsy, to have the surgeon wait until there is a permanent section, which takes longer, but allows you the advantage of good fixation of the tissue. Time also permits a conference approach with your colleagues. Then, if a mastectomy is necessary, it can be done soon afterwards.

Take a stomach or bowel situation. The patient is on the operating table, the surgeon excises a piece of suspect tissue, then generally he or she comes out of the operating room to view the specimen with us in the laboratory right next to the OR. In this hospital we're trained, as pathology residents, to go into the operating room to see where the tissue is taken from. You have to glove up and mask up and gown up because the patient is there, but you can see directly where the specimen comes from, and you know what's wrong with the patient. In some other places, the specimen comes through a chute to the pathologist. They never even see the OR. Sometimes, they never see the surgeon. Just "Breast biopsy—frozen section. Number 106." At Columbia, we've always had a clinically strong, interpersonal relationship. We each know, more or less, what the other is thinking about, and the decisions are made over the microscope. If there's a problem, we call up someone else from the department, perhaps with more expertise.

The majority of our work is done in our full-time lab in the surgical pathology headquarters. We start in the morning with preserved specimens from the previous day's operations. We take little bits and pieces of tissue, put them in wax, and put them in molds so that they can be cut. The cutting is very much like what you do in the operating room, except it's now in a wax medium instead of being in a frozen, water-like medium which you do up in the OR. The technicians then cut these into thin sections and put them on glass slides, and they're stained. By early afternoon we have slides on any tissues from the day before. The gross exam, the one done while the patient is still in the OR, will give a certain amount of information, but definitive diagnosis on malignant versus benign conditions is often delayed until you can look at the slides. Some cases are huge. A prostatectomy, where you have large amounts of prostate tissue, can necessitate fifty slides, and each one has to be looked at with every piece of tissue on it, because if you miss one little bit that has cancer, you can make the wrong diagnosis.

Pathology is always demanding. There's no way you could possibly know much more than a kernel of the information about all of the diseases that exist. So you try to reduce your scope. My scope is primarily liver disease. But even with liver disease, you can't possibly tackle it all. Pathology offers a much different vantage point, I suppose, from what people see who work with patients. A surgeon's life must be terrifically rewarding. Someone comes in with a problem and he can do something and send them home better, most times. A pathologist is expected to know everything. The gratification comes when you feel that you know a small part of it. It's knowing that you've made an appropriate decision, and you've helped treat a patient, and perhaps you have uncovered something in biology that we didn't understand so well before.

Pathology is only part of my life. Music and art make up the rest. I sing with a choral group in New York City, the New York Choral Society. When I was in London, I sang with the London Philharmonic. I also have a lot of art projects going. I'm working on a children's book right now. Also, I'm the faculty advisor for the Bard Hall Players, which is a theater group of medical students. Theater is one of my biggest loves. It's a perpetual interest. I've been doing sketches based on theater sets and productions for at least ten years, and I had a one-man show of them two years ago at the National Arts Club.

Fortunately, I've never really needed—knock wood—much more than five hours of sleep, so I go to bed at midnight and get up at five. To me, the morning between five and seven is the best time of the day. Last night I painted from eleven until one.

I guess I've turned into something of a showman. Pathology kind of requires it, because you're presenting information to so many people—most of the time to your colleagues. So you have to make it interesting and vivid, if you can. It's like, once you've sung in Carnegie Hall in front of four thousand people, a fifty-person conference at a medical morbidity and mortality conference is a piece of cake. I used to be terrified when I first started with the choral group. I was still in medical school, and I'd get out on that stage, my heart rate would pick up twenty beats, I'd be sweaty and have a typical anxiety reaction because I was always in the front row. But in two or three years that stopped. I just enjoyed being out there, even in the front row. And that experience put me greatly at ease in front of a class of medical students.

Last year I had to give a large seminar in front of a medical audience of over a thousand people in Chicago for the Liver Meeting. I made two, twenty-minute presentations. I have to admit that, even then, my mouth got dry, but I think it was easier to handle because of Carnegie Hall. So, thank you, Isaac Stern!

R. LINSY FARRIS, M.D.

Ophthalmologist

＝＝＝＝＝＝

"I was born in the small town of Patrick, South Carolina. My father and grandfather were Seaboard Railroad telegraph operators. On the other side of the family, my grandfather was a farmer and his father was a country doctor. My mother was a home demonstration agent in the South during the depression, and seeing a great deal of need, I suppose, for doctors, and knowing that her grandfather was a doctor, she began talking to me at a very early age about studying medicine."

He is fifty-five. His manner is of the true southern gentleman. He speaks softly, with a deep southern accent. His specialty is tears.

My grandfather had macular degeneration and was almost totally blind in his early eighties. I was a young teenager and I was allowed to go and spend a summer with him so that I could drive for him—in South Carolina you could get your driver's license when you were fourteen. We would sit on his porch and I would read to him, and together we would listen to the talking books that he had. I remember being quite affected by all this, and I think that experience impressed upon me how important vision was.

Tears are much more than just fluid. Actually there's structure to them. They're a fascinating part of the body because they change so rapidly. Normally, we each have about two or three big drops of tears in our eyes to let us see clearly. You can see much clearer through a wet surface that's continually renewing itself than through anything else. For example, when you go through the car wash and someone shoots a thin layer of water across the windshield, it becomes very clear, but when it dries up you don't see through it quite as clearly until it becomes completely dry. Well, this is the fascinating aspect about the tear film; it has to work just right to make your eyes feel good.

We probably secrete, in a day, somewhere in the neighborhood of a teaspoonful of tears. People who have no tears are essentially blind. That's because this living tissue that the tears flow across needs to have moisture. Our whole body is moist. On your hand, you've got a tough skin with a dry layer that protects and keeps the fluids in. But in the eye, the surface cells are not that well protected. They're succulent, water-logged cells that have to be maintained in a moist state in order to remain functional. The eye is the only unprotected surface of the body totally exposed to the elements. The only other thing similar to it might be the mouth. If you open your mouth and breathe through it, it feels dry, and that's where saliva plays its role. People who don't have saliva are terribly uncomfortable. They can't talk, they can't eat, their voice changes. In a similar but much simpler way, this is what happens to the tearless eye. Without tears, the surface of the eye just begins to deteriorate. First you have decreased resistance to bacteria and then, if you have any type of eye injury, however slight, it doesn't heal as quickly. Fortunately, you see very few people who have absolutely no tears—most folks just have a decrease in the amount.

We have a variety of things that we can do to help. First, there are artificial tear drops. If that doesn't work, we try other methods, one of which is a small plastic insert—you put it under the lower eyelid—which melts and puts a film over the eyes. In a way it's like spreading oil on water to keep the water from evaporating. We also can prescribe certain glasses called moist-chamber spectacles that have side shields of plastic. This provides the effect of putting a covering over the eye, just as you would cover a dish with a lid. They're sort of like goggles, but they're fitted so that they don't quite look as bad as goggles would look. We also have very tiny plastic plugs that we can put into the tear ducts to keep the natural tears and the artificial tears from draining away so quickly. Otherwise, they'd drain down into the nose. That's the reason your nose gets runny when you cry, because excessive tears run down. What we're doing is blocking that passage.

Some of my research has indicated that wearing contact lenses can lead to dry eyes because the tears have a special structure—you put this little contact lens in there, it disrupts that, and the tears evaporate more quickly. So anything that would disrupt the tears, for example, excessive eye makeup, could disturb the tear film enough to evaporate it more quickly.

Another cause of dry eyes is when the lachrymal [tear] gland itself atrophies. The gland is between your eyebrow and your hairline. From that gland, ducts come down and deliver the tears underneath the upper eyelid. So tears flush over the eye, then they drain out through the tear duct on the inside corner of the eye—right by your nose. That's the drainage duct down into the nose.

Eventually I think we'll be able to analyze tears and their role in the health of the eye as thoroughly as we have the blood. We still aren't sure what is actually in tears; we don't know the different fractionation of lipids in tears, for instance, like we do in the bloodstream. The reason they haven't been able to analyze what's in tears is due to the very small volume we're dealing with and the techniques that are required to analyze small volumes. With the current sampling methods, when you try to collect tears, you stimulate a totally different type of tear.

The best we've been able to do so far is to collect a tear very quickly with a very tiny glass pipette. The patient sits in a chair, and we just touch a little wedge of tears along the lower eyelid and very quickly we get a sample. We can take that sample and transfer it under the microscope to a drop of oil; the oil prevents it from evaporating. We freeze it very quickly, and then thaw it gradually, and as the last ice crystal disappears, we take that as a reading. This just tells us how concentrated the tears are as far as salt content. If you don't have enough tears, they're saltier than they should be.

It's amazing how we can take something so small and make something so big out of it, but that's the way medicine is. You can get a superficial feeling of what different aspects of medicine are, but the deeper you get into any subspecialty, the more you realize how much there is to know.

A lot of physicians feel that ophthalmology is at the fringe of medicine—that it's really not "real" medicine because it's not a life-or-death specialty. That's true. But I often feel fortunate not to have to deal with life and death issues that much. After a while you lose your ability to deal with it as easily as you did back in medical school and internship. I went through a part of medical training where I did deal with life-and-death situations, and it's difficult. But you get away from that in ophthalmology and it becomes stranger and stranger.

You still use the information you were taught—physiology and pathology of the heart and liver and lungs and all that—it's very important for you to have that background, but you're not using it every day. You have to be able to accept the fact that you're going to be a physician who really doesn't know how to read an EKG, and that you're going to have to rely on your colleagues for that. But it doesn't matter, because there's so much about the eye to learn. We laugh when people refer to ophthalmologists as not being real doctors, because one thing is we know very well is that when a person has trouble with his eyes, he's going to come to us. There's such a value placed on vision. We hear this so many times from our patients: They'd rather be dead than blind.

ROBERT DEMAREST
Medical Art Director

It's clearly an artist's room. A large drawing board—the top of which is covered with a number of incomplete drawings of the major leg muscles— butts up against the window. Illustrations of body parts cover the walls; some signed by him at the bottom. Bones are scattered casually on a shelf and a skeleton stands almost dead center in the office. An incongruous object, a gumball machine, rests atop an open anatomy book. He sits on a high stool, his back to his drawing board. An air of contentment pervades this office as the room catches the last rays of sun in this summer twilight.

He's been the medical art director for the last eight years. His day is spent drawing illustrations for medical journal articles and books contributed to by the physicians. He also provides anatomical drawings for teaching lectures and presentations at scientific meetings. He has won Best Medical Illustrator of the Year awards five times. "I hang these awards up because it's convincing to the doctors. Doctors are very print-oriented. So when they see these awards, they say, 'He must be pretty good; it says so here on the wall!' "

What you're really doing as an illustrator is communicating. Take the brain—I'm not drawing so much what you see, as I am drawing the epitomy of all the brains that you have ever seen and all the knowledge of brains that I can garner. The brain that ends up on the paper is really a prototype of a brain so that people can learn from it.

As a student of this field, you study from a cadaver. You learn to do a perfect dissection of the organs, the tissue. And when you draw something, if you're going to draw from a specimen, the dissection has to be classic. You really have to know your anatomy, know what to cut away so that you have good material to draw from. Also, as a student, you must spend time in the operating room. That to me was the most interesting time of all.

My first operation here I passed out right on the operating room floor. It was quite an experience, but one that taught me a few things. The first was, not to arrive in the operating room until the surgery was underway. On that particular morning, the phone rang real early and the doctors said to come right away, they were doing a procedure that they wanted to have illustrated and this was a particularly appropriate case. I rushed right over, put on scrubs, and went right in to the operating room. They hadn't really finished prepping the patient, and since he was still awake, I got to meet him personally. I made contact, one human to another.

The fact that he was semiawake wasn't what got to me. It was the identity with another individual and the fact that he reminded me of my grandfather. So when they started to cut into him, the next thing I knew, I was gone. It was also very hot, and I hadn't had breakfast, and that may not have helped matters.

When I came to, the surgeon was calling for a needle and suture material to sew up my chin! I broke a tooth, cut my tongue. What I learned from that was not to identify with the patient, but to identify with the job at hand. I have to admit for the next year or more I would always arrive a little late, in fact after the patient was prepped and draped, when all that was evident of the patient was what you could see through the open square in the sheet covering him.

The time a medical illustrator spends in the OR is valuable for things that might not be obvious to the layman. I'm looking not so much at the material in the field as I am at the way the retractors pull the skin, or the placement of the hands of the surgeon. All this adds a certain verity, a certain truth to the illustration. The actual material that is being operated on, whether it's a shoulder or a heart or a stomach, is done very symbolically, because I want to do something the camera can't do, and that is to eliminate the unnecessary material. I want to get rid of the fat, the blood, the extraneous tissue. The camera is not discerning; the human eye is. And in the end, a drawing will communicate more meaningfully than a photograph. It's the judgment factor. I think it's a question of what you eliminate, not what you put in the drawing, that makes a drawing meaningful.

One of the exciting things about medical illustration—where I get my biggest thrill—is when I have an assignment that involves a long operation. My task is to take that ongoing dynamic procedure and break it up into a number of two-dimensional drawings to tell the story; to take a temporal procedure and freeze it into half a dozen drawings that can recapitulate in the viewer's mind the entire procedure. Then, when the surgeon comes in to see my sketches and says, "That's it! Let's finish them up!" I know I've achieved my main goal. I've communicated that story.

I spend part of my day doing book illustrations—getting all the paraphernalia together. Also, there is hardly a day where there isn't some kind of emergency—doctors are always last-minute people when it comes to papers or presentations. They're always in a hurry, needing slides overnight or needing drawings in a very short time because their deadlines are real. There's a lecture to be given or there's a paper that needs to be in, so we usually respond very quickly to those.

My field is to be of service to medicine. Physicians and students see my work, and perhaps they'll go on to expand the frontiers of knowledge, and, I hope, make life better for my fellow man. It sounds very noble, and I'm sure it sounds corny, but my personal philosophy is: there's only the people. That's the final equation. I think in some small way I'm of service to mankind—I truly believe that.

There's probably nothing more intimidating than a blank piece of paper. Even after all these years, when I'm driving to work, knowing that I've got to start a new illustration for a particularly prestigious client, I worry about it. Yet I know in my worry that once I start putting pencil to paper and come to grips with the illustration itself there's no more worry. It's still intimidating, though, because I want today's drawing to be better than yesterday's. I want the next drawing to be better than the one I won a prize for last year.

Artists are the luckiest people in the world because they can never become the consummate artist or illustrator. There's always something more to do. There's always that drive to be better. I'm reminded of Okasi's—he's a Japanese woodcut artist, the most famous Japanese woodcut artist—deathbed comment. He was in his nineties when he died, and his daughter reports that he said, "If I only had ten more years, five more, even one more year, maybe I could learn to draw." I feel in some small way that I say that same thing; it's a continual challenge.

I've been here working around this institution for thirty years, in and out of the operating room, and while I love medicine, I never felt the need to be a doctor. In fact, I think I have an advantage that most doctors don't have, and that is that I can be an orthopedic surgeon in the morning, vicariously, and an obstetrician in the afternoon. I can even be a neurosurgeon. And indeed, while I'm doing my work, I am, at least in spirit, all those things.

VII
PEDIATRICS

For years Babies' Hospital has been noted for its advanced treatment of childhood diseases and its pioneering work with premature infants. Physicians at Babies' have made medical advances in the last four decades that are still used to diagnose and treat children all over the world. One is the Apgar scoring system that enables a physician to assess a newborn's physical condition within seconds after birth; another is a treatment for hyaline membrane disease, a lung problem associated with prematurity, which took the life of President Kennedy's infant son Patrick. Physicians here have developed new treatments for leukemia in children and participated in the first successful heart transplant in a child. On the twelfth floor of Babies' is one of the nation's most advanced neonatal intensive care units. Infants in crisis, often within hours of delivery, are routinely transported here in mobile intensive care ambulances from other hospitals. The progress in caring for premature infants in recent years has been dramatic. In 1972, 29 percent of babies weighing two to three pounds at birth survived. By the end of 1986, that number had risen to 95 percent.

But advanced medical programs tell only half the story of Babies' Hospital. The other half unfolds in the form of social programs—some unique, some commonly employed in other hospitals—all of which support the philosophy: What is good for the child is good for us. Among the programs are a therapeutic day nursery for abused and neglected children and their families and a day hospital for children with cancer and blood disorders. Three New York City schoolteachers see to it that children who are confined to the hospital continue their schoolwork. A foster-grandmother program, funded by New York City, is responsible for the presence of five women in their seventies and eighties who come in every day to be "grandma" to lonely children.

Perhaps the most unusual program, however, is the one involving clowns from the Big Apple Circus. Several days a week, two or three young men come to the hospital to make "clown rounds" for the children. One morning I followed two of them, Dr. Stubbs (Michael

Christenson) and Dis-Orderly Gordoon (Jeff Gordon) as they went like pied pipers from room to room, enchanting the children. In one particular room, "Dr. Stubbs," dressed like a hobo in torn and tattered clothing, knelt in front of a silent little girl, hairless from cancer treatment, who appeared lost in an oversized wheelchair. He pulled a wilted tulip from his bag. "A smile from you will make this flower grow," he said, softly. Her huge dark brown eyes widened. It took all her energy to manage the tiniest hint of a smile, but she did it. The flower stood up. The clown shed a tear.

At noon, when the children's lunches were served, the clowns and I headed for the empty playroom. Over tuna-fish sandwiches and Cokes, I asked them to tell me about the program.

JEFF: This all started when we came to the hospital to give a performance for the children on Heart Day, an annual event when kids who have had heart surgery here come back for a big party.

MIKE: There were probably about four hundred people in the audience. Dr. Peter Salgo, the NBC medical correspondent, who's an anesthesiologist on staff here, was there, and before the show he said to me, "Now look out in the audience. You see all these children?" I said, "Yes." And he said, "Every one of those children would have been dead fifteen years ago." I was very moved by that experience and it was then that I had the idea of creating a situation in which the clowns would go to the kids instead of the kids coming to the clowns; not as a special treat, but as an ongoing, everyday aspect of hospitalization. That was really the seed of the Big Apple Circus Clown Care Unit.

JEFF: The hospital is such a serious place. We believe there's room for fun, for satire and humor. Laughter, as everyone knows, is the best medicine, and that's something we're professionals at purveying. We've learned to be very careful to regard the child's room as a safe haven. It's their place, so when we come onto the floor, we don't just barge in. We ask permission of the child—"Hello, can we come in?"

MIKE: And the reactions range from, "Oh, golly! A clown! Come on in!" to frightened screams—few, but some. So we don't push it. The thing is, we know we're going to be back, so if we have a child who is fearful we can just let it go, and the next time they see us they're not quite as scared, and the next time, and the next time, and eventually we get close.

JEFF: Ronnie was a good example of that. She's a little girl who's spent pretty much of her life on a respirator in the intensive care unit. She can only communicate by raising her eyebrows and blinking her eyes. At first when we came by, she would cry. She was kind of afraid of us, so we kept our distance from her. Eventually, over a period of three months or so, she got more accustomed to our presence at her bedside. Now she brightens up when we go in there, and she smiles at us and mouths, "Hi, clowns," and we talk about bubbles, or her latest color nail polish. She's a different child from the first time we visited her. She's a special case for us because she's one who is always here. It makes us feel good that she's drawn us into her life.

MIKE: When children are in crisis, you can become very involved very quickly and feel close to them in a limited amount of time. One day we met a Portuguese couple whose baby was having heart surgery. After his first postoperative day we went to his bed in the ICU and blew some bubbles and began to play with him. During the next week he got progressively better until finally he was transferred to the regular cardiac unit. Over a period of a month and a half, we followed him from the ICU down into cardiology and on the day of his discharge, right out the door.

JEFF: We happened to be on the elevator the day he was leaving. And as fate would have it, to say good-bye to him as he went out the front door.

MIKE: That was glorious. The other side of it is that we were in ICU and we spent time with a young boy who was on his way to Pittsburgh for a heart and lung transplant. He was so sick. We spent fifteen minutes clowning around with him. He was cracking up through his oxygen mask. We all had a ball. Then we learned that he died just hours after he left the facility.

JEFF: It was our first encounter with a child passing away and we realized that it was an honor to have shared this child's last laughter.

MIKE: Our clown team consists of Dr. Stubbs, Dr. Schmutz, and Dis-Orderly Gordoon. We start rounds at the first child's bed. "Good morning," I introduce myself, "I'm Dr. Stubbs." We give a preliminary examination, if it's a new patient. As the doc, I'll ask the first questions. You know, "How old are you? Are you married?" They always love that one—"Are you married?" I say, "I'm going to have to get a few details for the record." I carry an LP record in my case so I haul that out and start writing on it. And I ask the normal questions that doctors ask. "Does your nose ever turn red? Have you ever had any problem with your funny bone? Are you ticklish?" I give them a thorough exam. And then I write my findings on a piece of paper, crumple it up, and file it, just like they do here!

If the parent is there, sometimes I give the parent a prescription. I say, "Make sure your child is looking at you, and then cluck like a chicken and flap your arms and bob your head three times a day. It's very powerful. No more than three times a day." And they start giggling.

JEFF: Since I play a dis-orderly, I'm usually making some kind of a mess. I blow bubbles that tend to drift and leave some suds on the sheets or on the floor. I always make a big deal out of cleaning it up with toilet paper. My costume makes me look as though I have four legs—I wear a coat that has fake hands in it so it looks like I have two hands and four legs and I walk around . . .

MIKE: We have a lot of fun with the kids but also with the regular staff. On our way to the different floors, we'll go through the regular hospital. I look like a weird sort of doctor, and I'm walking with my patient who has four legs. If we're on an elevator, I'll lean over to him and say, "Are you experiencing any pain now?" He'll say, "No, doctor, not at all." I'll say, "Wonderful. Next week we can start work on your arms."

There are times when we'll simply sit with a child, just be there and sit with him, because that's what's needed. We don't always have to perform. Just the fact that we're there is important. When we come onto a floor we check first with the nurse. Sometimes she'll say, "So-and-so in room such-and-such just received chemotherapy and it would really be great if you'd go in and spend a little time."

JEFF: This morning Mike did his first nose transplant. He took a clown nose and put it on a little girl's mother's face with forceps. And the child was just giggling like crazy.

MIKE: What we're really looking for are those parts of a kid's experience here that we can pull out into our world and give back to them in a fun, lighthearted way. For instance, doctors making rounds. It's very common for doctors to come en masse around a kid. If it's an unusual symptom, each one will take a listen, and they can be pretty obnoxious. So we've incorporated making rounds with the kids, and sometimes we'll look at the child and say, "Oh, we better have a conference." And we turn and we do "Warl, weah, yah, yah, rarh!" and I include some animal noises in that and then turn back to the kid.

JEFF: The intensive care unit is the most fulfilling and, at the same time, the most difficult unit to be in. It's where all the chronically ill children are. Some children pass away there. There's a little boy, two years old, Mikey, who was hooked up to an IV, waiting for a heart.

MIKE: But we didn't know that. We just saw him for a week and a half as little Mikey, our friend. I personally thought that he was just there and on his way out because he didn't seem . . .

JEFF: He was real chipper. We figured he was on the road to recovery.

MIKE: So a few days later we came back and Mikey wasn't there. The nurse on the unit gave us a little note that said, "Michael got his new heart last night." We said, "He was here for a heart transplant? We didn't know. Where is he now?" She told us he was over in the Presbyterian Hospital heart surgery unit, so we looked at each other and we both said, "So, let's go!" We have security clearance—we have two badges that say D. Stubbs and D. Gordoon—and we can go anywhere we want to in the hospital. So we got on the elevator in clown costume and makeup, with regular lab coats and our IDs. We go to the coronary unit, we pushed the door opener, and these two huge doors went "*KSSSSSHHhhhhhh!*" and we walked in. Someone said right away, "Yes?" We said, "We're following a patient from Babies'—Michael—he got his heart last night. Where is he, please?"

They took us to his room. It had a huge glass window, and we stood there waving at him, and he was a little out of it, but he knew us! And he managed to even smile just a bit—but we knew he knew we were there for him.

JEFF: And we feel that!

MIKE: Exactly. You experience such joy in that moment. You look at a child and you see him smile, or maybe a child can't even muster the strength for that, but you watch him as he tries, and right at that moment you feel it.

JUDITH BUSHELOW
Play Therapist

The children's playroom. Chairs and tables covered in old spattered paint are scattered helter-skelter about the room. Children's paintings line the walls and a colorful mobile of an oversized Clark bar spins from a string attached to the ceiling. Smells of finger paints and paste permeate the room.

She's in her twenties, but looks very much like a young teenager. She wears her long brown hair parted in the middle and she is dressed in baggy blue overalls and a bright yellow T-shirt. "One color we never wear around here is white. Anything but White to the kids means painful. People who wear white give them shots; people who wear white stick them for blood tests. So we avoid that."

We have a lot of chronic patients here—kids who keep coming back. Since I've been here, I've watched a lot of them grow up.

We get as many children as we can to come to the playroom, because we think it's important for them to be in an environment with other kids and doing something fun. We bring them in on stretchers, wheelchairs, crutches—however we have to. With infants, we do things that help them learn about the world around them—having them grasp rattles, getting them to hear sounds. We sit them up and we work their legs and their arms and help them develop strength. With toddlers, it's exploring the environment. You let toddlers loose in the toddler room and you might as well stick them in a candy store because they just grab everything. So we'll sit and we'll play with a toy with them and show them how it works.

With the older children, doing things together gets them talking to each other—about being in the hospital, what it's like, their problems. It's real nice, because they realize they're not out of the ordinary. Here, everybody has some type of problem and they all support each other.

A wonderful relationship formed just a couple of weeks ago between two boys—one was eight and the other was twelve. The twelve-year-old boy came here from foster care for a medical problem. The eight-year-old was here for cystic fibrosis. They were put in the same room and quickly became great friends. Neither would come to the playroom without the other. Recently, the eight-year-old was discharged, so his mother brings him every now and then to see the older boy. They speak to each other on the phone every day, and it's a wonderful relationship for this foster-care boy, who hadn't had a lot of steady relationships. Here is one that will probably continue for a while. We try to put children of the same age into the same room for just that reason, and lots of wonderful relationships have developed. Kids coming to visit say "hi" and quite often ask if I've seen their old roommate.

There are always kids you remember. Something happens to jar your memory and there they are. One of my patients—a fifteen-year-old boy who was half Jewish and half Catholic—learned that I was Jewish, and he enjoyed talking to me about Jewish traditions. One day we just sat there and talked about matzo ball soup. That's what he wanted to talk about. He knew he was very ill, and in fact he eventually died of cancer. But it wasn't like he said to me, "I want to see a rabbi," or "I want to see a priest." He just wanted to talk about making matzo ball soup, or why with Orthodox Jews the men sit downstairs and the women sit upstairs. We didn't get into God or his beliefs in that. We just talked about general, traditional things. He loved it. It made him laugh. That was the type of relationship I had with him. I would ask him how he felt. "How are you feeling today? What happened today?" And he would tell me, "Oh, they stuck this into me," or "They did this, and I've been throwing up," and this and that. But that's as far as he wanted to talk with me about his disease. There were other people who were working with him who he specifically talked to about his illness and who were helping him cope with the fact that he was going to die.

We keep lots of medical play equipment here—miniaturized hospital beds, miniaturized operating tables, dolls. We have syringes, we have casting materials, stethoscopes. And informally, we'll sit down with children and say, "You're the doctor today and I'm the patient. What do I need to have done today, doctor?" Or, "I need to have my blood taken." We'll act out as a child would—"Oh, I'm scared. It's going to hurt"—and we'll talk to them and as we're acting it out we'll tell them things that need to be done to help them cope with the situation. For example, if a nurse comes to me and says a child is petrified of needles, what I will do is bring in the dolls and the syringes, either to the room or the playroom, and let them be the nurse and I'll be the patient and say, "I have to get a shot because I need my medicine," or I'll ask, "Why do children get shots?" They'll either answer, "I don't know," or "They need medicine," or "They were bad," or "They didn't eat all their peas." Children can misinterpret things as punishment for something that they've done. "I got sick because I had a bad thought about my brother," and this can come out in play. If that comes out, we correct it. "No, children don't get shots because they were bad or had bad thoughts about their brothers. Children get shots because it's one way of getting medicine. Just like getting pills; just like having an IV." We emphasize that over and over again to them so that they learn that they're not being punished. They have trouble understanding why something that makes them well can hurt so much.

The hardest ones are the oncology patients. So many of them have such poor prognoses. I very much want them to be happy. I like the feeling I get when I can make them smile and laugh. Sometimes we'll have a kid that just got some chemo drug that will make him sick as a dog in about an hour, come over here and run around for an hour until he doesn't feel well enough to continue. There's something about these kids, there's such a . . . it's very hard to explain it. There's a survival instinct in all of them. They just fight so hard to go on and to enjoy every day. It's so wonderful to be able to watch them and be with them. They're going through the toughest thing a child can go through, ultimately dealing with the fact that they're going to die. Regardless of what age they are—I don't care if they're six or sixteen—they know it. *They know it.* They're not always told, but they know it.

Band-Aids are really important to children. They signify a lot of things, but mostly they signify an end. The shot is over, here's the Band-Aid. They signify that you went through something. You'll have a little two-year-old come to you and say, "Boo-boo," and you'll say, "Oh, you have a Band-Aid, you had a boo-boo." They're telling you that something painful happened to them and here's the Band-Aid to show it. Young children also think that if there is a hole in their body, all the fluid is going to come out, so they need a Band-Aid to stop it. That's why Band-Aids are so important. So we emphasize that: "Ask the nurse for a Band-Aid." I'll have kids come up to me and they'll put Band-Aids all over my arms and give me a "shot" and I'll sit there and I'll hold still and I'll say, "Ouch," or I'll cry—giving them control. Also, I'm telling them it's okay to say "ouch," it's okay to cry.

Balloons are wonderful ways for children to vent their anger. I'll say to some of the younger ones, "When that doctor pokes you and when that nurse comes in and sticks you with a needle, you take this balloon and you 'bam' it. You just hit it so hard." I give them lots of different balloons. I tell them to think about people who make them mad. One seven-year-old boy's mother said that within fifteen minutes of getting stuck one day he was smiling after punching all these balloons out. What was making him mad was that he had no say. These people would come in and stick him—he had a spinal tumor and he had to go through a lot of terrible procedures and he was just mad.

Forget it. If I don't have a balloon in my pocket, I'm in trouble. And if you asked me what the big answer is, I wouldn't even have to think. I'd say, just off the bat—balloons and Band-Aids.

JAMES WOLFF, M.D.
Pediatric Oncologist

He's seventy-two years old and still very involved with his practice. His interest in pediatric oncology goes back to the fifties, when the field was practically nonexistent and when children with leukemia rarely survived a year after diagnosis. He has watched the discipline grow to the point where today children with cancer survive much longer and, indeed, often become free of disease. Years ago, he established a pediatric hematology (blood) oncology (cancer) service at Babies' Hospital. It became a major training program and still remains one of the busiest children's cancer centers in the country.

It takes a certain kind of person to work with children who have cancer. Indeed, many physicians can't deal with it at all. And many people have gone into pediatric oncology, tried it, and dropped out. People I've known. But that was ten or fifteen years ago, or twenty years ago, when most of our children died.

When I started in hematology, the outlook for childhood leukemias was zero. Because of the statistics, I felt that it wasn't good to tell kids that they had a fatal disease. I felt the parent should keep it from the child. We counseled the parent not to tell the child anything. After a little while, though, it became apparent to me that this was the wrong thing to do.

I had a very illustrative experience regarding that. We had a kid with Hodgkin's disease who was about eight when he was diagnosed. He was an only child of a widowed mother and they were as close as two peas in a pod. When we made his diagnosis, she was absolutely devastated. By then my thinking had changed and I felt that anybody who had Hodgkin's disease, even a child who was eight years old, should know what he had. The problem was, I couldn't get the boy's mother to let me tell him nor would she tell him. He would ask her, "Why am I going to the doctor all the time if I don't have something really wrong?" and she'd give him some foolish excuse. So finally one day—he was an adolescent by then—she said to me, "My son asked me last night if he had Hodgkin's disease. I said, 'Why do you think a thing like that?' 'Well,' he said, 'I saw a program on television and the person with Hodgkin's disease was getting all the same drugs I get.'" I told her if he ever asked again she had to tell him. I felt quite sure the boy knew already. I told her she was just kidding herself if she thought differently.

The boy asked again that night, and this time his mother told him. She called me the next day and thanked me, and said, "We laughed for half an hour. He told me that he knew all along." He had known for years but he didn't want to tell her because he was protecting her, and she wouldn't tell him because she was protecting *him*.

So now we always tell the parents their child has to know. Of course you can't tell a two-year-old he or she has leukemia. But even slightly older children will ask questions. As they ask questions you answer them honestly and it gives you a wedge to tell them something about the disease. And they almost always ask. If a child doesn't ask, it's because he doesn't want to know. In that case, you've got to tell him. You've got to find a way of telling him.

They're trying to raise a million and a half dollars to establish the James Wolff Chair in Pediatric Hematology and Oncology. The purpose of it is to support the salary of the head of that service. I'm honored, although I'm not sure how it all got started. I think it came from the chairman of the Department of Pediatrics and from my successor as head of the Division of Hematology and Oncology. I think the two of them decided it would be a nice thing for me and it would help them raise funds, perhaps.

I suppose a large part of the reason for this "chair" has to do with the service I developed here. When I came to Babies', there was no department of pediatric oncology, so I established one. I had a training program where we always had one or two fellows, and we established a fairly active service, both inpatient and outpatient. I also developed a lot of the laboratory work in which they're now investigating how best to diagnose this disease. We became one of the major training programs in the country.

Over the years, this field has grown tremendously, partly as a result of the extensive research going on, but also because there are so many interested people. We work in pediatric oncology as a team now, using different disciplines such as pediatrics, pediatric oncology, pediatric radiation oncology, pathology, pediatric surgery, and other pediatric subspecialties. We have an equally strong crew of paramedical people—chemotherapy nurses and nurse oncologists. We also have people who are tuned-in to the psychosocial aspects of the disease, and they're very good at it. In fact, they're often better than the doctors. They're more appreciative of the emotional aspects and are better trained to handle them.

Today, because of the new treatments we can offer these children, an increasing number of our patients go into remission. Many of them are able to live semi-normal lives. They go to school and take part in all the activities. If they're symptomatic, if they're not totally in remission, they go as much as they can. Sometimes they have to drop out for a while because they have to come in for treatment, but we try to keep them in class as much as possible. These kids have such remarkable courage. If they've lost their hair, they go to school with hats on. The girls usually get wigs. Even the five- and six-year-olds. Some of the boys don't care at all, and others just put on a baseball cap and off they go.

There still are a number of areas where we haven't really found good answers. Certain diseases have not responded well to chemotherapy. So we look to other approaches. Bone marrow transplantation is something that has come to the forefront in the past few years, not only for leukemia and aplastic anemia, but for solid tumors as well. I think there's a great future for that. Then there's the area of monoclonal antibody treatment, where you identify an antibody against a certain type of substance on the cell wall, and you use these antibodies both for diagnosis—to show whether somebody has disease in some part of the body—and in treatment. That's in its infancy, but I think there's a great deal that might be expected in the future from it.

To be a good pediatric oncologist, you have to be somewhat objective. You can't spend every minute of your life worrying about your patients. Not that the people who are in it aren't empathetic to the children. They are. But you have to be able to say, "This is the state of the world—this is the way things are." The main thing is not to divorce yourself from the problems that the patients have but at the same time to know there are certain things you can't alter. Look, I still take these patients home with me—in my mind. I think about them at night. If I leave a small child who is critically ill, I always wonder if I've done everything I could have possibly done to make him comfortable, to give him a chance for survival. I think of them, of course. But I think about the good times, too. Like seeing a great majority of the patients getting well. Like recalling the days when we had a hundred percent deaths from leukemia, and knowing that now we get maybe sixty-five or seventy percent survivals. That's what you have to think about. That's the best part—seeing so many of these little children live.

MARY DAVENPORT
Foster Grandmother

She's seventy-seven years old.

A foster grandma loves a child. That's all we do. In this program, they assign us only one baby, and every day when we come in, we spend time with that one child. It's usually a child whose parents can't always come to visit or one whose mother doesn't come at all. When I get assigned a baby, he's mine until he gets discharged from the hospital—or dies. Everything that I would do for my own child I do for this baby. Everything. I've only had six or seven since I'm here—and that's five years now.

I think we get two-something an hour to do this. It's called a stipend. This way we don't pay anything out of what little money we get now. But anyway, we didn't come here for money. We came here to love a baby.

My baby now is Samuel. Samuel was born here, and he's been "my baby" his whole life. Thirteen months and he's never gone home. He has stomach problems. I'm not sure what it is, but it doesn't matter. We never really need to know the medical things about our babies. His mother comes, but she has other children at home who need her, too, so I care for Samuel in the mornings.

When I get here, first thing I do is put on my red jacket—all the grandmas wear red jackets—and then I go up to his room. I have this thing with him where I stand outside the door and he can't see me and I whistle. Soon as I do that you'll hear him say, "Grandma?" Then I go in and I love him up a bit, then I put a big tub in his bed and I give him a bath. He just makes a mess, Samuel does. Then I dry him off and put him down in the playpen while I fold his pajamas. In the meantime I'm talking, talking, talking and he's just talking right back. He can say so many words now. If the doctor walks in the room Sammy'll begin to pull to me because he sees the white coat. That's why we all wear red, all the grandmas. It's amazing how the red, like magic, takes that fear from him. Yes, red means love. And they love us.

We spend the morning together, and after his lunch I put him back in his crib and put him to sleep. That's when I visit with some of the other children. Sometimes they send me to ICU. I have a little girl there who was with me when she was about three months old and then she went home. Now she's three years old and she's back here again.

I still think a lot about one particular baby. Her name was Bonnie. She was a dream. She was the prettiest little girl you ever saw. She couldn't hear, she couldn't see, and she couldn't speak. And I spent all my time with this little girl. I didn't dare look at another baby. She was fifteen months when she died. She just died. They knew she wouldn't live. When I came in that morning, one of the nurses said to me, "Oh, grandma, Bonnie's gone." I said, "Thank God." I wanted God to take her. They had told her mother not to get too involved with the baby, so it wasn't the mother's fault that she didn't come, but you had to love her. I did every-thing for Bonnie, and I told the doctor, "She may not hear, she may not see, but she can tell something, because she always knows when I walk in that room."

We have so much to give to a child. We don't have to worry about caring for our own children anymore. We don't have the problem of money because we don't need that much anymore. We don't even have the problem of food, because foster grandmothers eat for free when we're here. But that's not the whole story. The best part of this is that it gives you the feeling of not being lonely, of being wanted, of family. Yes. That's it. You feel like you're part of a family again.

PENELOPE BUSCHMAN, R.N.
Psychiatric Nurse

As she talks she refers to the pictures of children that line the walls of her office. They're children of all ages, sizes, races. She calls them "my kids." They are children who have been struck by severe or life-threatening illnesses—children who have had cancer, diabetes, severe asthma, cystic fibrosis, and AIDS.

Even though much of the scientific literature says a child isn't capable of anticipating his own death or even of understanding death until he's well into his ninth year, I think children with severe, chronic, terminal disease—maybe as young as three—have a sense of their bodies not working, and have a very acute need not to be separated from their families.

I can remember when I was working as a pediatric staff nurse, when a very young child was near death, a red flag on the field for us was if the child stayed awake all night. Crying. Wanting something. Wanting some physical presence. I think what we hear from the very young children—the two- and three-year-olds—is fear in anticipation of permanent separation and a real inability to be absent from the mother. Of needing and wanting her. Very often a four- or five-year-old child will begin to talk about dying. Billy, one of our cancer patients, was five when he died. He talked about death much more than any of the other children his age. An aunt had died about a year prior to Billy's death, and he was absolutely intrigued; he wanted to go to the cemetery, and asked all kinds of questions about the box in the ground.

I can spend hours with these children and talk about all sorts of things, but rarely will they ask me, point blank: "Am I going to die?" If that happens, I'm interested in knowing what prompted the question. Was the child worried about dying or were there other things bothering him? I would also want to have some sense of where the family stood on that issue, and whether or not the child had asked the family. Did the family answer him? Did they say, "Yes, you are dying"?

I'm thinking of David, a nine-year-old boy who had a lot of difficulty asking questions about his disease. He had a form of leukemia that was very difficult to treat and that was fatal. Essentially his treatment would help him for a while, but not for a long period of time. He was a very troubled little boy and I remember there was a time when he needed some answers. But he planned a strategy first. What he did was, he threw a toy airplane under his bed and then called me into the room and asked me to get it for him. While I was wiggling under the bed to get his toy, he asked me for the first time, "What's wrong with me?"

Well, it took me a few minutes to crawl out from under the bed, so I had some time to think, and I said, "David, what is it that you're asking me? Are you asking me about your sickness or are you asking me about some of the other problems you've been having?" He said, "Right now I'm asking you about the infection." So we answered that question.

Now this is a boy who persisted at his own pace, and I think had I hurriedly answered his question there might not have been any further discussion. But there was something about the way he structured that interview that really allowed me to respond to him kind of slowly.

He was a classic example of how children anticipate things. He was an only child who had been adopted at about age five and he was dearly loved by his parents. His mother was here every single day with him. She didn't stay overnight. He had gotten to the point where he was able to manage pretty comfortably with the nursing staff and he felt okay about staying on his own. His father worked on one of the bridge construction crews way up on the high wires. Whenever we needed to get in touch with his father it was rather an elaborate procedure and we had to give ourselves a lot of lead time to allow him to get down and here.

Anyway David's condition had begun to deteriorate and at that point we had been talking with the family about the fact that the time was fairly short. David had called one of the student nurses who was working with him that particular day and asked her very directly if he was dying. She said yes, and he panicked! He was furious! He told her to leave and find me.

It was a shame it happened that way, but it was an error of innocence. She didn't know him. She didn't know the context and in a real effort to be honest and open and helpful to this child, she just said yes. She came to find me and she was in tears. She felt terrible. She didn't know quite what to do, so I took her with me into his room because I felt she was hurting. He was so angry. He said, "Do you know what she said to me? She told me that I'm dying!" "What did you ask her?" I said. "All she did was answer you."

Then he said, "So, well, am I?"

It was the first time he asked me, point blank. He had talked about his illness, he had talked about not getting better, but he had never asked, "Am I dying?" I said, "David, what is it that you want to know? You've asked something, somebody answered what she thought she heard. What is it that you want to know?" He said, "Am I dying right now?" I took the nurse's stethoscope from her pocket and I listened to his heart and I said, "You know, your heart is beating very strongly. You're breathing. We're talking together. You're moving about. Nothing has changed." He said, "Okay. My mother isn't coming in until very late today. Could you call her and ask her to come in a little bit earlier, and could you also call my father?" and I said, "Yes, of course."

I never take those requests lightly, so I called his mother and she asked me, "Has anything changed?" and I said "No, except that David asked that you come in earlier and that's an unusual request." She got here by midmorning and his father came in a few minutes later. And David died that afternoon at two.

I remember another lovely five-year-old boy named Jimmy, who was one of eight children in his family, and who had been diagnosed as having leukemia when he was about two and a half. There are a lot of poignant memories connected to that special little boy and to his family. He had been in remission for a good two and a half years and had done reasonably well and had even started kindergarten. His family was enjoying that wonderful time with him. It wasn't long afterward that he relapsed and soon after that he died here at Babies' Hospital. We had worked together and his mother and father had anticipated their child's death in the best way that they could, and they were here with him and taking care of him and, indeed, he essentially died in their arms.

The evening of Jimmy's death, his mother and father went home and suggested to the children that they each select a very special item belonging to Jimmy, something they would like to keep, something to help them remember him. Then they all put these things together into a box. There were some wonderful possessions of Jimmy's that went into what became "the memory box." One of the sisters found his old dirty, smelly sneakers and put those in the box because they always made her think of him. Others chose very sort of homey, special toys, clothing, possessions.

The box was kept in a very special place in the family room. The rule in this family was that neither the children nor the parents could look through the box alone. They needed to find a buddy. They went through the box very frequently at first. They would look at the box and inevitably there would be the tears and the reminiscing and this went on for a while. After a time, when the box was being opened a little less frequently, his mother decided that it should be moved upstairs, and it eventually moved up to their attic where it still resides. Occasionally somebody in the family will need to go back up to the memory box just to be close to him.

I find very often that children of all ages have certain things that they want to do when they begin to realize that they may not live. One very special young man, a sixteen-year-old, who died here very recently, had been diagnosed as having leukemia when he was about seven. We had known him and worked closely with him and his family all those years. He had had a couple of relapses, and with each relapse his chances for long-term survival diminished.

The last time he came in, the oncologist had to give him the news of his most recent relapse, and he was devastated. He came in with his father and they were absolutely shaken. The oncologist wanted to begin his reinduction treatment; she wanted to give him some treatment right away, and in a taciturn voice he asked for some time. He seemed to be struggling and I asked if I could sit with him and talk with him or listen to him or just be with him. His father took a walk; he just couldn't be there.

The boy said that there were a number of things that were very important to him. He knew that once he started on this particular form of treatment, he might not be able to leave the hospital for some time; indeed, he might not survive the treatment. He said, "You know, I have a girlfriend." She was away at school up in Massachusetts and he said, "I planned to visit her this weekend. I'd like to see her. I'm not sure that I'm going to tell her this, but I do need to see her. I also plan to see my best friend who is at school not far away from where my girlfriend is. I really need to spend some time with him."

There was real urgency to his request, and he said, "Can I ask for that time?" I said, "Why not?" So we sat down with the oncologist and she said, "Well, quite frankly I'm hesitant to say yes, because your count is low and you could get into a problem with some bleeding. You need to know that there's some danger in your doing this." He said, "I know that.

But right now it's most important for me to do what I need to do." So the oncologist, with a lot of grace and with her fingers crossed, agreed.

He traveled up to Massachusetts that weekend. He saw his girlfriend, whom he decided not to tell, and then he was able to talk with this very dear friend and bare his soul to him. Only then did he come back and begin a reinduction course of treatment. He lived for only a couple of months after that.

We're seeing more and more children with AIDS. Some of them are children of drug-abusing parents, who are born with the disease. Others come here because they have developed it as a result of contaminated blood transfusions. It's such a tragedy when a child develops AIDS through a transfusion, especially when the family has agreed to and encouraged transfusion treatment. These children are in an enormous amount of pain, and since there is no cure for AIDS, eventually they all will die.

I find that I remember many of the children I've worked with who have died, around the anniversary times that the families remember them. Very recently a mother called me—the mother of a young man who has been dead for about seven years—simply to say hello and to let me know how she was. I asked her what made her think of me at this particular time and she said, "Oh, it will be his birthday tomorrow." And I said, "It's curious, because I've been thinking about him." She said she needed to talk with someone who knew him and who remembered him and who could talk with her about him and not tell her she shouldn't talk about him now. You know, you never get over the loss of a child. Never, never, never, never, never.

There *are* happy endings here too. One young woman who was a patient here wanted very much to write a symphony. She was about fourteen when she was first diagnosed with Ewing's sarcoma, a form of solid tumor. She was treated here and did very well. Eventually, though, she had a recurrence of her disease and was told she needed to come back in for additional treatment. At that point, she said she needed to have some more time to complete her work before she could come back. And she did. She completed her symphony and then she came back. I don't know that she ever needed to do anything with it beyond that; it was not just a course requirement, it was, for her, something that she needed to complete in case she didn't have an opportunity to complete anything else. In the meantime she has gotten married and been able to start and finish a whole lot of other lovely experiences.

I try to let my day here end here, because I have healthy children at home and I need to make a transition so I can have a normal semblance of family life. It's not easy, though, particularly if I'm concerned about a child or about a family. I might be successful in blocking them from my consciousness, but I end up dreaming about them or thinking about them in some other way. Like early in the morning, while I'm still in bed, they'll pop up in my thoughts.

Working with these children and their families has given me an enormous amount of respect and appreciation for the resiliency of the human spirit and a real belief that that is the most important thing there is. It doesn't matter how much technology we're able to create to deal with the workings of the human body. Unless the human spirit is cared for, we're going to miss the mark altogether.

JOHN DRISCOLL, JR., M.D.

Director,
Neonatal Intensive Care Unit

He's a large man who appears all the larger as he stands over a tiny infant. He was a college athlete who played basketball and lacrosse. Now he coaches a grammar school basketball team. "That's my way of staying a kid myself.

"When I went to medical school at Bowman-Gray in North Carolina, I came under the influence of the chief of pediatrics there, a fellow named Weston Kelsey. He was a charismatic person, a small man whose lab coat came within four inches of the floor. He was a pipe smoker, wore a bow tie, and was a great storyteller. He was this mite of a man who drove a taxi in New York City and played linebacker for the Chicago Bears, if you believed the stories he told. But he was an extraordinary physician and an extraordinary teacher, and it was because of him that I went into pediatrics."

In 1972, when I started in the nursery, babies who were brought here with birth weights between two and three pounds had a twenty-nine percent survival rate. Seventy-one percent of them died. Babies under two pounds, ninety-five percent died. Last year, of babies between two and three pounds, ninety-eight percent survived, and babies of less than two pounds, around seventy-five percent survived. So that's all happened during my lifetime in neonatology. I think if you had told me when I started here what the future held, I would have thought you were crazy.

Neonatology is the field of medicine that deals with illness in the first twenty-eight days of life. But, in fact, the field is more correctly described as perinatal-neonatal medicine. Perinatal refers to the period of time from the twentieth week of gestation through birth, and neonatal goes from birth to twenty-eight days.

The field has changed dramatically, so that now in some cases we get involved with mothers before the baby's delivery, mothers who have medical problems, or mothers who develop obstetrical problems which in some way threaten the fetus. We're involved with families often for weeks prior to delivery of the baby. For instance, if we know it's going to be a high risk infant, we often transport the mother-to-be here so she can deliver her baby in our delivery room and we can take over immediately.

We have close to seven hundred and fifty admissions a year to our neonatal ICU [NICU]. More than fifty percent of them are full-term babies who are very ill. If it's a healthy infant, but under two thousand grams [four pounds], it will be admitted here. The smallest baby we've ever treated was four hundred grams, that's less than a pound, probably twelve ounces: You could hold that baby in the palm of your hand.

I've always felt very strongly, and as an institution we've been committed to this philosophy, that our goal shouldn't be solely to improve our survival rate. We must also assure a quality of life that is meaningful to the sick infant. In the early seventies one of the concerns was that reversing the high mortality rate would mean saving more and more small babies who would ultimately be impaired. Many of these premature babies were significantly impaired; they were blind, mentally retarded. There were institutions that were reporting rates of cerebral palsy exceeding fifty percent, eighty percent in their premies. But today, more gratifying even than the fact that survival rates have improved to the point where they defy belief is that the quality of life for these babies has improved as well. In our own unit, eighty-five percent of the premature babies we discharge are absolutely normal. Fifteen percent will have some sort of a problem, but the distribution of problems within that fifteen percent has also changed. There are children among that fifteen percent who have cerebral palsy, one of the complications of premature delivery, but in a fair number of those children, it's not the sort that you can detect by looking at the baby. It's slight. It won't allow the girl to be a ballerina or the boy to be top athlete, but they'll have their mental capabilities, and perhaps only a slight physical limitation to contend with. But we're not willing at this point in 1987 to sit back and say, "Well, we've done it all. Ninety-eight percent of the babies survive." Our efforts are now being directed at reducing that fifteen percent of impaired babies.

Another major problem is that premies' brains are not fully developed at the time of delivery. The brain grows during the first eighteen months of life. In the center of the brain, there is an area called the germinal matrix that provides cells that migrate out to the periphery of the brain, and that area has a very rich blood supply. There's a tendency for the premature baby to bleed into that area. Now a mild bleeding is not associated with any problems at all, but there are some babies who start out with a mild bleed into that area that then extends into the whole brain. Children who have that severe type of bleed are almost universally impaired, and their impairment is generally severe. That problem is currently under investigation in a lot of units around the country in an attempt to understand why they bleed and when they bleed. If we can understand that, the next step will be to prevent it.

But I'm not eternally optimistic. I think we're always going to have a nucleus of babies in whom something goes wrong, either very early in gestation or in the middle of pregnancy, that was unrecognized by anybody and that will result in a baby who will be retarded.

In this particular unit, it costs about six hundred some-odd dollars a day per baby. For the baby under two pounds birth weight, the average length of stay in the NICU is a hundred days. So it's not unusual for a baby to get out of here with a fifty- or sixty- or seventy-thousand-dollar hospital bill In my opinion, that is absolutely justifiable if the child is going to lead a meaningful life, is going to contribute to himself, his family, and society. But what about the children who go home—you've done everything you can—and it's not a good outcome? Does that mean it's not worthwhile spending that money? I have a lot of trouble with that, because we can't always tell what's going right and what's going wrong with these babies. It's not until later, down the road a piece, that it's obvious that we have a problem.

I think one of the paradoxes of what we're doing is that we're spending millions of dollars to provide care here, and when these children go home, there may not always be appropriate support. I think each one of these units ought to have—funded by state, city, local mechanisms—a follow-up program that looks at these children. Follows them along. Says, "Look, we may have a problem coming. If we do, here's what we're going to do to assure that that child can achieve his maximum potential." I see that as a continuity. It's not good enough to pour all this money into getting the fetus to the point where he or she can be delivered alive, continue to pour money into his care until he goes home, and then say, "Sayonara."

For as long as I've been here, we've felt very strongly that our goal is not to save life at all costs, but rather to respect life; to recognize when there are major problems with a given baby, to be forthright with families about what that problem is and what the immediate and long-term implications of that problem would be to that baby and that family. In the appropriate circumstances, we must give the family the information that will allow them to make a decision about whether they feel that care is appropriate for this baby or not. If it's not, you can either not initiate it in the first place, or discontinue it if you've already initiated it.

I think that families want information. They don't want to be protected or coddled. They want the facts as best we can give them, and then they need to make decisions. On the other hand, we are also the ombudsmen for the child and we have to be prepared for the situation where somebody is saying, "I don't want you to do this, this, or this," and we say, "Hey, wait a minute. This child is perfectly salvageable. The probabilities of a normal life are very high and we're going to go after this baby. We're going to treat this baby."

There are very few things in the nursery except for, say, chromosomal abnormalities, where you know by looking at the baby that the baby is going to be retarded. If they have certain chromosomal abnormalities— Downs' is not a good example because although these children are retarded they're quite happy and can lead meaningful lives—that have distinctive physical characteristics, you can say to the family, "Look, with this cluster of physical abnormalities it probably means the chromosomes are abnormal at such-and-such a position. It'll take us forty-eight hours to get that answer, but if in fact that's the case, you should be aware that fifty percent of the babies die in two months, eighty to ninety percent will be dead in a year. Of the ten percent who do survive, one hundred percent are retarded." In this situation our position has always been that if this child needs heroic care, we would recommend that it not be given, that we make the baby comfortable, feed the baby, nourish the baby, but if the baby requires respirator care, that it not be rendered to him. This is what we present to the family but in the end we tell them it is their decision.

There was recently a case where the parents didn't want the baby treated and the law made the baby a ward of the court and saw that she was treated. That wouldn't happen here when, in the opinion of our attending staff, keeping the baby alive is a reasonable decision. We've had very rare but occasional instances where families have said, "We don't want you to treat our baby," and where we've said, "That's not acceptable." I think there's a certain amount of trust that has to be established and I think we've been successful in establishing it here.

Every June we have a reunion in the garden of all our babies who have come through the neonatal ICU. We watch them as they grow from year to year. It's a great time for the staff *and* the families. And when families can't come, man, it's a major disappointment. In some ways, for many families, it's kind of a completion of the process. When they go out of here initially, they're awash with emotions—concern for the baby, fear of what's going to happen down the road. I think the first reunion often is their acceptance of that whole process. It allows them to express something they never have before, how grateful they are to the nursing staff and to the medical staff, for what the team did for their baby.

KATHERYN ROSASKO, R.N.

Research Nurse Clinician,
Neonatal Intensive Care Unit

She started as a staff nurse in 1972, when the neonatal nursery was about twenty-five years old and she was twenty-eight. Two years ago she stopped doing staff nursing because of orthopedic problems. She concentrates now on research projects, some of which include studies focusing on the best way to provide respiratory care for infants with underdeveloped lungs and the development of a formula that will provide the best nourishment to a premature infant. After five minutes with her, it's clear she misses working with the babies.

The dreams nurses dream tend to be alike. They're anxiety dreams: "Did I check this? Did I do that right?" You're a professional, so no matter what disasters happen with a baby, you have to be clear headed, rational, and you do what has to be done. But the emotions are always there. And they come out at times when you least expect them. For instance, I can be riding home on a bus and just suddenly I'll be wiping tears away and trying to be very discreet so that no one will know.

We have an ethics committee here, which was in the planning stage prior to the controversy over the Baby Doe regulations that the federal government tried to impose. We deal with highly sensitive issues such as when to support life artificially in a very ill baby and when to withdraw support. When I first came here there was the feeling that once you started treatment on a baby you really couldn't withdraw it. We now feel it is more appropriate to review each baby on a day-by-day basis; if it's initially appropriate, if you feel that there is any reasonable hope of benefiting the baby, then you go all out, but if conditions change over a period of time and you're faced with a losing battle, then it is appropriate to discuss the withdrawal of the treatment.

Historically, right back to the Hippocratic Oath, the approach has always been to do everything you could to sustain life. But modern medical technology many times enables us to sustain life in a patient where we're doing all the vital functions mechanically—the baby will never do them on its own. Take a very premature baby, a baby that was born close to the time of viability, who has developed complications involving multiple systems of its body, and who has developed perhaps the most ominous complication—a massive bleed into the brain, a type of hemorrhage that is incompatible with life afterwards. Do you treat that baby? This is an issue that might be brought before our ethics committee.

The ethics committee is made up of people from different backgrounds. In addition to doctors and nurses, we have a theologian, a lawyer, and a medical anthropologist. Dr. Driscoll is the head of it. There are different ways a baby is presented to the committee. A doctor caring for the baby might present the case, or another staff member—a nurse, for instance, who is uneasy about the way things are going. Even the parents could—if they wish—ask for a presentation.

Several months ago a doctor who used to be a fellow here and is now an attending at another hospital in New York called up Dr. Driscoll and asked if he could present a patient they were having a problem with. It happened to be a very small premature baby with a massive hemorrhage in the brain. It was on a respirator and needed other life support equipment. I think he knew that it was reasonable to withdraw support from that baby, but I think perhaps he didn't feel enough support where he was, and he just wanted some sort of confirmation from our committee that there was no other alternative.

The main purpose of the ethics committee is to explore the issues, to try to reach a consensus about what to do in each particular case, to make other people more aware of how to sort out the ethical issues and how to approach them. But we have no power to mandate a decision on how a particular baby will be cared for. For instance, if the doctor who presented it doesn't agree with the ethics committee's feelings, he doesn't have to abide by them.

In one case a baby's parents came to a meeting that was convened because we were going to try to save their baby using an experimental procedure that was to be done here for the first time. The baby was literally dying. He had a problem called persistence of fetal circulation as a result of being born with a diaphragmatic hernia. This is a problem whereby the pathways for circulation that exist in the fetus and are supposed to close at birth, remain intact and blood is shunted *away* from the lungs instead of *to* them. So the baby gets too little oxygen.

This was a full-term baby. But because of his diaphragmatic hernia, his intestines were in his chest, and so his lungs had not developed fully. The doctors first had to do a surgical procedure to bring the intestinal organs back into the abdomen, and then to repair the diaphragm. The only babies who survive with this problem are those whose lungs are not too small to sustain normal respiratory function. But his lungs weren't big enough.

You try to deal with this problem by using a respirator and giving certain types of medication, but in a certain number of these babies, that just doesn't work. And that's the point we had reached with that little baby boy on this particular morning when I came in to care for him. He was very poorly oxygenated and we were doing all we could for him. Then our respiratory care specialist began talking about this experimental procedure called extracorporeal membrane oxygenation [ECMO], which, at the time, only three other hospitals in the nation were doing, and they had only small numbers of patients to report on.

The doctors in our hospital who were working on the procedure had done it only on laboratory animals, but we knew that we were going to lose this baby if we didn't do something to help him. There was no question. This baby was dying.

It was decided that we should attempt it. So the process began—going through legal and administrative channels to get permission. The mother came in from the other hospital where she had delivered the baby two days earlier, and we all went into the conference room—the surgeon, the neonatologist, the parents, and me. They presented the baby's problem to the parents and described the experimental technique and told the parents all the possible complications. They explained that there were a few other places that did this procedure, but they were far away and the baby was much too sick to even think of transporting it. We said that we had only done it on a couple of laboratory animals, but that it was all we had to offer them. If they were willing to take the risk, we would be willing to attempt it. And so they agreed we should go ahead.

The procedure is done using a heart-lung machine, but with a special type of membrane that has been designed specifically to deal with the problems of very tiny lungs. Having the machine oxygenate the blood allows the spasm of the pulmonary artery to resolve on its own. Using ECMO, you take over the circulation for the baby, bypass the baby's heart and lungs, and you oxygenate the baby on cardiopulmonary bypass until the baby can be weaned from the respirator.

You can't use just a respirator on the baby at that particular time because if you allow the baby to remain in this condition while you wait for the lungs to improve on their own, you're risking brain damage and eventual respiratory failure and death. On ECMO, you're bypassing the lungs, but you're giving the baby very well-oxygenated blood. Then, gradually, as the lungs improve, the pulmonary artery spasm decreases. What you aim for is that point where you can easily wean the baby from the respirator within a few days.

The baby did *incredibly* well. It was wonderful. To go from a point when I was literally thinking of how I would help his parents in their grieving, to a time when I watched them take home a healthy baby boy who has been fine three years since—is just so wonderful. I can't explain it in words, but in all my years of being a nurse I have never before had such a feeling of winning one from the Grim Reaper. I mean, we really cheated him out of that one.

JERI MEHLING, R.N.

Nurse,
Neonatal Intensive Care Unit

She lives just over the bridge, in New Jersey. She went to nursing school straight out of high school, worked downtown for a while, and decided she wanted to be closer to home. "I didn't see an ad for this job. I just called them up, asked what they had in newborn intensive care. They said I should come up, which I did. It was awe inspiring, the whole thing. The hospital. Coming to this floor. Walking into the unit . . ."

To an outsider, the neonatal unit must look like something out of the twenty-second century. It's a conglomeration of lights flashing at you, buzzers going, machines hissing. And the babies. They really look like something from outer space. Since this is an intensive care unit, the babies who come here are either very, very tiny or very ill, or both, and the important thing is to constantly monitor their vital signs. To do that, we have to hook the baby up to all kinds of machines. A premature baby under three pounds is put into an isolette, which is like a small plastic box with a little mattress. She has little electrodes pasted on her chest with plastic disks which contain small wires, attached to a machine so we can continuously monitor her heart. Her blood pressure is measured through a line placed either into the umbilicus or into a peripheral artery. If she's very,

very small she may have aluminum wrapped around her, like a baked potato, to keep the heat in. They place a heat shield, which looks like a plastic bubble, inside the isolette so that when you open the isolette door, the cold air doesn't rush in. Sometimes we even put Saran Wrap over that because these babies drop their temperature so easily.

If the temperature drops on a baby, we come in with the heat lamps. When they're very small their liver is immature, so they'll get yellow or jaundiced. We treat that with phototherapy with an ultraviolet light. And then, while they're under that, because it's like staring into the sun, they have to have their eyes covered. We cover the baby's eyes with little gauze pads and then we'll put a hat over her head which we may bring down over her eyes so we don't have to use tape on the gauze pads.

So picture this sweet little baby, only about a foot long—a normal-sized baby is usually eighteen to twenty-two inches—wrinkled because it hasn't grown into its skin yet, lying there with all this paraphernalia. It's got to be so frightening to someone seeing it for the first time, especially a parent. We encourage parents to touch and to hold their babies, as long as the babies are stable. They can even put a little tape recording of their voice into the baby's isolette, if they want to. Or they bring a little music box, and we'll play it for the baby.

We have here what we refer to as a regional perinatal network. This is a network of affiliated hospitals in Connecticut, New York, and New Jersey. If any of these hospitals has a newborn in trouble, they call us and we pick up the baby. We go out with our transport team—one of our pediatric fellows and a nurse who has been trained. We have a transport isolette that's equipped with a respirator, a monitor, temperature controls, and a case with all the drugs and supplies we might need for the trip between the hospital where we pick up the baby and here. We go by ambulance, and there are always two drivers, just in case.

One particular transport, we were called to a hospital in New Jersey where a baby had just been born and was in terrible distress. The baby was very unstable and we had to bring him back here; he was only an hour old. When we arrived at the hospital, we went directly to the baby. We put him into an isolette and we took him up to see his parents in the mother's room.

We always take the babies to see the parents before we leave the referring hospital so they can see the baby, touch the baby. If it's a sick baby they usually hand it right over to the pediatrician in the delivery room; the mother might not have even seen it. So we always go to see the parents in the hospital room before we leave, even with the sickest of babies. Even if we just walk in for two minutes. This baby was on a hundred percent oxygen, which uses our tank really fast, so we wanted to get into the ambulance, onto the ambulance oxygen, and preserve our tank for the trip back.

In the ambulance, ten minutes out from Presbyterian, the baby started changing color and we had to stop. We had already stopped three or four times, because when we're rolling sometimes the monitor won't pick up real well and you have to watch the baby for color changes. So every time we thought the baby might have been in a little bit of trouble, we said, "Stop," so our tracing would come back to normal. Then, all of a sudden, the baby's heart stopped—he had arrested.

The first thing we had to do was pull over on the side of the Palisades Interstate, because you can't resuscitate a baby while the ambulance is moving. Then we started trying to revive him. You get so scared when that happens. That's why you have to be trained to go out on transport. When you're in that situation with only one doctor on board, you only have four hands. So either the nurse will be "bagging" the baby [breathing for the baby artificially, using a hand-operated device called an ambu-bag, something like a bellows] so the doctor can give the medication, or the other way around. This time the doctor was pushing the oxygen, and I was giving the drugs. He said, "Give this much of the bicarbonate that you're holding," and my hands were shaking, and I was saying, "Am I giving it too fast?" He said, "A little faster." I was trembling. "Okay, it's a little faster. Is it too fast?" "Okay, a little slower."

An arrest always seems like it takes hours when it just takes minutes. That time it seemed like forever. When we got his heart going again, we took off. When we arrived back here, they were waiting for us downstairs at the ER ramp. Members of the security department always bring us through the halls and onto the elevator. That night they were yelling, "Out of the way! Out of the way! Move, move, move!" and we were running through the halls pushing the isolette and everything else that we had. At last we got him up to the ICU and I could take a breath. I think we were up there about half an hour, forty-five minutes, and he crashed again. We lost him that time.

There are days when you could just cry, when you know you just can't do this anymore. If we're very, very busy and you have two sick kids, you feel like you're just not giving them everything. You're giving them all you have, but there's not time to give them more, and there's just not enough of you. It all comes down on you once in a while. But you keep going because of the ones you're going to save.

The first time I saw a baby die, it was awful. It was a real tiny baby girl. Her lungs weren't fully developed and she just wasn't able to breathe well enough to survive. The doctors had tried everything. She was getting blue and the decision was made by her parents and the doctors not to do anything more. I remember standing there, holding oxygen to this baby's nose because once in a while she would gasp, and when she gasped I wanted her to have the oxygen—not that it prolonged her life but it made me feel I was doing something for her. I've learned since then that it's not necessarily good to prolong it. It may be humane to let them go; to comfort them, or give them a little bath. Just to hold them . . . Since then I've held lots of babies and just let them die in my arms. We encourage the parents to do it, too, if they're strong enough. But this was one of my first times, and I stood by that isolette . . . Finally, I picked her up and we sat in a rocking chair and I rocked her while she was dying. I just thought it was nicer for her than to die alone in an isolette, you know, with nobody's hands on her, nobody ever touching her.

MICHAEL KATZ, M.D.

Chairman,
Department of Pediatrics

I was born in Poland in a town called Lvov. It's now in the Soviet Union, but it was in Poland fifty-nine years ago when I was born. I lived there until the mid-thirties when I moved to Warsaw with my mother and stepfather. When the war broke out in Poland in 1939, I was eleven. All men were asked by the Polish government to leave Warsaw and join the armed forces and so my stepfather left us. He eventually wound up in eastern Poland. The Soviet Union had attacked Poland from the east in 1939 after Hitler and Stalin signed their pact, and the country was divided. So our family was separated by what turned out to be a line between the Soviets and the Germans.

At the end of 1939, my mother and I sneaked across the border between the two halves of Poland. We traveled by truck and then on foot and eventually we wound up in the Soviet part of Poland in a small town where my stepfather was waiting for us. Together we went on by train to my grandparents' home in Lvov.

I began school in Lvov, and life became somewhat normal. Normal, that is, until June of '41, when the Germans attacked the Soviet Union. Our family had an opportunity to escape eastward, but both my mother and my stepfather, originally refugees from the Russian Revolution, absolutely did not want to do that. And that turned out to be a fundamental error of judgment. Had they escaped at that time, they would have survived.

We stayed in Lvov, assuming that the Germans would be somewhat civilized, but I don't think anybody fully understood the situation. We were immediately overcome by the Germans and then things began moving very quickly. The Germans began sending in the *Einzatzgruppen*, groups whose task was to shoot all the Jews. They went to the small towns and villages, and we heard that in the smaller communities where the population was predominately Jewish they made the Jews dig their own graves and then they killed them all.

It was a tentative period. I couldn't go to school because Jews were not allowed to go. We couldn't use any public transportation, for example, or sit in the parks. Things became progressively worse. One night, my stepfather was suddenly taken away on the pretext that he was involved in some shooting that had occurred in the street. We heard a few weeks later that he was shot.

Eventually they took all the men in Lvov, and the only males left in our household were my grandfather, who was in his sixties, my ten-year-old cousin, and I. No one quite knew what to do. I began working, as everybody over twelve had to; I worked for a German army automobile depot as a mechanic servicing military trucks and cars. Although I wasn't a mechanic, I became one very quickly.

In August of '42, all of a sudden our new ID cards were taken away from us, processed and returned very quickly, stamped by the Gestapo. My card had a stamp outside but everybody else's card in my family had a stamp on the inside. At that time no one knew the significance of that. The significance, as it turned out, was life and death. I went to work one morning and I heard that the place where my mother and my grandparents worked was being evacuated. I ran to find my mother. She was all the way across the city. Because of my stamp the patrols had to let me through, although I was stopped periodically. When my document told them that I had to be allowed to go, they hit me and once even made me crawl on the ground and eat grass like a cow. Except for a few bruises, I managed to get through intact. But by the time I got to where my mother worked, about eighty percent of the people were gone.

My mother was among them.

The people left described an absolutely brutal evacuation—beatings and torture. Presumably all those people were taken to Belzec, which was an extermination camp where people were gassed within forty-eight hours. We knew nothing about that then, though, so there were all sorts of interpretations of what was going on. Most of us expected the worst. This episode was followed by a period of relative peace for the following few days, and then my co-workers and I were all locked up and moved to a concentration camp ourselves.

We continued to work for the army, except now we were escorted every morning by the Ukrainian police. Then one morning we were led to a quarry, and I was given a pneumatic drill that I could hardly handle—I was only fourteen years old—and I decided then and there that I was not going to survive if I didn't do something drastic.

Several nights later, I stayed outside of the barracks after the curfew, hid behind a barrack, and waited until it got very dark. Then I crawled under barbed wire to the adjoining cemetery and hid there till morning. And then I ran. This was before the time when they put people into those blue-and-white pajama-like garbs in the concentration camps, but they did paint stripes over whatever you were wearing. I was wearing overalls because I was working as a mechanic, but under the overalls I had a suit, so I buried the overalls. I probably reeked with the stench of someone who hadn't washed or changed his clothing for six weeks, but, nevertheless, I went out into the city and managed to lose myself in the crowd.

I didn't wear an armband and I had no ID, but no one stopped me. I went to see some people I knew and asked them to help me. They had some of my mother's jewelry. I know they didn't wholly release all of it, but they did help me to buy someone else's birth certificate, and I took what they gave me, changed my clothing, changed my name, and I went off to Warsaw.

In Warsaw I played the role of an abandoned Polish child whose parents were taken away by the Russians. For the initial five or six days I slept in the waiting room of the railroad station, and then I found a job in a bookshop owned by two high-school teachers who couldn't teach because there were no high schools. One was a very nice guy and the other was an absolute swine who was very pleased with what the Germans were doing to the Jews; of course he didn't know that I was Jewish.

It's funny. I never felt sorry for myself. I suppose I just didn't have the time. What I felt was very angry. The next job I found was safer. It was in a factory that made artificial coffee out of sugar beets. I worked there until one of the foremen jokingly—but one could never tell—made some allusions to my background and said, "Oh, you're as smart as a rabbi." That could have been a perfectly innocent comment, but I began worrying about it. I quickly found another job as an office boy for a big German industrial office. While doing that I joined the underground, and I began working with the resistance forces. Since I was an office boy, I had run of the city, so I was able to act as a messenger and carry documents and ammunition.

In 1943 there was an uprising in the ghetto and, being a part of the underground, I volunteered to bring weapons to the ghetto, which I did by traveling under the city through the sewers. By August 1, 1944, Warsaw was in turmoil. We emerged from underground and attacked the Germans and spent two months fighting in the streets. We eventually lost because the Russians, who were right across the river, would not cross to help us. We knew the Germans had to treat us as prisoners of war if they caught us. As a result of the Geneva Convention, they couldn't, at least openly, do any harm to us.

I was in a position to be taken as a prisoner of war, and I lived in fear that my true identity might come out. I was still using my pseudonym, even as a member of the Polish resistance, and still no one knew that I was Jewish. I was afraid that if I were taken as a prisoner I would have to use a public bathroom—I am circumcised, which would have automatically revealed me as suspect.

It so happened that the barricade I had manned for six weeks during the uprising was next to a makeshift hospital run by the Polish Red Cross. They were looking for someone who was fluent in German and Polish as their gofer. I joined that hospital and stayed in Warsaw for six more weeks, part of a group of six hundred—the last human beings in a city of a little over a million people. The city was demolished during the uprising, and subsequently the Germans flattened it. It was a surrealistic experience, walking through a city that was turned to rubble, not being able to recognize where we were.

We stayed there until we were evacuated to Krakow in western Poland. I continued to work with those people until the Russians came to Krakow, which was in January of '45. They took Warsaw shortly after the uprising, after the city was destroyed. Then on January 14, 1945, forty-two years ago, they came to Krakow and "liberated" us.

I decided soon after that I didn't want to stay in what was fast becoming a Soviet satellite. My first objective was to go to school somewhere and finish my secondary education. I hadn't gone to school at all during those years, but I studied as much as I could on my own. In fact, when I worked for the bookstore, one of the teachers gave me a whole outline of a curriculum that I should follow. When the schools opened again in Krakow, I decided to attend.

I presented myself as a year ahead, and while I don't think I covered myself with any scholastic glory, I was admitted to the last year and finished it and got a diploma. I had to leave it with my friend because I had decided to leave Poland and I decided I was going to travel as a Greek. There was no legitimate way for me to get out of the country except by not being Polish.

I became a Greek with yet another name, a Hebrew name, but I was supposed to be a Greek Jew. I proceeded out of Poland through an underground railroad, traveling through Czechoslovakia to Hungary, allegedly on the way to Greece, pretending that I spoke no Polish or German and could not understand any other Slavic languages. I was with a group of people trying to escape. We got to Budapest, then we changed and became Austrians returning to Vienna. In Vienna we became Austrians going to Graz. That was the most difficult step, because we would be then leaving the Soviet-occupied zone, and going into the British-occupied zone of Austria. It was in October of '45. The underground railroad was run mostly by various Zionist groups who were trying to get most of these people to Palestine. So they got us to Graz. And then they abandoned us.

———————

He continues to tell of being arrested in Graz by the British because he had no legitimate reason for being there. He was put in a camp but escaped within a few days. "Escaping from the British after four years of German occupation was child's play." With money he had been given by the underground, he and a friend went to the railroad station and bought tickets to Salzburg, hoping to make it to the American zone.

When the train arrived at the border between the two zones they were taken off and detained by an American MP because they had no passes. The train, which was still in the British zone, left without them. He and his friend headed for the mountains on foot and spent the night with a farmer. Early the next morning, they began trekking toward the American side. From there he took a train to Salzburg and made contact with another underground railroad. It was then that he was told of a place outside of Munich where there were displaced persons' camps, and that if he could get there, he would be made legitimate. "So that became my single goal."

He was just seventeen when he arrived at the camp, which was run by UNRRA—the United Nations Relief and Rehabilitation Administration. There he met and became a translator for an American UNRRA officer. Not long afterward, the woman became the immigration officer for that camp.

———————

President Truman declared that all the refugees who were in West Germany before December 22, 1945, were presumed to have arrived there legitimately. So all of a sudden I ceased being a bastard and I was a legitimate person! I received a document which said my name, and I had a foundation from which to start building the next step.

Truman said that the immigration quotas that had not been used during the war could be used, so the woman from UNRRA signed me up. I was number seven—the seventh person allowed to go from that camp. And so in June of 1946, at the age of seventeen, I was on my way to America.

My mother's distant relatives came to New York to meet me. One of them had just become a widow and had no children so she invited me to stay with her in Philadelphia. I went to work as a dishwasher in a luncheonette in the business district of Philadelphia, and I immediately applied to the University of Pennsylvania to go to college. They didn't know how to classify me. "Where are your high-school documents?" There were none, of course. I'd had to leave them in Poland because I was traveling as a Greek. I said I had written to my friends to send them to me and that they would eventually come. So they allowed me to start college as a special student for no degree until this was clarified.

My mother's relative paid my tuition the first year, which was the extraordinary amount of seven hundred dollars, and I got a job for extra money. I worked first as a dishwasher in a small restaurant. At six o'clock in the morning I would open up the place, start coffee, serve some breakfasts. Then at eight o'clock the regular crew came and then I could go to school, come back in the afternoon after school and work some more. Eventually my documents arrived and I was reclassified as a regular student. I got quite a lot of credits for the Polish secondary school because Polish secondary school, when completed, is equivalent to the first two years of college. So I had a lot of credits and in 1949, after three years of studies, and with more credits than I could possibly need, I graduated.

In retrospect, I suppose determination was a major ingredient that kept me going through those lean and tentative years in Europe. I don't necessarily know where it came from, although the one thing that pervaded all my plans was the desire to be educated. That I had never abandoned. And that, of course, was the legacy of my mother and father.

After graduating from the University of Pennsylvania, he attended graduate school, where he did research in cell physiology, and then went on to medical school. He began his internship in surgery at the University of California but his training was interrupted when he was drafted into the navy. During that time he was sent to work in a Korean orphanage, which was where he first became interested in children. After Korea, he came to New York to finish his training—he had decided to become a pediatrician— and he started a residency at Babies' Hospital in January 1960. At the end of his residency he had a fellowship at the Columbia University School of Public Health in pediatrics and infectious diseases and spent a year in Uganda doing research on the effects of malnutrition on the immune sys-

tems of children. In 1965 he went to the Whistler Institute in Philadelphia to continue this research for six years. Upon completion of the project in 1971, he returned to the School of Public Health as head of the Division of Tropical Medicine. In 1977 he became chairman of the Department of Pediatrics.

VIII
THE OPERATING ROOM

At 6:15 A.M. most of the patients on Nine West are sleeping. In room 911, Arnold Miller, a fifty-six-year-old business executive from New Jersey, is nervously changing from his pajamas into a blue hospital gown. He pauses for a moment and looks out the window as the rising sun begins to bathe the city in light. His pensiveness is disrupted when a nurse enters the room. She gives him a sedative to relax him while he waits for the stretcher attendant to take him to the operating room. He is scheduled this morning for coronary artery bypass surgery. If all goes well, in less than an hour Arnold Miller will be fast asleep on the operating table.

Nine floors higher, the OR personnel—the day shift—have started filtering in. Eighteen is given over largely to the operating suite, a complex of fourteen operating rooms, six anesthesia rooms, central supply, a bone bank, central scheduling, and the doctors' and nurses' locker rooms. This morning, as usual, Joan Lawson, the scheduling nurse, is the first to arrive. She goes directly to her desk to scan the form that lists the day's cases. Arnold Miller will go into OR-C, one of two rooms specially equipped for open heart surgery.

By 6:30 the day shift has traded places with the night shift, and the entire operating suite has come alive with people. Four nurses in the locker room are changing into "scrubs," a blue cotton dress, paper shoe covers, and a hair covering that looks like a paper shower cap. As they change, they converse about a party they're giving for a nurse who retires next week. Two of the women, one a circulating nurse and the other a scrub nurse, head for OR-C. The circulating nurse will direct the operating room during surgery. She is charged with keeping the the sterile field around the patient uncontaminated by anyone not "scrubbed," or, as they're called in the operating room, anyone "dirty." She is the person who leaves the room for extra supplies, if necessary, and is responsible for recording pertinent events, such as precisely when the initial incision is made, the time the patient goes on bypass, and the time the last suture is placed. Right now, though, she helps the scrub nurse set up the instrument tray for Mr. Miller's surgery.

The scrub nurse has been working with the heart team for over twelve years and could, as she puts it, "probably do the operation myself if I had to." During the surgery, she will stand next to or across from the surgeon, ready to hand him instruments as they are called for. She is called a scrub nurse because she is subject to the same scrubbing ritual as the surgeons who perform the operation.

OR-C is a twenty-by-twenty-foot chamber with green tile walls and stone floors. The room is larger than most of the other operating rooms in the suite in order to accommodate the large machinery, such as the heart monitors and the heart-lung machine, that will be the patient's lifeline during part of the operation. It must also hold the nine or ten people present during most of the surgery. Perched high in the corner of the room is a TV monitor that will display the patient's heart rate, EKG, and blood pressure, so that the surgeon need only glance up to see the patient's vital signs.

By 6:50 A.M., the anesthesiologist and his resident have come into the room and are preparing their machines and the drugs and anesthetic agents that will be used during the operation. In a small, adjacent room, two perfusionists are setting up the heart-lung machine, which will temporarily take over the function of the patient's heart and lungs while the surgeon implants the bypass grafts. At 7:10, Mr. Miller arrives on a stretcher. Still awake but a bit drowsy, he is transferred to the operating table, a pedestal covered in green cloth that stands in the center of the room. Just outside, two assistant surgeons are scrubbing at the sink— fifteen strokes on each finger for the first go-round, ten strokes for the second, and five for the third.

The senior surgeon, wearing scrub suit, cap, and mask, strides through the door and goes directly to his patient. He places a reassuring hand on his shoulder. "How're you doing, Mr. Miller?" he asks. The patient nods and says, "Did you get a good night's sleep, Doc?" The surgeon's eyes smile. He has been asked that question, or one like it, almost every morning for the last thirteen years. "Slept like a baby," he says.

As the surgeon leaves the room to scrub, the anesthesiologist straps a blood pressure cuff onto Mr. Miller's right arm and inserts an intravenous line into a vein in the left arm. "Ready to go to sleep, Mr. Miller?" he asks. Miller nods. The anesthesiologist places a black rubber mask over the patient's face. "Breathe deeply," he instructs his patient in a soft voice. "Just one or two big breaths." Before he takes his second breath, Mr. Miller is fast asleep, his tense body melting into a mass of relaxation. The anesthesiologist's role in the operation is as vital as the surgeon's. For the duration of the operation, he will be responsible for Mr. Miller's respiration, heart rate, blood pressure, and temperature. He is charged with keeping Mr. Miller alive.

With the patient asleep, the staff shifts into high gear. Various electrocardiographic wires and other monitoring lines are put in place. Mr. Miller's skin, which was shaved from neck to ankles last night, is lightly shaved again and painted with an iodine-colored antiseptic solution. The resident and his assistant place linen drapes over the patient's body, leaving only two operating fields exposed, the middle of the chest and the right leg, from the knee to the ankle. It is from this leg that the surgeon will take the veins used to bypass the coronary arteries.

After the patient is draped, everyone moves into place around the table. The first assistant, the resident, and the scrub nurse are on the left side of the operating table. The anesthesiologist and his resident are at the head. The two pump technicians are on stools behind the heart-lung machine. The surgeon backs into the room, arms bent at the elbows, hands in front of him. The circulating nurse helps him into his sterile gown and ties it for him at the back. She snaps open a bag containing a pair of rubber gloves, being careful not to touch them. The surgeon plunges his hands into the gloves, tightening them with interlocking fingers, and steps up to the table.

The room becomes still, full of expectation; the only sounds are Mozart's Fifth Violin Concerto playing softly in the background and the steady beep of the cardiac monitor echoing the beat of the patient's heart. At once one wonders: In how many operating rooms, in how many hospitals, in how many countries, for how many years has this scenario been repeated? And always, the opening line is the same: "Scalpel, please." Without a word, the nurse places the scalpel into the surgeon's outstretched hand and the operation begins.

JOAN LAWSON, R.N.
The Desk
Administrative Nurse Clinician

―――――――――

She sits behind a counter facing the entrance to the eighteenth-floor operating suite. Anyone who enters must pass her desk. A small woman with sharp eyes, she is dressed in operating "scrubs," her hair is covered by a blue paper cap. She speaks with a Scottish accent that she has retained even after twenty years in this country.

―――――――――

People around here refer to me as "the desk." Everybody knows me. The nurses. The doctors. Everybody. The doctors know if they can't get the OR time or the room that they want, it's nothing personal on my part. It's strictly "the desk." The nurses, too. When they give someone information from me, they say, "That's what the desk said."

Basically speaking, every OR has one of me, regardless of what they call me. I'm responsible for the operating schedule—for making sure it works and that every operating room has the right number of staff in it. I'm really just dealing with numbers—getting the right amount of people in the right rooms at the right time. I know that in order to start surgery tomorrow, we have to have so many nursing staff for so many rooms. So my job is to see that we have it, twenty-four hours a day.

I'm also responsible for seeing that all patients who are scheduled for elective surgery get their operation done that day. The hard part is when every operating room is full and we have to squeeze the emergency cases in. For example, I get a call from the emergency room and they've just gotten a patient with a gunshot wound to the abdomen or chest. They'll call me and say, "We're sending a patient up, *now!*" When I get a call like that, I know I *have* to get a room. So I go looking in every operating room to see who's almost finished. I move the schedule around; some cases get delayed. A lot of people complain. But we manage to get that patient in. We haven't yet had to operate in the hallway or the anesthesia room. I'm always terrified that someday it will come to that.

The operating room is constantly on the move. Every day I experience every emotion known to man, with the exception of boredom. I can honestly say I've never ever been bored because no two days are the same. You get good days and bad days. The good days everything runs smoothly. The bad days are when I come in at six-thirty in the morning and two rooms which are scheduled for seven-thirty cases have emergencies going on—like a bleeding open-heart and an aneurysm—they may have been there for hours and they may have hours to go. I know right off that those cases are going to hold up everybody else, so I have to start shifting people around and start thinking about what I'm going to do later that day.

I've been here for such a long time, I can remember a lot of the doctors when they were interns. Now they're big-time attendings. It would appear to me that doctors speed up the ladder much faster than nurses. In no time at all. There was an attending the other day complaining to me that he was going to be thirty-one this month. Thirty-one! What I wouldn't give to be thirty-one again.

MAUREEN SPRINGER

Stretcher Attendant

A native of Barbados, she came to this country in 1968. Two years later, she sent for her small son. "He's married now, with two kids." She's been at this job for seventeen years. She's forty-three.

Going with the stretcher to pick up a patient is not something to be taken for granted. There's a strict procedure to be followed. When I take the empty stretcher to the floor, I let the floor nurse know I'm there. Then I go in to the patient, I check his identification bracelet against the name I was given. If the family is there I ask them to wait in the corridor while I transfer the patient to the stretcher. If there aren't too many people, I'll let them walk me to the elevator and then they get their hugs and kisses before we go up on the elevator.

Patients usually start talking to me as soon as the elevator doors close. Sometimes they ask questions about the operating room, or they'll talk about the weather, or they ask me where I'm from. You transport enough patients, you get to know what to expect. If they close their eyes and don't want to say anything, you know just to bring them to the OR. Period. If they say, "So, how are you? What's your name?" then you feel free to make small talk. But you don't discuss anything about the hospital or their operation. You just discuss yourself or the weather or whatever. That's it.

When you arrive in the OR, you have to know which room you're taking the patient to. They're scared and upset enough; imagine what would happen if you wheeled them into the wrong room. Here you have a patient who is going in for abdominal surgery and the doctor comes in and starts looking at the patient's foot. Now what's that patient going to think? It doesn't happen, of course, but it could. Here again, we're very careful. So even though you may be sure, you always stop and ask the desk again. "The name of this patient is So-and-so. What room does the patient go in?" And she tells you.

It depends on your personality as to how you can cope with certain patients. I have brought patients up who are very, very scared. You know, if you're a patient, when you're wheeled into an operating room, every book that you read in the last ten years about someone dying under anesthesia is going to come right back to you. Is that going to happen to me? Many people ask questions and you have to at least acknowledge those questions. You can't just ignore them. So you just say you don't have any medical information and you suggest they talk to their doctor. I guess when someone asks me about their operation it's because there's no one else there at that moment to talk to. They don't know what's happening. They're scared, so they turn to the person pushing the stretcher because we're right there.

I never see them afterward. If a patient says, "Come and see me after my surgery," I say I will, but I don't go, because they always ask more questions. "Was I out? Did I say something I shouldn't have?" I don't want to answer questions like that, so if I pass them again in their room or in the hallway, I just wave and smile and I keep on walking.

JOSEPH PRESTIPINO

The Barber

~~~

He's fifty-three. For the last ten years he has run the barber shop on the main floor of the hospital. The three-chair shop, which has two other full-time barbers, smells faintly of shaving cream and talc. Clients include hospital staff, patients, and people from the neighborhood. He takes pride in the fact that the hospital president has his hair cut there. A shave and a haircut cost $13.00.

He usually only spends his afternoons in the shop. In the morning, he's either in the operating room or in the Neurological Institute, where he shaves the heads and backs of patients about to undergo neurosurgery.

It's a job. My friends all kid with me. "Hey, Joe, what are you doing over there?" But it's a job, like anything else. It's work. I got a family to support.

I started by myself here. Now there's three of us. We all give haircuts, but I'm the only one who also works in the OR, so I have to keep myself on a strict schedule. I get up at four-thirty every morning. I take my shower, make a cup of coffee, and come to work. Here, I do a little cleaning in the shop or whatever needs to be done, and then I go across the street to the Neurological Institute to the operating room. I get a schedule for the day's operations, and I see what's got to be done. I shave four, five, sometimes six patients a day.

The first few times I shaved a head for an operation it bothered me. But after a while it became nothing. My talking with the patients is so fantastic. Maybe they ask me, "Joe, how much of the hair are you going to cut?" I answer them nicely, because everybody's frightened when they get an operation. So I will say, "It's not up to me, it's up to the surgeon. I'll try to do the best I can, not to cut it too much." You got to know how to talk, when to talk, and how to sneak the words in. There's a lot of angles that you have to learn to make patients feel a little more relaxed. You just pick them up as you go along.

Nobody showed me what to do in the beginning. I picked up most of it on my own. With backs, it's easy because you shave the whole back. But with the heads, it's a little difficult—especially when a woman is involved. We do a lot of suboccipital—that's the back area of the neck. I lift the hair up and I cut underneath where the surgeon is going to operate, and then the top of the hair, if it's long, will cover it up.

I save the hair when I cut it. I pick it up and put it in an envelope. Then I stamp it with the patient's name on it, and turn it in to the ICU so they can give it to the patient. Some people are peculiar. They want to keep their hair. Even the men. Some people say it's in case of a mortality. I don't know for sure. But I don't want to have them saying, "Why do you keep the hair? Maybe you're going to do a wig or something . . ."

Usually I only do patients having neurosurgery. So I shave just heads and backs, and axilla [armpits] sometimes, arms, something like that. If a patient needs a shunt, then I'll shave the head, neck, chest, and abdomen. Sometimes, though, they call me for some difficult case in the regular OR, like an orthopedic case. Or a few times they called me for open heart surgery, to shave the whole body. They only do that if the person has so much hair on them that it would be difficult for a nurse to do it. One time they had a patient who had hair just like a gorilla. It took me about three hours to do his body. I had to clip it first with a machine, and then shave it with a razor and soap.

I mostly do the heads in the operating room. I ask the surgeon what he wants before I start, because head preps are not always the whole head. Sometimes it's only a partial. And sometimes if the patient is a little scared, the doctor may put the patient to sleep before I start. To eliminate any trouble, I don't touch the patient, especially if he is having a craniotomy, unless the doctor says to me, "Joe, on that patient, do a full head prep." Or else, I prep them in their room with the doctor's supervision. That way, I don't get in trouble; the nurses don't get in trouble; nobody gets in trouble. My work is done with no problems, and everything works smoothly.

This morning, a patient called the anesthesiologist. He says, "I want to talk to the barber." Now on this patient the doctor is supposed to do a partial craniotomy, so I would only need to cut a little bit of his hair. But when I went in there, the patient says to me, "Take everything off. This way, when it grows back, it's all nice and new." Some people want it that way; some people don't want it that way.

Sometimes I walk around the floors, I kid around with the people. I say, "Hi, how are you?" Then they point at their shaved heads, "Look what my doctor did to me!" They don't even know that *I* did it.

I do a lot of babies. Very small babies. All kinds. It's very sad. When the parents are in the room when I go in to shave the head, they want to know if the kid can get well. It's not my place to talk about that. I can't tell them anything. I tell them I'm only a barber, that I cut their hair. That's about all.

When I finish in the OR, I see if I got anything to do on the floors. Then I go to my little shop. Sometimes during the day, I get emergency calls from the operating room. If I have a person in the chair, I have to leave him and run to the operating room. Then I come back and I'll finish the customer. Maybe they'll wait a little while. I do my work. I try my best. I try to leave everybody satisfied.

Today, I make a living. I'm not getting rich. Now I got something else going, too. I'm a big man at the racetrack—I got a big window. I take bets. I've been working there now for fifteen years—Yonkers. And I handle a lot of money—I'm a pari-mutuel clerk. What I could sell you in two minutes, you'd be surprised. To get this license, you got to clear completely of anything. Otherwise they won't give it to you. I figured, I don't earn that much money as a barber. If I needed something, I don't want to work doubly hard to do that, so let me have another little job, maybe. So that's why I do it. Also, it keeps me young; it keeps me alive.

People in this country—they have a family, they have it nice. They have a car, they got a girlfriend, they got this, they got that—they don't know how lucky they are. It was not easy for me. It was tough. I came to this country alone at nineteen. I spoke no English and I had to work really hard. In Sicily, I was used to the good life. I had three sisters, they used to care for me—cook, press my pants, this and that. Here it was hard. I opened my own shop, things were going along. I got married, had three kids, and then the long hair came in. The hippies. And there was not enough work to support my family. I had to find other jobs. I worked in a gasoline station on Sundays. I worked on the newspapers at night, and weekends—I used to deliver newspapers to the stores. It was very discouraging until one day my friend, who worked in this hospital, told me he was going to retire. And that's how I got here. I took over his place.

Everything seems happy today. I'm just an average guy, life hasn't been easy. I've been working all my life. But tomorrow, even if suddenly I get rich, I say with all my heart, I could never stop working. I love the work. I like to work with the surgeons, especially with the neurosurgeons. And they like me too. They have no problem with me whatsoever, because they know I can do my work with one eye closed and one hand tied behind my back.

LEONA VINCENT
The Bone Lady
Orthopedic Technician

She works in the rear of the operating suite, in a small room lined with metal counters upon which are stacked hundreds of gleaming, steel surgical instruments. She is responsible for all these instruments. She is also in charge of cataloguing and storing bones for the bone bank, which is actually just a large upright freezer. She is thirty-six. She has a brilliant smile and speaks in the soft, sing-song rhythms of a Caribbean native.

Not too many people ever heard of a bone bank. Most hospitals don't have one. Here, we save any extra bone that might come from one patient and use it for another patient who might need it. For instance, if a patient comes in to have total hip replacement, or if someone has a bad fracture and some shattered bone needs to be removed, we save the bone that is removed. Instead of throwing it out, we keep it for the bone bank. We also get ribs from the kidney patients. Doctors remove a patient's rib when they do a kidney transplant but they don't put it back because the patient really doesn't need it.

If a patient comes in with a lot of broken bones and the doctors need to fill a cavity in, they use pieces of bone from the bone bank to make the patient's broken bone stronger and more smooth and even. It's like a transplant. Years ago you used to see people with big holes in their foot from some problem, like maybe a tumor was removed. Nowadays, during surgery you can fill them up.

There are rules and techniques that we follow. When the surgeons remove a bone from a patient, they bring it to me in a jar, all sterile. I register it for my bone bank under a number, and I send the piece of bone for all the cultures to make sure that it is safe to be used on any other patient who might need a bone graft. If the lab says the bone is healthy and can be used, I store it in the freezer.

When we have a case, especially when they're doing major revisions, the doctors will say, "Hey, Leona, we need a femoral head," or "We need a rib." And I'll check and make sure I have a rib and a head. And I say, "Give me fifteen or twenty minutes to thaw it." Sometimes the guys come over and open the freezer and choose what they want. It's not a big bank. It's just for our use.

I'm also responsible for the orthopedic instruments. I clean them, oil them, and make sure they don't squeak. When I get here in the morning, the first thing I do is check on all the things they'll need that day and I make a tray and park it right outside the door of the operating room. Then all they have to do when they're ready is pull it in. Next, I look for the instruments that I sent to Central Supply to be gassed the day before, and make sure that I have all my equipment back. There are four orthopedic rooms, and they're all going all the time. After each case they bring the instruments back to me and I clean them for the next case. And that's how the days run.

Even though I rarely see the patients, I always ask the doctors, "How is Mary Jane? How is Harry?" I remember these people if it's really a tough case, like a total hip revision, or when Dr. Dick has a big tumor case. I'm so fascinated by the way it's done! It's like building something wonderful—building back a leg.

I get very emotional when we work on children because I have two of my own. If a little kid is born with no fingers, Dr. Dick removes the toes and puts them on their hands so the child will be able to hold a cup of tea or a little toy. I think that's really amazing. Sometimes they come back a few times. So if I see a child's name on the OR schedule and that name looks familiar to me, I go into the anesthesia room and chat and say, "Hi, how are you doing? Good to see you!" And then I sneak a quick look at the fingers.

I started in this hospital as a housekeeper in '75. I did a year and eight months of housekeeping. But that's not really what I wanted, because I'm very good with my hands—taking screws out, putting screws in. I just thought that I was wasting my time cleaning, so I decided to change and get into the nursing department as an aide. And that's how I got started here—I was a nurse's aide assigned to the operating room. They trained us so we could rotate through every surgical department. We used to do the instruments, open heart, everything. My last rotation was in orthopedics, and when I got there, they said I was perfect! Instruments that they had never taken apart I took apart, cleaned, and put back together. I didn't even think about it. If an instrument was dirty, I just cleaned it.

When I was a little girl in Trinidad, all I ever wanted to be was a nurse. But I was the second of fourteen children and only my older sister got to go to school. So she became the nurse. The second child had to be home and help Mama raise the little kids. I came here in 1968, at nineteen years old, to find a job so that I could help my family. I worked for a year as a housekeeper in New Jersey, then I got married, came to New York, and lived right on this street.

For three years I tried to find a job but I couldn't find anything. I tried to work at this hospital, and I put in an application, but every time I came, they told me, "No jobs. No jobs." I would have done anything.

Now at that time there was this lady who lived in the building next door to mine. Our kitchen windows faced each other and we could see each other in the kitchen. Every morning this lady would open her shutters and every night she would close them. Then all of a sudden I didn't see her shutters open for quite a while. I got scared. I kept telling my husband, "Something must be wrong; that lady must be dead." Finally I decided to go next door and look on her mailbox to see what her name was. Then I looked her up in the telephone book, and I called her. When she answered, she answered me so low. I told her who I was and asked what happened to her.

She said she had been sick and I asked her if I could come to see her. When I got there, I couldn't believe it was the same lady. She was so thin! She was also very weak, so she asked me to call her job supervisor and tell him she was sick. She was in housekeeping here.

Anyway, she got even sicker. And I used to take her to the doctor because I was at home at the time. I'd take her to the doctor, back and forth, go fix a little breakfast. I used to give her a bath and everything. I got very attached to her. I had a little baby at the time and my husband used to work evenings and the minute he left for work, I'd take the baby and go there and stay with her. And just before he'd come in, I'd go home. And from time to time, I would call her supervisor in housekeeping—Mr. Fields—and say how the lady was doing, which was very poorly. And Mr. Fields got to know me from my voice.

This went on for about six months. The lady, who had been so fat, all of a sudden just shriveled away. It was cancer. Then one day I noticed she was vomiting, and it was black. Now I knew nothing about nursing but

I knew something was wrong, so I took her to the hospital. The doctor told me she wouldn't make it and the next morning, when I went in, they told me she was gone.

After she passed, I went to the funeral service and it was there that I met her supervisor. He said, "So you are the Leona I always talk to! Well, Leona, Mrs. James told us that you took such wonderful care of her. She said if she died she wanted very much for you to have her job. So now her position is open, Leona. Her job is yours."

ERIC WHITE
The Plaster Man
Orthopedic Technician

We're in the plaster room, where patients are brought if they need to be put in traction or to have casts made. In the center of the room two treatment tables stand alone, like small black islands. Old plaster body-jackets, some with heart designs cut out at the belly area, line the walls. "These are special designs," he says, "but only for the young kids. It always makes them smile."

He's wearing a white uniform, bits of plaster are stuck to his arms and in his hair. He has just finished casting a four-year-old little girl with a broken leg.

"My name tag used to say: 'Eric White—Orthopedic Technician.' And people I worked with would say, 'An orthopedic technician. A real big shot, huh? Well, I remember when he was just an orderly.' So I got rid of that and now I wear just my name: Eric White. That's it. "It doesn't matter, anyway. Whenever I walk through halls people say, 'Look! There goes the plaster man.'"

I've been putting people in casts for twenty-two years. If you were to break a leg, the doctor would maintain the position of the fracture and then it's up to me to put on the cast. In most small hospitals, the doctors do the majority of the casts themselves, but in the last ten years in large institutions like this, it's guys like my partner Milton and me who do the casts.

Whether a doctor stays in here with me depends on whether the fracture is stable or unstable. Certain things we can do without a doctor's assistance. They just give us instructions on what they want and then we do it.

Not everybody understands when a technician does the cast. They want the doctor to do it. Especially when you walk into a private room in a private hospital where they have private physicians, private-duty nurses, private this and private that, they're not going to let just anyone come in and do just anything to them. I know *I* would prefer a technician in a specialty working on me any day because technicians do just that one thing all day long. You do something over and over and over again, even if you don't have anything on tap, you have to get good at what you're doing. And when you do as many as we do, you do them better and faster than just about anybody.

Milton and I can put on a whole body jacket—that's what they use for curvature of the spine—in about seven minutes. That's a record, we think. And believe me, speed counts! You take a patient. That patient is already upset because he doesn't want to be in a body cast in the first place. Add to that that the table's not the most comfortable place in the world, you have a little belt running down your back, and most patients think they're going to fall off. Then we we have to put traction around the waist and traction on the curve to straighten it a little bit. So right away you can't take a real deep breath because of the restrictions. You get all that and some patients really panic. We *have* to hurry.

Doing a cast right takes a lot of thought. For example, when somebody asks me, "How many rolls does it take to cast a kid's broken arm?" I say you have to look at the individual. Actually, you have to look at the area that kid comes from. If the kid is from Princeton, New Jersey, or any rich neighborhood where you know they're well taken care of, you can get away with light casts. But if he's from an area like this, where you know the mother and father work and the kid's on the street all the time, you have to make that cast stronger than you would ordinarily do. If I'm working on a young kid, let's say a ten-year-old, and the first thing I hear the mother say when she comes in, bitching and moaning about being here, is "I'm tired. I can't stay here. I'm gettin' tired of runnin' back and forth!"—right away, I know this mother's not too concerned about her kid's health and she's not going to watch out for him. She's more concerned about going home and watching her soap operas. So what I do is, I add an extra roll and make the cast stronger.

It also depends on the season. In the summertime a kid is more active, he needs more material in his cast. In the wintertime, he's not going many places, so you can get away with a little bit less. When I'm teaching the residents, and it's summer, I always put an extra roll on and they want to know why. I say, "You put on three rolls for the patient and an extra roll for the park."

Sometimes I've been asked, "Doesn't it bother you, little kids screaming?" It bothers me, sure. You don't want to see a kid cry. In fact sometimes I'll go home and I'll grab my daughter and hug her and squeeze her, and she doesn't know why. But if you see some kid that's not going to ever walk properly—some kid born with cerebral palsy, or some kid born with a bone disease like osteogenesis imperfecta, where every time the kid moves in bed he could break a bone, you just thank God your kids are healthy.

We had a little kid upstairs once, his father was quite a wealthy man, and we had done some hip surgery on him. After six weeks he came back into the hospital to have the cast off and my assistant went up to remove it. Now, it normally takes about five minutes to take off a cast, but five minutes go by, ten minutes go by, half an hour—so I called upstairs to find out what was taking so long. My assistant said the boy just wouldn't let him take the cast off. Well, this kid's six years old! And I remembered him—a real fresh kid. So I went up and I walked into his room and right away he makes a face. I picked up the cast cutters and the kid looks me in the eyes and says, "I'm gonna' hit you." Well I looked right back at him and I said, "Remember the last time you were here? You called me a 'nigger.' Well," I said, "you can call me anything you want. You can scream and you can holler. But you're not gonna' hit me! You got that?" So then the mother, who was sitting there the whole time, says, "I apologize for him. I don't know where he got that word from." And I said, "Well, I don't think kids are born with that word in their vocabulary. They have to learn that somewhere along the way."

There was this one little girl who was born with spinal problems and other medical problems. They told her mother she would never walk properly. She would be a wheelchair patient all her life and she would never be able to control her bowels. Well, her mother couldn't deal with that so she put her in a foundling home. During that time, before the utilization rules were so strict, the child would come into the hospital and sometimes stay for three months. And I got very attached to her—maybe partly because I had recently lost a child. Anyway, by the time she was two years old I decided I wanted to adopt her. I wanted to take her home. They discovered she had mild retardation, but to me it didn't matter. I mean, her mother didn't want her. But it turned out that the only thing her mother had to do was show up once a year and sign some papers and she couldn't be adopted. To me, that was being cruel. She never visited her, she never brought her anything. But still she kept her. As the child got older, every time she came back into the hospital she would ask for me. And over the years we became very close. She's thirteen now and I don't see her as often. But I hear she's doing okay.

I guess the thing I like best is the kids. I mean, just making a face at a kid and seeing that kid smile. You see some kid come in that really did a job on himself, and you take care of this kid, sometimes for up to a year. And then you take his cast off and watch the kid walk out of here. And even better, the next time he comes back to the clinic he comes in running. You know, that's the reward you get. The money part of it you can keep, but just the reward of knowing that you helped that kid run again—that's the payment.

ALBERT ANTHONY ALFARO, L.P.N.

Scrub Nurse

———✐————————

He's a slight, balding man who has been working as an OR scrub nurse for twenty-eight years. He has recorded thirty thousand operations in which he took part.

━━━━━━━━━━━━━

I've always done a lot of overtime because I had to put five children through school. I put my oldest daughter through nursing school. My second daughter is a Berkeley graduate and now an executive secretary. My son Albert I put through X-ray school. My fourth, a daughter, is a professional singer who I hope to see doing records. My youngest daughter is studying psychology. So I've had to work the overtime. But I'm used to this life-style. And when you have five kids and you're a scrub nurse, what else can you do?

I'm the only male scrub nurse in the OR. My role is to stand across the operating table from the surgeon and hand him instruments. Before the surgery, I set up all the instruments, I get the OR table ready.

We have a card for each of our doctors. On it, we list the doctor's idiosyncracies, which instruments they like, what type of suture they use for which operations, basically what they like and don't like. So we set up for the operation that way.

The five-minute scrub is a ritual. It's half a minute on each arm first, then half a minute on each hand. Then you do it again. Last, you do your nails. Total should be five minutes. You watch the clock. The only time you would do it in less time is when you already have the gloves on and you're rescrubbing. But I always do it for five minutes—that's one thing that I stress. You never know when you may have a hole in your glove during a case.

After the scrub you get the instruments ready. You have your sutures lined up, your abdominal pads, four-by-fours. Then you help drape the table and bring the portable canopy up to the table and give the surgeon a wet four-by-four to make sure the powder is all off his gloves.

Before he takes the scalpel, the doctor asks the anesthesiologist, "Can we begin?" The anesthesiologist is sometimes behind the drape that shields the patient's head. He can't see what's going on so he likes to know when we're starting. At the moment the surgeon cuts the skin, the circulating nurse will record the exact time and that's what we call the beginning of the operation.

It's all second nature now. But what got to me at my first operation was seeing the abdominal intestines lying on top of a white towel and still attached to the person—that was kind of eerie. The only other time I took a step back was when they handed me an amputated limb and I had to hand it to another person. I'm so used to it now, it doesn't bother me. I can understand, though, how some interns pass out the first time they see something like that.

A lot has changed in surgery here since I started in the late fifties. To begin with, they did about forty-five elective surgery cases a day versus ninety-five now. Then, we had no electives starting after two in the afternoon. Now we can start them as late as eight at night. The number of trauma cases we have now is enormous. We had maybe three gunshots a year versus one or two a day now!

Our operating time has shortened tremendously, basically because sutures and other materials that we work with have really improved. In the early days we would recycle our silk thread rolled up on a thin roll of rubber with numbers on it to determine the size of the suture. We'd recycle the gloves. We used glass syringes. We used everything over and over and over. Now everything is disposable. And the nurses used to stand there threading hundreds of needles at a time; now everything is prethreaded. We use surgical staples, which also cuts way down on the time. They just use a staple gun like you see anywhere, but it's for surgery, of course; it eliminates all the suturing with one press of the gun.

In plastic surgery, you name the operation, I've seen it . . . patients who come in with no ears have them constructed with cartilage from the rib area. I've seen surgeons rebuild a forehead area crushed in a car accident.

Patients born with a deformity of the eye have a normal face built up with muscle slings. It's very encouraging to see these people before and after. Sometimes they'll come for secondary revisions and you can see the highlights, the difference in their face. There are some women who have enormous breasts. They'll come in with forty-eight measurement and go out with a respectable size thirty-four. Young women. In their twenties.

The high point of my career was being the scrub nurse for the delivery of the Kinnast quintuplets. We were looking forward to that case all week. We knew it was going to be a multiple birth, but they didn't know when the lucky day would be. And I was the lucky one to go down on a Friday night and I double scrubbed. We had two teams—the sponge nurse and the scrub nurse. I was the scrub nurse. It was so exciting! The mother didn't look to me like she was going to have such a multiple birth, but there it was. Five!

It was real hectic. We had interns. We had residents. We had traffic all over the place! I tried to keep as many people as I could away from the OR because you don't want too much traffic when you're operating. I was set up for a C-section but we didn't have to do it. They were born spontaneously. "Here's one. Here's the second . . ." I mean, it was just something!

I was going home that night, this was when I lived downtown, and the bus driver says to me, "Say, did you hear about this lady who just gave birth to five babies?" She was already famous, and I was part of it. But I didn't tell him that. All I said that night to the driver was, "Oh, yes. I guess you could say I heard about it."

ROSEMARY MARTINO
Microsurgery Technician

In one corner of the microsurgery research and training laboratory, a table holds two large microscopes. The rest of the room houses laboratory benches and sinks. A faint smell of formaldehyde hangs in the air. She has been at this for two years. Before this she was a research assistant, but "it was too far from the mainstream of things. I wanted to be around people." She's twenty-eight.

My job is to teach surgeons and medical students the techniques of microsurgery. This means they learn to suture with tiny needles the size of an eyelash and almost invisible thread, while looking at the operative field through a microscope. Six departments participate in the program: orthopedics, plastic surgery, OB-GYN, urology, neurosurgery, and general surgery. It takes about forty hours to learn to do it properly.

The needle we work with is actually thinner than a human eyelash, but it has the same curve and size. The diameter of the suture is about one quarter the diameter of a human hair. With materials so small, you have to have very fine instruments to hold the needle and to help tie the knots. We use jewelers' forceps, which are aligned to a thousandth of an inch and have a pressure of several tons per square inch. You need a microscope to se what you're doing.

For someone who's never worked with one of these microscopes, it's a horror in the beginning. And if you take somebody from a subspecialty who's not as well trained as a surgeon, they're nervous at first. But I tell them if *I* can learn, anyone can learn. You have to be able to concentrate—that's all. We'll start by tying tiny knots on a piece of latex-glove rubber, which is about the thickness of an artery. As soon as they're proficient on latex, we move on to silicone tubing about the diameter of a drinking straw. They learn to sew two pieces of tubing to each other end to end, much the same way you would sew vessels. This may sound easy, but under a microscope it's really tough. You have to stitch the ends together while keeping the inside path free. When they have that down, and they have a very light touch which they've learned from sewing on the glove latex, they're ready for the rats.

A rat's femoral artery is the first live tissue my students work on. They sever the artery and then try to repair it with the same end-to-end process they used with the silicone tubes. It'll take maybe five of those to get good at it because a rat's blood vessel is like tissue paper and it just sort of falls away. If they get really advanced, they do a "free flap"—they remove an area of the rat's groin and they completely sever the blood supply. Then they sew it back again and in two days you can see if the tissue lived or died. That is, if it received blood supply or not. If it did, they can feel very successful at the techniques of microsurgery—on rats, anyway.

A couple of years ago, at ten o'clock one morning, Matt Putnam, a fellow in hand surgery [a medical or surgical resident who is doing an extra year or two of training, usually in a subspecialty] called me from the OR and said, "Rosemary, bring the microscope up this minute! Don't ask any questions, just bring it up." I couldn't imagine what they wanted it for. I knew they already had a microscope up there. What I didn't know was that some lady had just been brought into the emergency room with her two arms cut off. Actually, one was hanging by a thread, but the fingers of that hand and the other arm were totally off her body. The guy who attacked her hacked them off with a machete. He then went for her neck; just missed her spinal cord. God knows how she got here alive. They had to give her forty-eight units of blood in the ER.

The medics brought her to the ER, her arms with her. They were incredibly efficient. Normally we're not set up to do re-implants. They either go to Montefiore or to Bellevue. But this woman was so far gone, and we did have people with the capability of doing the operation, so she was brought to us. What equipment and personnel they mobilized to do this case! Two surgical teams. One OR had the team that worked with the one arm that was still slightly attached to her and her body. The other team was in an anesthesia room which had been set up with a sterile field and converted to a mini-OR. There, they were working on the severed arm, isolating all the structures with little loops so they could identify them when they had to put them back together again. They had three microscopes going at one time. One was being used by the team of surgeons working over the stump of the arm that was hanging by a thread. One was in use for the other stump where the doctors were tagging arteries and veins they would have to sew back together. The third microscope was in the anesthesia room where another group of surgeons was working over the severed arm. It was amazing. They had lines running all over the place, and so many people.

They kept it very low as far as publicity because this is not a re-implant center and you don't want people coming here all the time for re-implants when we have two places in the city that do them. This was an emergency, though. Maybe she could have been moved after she was here, but it was felt that if she had been moved, she would have lost the arms. They couldn't afford to let the arm be that long without blood supply. You can only leave an arm off for a specified amount of time without it dying.

They had the residents and a few of the medical students, and I was allowed up there. I saw some of it. It was really a sight—and what was so amazing was I saw the people I had trained doing what they learned from me! It was so wonderful to see how my work was translated into the operating room. To know because of what I did, somebody could go out into the world and do something totally constructive for somebody else. It was immediate gratification. Just like a surgeon!

MELVIN ROSENWASSER, M.D.

Orthopedic Surgeon

He grew up on a farm about seventy-five miles from New York, in a small town called Walden. He went to college in the late sixties and early seventies. "That was during the Vietnam uproars and medical school was very hard to get into. If you considered it, you had to excel in all your classes, and yet there was all this unrest on the campus—the traditional kinds of goals were being questioned. People wanted to take things pass-fail, didn't want to have to be ranked or graded." He is a P&S graduate.

Orthopedics has become more and more the specialty of the eighties, and the brightest, best students want to go into it. That's probably because it's so wide open and vast and interesting. Not only does it have a surgical bent to it, it has a research bent to it. In orthopedics, there's always something to offer a patient who comes to you with a serious problem, whether it's a baby with a club foot, or an old person with osteoarthritis, or somebody with a sports-related injury.

I constantly tell the residents that every case, even one that seems simple, requires the discipline of doing everything right and not taking anything for granted. I've seen simple things turn into disasters and very complicated things turn out fine. Some of that is predicated upon the skill of the surgeon, but a lot of it depends on training. Surgery is a discipline and there's a monotony to certain steps, but you have to follow every one of those steps anyway or something is going to fall through the cracks.

To me, orthopedics is fun—it's hard work, it's challenging, but it's fun. And you *never* know what's around the corner. Not too long ago I got a call from one of the residents in the emergency room saying there was a lady down there who had both of her arms chopped off. At first I thought they were just kidding around. But the resident said, and I could hear the urgency in his voice, "No, really, Dr. Rosenwasser, that's the situation! Could you come down? *Now.*"

I got down there in a matter of minutes. It was difficult to examine her, obviously. She was in shock, but she was awake. It's interesting—when patients are subjected to major trauma like that, they're not in pain. There's a self-protective mechanism whereby the brain secretes endorphins, natural pain-relieving substances. So people who have had horrendous injuries can be sitting there and they can talk to you and basically they don't feel the pain.

It's a shocking thing, dismemberment. There's a grisly connotation to it. You read about these things in police gazettes, people being found in boxes and trunks and what have you. But you hardly ever *see* them in person. They're used to all kinds of trauma in our ER—but there's something different about seeing body parts away from the body. It's not the same as seeing a dead body. The staff down there was doing their usual things to keep this woman alive, but they were really in shock. You could tell that right away.

After we determined the extent of her injuries, we called the desk in the operating room. We told them we *had* to come up—fast! Usually there's a lot of negotiating, but we said we had a serious problem and time was of the essence, and they said they'd be ready for us. So we headed for the eighteenth floor.

There are six elevators in the lobby. One is expressly for emergencies and patients. The problem is, to get to the elevator you have to wheel the patient down a crowded corridor and past the bank of elevators where all the visitors are waiting. For the people in the corridor, it's not a terrific sight—under any conditions—to see a blood-covered patient. You look at a stretcher, you can always see that there's someone on it, even though we try to maintain the patient's privacy. To someone who might be going to see his newborn son, it has to be shocking.

Anyway, we got to the OR, and we knew right away we were faced with a very involved problem. The woman had lost a lot of blood, so first we had to give her blood and fluids. Then we repaired the neck lacerations, because many arteries were still pumping blood all over the place. At the same time, I called for an extra microscope so we could dissect the vessels out of both the severed arms and also from the place where they were going back. Reattaching an arm or a hand—and we were doing both—is a very complex procedure. It's like cutting a telephone cable. Each thing has to go back exactly where it came from if you want it to work properly. It's an all-or-none phenomenon. You have to fix everything or you can forget it altogether. First you want to reestablish the circulation. And once you know that the part is viable and is receiving blood again, you have more time to reattach all the nerves. And you have to know it's going to take a long time. People always ask me, "How can you sit there all that time." But I don't have a sense of time when I'm working. You just keep working until there's nothing left to fix. And I'm always amazed—the whole day is gone.

This particular case took us twelve hours. You get fatigued. I mean, you're not Superman. I sat there for twelve hours—using the microscope, not using the microscope—always concentrating. I only got up once, and that was to answer the telephone. The unit manager called to say he wanted to have television cameras come up and interview me; they wanted to get the inside story. I said I couldn't—no, I *wouldn't*—leave the room. We were still working on her. Besides, I really felt that it was inappropriate to discuss it. After all, she was still in the operating room. What if she died?

We had two rooms going. One with the patient and the other, which was really like an induction area, where another team was working on her severed arm, reattaching the hand. It was a circus, because everybody was peering through the windows. The woman had had nail polish on, and her arm was sitting on a table. It was so bizarre, this hand with her ring and her nail polish . . .

When it was over—twelve hours later—we took her to the surgical intensive care unit. She was a real celebrity over there. Every hour or so we checked her circulation because these replants sometimes can go bad the first day—they can look good now, but six hours later the vessels clot off and you have to go back to the operating room. But it just didn't happen. She did fine.

She got out of the ICU in a day or two and she went to the floor. We kept her there for a very long time, partly because of her social situation and because she was concerned for her safety. That's when they gave her a pseudonym. Her name was Florence Ramirez, but they gave her a totally different pseudonym, something like Ellie Bernstein. She was down in one of the private rooms in Harkness for quite some time and everybody got real attached to her.

She spent at least a month with us. Everybody was going in and out of her room all the time—the therapists were very involved, and the hand fellows, as well as me. We were very happy that it was working, that she was going to have functional limbs, because there really isn't anything like an arm. You can walk very effectively with an artificial leg, and you can do just about everything, including swimming and running. But the arm is so specialized and has so many complex functions, and the types of devices that we put on are so crude—even the newer ones that are computer generated and open and close voluntarily—they're still so crude. So to save an arm or a hand is really a great thing.

Both hands are functional. Are they as good as new? No. But it's a question of are they useful, and can they do the things that she needs? Help her dress, help her eat, help her do things. And yes, they do. And very effectively. Both of them.

One of the problems we had with Florence was that she didn't come back after we discharged her. It's hard to reach people who don't have phones or who use different names. That's probably the most disappointing part of the whole thing. Although we had a close relationship with her when she was here, when she left, we had no way to make sure she would come back. And in fact, she never did.

IX
ADMINISTRATION

"The man was a genius! I tell you, he was an absolute genius!"

Dave Ginsberg, who is in charge of planning, is practically shouting, although he is less than two feet away from me. We're standing in the middle of Fort Washington Avenue, a street that runs parallel to the Hudson River and marks the dividing line between the old Presbyterian Hospital and the new one. The street has been closed to traffic for several weeks now while construction continues on the four bridges which span across the street below and will ultimately connect the two hospitals. We pause to watch as hugh cranes lift the steel beams. "It's amazing," says Ginsberg, indicating the new structure, "when you consider that less than five years ago, what we're looking at today was nothing more than a blueprint and a dream."

The old medical center was once a dream, too, in the mind of Edward Harkness, the man Dave Ginsberg describes as a genius. As we're watching the workmen, Ginsberg asks, "Do you know the story of how the medical center was put together?" We head toward the garden for a short walk as Ginsberg begins his story: The venture was the brainchild of a Presbyterian Hospital trustee, Edward Harkness. Going against the conventional wisdom of the day, he saw the possibility of great advantages from combining in one setting patient care, medical education, and research. Harkness thought a hospital and a medical school should be interdependent. On one hand, the medical school would supply the hospital with future doctors who need a setting in which to get clinical experience and a place where they can be taught by practicing physicians and scientists. At the time, P&S students had little such exposure because most New York hospitals were opposed to allowing students to train on their wards. The two facilities available to the school, Vanderbilt Clinic and Sloane Hospital, did not have enough teaching cases to meet the needs of the students. On the other hand, Harkness said, Presbyterian wants to have the best-trained doctors taking care of its patients—those doctors are generally found on the faculty of a good medical school. Armed with this argument, he convinced the board of Presbyterian Hospital to look for a school with which to affiliate.

The concept of affiliating a hospital with a medical school was not a new one. It dated back to Doctor Samuel Bard (for whom Bard Hall, the freshman medical student residence, is named), a professor of medicine at the then King's College, who in 1769 wrote about the benefits to students of exposing them to patients with the diseases they had been reading about in the classroom. After the Revolutionary War, King's College merged into Columbia College of Physicians and Surgeons, but it was not until the early 1900s that a search was begun for a hospital affiliation.

In 1911, both Presbyterian Hospital and the Columbia College of Physicians and Surgeons achieved their goals by joining together in what would be called Columbia-Presbyterian Medical Center. The first order of business was to find a proper site for the new center. Here again, Harkness's imagination was exceptional. His view that the center should be constructed far to the north of the population concentration of Manhattan prevailed, and he helped find what he considered a perfect location, in the semirural Washington Heights area. The site he selected was the home, from 1903 to 1912, of the New York Highlanders' baseball club, the future New York Yankees.

After a decade of negotiation, interrupted by World War I, an alliance agreement was drawn up in 1921. Because of the difficulty the institutions had had in reaching agreement, Harkness decided to create a legal document between the hospital and the university that would force the two to work closely together. The agreement stipulated that the chairman of each department at the university be at the same time the director of service at the hospital. In addition, the hospital could not appoint physicians to its staff who had not already received an appointment from the university. To interlock the two even further, he divided a major part of the land with a line running north and south. East of the line was hospital property, and west, the university's. He then proposed that the hospital be partly constructed on university land and the university partly on hospital land. So, in order to build in the future, each institution would have to go to the other.

Ground breaking at the site took place in January 1925. Three years later, on March 18, 1928, Presbyterian Hospital and the Columbia College of Physicians and Surgeons moved into their new quarters. The move represented the operational beginning of the first medical center in the United States. "And so here we are today," concludes Ginsberg, "a consortium of nine institutions packed onto twenty acres with a nursing school, a dental school, a public health school, even our own nursery school. And when the construction crews pull out in 1989, we will have a new hospital here, a community hospital uptown and four ambulatory care centers scattered throughout the community. Not bad for a place that less than sixty years ago was a baseball field.

"So you see," he says, "Harkness really knew what he was doing all along. And here we are, sixty years later, perpetuating his dream."

We have started walking back to Fort Washington Avenue to watch the progress of the bridges. By now, two large groups have formed on the street, one at each end of the block. A hospital security guard faces each group, preventing anyone from passing. No one wants to. Every face is looking up expectantly as the crane lifts a twelve foot steel beam and delivers it to the six workmen, three on each end of the structure. As the missing link is laid into place, a cheer goes up from the crowd. For the first time the two hospitals are connected.

When the guards allow us to pass, Dave Ginsberg and I head for his office.

THOMAS Q. MORRIS, M.D.
President

―――――――――――

His is an expansive office in the administrative suite in Atchley Pavilion.
Portraits of past presidents grace the walls. It's a clear, crisp day outside,
and looking south through the windows, all of downtown Manhattan ap-
pears to be in view.

He's an affable man, tall and stately, with a quick wit and an easy laugh.
He came up through the ranks: P&S medical school, class of 1958, acting
chairman of the department of medicine, vice-dean of the medical school,
and, as of January 1, 1985, president of the hospital. This morning, as
always, he is wearing a white lab coat, a reminder that even though he
occupies the president's office, he is still, first and foremost, a physician.

We settle into a comfortable sofa, the tape recorder between us. I ask
about a typical day. He opens his appointment book to yesterday.

―――――――――――

I got up at about five-thirty. I have a fairly long drive, about thirty miles
each way. But I've been making that ride for twenty-plus years now, so it's
not really a factor. I generally get here at six-thirty, when all the surgeons
do. When I come in from the parking lot, all the surgeons are walking in.
When I go home at night, the internists are leaving.

A lot of calls come in between a quarter to seven and seven-thirty
because people know I'm here and that I'll answer my phone. The other

day I met with our newly designated acting director of radiology. He wanted to make sure that he had access to me if he encountered any problems as time went on, and I said he certainly would. I told him that I'm always here early in the morning and he can call me. So the next morning at six forty-five the phone rang. It was he. He said, "Just checking . . ."

At seven-thirty, I had an informal meeting with the executive vice-presidents. That's something I do almost every day. There are three of them. Joe Corcoran, the executive vice-president for administrative affairs, is responsible for making the hospital run in terms of day-to-day operating problems and he's responsible for the financial picture. Dr. Gerald Thomson is executive vice-president for professional affairs. His responsibilities are to see that patient care in this hospital is delivered in an expert and timely way. The medical and nursing staffs report to me through him. Dave Ginsberg is the executive vice-president for planning and program development, a monstrous responsibility today, not only because of all the new construction we have going on around here but also because of our involvement with the new ventures that are emerging in medicine—health maintenance organizations, institutional networks, and so on.

These early morning meetings deal with everything from construction of the new hospital to recruitment of new doctors, nurses, and technicians. We can have all the best bricks and mortar in the world holding that hospital up, but if we can't staff it, we can't open it. So yesterday we talked about recruitment, where the money is coming from to make it possible, and what kind of programs we're going to have.

When the meeting was over I had my Spanish lesson. I've been studying Spanish with Margaret Hawkins, one of our employees in Training and Development, for a couple of years now. I'm trying to get myself to the point where I can at least be reasonably conversant at community meetings and with patients. So much of our community is Spanish-speaking that I think it's important to have the hospital be sensitive to that, and try to participate in some marginally reasonable way. Unfortunately it doesn't look like I'm ever going to be the equivalent to the José Greco of dance. But I did get a B-plus for the day's lesson.

Along the same vein, I met next with Helen Morik who is the director of our Office of Government and Community Affairs. That department more or less acts as a liaison between us and the community. We spent a half hour talking about our relationships with the community and the elected officials in Washington Heights.

At ten o'clock, I went to a memorial service for Dr. André Cournand. This relationship goes back thirty years for me. Dr. Cournand was ninety-two when he died. He won the Nobel Prize in 1956, he and Dickinson

Richards, both of whom were on staff here, and a man from Germany named Werner Forssmann. The three of them won the prize for cardiac catheterization. I met Dr. Cournand for the first time when I was a medical student in '56, right after he became a Nobel laureate. He and Dr. Richards lectured to our third-year class. When I did my training at Bellevue, he was working there so I got to work with him directly. I did a fellowship in his lab. Years later, when I was acting chairman of the department of medicine, the shoe was on the other foot. Dr. Cournand was an emeritus professor and directing programs in social medicine on this campus and he wanted me to think that *he* was working for *me*.

I think the most important impact anyone has on you, more important than the subject matter that they're teaching you, is the way that they teach you to approach problems. In that respect both he and Dr. Richards had substantial effects on me. I would never have ended up coming back to this medical center to do research unless I had been with those men; so I would never have ended up in this job. I've always felt their impact on my career has been rather substantial. It's terrific to be around people like that, who not only have great accomplishments, but make themselves totally available to you and make you feel very comfortable with them. And that's what both of them did. You never had the feeling that they were anyone special.

The memorial service ran longer than I expected and I ended up with a tight time-frame, but I was back up here by noon for the Management Committee meeting. Management is made up of all the hospital vice-presidents and the directors of a number of major areas—about a dozen people. The agenda for the meeting varies but one thing we always do at these meetings is hear a media report from Richard Zucker, our director of Public Information. It's important for us to know where we're being highlighted, whether it's in broadcast or print, and what's coming up. We have to know in advance when there's going to be a horde of TV reporters running throughout the hospital so we know what to expect. For example, Channel Two's program, "48 Hours," is planning to follow one of our heart transplants for an upcoming show. I'm sure they'll be here with crews for quite a while.

We try to give open and fair access to the media. Not to the detriment of the patients and not to the detriment of the institution, but in a balanced way. Patient confidentiality has to be top priority and we talked about this at the meeting. Lots of media events surround our patients. It was all over the papers when Mayor Koch was brought here. Also Hedda Nussbaum and Sonny von Bulow. Lots of members of the entertainment world come in for treatment. They deserve privacy when they want it, and we provide it. The problem is, our staff—clinical or administrative—is frequently confronted by members of the police who want information. We have to be careful in those situations. Just because someone's wearing a uniform doesn't entitle them to confidential information about a patient. So our staff is trained never to give out any information to anyone. No matter who they are.

We also talked at this meeting about cost containment. We're doing all sorts of things now from looking at how we turn lights on to how many bulbs are in each fixture. We install reflectors in various sorts of fixtures and use half the number of bulbs, and therefore halve the cost. We're trying to increase the number of voluntary blood donations—we want to double that this year. So we talked about those things. Media, revenue enhancement, cost containment, confidentiality.

After Management Committee I met with the Dermatology Search Committee—we're looking for a new Chairman of Dermatology. Then I grabbed a sandwich and went off to another meeting. I'm a member of a steering group called Health of the Public. We have received a grant that involves Presbyterian, Columbia, and Harlem Hospital. We're trying to develop programs for the integration of public health and education for medical students, nursing students, and public-health students. At this particular meeting we went over such things as the summer seminar they're going to have, special courses and how they'll be paid for.

By then it was three o'clock. I spent the next hour with the dean of the medical school, Dr. Bendixen. We discussed a whole host of things regarding joint activities between the hospital and the medical school. We do that regularly so that each is kept abreast of what the other is doing.

At four, I attended a meeting of the board of trustees. We have thirty-two members on our board. They're the governing body of this place. I can never predict what's going to happen at these meetings, but it's always interesting to see the trustees' different perspectives and points of view. They want to know that we're doing important work in the hospital, that we're recruiting high quality staff, that we're making new advances. Some board members want to make sure that we're providing support for the community. Others have particular areas of interest, and they want to know what's happening in pediatrics, or what we're doing in neurology.

The board of trustees must approve all policies set in this hospital. Basically, there are two kinds of policies: medical and administrative. Medical policies determine how we manage various medical situations. First the situation is brought to the attention of the medical board—an appointed and elected body made up of directors of service and practicing staff in the hospital. I'm on the medical board and so is Dr. Bendixen. All regulatory policies that affect direct patient care are brought to the medical board.

A good example is the new state guidelines on "Do Not Resuscitate" [DNR] orders. It's an in-house decision as to how to comply with outside regulatory guidelines. They come from the New York State Health Department, and they're interpreted by our legal staff and discussed with the physicians. In the case of DNR, it involves everything from who communicates with the patient, who communicates with the family when the patient's not competent, who handles the communication, to how it is documented. If there's a dispute, what is the mediation process?

The medical board deliberates on these questions and makes recommendations to the hospital and then it goes to the board of trustees. As the governing body, they have the ultimate responsibility, and they have to be comfortable. Suppose they totally disagree with it? Suppose the doctors said, "We will not resuscitate anybody." The trustees, when presented with that policy, could say, "That's crazy. You can't do that." Now, I must say our medical staff is extremely reasonable, and the policies that they develop are always appropriate, but the trustees do have the ultimate authority if they disagree with the staff.

Administrative policies are developed by the administration of the hospital, and they can include all sorts of things: hiring and firing of personnel, negotiations with unions. Those policies are first developed by the various sections in the hospital, and then brought to the HAC Committee—which is the Hospital Administrative Committee—and that body makes recommendations to me. Unless I think they're way off base, I endorse them. Then they're presented to the board of trustees.

Every trustee in every institution is worried about liability these days—personal liability. That's because there have been so many instances of hospitals being pursued by the press concerning care of particular patients, or what is viewed by the state as an adverse incident. The state directs that responsibility right back to the governing board.

The governing board is ultimately responsible for what goes on in this hospital—house staff and attending physicians included. The residents are hospital employees. All the physicians are our responsibility as well. We have given them privileges to practice here. If a physician's personal conduct or medical practice as it affects patients is inappropriate, it's our responsibility to intervene. It's a pretty clear responsibility. That's why trustees in many institutions in New York State are fleeing their jobs. They're resigning left and right. It's a serious problem in some areas.

A hospital is always in a state of flux. That's partially due to several external factors which are totally out of our control—I call them the three Rs of health care: the regulatory, reimbursement, and regimentation aspects of medicine. Those things are changing all the time and we're always caught having to respond to them.

For example, suddenly the state puts out a new series of regulations about house-staff training—the number of hours that residents can work. So we're going to have to change a whole lot of schedules; add staff; all sorts of things. Another example: there's a new regulation in New York State requiring every patient to sign a letter as he or she is about to be discharged. If the patient agrees that he's ready to go home, he signs the letter. That means we have to deliver forty-five thousand letters every year—one to every patient who is about to leave. We're not quite as good as the U.S. Postal Service; it's a huge job for us. Who delivers those letters? Should it be the nurse? Should it be the doctor? Should it be the social worker? Should we hire someone to do it?

If a patient doesn't want to go home, he can appeal the discharge order and we must keep him for at least twenty-four hours while a third party designated by the state comes in and decides if he should go or not. I think the state, in its enthusiasm to implement this system, neglected to consider a number of aspects. One, which doesn't apply so much to us but still exists, is that every prisoner who is hospitalized gets a letter like this. And so they all say they're not ready to go back. Why would they say otherwise?

So we talk about these things.

By the time the board meeting was over, it was after six. That left me very little time to meet with my secretary—so she could tell me what I hadn't done that day—and to dress for dinner. Some weeks I'll go to as many as three or four business dinners during the week. So last night was another. And I always seem to cut the time very close. No problem, though. I can now get into black tie in seven minutes.

I was the host at last night's dinner. It was for members of the New York Medical-Surgical Society. That's a group of New York's leading physicians, practitioners, educators, and administrators. They rotate the hosting for the dinner and the host picks the topic for the evening. Frequently it's dedicated to discussions of difficult problems in clinical medicine, or anything, actually. I picked medical education. I think one of the things that cries out for action is change in the whole educational approach, not only at the graduate level or resident level but at the medical-student level as well.

I spoke to the group about how, if I were a medical student today and went back and took the medical-school curriculum, I would find it very comfortable. That's because it's basically the same as it was thirty years ago. We're all lamenting about changes that are occurring around us, but we're not doing anything about them. Fewer and fewer young people are going into medicine. Why is that happening? Well, those three Rs certainly play a role, but what are *we* doing to make it an exciting, challenging, fun career for people? There's something wrong with pushing students through the same curriculum that we had thirty years ago, when we know at least on the clinical side that patient stays are shorter, the patients are sicker, and there's not enough time for the students to really learn from those patients. And yet we're jamming them into this day after day, month after month, and the students come out and say: "Boy, that was terrible!" That's a pretty loud message. Even our basic-science curriculum is essentially the same. I think the mandate for change in medical education is screaming at us loud and clear.

It turns out that the discussion that ensued was extremely active but in total disarray; nobody could agree on anything. That's not a bad thing though. It simply shows that we ought to get together and figure out what we want to do.

The dinner was over by ten and I headed for home. It was a full day, but that's not unusual. This place is a big responsibility. They tell me twenty-five thousand people walk through here every day. And I can believe it. To start with, we have about six thousand employees, six or seven hundred admitting physicians on top of that, and the college has a few thousand employees; so you get up over ten, eleven thousand very quickly. Then you think of the number of visitors—we have twelve hundred patients in the hospital every day—each one has one or two visitors. The numbers just catapult.

The thing that impresses me most of all is how many people it takes to make it all go properly. I walk through the emergency room from time to time just to see how it's going; I walk from there over to the walk-in clinic, or upstairs to one of the group practices in Vanderbilt. And you see all those people, carrying out their responsibilities under either good or adverse circumstances. They're committed and they're dedicated and that's what makes this place so great.

Before I moved into the presidency, I spent three months observing what goes on in the hospital. I spent most of the time walking around, seeing different areas, and just saying "hello" to people. One of the places I went to was the laundry. As they took me through, they used the opportunity to show me one of their machines which they were not pleased with, a machine that dries and folds sheets and is called a mangler. They did a little campaigning with me, and so not too long thereafter, along on the capital budget came a request for a new one. It was a new model but it went back to the old style and they said they could feed in the sheets faster manually than they could with this semiautomated gadget they had. So we approved it. After the new machine arrived, they invited me back to see it in action. There was a team of four people working on this new machine. Apparently, several weeks before, they had processed over one thousand sheets in less than an hour, more than had ever been done before, and the laundry manager gave them an award. The day I went over, I was introduced to the award-winning team. Everybody was very excited about it. And it *was* exciting and it was *important*. If you consider all the things going on in this place, and the number of people we serve, you realize how every person, every facet of this hospital, has its own importance. And that includes the laundry. I mean, there's no way you can run a hospital without sheets. At times we've tried . . . it doesn't work.

KEVIN DAHILL

Director of Activation

The picture window in his office is less than fifty feet from the framework of the new hospital. It is noon and the construction workers outside are just breaking for lunch. Five men, in plaid shirts, jeans, and hard hats, sit on the steel beams eight stories up, legs dangling, eating sandwiches.

His is one of the Horatio Alger stories of the hospital. A young boy starts his career working as a part-time messenger and now, sixteen years later, he's a hospital administrator.

This hospital played a big part in my growing up. I lived in this neighborhood, and if I got hurt playing stick ball or whatever in the street, my mother brought me here to the clinic. Everyone in my family has worked here at some point in their lives. My mother was first. A little over twenty years ago she took a part-time job in the evenings in the record room. At that time, the evening shift in medical records was made up of housewives from the neighborhood. It was the famous "seven-to-eleven shift"; seven in the evening to eleven at night. These women all became very close friends. A social network developed from it.

My father, who was a Teamster official at the time, took early retirement at age sixty. So for something to do, he latched onto a job here in the cashier's office. After what he had been through—major contracts with the

Teamsters and getting involved with milk strikes in New York—he thought this job was a joke. He'd walk in here in the mornings and he'd work behind the window and cash checks and set payments on bills. He'd stroll home for lunch and watch a couple of soap operas and then stroll back and do his afternoon's worth of work. He always used to tell us, "A second grader could do this job. It's so easy." But he loved it. The only reason he retired from here was because at that time, if you were sixty-five, you were out. There was no question about it.

By then I had started college and worked here as a part-time messenger. My sister worked in patient accounts, and on down the line. I have three other siblings and every one has worked here in some capacity or another. So this place has played a large part in my life. And I'm sad but in some ways I'm happy to say both my parents passed away here.

My first full-time job was in 1969. I worked evenings at the information desk. Then I became evening supervisor of admitting, and then I was the night manager of the hospital for five years. It's a strange life, working nights, but it's interesting. There are people who have done it here throughout their entire career, but it's a very strange life. Your sleeping habits, your eating habits, are totally different than the normal routine that everyone else has. People look at you strangely when you pour yourself a Scotch on the rocks before you go to sleep at nine-thirty in the morning. Or you have a hamburger and French fries at six in the morning. Things like that. In my case, as a night manager, it was even more peculiar, because we would break up the week. I would do three nights a week from midnight till eight A.M., have two days off, and do two evenings of four to twelve. The police department always complains because they go week to week and they swing shifts. They do a week of midnights and a week of four to twelves. We broke it up right in the middle of the week. So your first day off was spent mainly sleeping, just to catch up.

It was sort of like a jet lag and I began to relate to childhood friends of mine who had fathers who were cops and firemen. When you went to their houses after school, you had to be real quiet. You always got the feeling there was something wrong with someone who slept all day.

But I liked nights. And as I look back on it, I even liked the environment. It's amazing what an *esprit de corps* there is on nights—the grave-yard shift, as they call it—among everyone who is on it. The doctors need the porters much more at night than they do during the daytime and they can relate to them better. There are centralized locations where everyone goes for coffee and Danish, as opposed to different places where the doctors and nurses eat during the day. At night you're all the same. There's much more of a family-type atmosphere.

Toward the end of that period, the hospital created a department of patient relations and I was put in as the director. From there, I was promoted again to the new position of director of Government and Community Affairs. Then, towards the end of '86, I got a call from Joe Corcoran, the chief operating officer. He said, "Look, we've got these buildings going up and ultimately we're going to be moving the old hospital into the new one and we need a person to be in charge of the move, and we want you to do it."

So as of January first this year, I've been the Director of Activation. It's a huge undertaking, moving a whole hospital, and it requires a large staff to look after things. Equipment has to be tested and monitored, people have to be trained to work the new equipment. There are big things and small. The furniture has to be in before the staff moves in. We even have to plan for things like wastebaskets.

It's a job just getting people to pack, asking them to make major decisions like whether or not to throw out documents from 1958. I'm thinking of staging a contest as part of the major move, for the department that discards the most hard-copy records, because I think people just hold on to things in order to hold on to them. We would have some sort of a special prize—a trip or something like that.

We're probably going to move in floor by floor, mainly because we're going to get the building turned over to us by the construction people floor by floor. When they turn it over, they're turning it over in bare-bones fashion. We've got to get the equipment operating and make sure it works and that our staff knows how to work it. We've got to clean up the place so that the state can come in and review it and make sure it meets code requirements and so on. That process takes a lot of time.

Moving the patients will be no problem. Even patients with respirators and IVs. On a given day we're going to decide this is "orthopedics' day." So we'll move all the ortho staff and their patients to the new unit. If somebody is in traction, then they'll stay in the old hospital until they can be safely moved. We'll decide in advance which patients are going to be moved that day. We'll have a schedule on that morning. We'll know that John Smith, who is now in 401, bed 3, in the old Presbyterian, is moving to Garden North, 812, bed 2. I envision a cadre of transporters and volunteers. There'll literally be a parade of patients coming across the bridges over Fort Washington Avenue. It's not difficult, when you think about it. It's like moving a patient from one room to another; it's just a longer trip.

In terms of what keeps me awake at night when I consider the move, the transfer of patients is not it. Sure, we may lose a patient temporarily, a patient may end up in the wrong room for a little while. I mean, it's realistic to expect that *somebody* will have made a wrong turn *somewhere*.

But that's not what worries me. I'm concerned about the human dynamics of the staff moving to the new building. The way I see it, our entire organization has to change. Take orthopedics again. We're bringing what are now four different inpatient orthopedics units together onto one floor. We have four head nurses moving into one unit. So now who supervises the floor? Will they get along? What happens to seniority? Now maybe I'm barking up the wrong tree, but I think that these are going to be issues we'll have to contend with. I think that kind of thing is going to transcend the overall activation effort. But I also think if we do this right, we can make it a positive experience. Theoretically this should be an exciting adventure.

A lot of my outward calm is strictly for show. I'm convinced that if I, above all people, show any signs of nervousness or apprehension, then we've blown it. I've got to instill confidence in people; not just in me, but in the process. There are times, though, when I just go somewhere and scream to myself or I whack a golf ball in an effort to work it out.

A lot of people say you shouldn't stay in any organization too long, and for years I disagreed with that. I've been very lucky in this hospital. The opportunities that I've had here have been wonderful. There's been no reason to leave. But now . . . now I think maybe I should give that some thought. I think most people resist change, and it's possible that after I get them moved, they're not all going to like me a whole lot. So after the new hospital is open, maybe I'd be better off like the Lone Ranger. Maybe I should just get on my white horse and ride off into the sunset.

JOAN MCGANN
Administrative Secretary

———

She is secretary to David Ginsberg, executive vice-president for planning
and program development.

*"I was already here by the time Dave came in 1978. I was a secretary to
the board of trustees so I worked in this same area. I remember I used to
sit and watch Dave's people come scurrying past me. Everybody was always
running, and I'd say, 'Boy, am I glad I don't work in Planning!' I think I
meant it then. I really do. I thought it looked so hectic and they had all these
deadlines to meet. Then, six years ago, Dave's secretary retired and I found
myself hoping that he would choose me to replace her. I figured, I could
learn to run."*

We're a big department of twenty-five people, almost a company unto
ourselves. We're very much a part of everything: planning, marketing,
project coordination, and development of locations for our physicians to
see patients off-site of the hospital. We have a building for our doctors in
midtown Manhattan, another in Riverdale, and now we've got small-
practice sites scattered throughout the Washington Heights community,
almost like store-front offices that will serve the neighborhood.

What I do for Dave keeps me plenty busy. For starters, I keep track of
his calendar. I make sure he goes where he's supposed to go when he's

supposed to go there, that he sees who he's supposed to see, and that he fits in everyone who needs to see him in a day. I'm also in charge of payroll, making sure everyone gets his or her timesheets in on time, keeping track of vacation days, paying the bills, and ordering everything from supplies to personal computers to lunch for visitors when that's indicated.

I'm not one to take a lot of initiative on my own, though. That's probably the result of how I was trained at secretarial school. We were taught to let the boss make the decisions. I would never even have called Dave "Dave" unless he said to, because in those days secretaries didn't call their bosses by their first names. It was always "Mister." In the beginning it was hard to get used to because he was always Mr. Ginsberg from the day I met him.

I think a successful boss-secretary relationship comes out of understanding each other, being conscious of the other person's needs, understanding each other's moods and temperaments. I think we have a good relationship that way. Dave goes nonstop until once in a while I say, "Give us a break! How much typing can we do in one day?" and he'll slow down—temporarily. But I really respect his drive and his energy and I like that part of his personality.

I'm always curious when a new secretary comes to work here in the administration offices to see how long she'll last. With some you can predict it, others you can't. Sometimes the constant pressure gets to them. When that's the case, you can see it right away. Others just don't really want to work very hard. Some of them are stunned by the type of work we do. I think it's not what they anticipated. They hope to have a few little letters to do, and things like that. We do detailed reports; we're constantly updating and revising them, and rushing to meet deadlines for one thing or another. They want a more glamorous type of position. I think most young secretaries today want glamorous jobs. And why not? But they can't expect to find that here, and they have to see that when they come for an interview. To me, it's no big deal. But that was our ethic. We worked hard. There was no women's lib when I went to secretarial school.

I grew up in this neighborhood. I lived two blocks from the hospital, but interestingly I wasn't in here as a patient until my children were born. The hospital was not a place we came to. In fact we hoped *not* to come here.

Where the service building is now, there was a tennis court for doctors. Come to think of it, you never saw a nurse playing tennis there. The fence was fairly high and they had those green tarpaulins so that you couldn't see through the fence. But there were always a few holes—air vents—so we used to look in and we thought it must be so exciting to be in there, playing tennis. For some reason that remains, for me, a strong memory of Presbyterian in the old days.

In the forties and fifties, the street that I lived on—163rd—was a melting pot. We had just about every nationality—Irish, German, Jewish, Polish. It was great. There was a Japanese lady married to a Jewish guy. I remember we were all awed by that because it was during World War II. I had a boy in my class whose mother was an Aztec Indian, married to a Mexican man. There were a lot of interesting people. It's still a beautiful area. It's very high above sea level, supposedly the healthiest spot in New York City. You could walk a block in any direction and still see trees.

I've learned more about my neighborhood working in this job than I learned in all the years I lived here. Statistically, that is—how many elderly there are here and how many maternity cases we have and how many births we have. Things like that. Demographics is a big part of this office.

I guess most people, when they go to work every day, come home and say, "Well, I had another day at the office," but I feel that I've accomplished so much. So much is done in our office, and I'm part of it every day. It's funny to look back . . . the days when I saw Mr. Ginsberg and his crew running by me—I never thought I'd be a part of that, and I never thought I could keep the pace they kept. But I suppose I've become one of the runners without even realizing it.

DAVID GINSBERG
Executive Vice-President,
Planning and Program Development

He's a stocky man of medium height with a kind face framed by a fringe
of gray hair and thick white sideburns. He is full of enthusiasm and anima-
tion as he points out demographic charts, maps, and sketches that line his
office and show the growth of the hospital and the community. An architect
by profession, he first came to Presbyterian as a consultant while working
with another company. In 1979, the hospital created an office of planning
and hired him as the director.

Ten years ago, Presbyterian hired the architectual firm I was associated
with to evaluate the hospital and to create a master plan for the future.
The general perception here was that everything was fine and we were
being hired strictly to recreate the institution as it was; to restore it to the
original. As we started to look at the institution, we realized that it had
so many other, more systemic, problems, that it just plain wasn't ready for
a restoration, with the roof leaking, figuratively speaking.

It was very hard to talk about the future, though, when the institution
was literally the same institution that was built in 1928. It had the same
open wards, the same un–air-conditioned space. Other than the fact that
a few lighting fixtures had been changed from incandescent to fluorescent,
not much was different in 1978 from how it was in 1928.

To understand what was happening, you have to go back to the late sixties, when fifteen to twenty percent of the patients who came here lived on the east side of Manhattan. For a number of reasons, as time went on these patients began to go elsewhere. For one thing, the hospital had just not kept up with the newer hospitals in midtown Manhattan and many doctors on our staff started practicing elsewhere.

As our population of Upper East Side patients fell off, it was quickly replaced by people in this neighborhood who had no other hospital to go to, because all of the other hospitals in the community had closed. Many of these people had no financial means and no insurance. But we took them in anyway, and as a result we began to lose a lot of the money we were used to. We were headed for a particularly difficult financial time.

This is a heavily endowed hospital and historically it has always used income from its endowment to support care for the poor. But in the three years prior to 1977, they used about twenty-five million dollars of principal of the endowment to keep going. The trustees were very, very concerned, obviously, and they decided it was time for a major reorganization of the hospital.

A new president, Dr. Felix Demartini, was appointed, and he recruited Ed Noroian as his executive vice-president. They were told by the board of trustees to create a long-range plan for the hospital, and that set of events, starting in the fall of 1977, changed the direction of this institution. The first step was to hire an architectural firm, which is how I got involved. My company was called in to look at the facilities.

Our first suggestion was that the hospital consolidate its facilities and achieve an acceptable occupancy level. To do that, it was agreed that the hospital should close down two hundred of the fifteen hundred beds that were within the complex. At that time the hospital had something like four hundred and twenty-five physicians with admitting privileges, a number that was declining every year. We also suggested that they figure out a way to recruit at least two hundred additional doctors. The third thing we said was, "Before you do any master planning, you have to spend some money to make this place more livable." And so we created a program that we called the Priority Projects. The hospital actually spent about thirty million dollars over a period of five years, and even then the place was so big that we only put a Band-Aid on the institution.

At the time, Presbyterian Hospital, which is the main building, consisted mostly of open wards. So we spent about a third of the money closing the wards and making them into semiprivate rooms with bathrooms. Harkness Pavilion was getting shabby because it hadn't had anything but a few coats of paint over a period of time, so we spent about a million dollars making Presbyterian and Harkness into at least habitable spaces.

We spent about five million dollars making the clinics in Vanderbilt look a little bit more like doctor offices. We spent about three million dollars in the emergency room, and about five million dollars in Babies' Hospital. Our obstetrics facility was just awful, so we built a new obstetrics unit on two floors in Babies'. We spent about five million dollars updating equipment. Then we did a little in the Neurological Institute, a little in the Eye Institute. It was a collection of hundreds of little projects, but when we finished it, at least you could walk around the institution and say, "All right, it's an old hospital but at least there is some degree of *humanism* in the place." It at least gave us time to do a decent job of master planning. Now that the roof wasn't leaking anymore, we could start talking about the future.

As the Priority Projects got underway, a very interesting thing happened. In order to get the projects going, we had to make an application to the state for approval of what we were doing. Part of that application included a community review. When the community began to look at what we wanted to do, they agreed the project was a good idea, but on the other hand, they said they didn't really know very much about this place at all. We were here in their neighborhood for all these years, but they really didn't know much about us. And why would they? We had never had any real contact with them, we were never really a part of them. So we began an all-out effort to meet our community, to get out there and get to know them and let them get to know us.

We joined every major community organization. We started to work at the community board, in the Little League, in the Boy Scouts, in every program that you can imagine, because we realized, as the largest economic force in the community, we had responsibilities that were not just health-care related.

Even today, we have a group of about twenty-five people who participate in each of these activities. We sometimes support them financially, we sometimes just support them with expertise; sometimes we just volunteer in the programs, but we have become a major center of activity in the Washington Heights neighborhood. It's been a very exciting time, and the end result is you walk out on the street and people are saying, "This is our hospital."

With community approval and state approval, we started our renovation project. And things began to turn around. As the hospital facility improved, we began to get additional doctors on staff. Many came because of the prestige of the institution. Many were people who trained here and chose to stay on. Some were motivated simply by wanting to work in the area. With the addition of new physicians and a livable building, it wasn't long before patients from the East Side started coming back. And that, combined with the fact that many hospitals had closed in this area, was the beginning of the idea that we needed more beds and more space.

So we opted to build a separate community hospital that would serve the people in the area who don't need to be in a medical center. It would be part of Presbyterian but would be three miles uptown in the Inwood section of Manhattan. It's to be called the Allen Pavilion. It will have a maternity service, a medical service, a surgical service, an orthopedic service, a psychiatric service—like any other community hospital.

So now, with the Allen Pavilion almost complete and the new Presbyterian hospital, which will be ready in early 1989, we'll have fifteen hundred beds again.

JIMMY GILL
Unit Manager

He's forty-six. A short, energetic, bright-eyed man with dark, curly hair and dark-rimmed glasses. He worked at Presbyterian as a part-time messenger when he was seventeen. At eighteen, he went into the army for four years. "The government had this program that if you go into the service, the place that you were working is required to take you back. When I came back, there was a letter stating that I had a job here. I wasn't really planning on staying in New York. In fact, I didn't want to stay in New York at all, but I didn't have any money so I figured maybe I'd go back there for a while, get some funds, and then take off." He's been here for twenty-four years.

This is the unit manager's office. We're in charge of the day-to-day operations of the medical center. We take care of any operational problems and we take care of any immediate crisis situations that come up. Our number is listed on every nurses' station and in just about every area of the medical center, so if something happens, they're supposed to call us.

There aren't two days that are the same in here; always something different. It's not the type of job where you come in and you generate so much paper work and then you leave. We're always dealing with a situation and handling some kind of crisis. Right now we have an unknown male who was a jumper—fell eight stories to the street—and has been here, unconscious, for several weeks. The police have been trying, unsuccessfully, to identify him. We've taken his fingerprints and pictures and we still haven't been able to determine who he is. But we'll keep working with the police until we get something on him. Usually, when someone like that is brought in, he's worked over in the emergency room and he might go to the OR and somewhere down the line the police will notify a family member or friend and they'll send them to us to tell them what's happened. Or if a patient from the ER dies, especially if it's at night, we're the ones here to talk with the family.

We had a city blackout about ten years ago. Practically everything here went down except the emergency lights and the elevators that operate on emergency generators. We set up flood lights so people could see to come in. People from all over the neighborhood came into the emergency room to wait it out. So we had those people to deal with as well as true emergencies. Every floor has certain rooms where, if the electrical system goes down, emergency generators go on. That night, it was our responsibility to coordinate who needed special attention and to get those people moved as fast as possible to rooms where they could be monitored properly. When you have a situation like that, people who are employed here—administrators and managers—automatically come in. They hear there's a problem, they come. If we need even more help in certain areas, then I start calling from my list of supervisors, managers, and directors and everybody shows up.

One thing about this office, a call comes in, you pick up the telephone, you don't know who's going to be on there. I've talked to presidents; I've talked to people calling from the White House; I've spoken with the governor's office; I've talked to just about anyone you can name. All the crank calls are transferred here, too. We get the heavy breathers or callers on some sexual hangup. For the most part, I'll talk to the cranks because you never know. We've gotten our share of bomb scares. Usually the caller is a weirdo with nothing better to do. But we never count on that. Anytime someone calls the hospital and says, "I planted a bomb,"—or any unusual call, for that matter—the operators give the call to this office. The last time the caller said he planted a bomb in the boiler room. As soon as he hung up, I called the police and then I called our security department and we started a search. The police sent the bomb squad down to help us. Now, I've been to the boiler room a few times, but I never realized how big it was. It's like a whole city down there! The caller didn't say anything except that he put a bomb in the boiler room. I called in our maintenance people to help and, with security and the police, we spent three hours down there. Combed every corner of the place. It was a hoax, of course, but we take these callers seriously.

I've had people call up and say they're going to commit suicide. A couple of years ago, I remember this woman called the operator and said that she had ingested a bottle of sleeping pills. The call was transferred to me and I started trying to pump her for any information I could get. She was all drugged up and she was talking very slowly and she kept saying that she was going to die and that nobody cared about her. She said she was telling someone. Imagine. She was telling Presbyterian Hospital! I tried getting the call traced, and fortunately she stayed on the line long enough. But you don't trace a call so easily. We just got lucky. The call was traced to a place in Brooklyn, an apartment building, and we got it isolated to a certain area. While I was on the phone with her, I was also talking to the police and they were able to locate the apartment. They had to break down the door. She had taken Valium or something and they brought her to one of the hospitals in the Brooklyn area. Yeah, we got lucky that time.

Once I had a lady on the line who was telling me she had taken a slew of pills. It was so hard to understand her; she was slurring and going into this drowsiness. "Lady, stay awake! Where are you?" I kept yelling into the phone. And then the phone on her end just dropped. It's so frustrating not knowing whether she died that night or if she just dropped the phone and decided to . . . I looked in the paper after that but I never saw anything. Those are the ones where you always wonder if you did enough or if you asked the right questions. But you can't blame yourself. There's nothing you can do about a call like that.

X
THE MEDICAL SCHOOL

On August 21, 1987, toward the end of the hottest summer New York had had for two decades, 148 students, chosen from among over 2,400 applicants, convened in Alumni Auditorium of the Columbia College of Physicians and Surgeons. At ten o'clock, Dr. Henrik Bendixen, dean of the medical school, stepped to the podium and addressed the class of 1991 for the first time:

Welcome to the College of Physicians and Surgeons—P and S for short. What we are welcoming you to is a professional school. In college, if you did it right, you interacted with your university and with the faculty serving it, hopefully, as sources of knowledge—Sherpas guiding you toward the altitudes. The intellectual scope of *this* professional school is not smaller than that of the college you left. It is, in fact, more than a match for that of *any* college. The real difference between your college and your medical school is the presence of a third party. In medical school, you will never get away from the patient. Whether as an individual, a family member, or a population—the patient is always present. Our respect for scholarship is high, and knowledge for its own sake is treasured. Yet, in our setting of goals, in our thought processes, in our behavior, we constantly acknowledge the presence of the patient. We function to live up to our own expectations—by all means—but we can ignore only at our peril the need to live up to the expectations of our patients, even when, at times, they may appear unrealistic.

Looking over our shoulder is the profession. You will soon find out that you are expected to live up to its standards. You will be reminded of that again on graduation day, when you speak the Hippocratic oath, which commits you to duties to your patients as well as to your profession.

The years ahead of you will be strenuous, yet exciting, as you learn and grow, and as you experience with awe what it means to be a physician. New knowledge will be coming fast and furiously. Remember, though, that knowledge does not keep any better than fish. Learn how to learn, and how to keep learning.

The greatest changes in our lives are caused by two impacts: Firstly, the profession is beset, perhaps deservedly, by regulators. Among other things, society wants to be protected against the so-called impaired physician. Yet the stresses which prompt a physician to become impaired do not differ substantially from the stresses which cause a medical student to become impaired. From the first day in medical school, you must recognize that some medical students become impaired, and that for some it is the end of a career before it begins.

We have an honor code here. You may choose to reject such a code because you do not wish to report a classmate for cheating on an exam. But you do not have the freedom to turn your back on your responsibility to intervene, just as you must if you observe a classmate to be an impaired student.

The coming years will be tough—physically and mentally. You will need to have tremendous resources of inner strength. Also, you must realize that you cannot do this alone. You must lean on someone—from spouse to friend—from peer group to faculty. You will help each other in any number of ways. But you have to go beyond that. As future physicians, you have entered a social contract to watch out for each other, mindful of the patient, the profession, and society. By early action you may prevent a lasting impairment and save a career—by inaction, you will have failed the patient, society, and the friend you wanted to protect. You will be under this obligation from the first day of medical school.

The second major impact to be mentioned is AIDS. We have known for some time that nature is capable of sending us new diseases, but the deadliness, intransigence, and wiliness of this virus is having a profound medical, social, and economic impact on our era. You will soon encounter patients who have one of the diseases caused by this virus. We cannot protect you from such encounters for many reasons. One is that we have no way of knowing if your encounter is with an individual carrying the virus, unless that individual already *has* the disease.

As a medical student, when you do a clinical clerkship, you cannot refuse to care for a patient with AIDS-related disease except for good reason. And there are very few. It is our obligation to see to it that you have the means to protect yourselves against a risk which is small, certainly far smaller than that posed by hepatitis. Above all, that means education—including education about fears, both rational and irrational. It also means that we must keep you informed about protective measures to be taken by hospital staff dealing with AIDS-related patients, blood samples or other body fluids. Your course directors have the responsibility to introduce you to these protective measures, and you have the responsibility of reading and understanding the most recent set of guidelines distributed, learning what they are.

I make no apology for the seriousness of my remarks. But I am pleased to add that medical school offers wonderful, rewarding, lighthearted experiences literally every day—as does the life of a physician. Don't ever forget that it is a special privilege to be a physician—able to help fellow humans and worthy of their trust.

Welcome to P and S.

HENRIK BENDIXEN, M.D.

Dean,
Faculty of Medicine

———

Despite its imposing size, his office has a certain warmth. The wood-paneled walls are hung with portraits of his predecessors; family photographs rest on a shelf behind his desk. In the center of the room is a massive antique library table of magnificent wood.

A calm, unpretentious man, he's well over six feet tall, lanky, white-haired. He wears wire-rimmed glasses and a bow tie that lies slightly askew on his white shirt. His jacket is nowhere in sight.

He has been dean of the medical school for three years. Before that, he was chairman of the Department of Anesthesiology. His daughter attended P&S and is now a second-year resident on the medical service. "It's absolutely wonderful. She's pretty good, too. So now my colleagues, who should know their genetics better, make the assumption that if the daughter is smart, the father must have something . . . That, of course, is nonsense."

———

I don't think students have changed all that much since the time I was a student thirty-five years ago. I think the world has changed more than the students. Over the years, we've always had bright kids, and this year's class is the same—bright, spirited kids, well motivated. They're wonderful. I think we're fortunate in having good students who are lively and interested not only in their profession but in mankind in all its aspects. Those are basic ingredients, and over the years, that still has not changed.

It's hard to describe the role of a dean of a medical school—it's so diversified and changes so often. Because every physician in this medical center is appointed through the medical school, an important part of my role here is to see that the right committees are looking at the credentials of people who are being suggested for appointments. That's very important, both for our sake and for the sake of the physicians we appoint.

I get involved to a degree with what students are taught. There are one hundred twenty-seven medical schools in this country, and in most the basic curriculum is the province of the faculty. If you're a wise dean, you never even appear to tell the faculty how to handle the curriculum. But periodically I meet with the chairman of the curriculum committee. He and I talk about things and exchange views. My most important role in that area, though, is to see that the curriculum committee is alive and that they do things. If that happens, then I have done my job, strictly speaking.

A large part of this job has to do with personal relationships. There are approximately thirty-five people, mostly department chairmen, who strongly believe that they must have access to me, and it happens that they are right. When I was a chairman, I would have been deeply insulted if I had a problem and I couldn't see the dean fairly promptly. In this job, you have to do everything from the very practical day-to-day affairs to just being willing to listen. There was a medical school dean at Case Western who was a psychiatrist. After a while he was asked, "Now that you're dean, what has changed in your life?" His answer was, "All that has changed is that my patients have stopped paying me."

Few people outside of the academic community realize how important research is to a medical school. No medical student in any country ever paid the full cost of his or her education. Medical education here is subsidized by clinical practice and by research. We have an enormous faculty of physicians who practice in the hospital and who teach the students for free. In basic science, since there's no clinical practice, the larger part of the teaching expense is piggy-backed onto research. All of these basic-science departments have millions of dollars worth of research grants coming in every year, paying for faculty, who in turn teach students.

Educating a medical student requires a phenomenal amount of money. If a student really was to pay the full cost, the tuition would have to be five to ten times higher than it is now. It's hard to judge just how much is spent on a student, because when a medical student sees a patient with a clinician, he's learning something while the physician is taking care of the patient. Does it take five minutes longer for the physician to see that patient just because the student is there? Does it take ten minutes longer? You don't know. What we do know is that there's a very interesting reciprocal effect—because the student is there, chances are that the physician is doing a better job.

In a medical center, you're involved in patient care, teaching, and research. What comes first? I'm a firm believer that you always put the patient first, although the three things are so intertwined. If you don't deliver good patient care, then you don't have worthwhile teaching. If you don't have good research backing up the patient care, chances are the patient care isn't first rate. We have absolutely fascinating research programs going on. In neuroscience, we're figuring out how the brain and the mind and the nervous system work together. In molecular medicine, we're figuring out the genetic explanation for a given disease. We're strong in immunology, the study of the body's defense system. We have a large cancer center here, doing spectacular research funded by what is probably the largest National Cancer Institute grant in the country, and we're well on our way to having some very significant results in AIDS research. We have an AIDS clinical effort and we have an AIDS basic-science effort going on in our labs.

There are a number of people who feel so strongly about the threat of AIDS that they're leaving the work they're doing or they're changing the focus of their work to try to find a solution to it. Many people see this as something which could approximate what Barbara Tuchman wrote about in *A Distant Thunder*—a very serious plague.

Medicine has always been a slightly risky business. Yet the risk of AIDS being transmitted to those taking care of AIDS patients is exceedingly small. The fascinating thing is that the precautions that we're in the process of developing are likely to have their greatest effect in reducing morbidity and mortality from hepatitis. It's thought provoking that five or ten years before we knew of AIDS, we knew about hepatitis, but we never really thought of it as enough of a reason to take very strict precautions. That's because hepatitis is not invariably fatal, while AIDS seems to be.

The worst part is going to be once we get to testing. First we'll test patients, and then we'll test personnel. What everybody is worried about, of course, is that we'll be expected to walk around with buttons or ID's or pink stars, or something like that. In other words, we could be headed for the pest houses. Not having the right to test, a lot of the time we don't know that patients have AIDS. If we knew more about which patients had it or carried the virus, we'd probably have more difficulty with the patients who were AIDS-free. One of the things that's going to happen is that the patient without AIDS will ask, "How can I be sure that the patient in the next bed does not have it?"

There's no question that the first step is going to be for a place like this to centralize the care of patients with AIDS in special units. You'll undoubtedly see some of what has been seen and reported from Milwaukee and other hospitals, where cardiac surgeons say they won't operate on patients with AIDS. I strongly disagree with that attitude. The only way to approach it at the moment is to take the precautions necessary against AIDS against all patients. The interesting thing is that the greatest exposure to blood is not in cardiac surgery, but in obstetrics. Interestingly, we haven't heard a peep from the obstetricians; or rather, we have not heard them say that they will not deliver a baby.

Before my appointment to dean, I was chairman of the Department of Anesthesia. I don't have much contact with my old department anymore, and that's very deliberate. I want to stay out of the hair of my successor. I think there are too many people who stay around and play mother-in-law, and that's awful. I won't do that. In fact, when I retire as dean, I don't intend to stay around being a senior adviser or anything like that. I intend to get out. What played a role in making me accept this job was that I had spent my entire life telling people, who really didn't want to listen to me, that nobody should be a chairman for more than ten years. Well, I had been chairman for over ten years. And although people would probably have been too polite to remind me, I remembered.

I've found this job very interesting, but in a couple of years I'll quit this, too, and then we'll see. If I don't go back to patient care, who knows? Perhaps I'll become an olive farmer in the south of France.

TOM BARTLETT
Medical Student, Third Year

———✦———

He's a Harvard graduate, blond, cheerful, twenty-nine years old. Before deciding on medical school, he worked for several years in a bank but left because "there was not enough direct contact with people." He has also spent several years as a scholar in Egypt.

We're in his apartment in The Towers, a complex of high-rise buildings housing students, nurses, and other staff members. He lives with three other students. The apartment has three bedrooms, a living room, two bathrooms, and a kitchen. The walls are covered with pictures, an afghan is thrown over the arm of an easy chair. The place, which is filled to capacity with old furniture, looks like it has been lived in for years, but it's tastefully done and is not at all what you would expect from a group of students who know their time there is only temporary.

He gets coffee from the kitchen. We settle into two overstuffed sofas.

———————

Medical school was a hard adjustment for me. Especially the first year. Being older and having worked and supported myself for a while, I missed not having a paycheck and the financial independence to come and go as I wanted to. I disliked having to depend on my parents and other sources and having to work within a fairly careful budget. I wasn't lavish before, but at least there was money if I wanted to rent a car and go out of the city for a weekend once every few months. Now that kind of thing is gone. Another thing that bothered me was moving into a tiny little room in Bard—that's where the first-year students live—it was no more than a cubicle.

The courses for the first year include gross anatomy, biochemistry, cell biology, histology. Gross anatomy made the greatest impression on me. That's where you dissect a cadaver and you learn about the human body, firsthand.

I remember the first day of class. We all walked into the lab, all hundred forty-eight of us, and we looked straight ahead at about thirty tables, lined up in rows, with yellow sheets draped across the top and numbers hanging over them. Lists had been posted so we all knew which table we were assigned to. Five students were assigned to a table. We all surrounded our tables and suddenly the room became perfectly silent. It was eerie. We waited for the professor to tell us what to do next. We knew, of course, what he was going to say: Peel back the sheet.

I was a little surprised that nobody passed out or even felt the least bit sick at the first look at these dead bodies lined up. You expected *someone* would have a problem, but no one did. The smell gets you first. Not of the bodies but of the preservative. Eventually, of course, you get used to it. For a medical student that first day in gross anatomy is one of those rites of passage. We all do it and we all remember it.

The body on my table was an elderly lady. She was kind of heavyset, with gray hair—she looked like somebody's grandmother. We named her that day. We called her Erna. No reason, just that Erna was as good a name as any. The whole time I worked on Erna, I couldn't help but wonder what the woman was like. You just have to wonder about where she came from, what she was like when she was alive.

Over the seven-month period of the class, you dissect the body section by section. You start with the chest. You do the lower extremities next. Then you do the pelvic region, upper extremities, and head and neck last. As you dissect the body parts, you remove them and place them in a numbered bag. This number corresponds to your table number. The bags are all kept separately so that at the end, when the body is cremated, it is cremated in total.

A lot of what you're doing is to see things lying "in situ," which means in place. You open the chest and you see the ribs and the lungs and the pericardial sac covering the heart, and the veins and arteries and nerves. You want to see them as they lie. We have a very detailed dissecting manual which explains where you cut, where you peel. That kind of thing. It's essentially the same techniques that are used in surgery in the sense that you make an incision, you peel back the flap, and you dissect whatever is presented without damaging the structures. You have to be pretty careful about not cutting the nerves or losing them.

The smell is with the lab and in the bodies forever. They're very heavily embalmed. By the time we get them they've been sitting in preservative for at least a year. They've had preservative flowing through them. The school has an undertaker whose only assignment is to procure and embalm bodies for the students. He's a real expert at it, too. He has to be good, because if the bodies decay, we can't really see the structures. His name is Mr. Rogers. Everyone calls the gross-anatomy lab "Mr. Rogers' Neighborhood."

There's some black humor to all this, but there's also respect. There really is respect for the bodies. The faculty and Mr. Rogers made it clear they weren't going to take any overt fooling around—no abusing body parts or cutting them off and holding them up and waving them around. Nothing like that. On the other hand you know there is going to be some joking around. I've forgotten the cadaver jokes, but they're standards, like "This lady is a real stiff!" You have to. If for no other reason, it keeps your sanity.

At the end of the class, around the time of finals, there's a memorial service for the cadavers. It's attended by all the students as well as the other people who have come in contact with the bodies. It takes place in the chapel and lasts for half an hour. There are readings and meditation and prayers, to give thanks to these people for having done what they did for us and to pay our respects to them.

There's a lot about the first two years of med school that makes you very frustrated. You don't get a lot of opportunity to think. What you're doing almost completely is memorizing lists. No matter how you cut it, what they're really doing is feeding you large quantities of material that you have to memorize and spit back on exams. If you feel the need to be creative, you can always make up mnemonics. I ultimately got very good at that. For example, there are two mnemonics for the twelve cranial nerves. The classic one is: On Old Olympus's Towering Tops, A French And German Vended Some Hops. The nerves are olfactory, optic, oculomotor, trochlear, trigeminal, abducens, facial, auditory cochlear, glossopharyngeal, vagus, spinal accessory, and hypoglossal. The more modern version of that is: Oh, Oh, Oh, To Touch And Feel A Girl's Vagina—Such Heaven. I used to make up a lot of them. One I used for memorizing part of the medical status exam for psychiatry. A Trained Tiger Prepared Mako Shark. And the second half of it was: Instant Justice Makes Fools Of American Attorneys. Intelligence, judgment, mood, fund of knowledge . . . I can't remember all the words. It's been a while since I had to use these. But anyway I memorized this stuff and regurgitated it for exams. You can't memorize this stuff otherwise. I had a terrible time with some of that the first year.

Here's the basic tension for both the first and second years. You know that what you're learning, at some level, in some way, you will need to be able to recall to treat a patient. Yet it's given to you in sort of list form, as dense and as fast as possible, because there's so much of it. So you say to yourself, I've got to get through this so I can get to what I came to medicine for. The fact of the matter is you can't be a third- or a fourth-year student unless you've learned this stuff. There's just no way around it.

Finances are another consideration. My medical education is being funded through a variety of sources. I have some money of my own, which I have either inherited, saved, or earned. My parents are helping me and I'm getting some student loans. But it's a terrible problem. Even if you have no debts coming out of college, it costs about twenty-two, twenty-three thousand dollars a year here—that's for tuition, living expenses, books, uniforms, transportation—the works. Maybe you could pare it down to twenty. Four times twenty to twenty-two is eighty to ninety thousand dollars.

Different loan programs have different repayment schedules. Some of them allow you to defer paying back until you've finished two years of residency. But if you're doing a three- or four-year residency you have to start to pay back some of your loans in the middle. How do you do that? It's a nightmare for some students. It drives people into doing one of two things. It drives them into going into practice a little earlier, so they don't have the chance to do fellowships and specialize. They have to go into internal medicine or one of the quicker residencies. It also drives them to go into higher paying things. That's detrimental to the country as a whole. It doesn't make sense for more people than is necessary to want to be surgeons or do procedure-related specialties like gastroenterology or basic cardiology.

I've been in my third year now for only a short time, and already I can see such differences between this and the first two years. These are the clinical years. We see patients and we're all beginning to know what we came to medicine for. One of the things you do in third year is rotate through the different services. You keep the schedule of an intern, more or less, and so you're on nights as well as days.

One of the first nights I spent on call was in the emergency room—I was on psychiatric rotation. It was real late at night, and this middle-aged, unshaven man, smelling of liquor, walked in and presented himself to the emergency room guard saying, "I want to kill somebody. I'm going to kill myself if I don't kill somebody first. I'm going to hurt somebody." He said the devil was telling him to throw himself in front of a subway. That kind of thing. The guard brought him to the back and I had to interview him first because that's the med student's responsibility. Then the resident would see him, discuss his situation with the attending, and make the real judgment.

I was very nervous, I have to say. My first thought was, "Oh, my God! I've got a real crazy here. This guy, if we turn him loose, he's either dead or he's going to hurt somebody! This man is paranoid! He could wipe out Manhattan!" Well, somewhat apprehensively, I interviewed him. I asked him about what he did, how long he'd been having these feelings, what had happened. And he gave me these real pat answers and spoke of feelings of depression and anger and psychotic delusions and he described in some detail the voices which were telling him to do these terrible things. I thought, "My God, we've got to admit this man! Put the straitjacket on him! Lock the man away until he calms down!" But what I said was, and I said this calmly, "All right, sir, you sit here in this little room and I'll get the resident." Well, I went out and I explained the situation to the resident and she sort of looked at me strangely and she said, "What does he look like?" So I told her, and she said, "What's his name?" So I told her. She went back into the files in the emergency room—the psych people keep a special record of emergency-room visits—and she looked up his name. "I knew it!" she said. Apparently he was a regular. He'd been in the emergency room once every week or two for the last six months with exactly the same story. All he wanted was a hot meal and a place to spend the night.

The resident examined him anyway, just as if he were a first-time patient. She did the whole workup, talked to the attending, and then she came back and asked him a few more questions. "So, have you ever hurt anybody before?"

"No."

"You know, we haven't any beds here."

"You haven't?" he said. Then he said, "Well, can you call another hospital and see if they have any beds?"

"Sir, I'm sorry, but there are people who really need to be in the hospital."

"Well, could you at least give me a token so I can get home?"

"We can give you a token so you can get home, sir."

And so my "killer" took the token, smiled and said thanks, walked out the door, and that was the end of it. I never did save Manhattan.

PAUL ROGERS

Chief Anatomical Technician

He is responsible for procuring bodies for the medical students to dissect in the gross-anatomy class. His home base is the anatomy room.

We're in the lab that connects to the anatomy room. It is dimly lit and appears to be unchanged from the day the building was built. Even the door, a wood frame with a frosted-glass panel, tells the age. The room is lined with shelves. On the higher shelves, fetuses in glass jars are curled up in formaldehyde. "Some of those things are forty years old. They've been here way longer than I have." Lower shelves hold bones and organs.

We're sitting on stools at a zinc counter that runs along one wall. At one end of the counter, looking incredibly out of place, are four flowered porcelain demitasse cups and saucers and an unplugged coffee pot.

"This is the Department of Anatomy, where we keep most of the specimens. These are all human body parts that were preserved years ago—not by me. You have a complete male and female crossected from the top of her head to the bottom of her feet, in slices one inch thick and preserved under glass. All the material in these cases is from real people. My office is next door, but I sit here and I have my coffee and meet with students."

My title is chief anatomical technician. It means I take care of all the bodies in the anatomy labs, things like that. I have my own morgue. It's not connected with the hospital morgue. Mine is strictly for body preservation. See, people come in and they'll donate a body to science; their mother, their father . . . whoever it may be. Being that I'm a state-licensed funeral director, I interview the families and let them sign the necessary papers. Then my men move the bodies in. I have my men clear everything with the medical examiner's office first, so later on, say in two years when I decide to cremate, I can do it without any problem whatsoever. So they'll bring me the body, cleared for cremation and all, and I embalm it. Then I'll put it away in my refrigerator for a while till it's time to use it.

I always keep the bodies in a vertical position. Robin Cook, I understand, got his idea for his book *Coma* when he saw those bodies hanging vertically in plastic bags in our morgue. I keep them upright because gravity assures that the embalming fluid will seep downward. That way we know that we're going to get capillary distribution of the fluid right to the very tip of the toes. The body is in this position for at least six months. We won't use a body sooner than that under any condition.

Procuring a body to be used for the students is a highly involved process. When a person expires in a hospital, the admitting office, the doctor in charge, whoever it may be, must ask the family if they wish to donate any parts. If the story is the person has cerebral damage, let's say, but he has a good heart, the doctor himself will ask the family prior to the relative's death. At the time of death they're asked if they wish to donate their eyes, or if they wish to donate their body to science. We've made up some brochures and sent them to all the different hospitals in the area so in case people do want to donate, they'll know where to call.

A lot of times when a family donates a body it's because they've heard by word of mouth that somebody else did it and had a good experience. It's like in the funeral business. If you give someone good service they'll turn around and tell their friends and relatives. Well, the same thing happens here. We try not to make a family pay anything at all. If a person dies within the five boroughs, we will assume the obligation of removing the body from the hospital, from the house, wherever it may be. I explain to the family what we do with the remains and tell them what different forms of study the body is being used for. I also tell them that at the end we'll cremate the body and we'll bury the ashes or, if the family prefers, we'll scatter the ashes or we'll return them to the family.

Donating a body is the greatest gift that anybody can ever give. You can't give more than that. And most of the people who do it are well educated. They knew in advance just what they were doing. When a family comes in to donate a body, you have to be so grateful. I mean, just think, it's like all the encyclopedia volumes in the world in one body. And we can study from them. Without this gift, our students could not become decent doctors.

I have met a lot of these people personally. Maybe an individual before his death came up and made arrangements with me, or maybe I met the family. So when I walk into my morgue, I remember when I look at a body. There isn't one name that you could tell me that I wouldn't remember. I remember it all. Every one of them. They could call me now and ask me about So-and-so and I'd say she was buried last year. I'm going back nine years now, but they say a name, a bong goes off. Don't ask me why, but it does.

I need about forty-five to fifty bodies a year to run my course. So far I have acquired that many every year. A lot of medical schools will order bodies from out of town because they don't have enough bodies to run their course; not enough people are donating. But when you order bodies from out of town you get formaldehyde-embalmed bodies. When the students work on formaldehyde bodies, the minute they start to dissect the body the fumes can kill them. And with those bodies, the tissue is not the same. It becomes shredded, it becomes whitish-grayish in color; it becomes very hard. Mold grows on formaldehyde. For all these reasons it's not the best. But, if you don't have, you don't have. You've got to take what you can get. I, on the other hand, use very little formaldehyde in my fluid. I use other ingredients like phenol, which is much, much better to use. So my bodies are softer, they're easier to dissect, they keep the same color, mold doesn't grow on them, and the student doesn't get sick.

During lab time I just wander around to make sure they're cutting right and all that. The professor's job is to teach all the structures and everything else, so if a student asks me, "Is this the brachioplexus?" even if I know I say, "I can't answer you," because that's not my field, that's theirs. I *can* instruct them in how to dissect, using the scalpel or things like that, and when it comes to death, to dead bodies, to the legality of it, the doctor sends them to me for information.

As I wander around the room, I talk to the students. In talking to people you'll find out when something's bothering them. I go to the table and I kid around. I'll say to a student, "You don't look too good. What did you do last night? You went out and got drunk?" You've got to be able to rap with students.

I remember some of the kids. I see them now and they're doctors on staff here. One student in particular comes to mind. When we did the brain, he'd say to me, "Mr. Rogers, what is this?" Bop! He'd break it. I said, "Whatever you do, don't ever become a surgeon!" Do you know, he's a surgeon today. He's an orthopedic surgeon! He comes here and he says to me, "Mr. Rogers, can I have a knee? Can I have a leg to work with?"

Some doctors come to me when they have to do an operation on a patient who has cancer of a certain area. I give them a body, and they do the operation in my lab here, and the next day they go do it on the patient. This way they know where all the nerves and everything else are. They know that you shouldn't sever this nerve or that nerve. The initial approach is very important in any operation, which is why it's so advantageous to have a cadaver.

At the end of the year we have a memorial service for the people who gave their bodies to science. I set it up seven years ago and we've continued it ever since. All the students and the faculty come. The chaplain performs a nice little service. He says a little poetry, a little prose. It's a nonsectarian type of service. It's only respect for a human being who gave his utmost to science. I mean, if we can't just have a little memorial service for them, there's something wrong with us.

———

At the end of the service, he always gives the people who are in attendance a plastic card as a remembrance. "They can use it as a bookmark, and they will remember," he says. On the front of the card is a picture of a sunset. On the back is a quotation by Robert N. Test. It reads: ". . . and let my body help others lead fuller lives. Give my sight to the man who has never seen a sunrise. Take my bones and try to find a way to make a crippled child walk. Explore every corner of my brain so that someday a speechless boy will shout at the crack of a bat or a deaf girl will hear the sound of rain. If you do all I have asked, I will live forever."

DAWN MCGUIRE

Medical Student, Fourth Year

⌇⌇═══════════

She's from Grayson, Kentucky, a town of twelve hundred people. She went to Princeton with the intention of being a philosopher, but realized that academic philosophy just wasn't for her. "It was too business oriented." After college she spent a couple of years writing—her first book of poetry was published in 1981—and "having to deal with ten different jobs to support myself." She formed an all-woman blues band called "Too Damn Mean" that played in Greenwich Village and in which she sang and played bass. At the same time, she attended Union Theological Seminary for a master's in divinity and found, while studying psychiatry there, that medicine was what she really loved. In 1983, at the age of 29, she entered P & S.

═══════════

There are two fundamentally different experiences in medical school. One is the first two years in the classroom and the other is the third and fourth years when you're working with patients. The first two years you feel as though you're on a tiny little island with a hundred and fifty other people, and you become remarkably knowledgeable about one another. You're in class eight hours a day, five days a week, for two years, with the same people. During this time, the intensity waxes and wanes depending on the exam schedule, but it's a fairly predictable two years and you can be as isolated or socially active as you choose. In fact, there's a lot about those two years that is in your control even though you're spending forty hours a week in class. You definitely have more control over your life than in the third year, which was, for me at least, an experience of intense unpredictability. The third year is when you start your clinical rotations through the hospital. You learn early in that year about the special vulnerability between a medical student and a patient; this interface between wanting to learn—and therefore feeling that you really are taking a somewhat parasitical stance on this patient's disease—and wanting to serve, because, after all, that's why you came to medical school.

My clinical rotations started out in pediatrics. It's a nice place to start because you're not expected to perform procedures on pediatric patients. It's an opportunity to get used to the hospital and to doing presentations. You don't have to feel like you might hurt somebody. They don't let you.

The rotation goes in a certain order. You follow pediatrics with OB-GYN. Here you see wonderfully healthy women, for the most part, with enormous veins, so if you're trying to learn how to put in IVs, you have people who you're much less likely to hurt while you're learning. By the time you get to the rotation in medicine, where you see lots of elderly people who have frail veins and fragile skin, you feel like you have some confidence.

During that third year, and in fact this year as well, I met so many patients who had such an impact on me that I know I'll carry their stories with me for a long, long time. One patient was admitted when I was doing six weeks of medicine. She was a woman in her early forties who was a nun. Not the black-and-white habit sort of nun, but a jeans-and-flannel-shirt sort of nun who runs a women's shelter. The admitting intern in the emergency room had indicated on her chart that she'd come in with shortness of breath. That was her chief complaint. He noted, too, that she had traveled to South Africa in the past six months, presumably to be included in any infectious cause for her shortness of breath. When I saw that I said, "I want this patient." I thought anybody who had gone to South Africa was going to be really interesting. And a *nun* who went there was bound to be fascinating!

From the moment I walked into her room, I had this distinct impression that she was going to do a lot more for me than I was going to be able to do for her. There was something very solid about her. As the workup proceeded, though, I got a real sinking feeling because, to my mind, her problem was looking more and more ominous. Her shortness of breath came from a pleural effusion [fluid in the lung cavity] that was quite extensive, and she also had some fluid in her abdomen. This was a woman who hadn't had a gynecological exam for seven or eight years, never having had children or been pregnant. Warnings were going off in my head that this could be an ovarian cancer. The workup proceeded and pulmonary specialists were called in to tap her lung, and the tap came back bloody, which is strongly suggestive of a malignancy. One afternoon I walked into the room while the doctors were doing the tap and it was a very difficult scene. She was sitting with her back to the door and they were tapping her lung. Her hands were gripped together and tears were streaming down her face. She wasn't saying a word, so the doctors weren't even aware she was crying.

I called her by her first name, asked her if she was doing all right, and went over and did the thing a medical student is very good at—I held her hand. At that point, she just started sobbing. At the same time, I felt like crying myself, actually, as they were drawing off this bloody fluid that had such an ominous significance for me.

When her workup was complete and she was diagnosed as having cancer, she decided to go for treatment to another hospital where she had a relative who was a doctor. I was relieved because I didn't know how defended I could be against what I thought was going to be a pretty precipitous downhill course in this person who could have been a friend, could have been a sister, could have been one of my teachers. Another thing that was difficult to defend against was the sadness that someone who has really given so much to people who are vulnerable, that someone like this should be afflicted. It was hard for me to be dispassionate about that.

Very soon after she left the hospital I had a wonderful dream about her. She was on a farm, and she was in her jeans and flannel shirt. It was a dairy farm; she was getting milk from a cow. She sort of looked up right as this bright sun was coming over her eyes and she looked up and the light was on her face. She had this wonderful expression of total enjoyment of that moment; of total affirmation of the experience of living.

I think the proper role for a physician with a dying patient is to enter into a partnership where there is a sense that that partnership is not going to end with the end of medical therapy. But we're not trained for that. Most of us feel totally inadequate and have found our own defenses, including abandoning the patient. It's been confusing to me and a constant source of frustration.

What brought this point home was a patient I had in my surgery rotation—an eighty-two-year-old man who had never, ever been sick in his life. He presented with back pain and his workup revealed that he had widespread, inoperable pancreatic cancer. He was becoming progressively more sick with this tumor and obstructed and not able to hold down food.

His doctor, who is one of the people at the medical center I respect the most—a very decent doctor—kind of abandoned him. I don't think it was callous at all, but that's what happened. And the residents just don't have the time to be very compassionate. They're much, much too burdened just taking care of people with conditions they can do something about. So I spent a lot of time with this man. It was the end of my surgical rotation, I had some time, and I elected to spend it with this patient.

I visited with him for a while every day, and we would just go over his life. He would say, "What am I going to do, doctor? Tell me what to do. I'm a dead duck." He wanted to talk. He wanted to talk about his marriage and his celebrations, of the things he regretted, what his family had been like, and his experience in Europe. He talked about the qualities in himself he wished he had better mastery over. Through it all, I didn't feel like this was extra. I felt like I was doing the best I knew how to do at that time for this patient. At the same time I felt, had it been known that I was doing that, it wouldn't really have been respected. Now that may or may not be true, but that's what I thought.

He died in the hospital at the end of my rotation. We had a ten-day break, and after I came back from the West Coast I went straight to his room only to find he had died the week before. His is one of the stories that's going to be with me. He taught me a lot; he allowed me to teach myself a few things.

What I think about third year is, if you've got any grandiosity you're certainly going to be delivered from that. I think it's also true that if you have any humanity you'll be delivered *to* that as well. I do consider medicine a public service. That's sort of a minority report, perhaps, but that's the way I see it. You really have to fight to keep that intact, that sense of priority of being in public service, of its importance. I think I realized that I had to fight for the first principles that I had, and I don't mean fight against someone. I mean fight to keep myself intact in the face of cultural pressures, of the big business of hospital care and the more-or-less technological approach of our age.

My first principles were pretty simple: The people I deal with are human beings. They are suffering human beings and they're much more like me than not. As simple as those feelings are, they can be very strained. It's difficult enough to deal with patients when you're also dealing with your own sense of inadequacy, all those things that trip us up when we encounter new circumstances when we're not quite on our feet. There's also a tremendous amount of pressure to make the same adaptation that everyone else is making, which is to objectify patients. Some say it's in your best interest to maintain a distance from them, to consider yourself less like them, rather than more like them. It's an understandable defense which probably begins toward the end of medical school. I think it waxes in residency, but I hear from the attendings that it wanes later on. They say the original attitudes of compassion come back. Lewis Thomas says in order to be a physician you have to have affection and curiosity. I think those come back. I've had attendings tell me that's the natural history of medical training, so don't lose heart; it will come back. They now really enjoy being with patients, spending time with them, becoming involved with them. Whereas that might have been the last thing they thought they would enjoy early in residency or earlier in their professional lives.

The other pressure is to continually maintain a community experience, an *esprit de corps*. It's incredibly important to your sense of well-being and to your survival to have a sense of connectedness and association with the other students and house officers. You need those social connections.

I'm applying for a residency in neurology. I think the personalities of the neurologists connected with this institution are wonderful. Eccentric, perhaps, but understandable to me. There's a really good collegial atmosphere. They have tremendous egos yet they make fun of each other in a very congenial way. It's an atmosphere of intense academic drives and at the same time broader interests. I find most people in neurology are widely read, really well versed in literature or history. That tells me a lot about the nature of the profession and what it may quietly expect of its members. Also about the kinds of minds that are drawn to it.

Throughout medical school I've tried to keep some semblance of a life outside of the hospital. I have a wonderful set of friends whom I've had for years, and I try to honor those friendships with as much attention as I can. If you're studying to be a doctor, your friends will let you become a prima donna. I think it's easy to fall into the pattern of being unpredictable and unreliable because you're under so much pressure. But I've tried to avoid that because I think it's tacky and it's unnecessary.

I've been politically active for a long time. I really came of age at the end of Vietnam, and social activism and social responsibility were more a given in my world view than they have been for some of my younger classmates. It's second nature for me to be involved in social issues.

Outside of school, I'm committed to political work. I've been involved with Physicians for Social Responsibility and the International Physicians for the Prevention of Nuclear War. I was in Budapest two summers ago as a delegate to the Fifth International Congress. I do work with a health-care group that supports Central America. They send medical aid to Nicaragua and El Salvador.

If you want to know what I do for fun, I'd have to say I read. Right now

I'm reading *Moby Dick*. It's such an unbelievable book! So Shakespearian. Such a work of genuis. I didn't read fiction at all in college, and it's been hard to find time to read for pleasure during these past four years. I feel I'm behind in the great works. Well, what better thing could you do with your time than read *Moby Dick*?

KENNETH FORDE, M.D.
Chief of Surgical Endoscopy

───

He is a member of the medical-school admissions committee whose career at the medical center spans thirty-three years. He started as a P&S student in 1954. Today, he's a full professor. He has just been elected a governor of the American College of Surgeons, one of the highest honors that can be given to a surgeon in this country.

"Presbyterian Hospital is up in the 'Heights.' I remember years ago, when I came to medical school here, there were a lot of European families, many of them middle- to upper middle-class who had done well or were well placed in their family backgrounds. You could come up here, and you could look down, and Harlem was down there, below Sugar Hill. I remember in Harlem, people referring to going to Medical Center, not even the medical center. To Medical Center. That was it. The ultimate."

───

I made up my mind when I entered City College in 1951 that I would be a pre-med, even though I was discouraged by a lot of well-meaning people. A famous minister, for example, in our community in Harlem, didn't think it was a practical goal for a black—we used to say "Negro" in those days—youngster to think of getting into medical school, especially from a city college. He said I should think of being a teacher—it was a more secure goal. When the time came to apply to medical school, I was discouraged again by a faculty adviser at City College from applying to the Ivy League places like Harvard and Columbia. But I did it anyway. When I was accepted here, I became the darling of the City College faculty. Before that, Columbia had taken zero to one person from the city colleges, and about the same number of black students. When I came here to med school as a freshman, I was the only black in my class. And that was out of one hundred and twenty-eight students.

Back in the sixties, the alumni council of the medical school—a very active and powerful group of physicians who graduated from P and S—had one of the most important meetings in the history of the school. At that meeting, two black medical students, Cliff Latting and Ross Hamilton, had the courage to stand up and say that they felt that there weren't enough black students and black faculty in the school—an assertion that astounded many. Including me. Although I had lived part of my life in Harlem and spent four years in medical school here, the question of minority enrollment never entered my mind. Sure, we noticed that there weren't many minorities here, but doing something about it honestly didn't come up. And when these students got up and made the challenge that some of the few of us minority graduates hadn't ourselves addressed, I was frankly embarrassed.

As a result of that meeting, a committee was formed that went to the dean and said we felt the school ought to be concerned about the lack of minority students here. Soon after, I was appointed as the first minority member of the admissions committee. And in the alumni association the first committee was established to look into minority enrollment and admission to this medical school. I was the chairman. We extended our concern to minority students in general, not just black students. We made recommendations and we immediately got involved in the business of recruiting minority students.

We didn't take a large number at first. Perhaps only three or four students per class, less than three percent. But it's necessary to remember the climate of the country at that time. It was the sixties. Affirmative action was in the air. And many administrators felt pressure to demonstrate that we were going to conform. Some were concerned that we might feel guilty and let our standards down. On the admissions committee there was a lot of discussion and a lot of different feelings were voiced. My own feeling was that it was not in anyone's interest to admit a student who we thought could not make it through medical school. That would be a tremendous detriment not only to the community that student would ultimately serve but to the school's reputation as well. But if you looked out there, there weren't many students who were prepared to apply to a school like ours, so the pool we had to choose from was small. In addition, schools like Harvard and a few others were ahead of us. They had already looked into minority recruitment and they were offering attractive financial packages. So we found ourselves in stiff competition for the same small groups of minorities.

We stuck to our guns, and we did not precipitously admit a lot of minority students who we felt couldn't make it. In the beginning, the students who were admitted were not of the highest possible caliber, but they were the highest possible at that time, and in those days we were happy to see a student who would make it through. There was *some* dropout, but fortunately not a lot. Some was predictable because we didn't have support mechanisms for counseling and tutorials and that sort of thing at that time. There was also the concern among some in the student body and the faculty about reverse discrimination. What if we worked too hard to bring in minorities? I agreed this might be true—but I thought that at that time that was a commitment to society that we, as a microcosm of society, needed to make.

The first few students we accepted under this new program were looked at as test cases. How were they going to do? There weren't enough of them to be able to run the spectrum. In any student body you'll get students, some of whom will be good, some bad, some mediocre. But when you have only a few of a minority they don't have that "privilege." So they were watched.

I know very well how that feels. As a minority, you're always on parade, on display. It doesn't keep me jittery every minute but I'm aware of the importance of presenting an appropriate front, so to speak, both for the majority and minority. Because you're a leader, you're an example. Sometimes, if you slip, this may affect people's accepting you or future minorities of your same group. They may say, "Remember the last time we had a black student here? He didn't do so well. We've got to be careful before we do that again."

When I was in medical school, I couldn't apply or even be considered for internship in some places. Even at Columbia-affiliated hospitals. There was one Columbia-affiliated hospital to which I applied for a residency and was told flatly that it would not be possible for me to be considered because a minority had never been taken there before. I was told what was and was not appropriate for me to look forward to. This is something you learn as a minority all along the way. Then, when you're finally established, you face other interesting challenges. For example, as you came along in your career, your colleagues, who had patients to refer, would worry about how their patients would accept you. Or you'd go in to see someone and realize the patient had been primed by his physician because they'd know inappropriate things about you, things that wouldn't have mattered in the ordinary exchange or referral. Because the doctor was concerned about acceptance and what have you, both to protect the patient and sometimes to protect you from embarrassment, they'd prime their patient.

You could tell a patient was primed because they'd recognize you immediately. You walk into the room and before you introduce yourself they say, "Hello, Dr. Forde." People, in their description of you, mention your color. And it comes out. Some patients whom you get to know later as good friends will say, "You know, Dr. So-and-so did ask me whether I would mind being taken care of by someone of your ethnic persuasion."

The acceptance is easier from the patient, sometimes, than from one's peers. Remember, surgeons are conservative and physicians in general are, too. There's a certain reluctance to venture into the unknown. You might ask, do I face it now? Yes, in some ways I do. But fortunately I think I have established such a reputation, not only professionally but as a person, that I'm sure a lot of people don't even think about it twice. And there are some totally color-blind people, I'm convinced, in this world.

From the beginning of minority enrollment and affirmative action there has been the hope of many, both majority and minority, that by increasing the numbers of minority positions, one is going to deliver better medical care to the minority community. That's not necessarily so. For one thing I personally tell every minority applicant who raises the issues or tries to persuade me that he or she is definitely going back to Bed-Stuy or Harlem to practice, that you don't have to have that goal. That I think by being a professor at Columbia University up on the hill, I am contributing as much as if I were a general practitioner in Harlem. I think one has to function in different roles. I think we need the excellent general practitioner in Harlem and we need an excellent researcher at Columbia University. We need superb clinicians too. I'd like to see minorities in all these roles rather than just assuming that because you're black and because you had an opportunity to go to medical school, you should go back and practice in the black community.

The process for admission to P and S begins when we receive a student's application. The application is reviewed by one or more members of the committee and promising students are invited for interview. We receive a few thousand applications for a hundred and forty places, and we interview perhaps a thousand of these students. We look at several things, not only academic achievement and potential, but recommendations from faculty, outstanding qualities, interest in humane values. Different members of the committee will place emphasis on different parameters. Some are looking for researchers, some are looking for practitioners, some are looking for great teachers. We all look for students also who are good and interesting human beings, whether one is a lutenist or a flautist or a good football player. We think that a physician should be more than just a scientific scholar.

We evaluate the prospective students and then record our thoughts, and then get together in subcommittees and review each other's evaluations. Then, as we look at the whole group of students, we decide on which ones we are going to admit. It's the hardest job I do for the medical school; the most soul-searching, the most challenging, physically and intellectually. One reason it's so hard to is because the decisions of this group may be pivotal for someone's career. There are many, many brilliant and deserving candidates whom we cannot possibly take.

Different interviewers have different techniques. I can only speak for myself. With experience you can pick up a lot of things, but you recognize your limitations. You depend a lot on what others have said about the students. Unfortunately some people indulge in a lot of hyperbole—but you get to recognize them after a while. You know, "Jim is the best student I have ever taught . . ."

What you talk about can range widely. I rarely use the interview to try to gain some idea of a student's academic knowledge. That's usually a matter of record. But I let them express themselves, and that can range from discussions about books, music, trips, or their summer job as a stevedore for three months. You're trying to find out a little about how the person conducts himself or herself, what the goals and interests are.

I've been pleasantly surprised that despite a lot of the negative press that medicine has gotten in some quarters—the suggestion that doctors are the "fat cats," and have all the money, and perhaps are not as concerned as they used to be—that students don't believe it. I always ask them in their interview how all of this has affected their thinking. And what I've found overall is that they are still as idealistic, thank God, as we were.

SOLANGE MACARTHUR
Medical Student, Fourth Year

She was a professional ballerina for nine years before leaving the ballet to return to college. In this large, sparsely furnished apartment, the only signs of her career are two small photographs hanging over her bed. In one photograph, she is performing Swan Lake *with the corps de ballet. In the other, clipped from a newspaper, she is part of a group gathered outside Lincoln Center, picketing the American Ballet Theater.*

She curls up with her cat in an oversized chair, looking smaller than her five feet six inches. She still wears her long, straight brown hair tied back from her face, ballerina-style. Her voice is soft, a little hesitant. I ask about her unusual name. "My father was a foreign correspondent for the United Press after the war. That's how he met my mother, who is French. So I have an excuse for my name. Solange MacArthur. It tells the story: American in Paris meets French beauty and they get married."

I was five when my mother first took me to the School of American Ballet in New York. I still remember it. There was an audition for little children. All around the room there were ballet bars, and I remember thinking if there were bars, you were supposed to hang by your knees on them. And so I just hung. My mother says that whoever ran the audition was horrified.

She told her, "This child is *certainly* not ready yet. Come back in a couple of years."

By the time I was six we were living in a suburb of Chicago and I got started in a local ballet school. By thirteen, I had become reasonably serious about being a dancer. When it came time to go to college, I went, but I didn't go willingly. I wanted to dance, not study. I enrolled simultaneously at the University of Pennsylvania and at Pennsylvania Ballet School. I scheduled all my classes at college from eight until eleven in the morning so I could go to dance class every day. That lasted about a month. I hated the University of Pennsylvania. I loved dancing, and all the logic of why go to college if you want to do ballet, struck me full force. So, after only a month at school, I quit and became a trainee at the Harkness Ballet in New York.

I was eighteen then, and I stayed with the Harkness for a year. Then I started to move around, going from one professional company to another. First it was the National Ballet of Washington. Then I went to Europe, where I danced with a company in Germany and one in Switzerland. When I was in Switzerland, the American Ballet Theater performed there, so on a day we had no rehearsal, I went where they were dancing and I asked for an audition. It so happened they were one person short in the company in Europe and they thought I was good enough, so they asked me to join them. Then, when we returned to New York, they invited me to join the company. It was very exciting!

The first year I had a wonderful time and I thought, this is as good as it's going to get in ballet. But by the second year, my tenth year as a professional dancer, something happened. I don't know, I just felt like I didn't want to do this anymore. I would sit around rehearsals and if I wasn't dancing, there was no excitement. It just wasn't like it had been. I'm not sure why, but I started thinking that maybe I should be doing something important in my life. I felt ballet wasn't important enough. There was something petty about it. The atmosphere was too hard. Everybody wants the part; everybody is fighting for their place in the limelight and for the director to like them. I don't know why I just didn't want to do it anymore.

Right around then it was confirmed that Baryshnikov was coming to be director of the company and I figured I should stick around for a while and see what happened. But by that time I had been with five different companies and it was always the same thing, the same politics, the same battles. So I started thinking maybe I should try school again. And because I liked science, I thought about going into medicine. Besides, it occurred to me, here I am at age twenty-seven. If I stay with ballet, I'll be at the end of my career in six or seven years. But if I go to medical school, by age thirty-five my career will be just beginning. So in February of 1980, at the ripe old age of twenty-seven, I left the American Ballet Theater and entered Hunter College as a freshman.

It took me three and a half years to get through Hunter, and in September of '83 I started medical school here. My first year here was dominated by a series of personal disasters. In fact, as I look back, I realize that medical school was the only thing that provided structure for me and a relief from what was going on in my personal life. First, my dad was diagnosed with pancreatic cancer. From my little bit of knowledge, I knew he basically had about six months to live and I knew exactly what was going to happen to him. Then, in the midst of all of this, at the end of my first year I found a lump on my neck. You know how medical students are. You think you have everything you're learning about, and what with my father dying and all, I was sure I had cancer, too.

The surgeon who biopsied it told me I had to have surgery. I asked if I could wait until I finished exams and he okayed that. Meanwhile, I started becoming a thyroid expert. I read a hundred papers on thyroid and the management of thyroid nodules and I was relieved that, well, if you're going to pick a cancer to have, pick thyroid cancer. It was a single nodule and they're very slow growing so it was okay to wait a month to have it out.

I asked the surgeon if I could watch him do an operation like the one I would have, before he operated on me. In your first and second year you don't get to watch any surgery so I had not yet been in the operating room. I remember his saying, "Think about this, Solange. The first time a student sees surgery, sometimes they feel pretty squeamish. And when you think it's going to be you in a week . . . Are you sure want to do this?"

I was sure. In fact, I was looking forward to it for some strange reason.

From the first minute I stepped into the operating room, I became terribly excited. I'm sure that that's when I decided to be a surgeon.

One of my most memorable experiences, in fact, was when I was on call during my general surgery rotation early in my third year. A guy with a gunshot wound came into the emergency room. My team went up to the operating room and I was the only student there. They opened up the guy's belly and his abdomen was full of blood and they pushed away all his bowel and small intestine and there was blood coming out from somewhere and the resident said, "Okay, Solange, here's your job." And he took my hand and placed my finger so I could put pressure where the bleeding was, and that stopped it. Then he said, "Okay now, whatever you do, don't move!" I was there for I don't know how long—at least an hour and a half in one position with my finger sticking into a jag in the guy's body where the bullet had shattered some bone. I was *petrified*. Every time I moved my finger just a millimeter, the blood would start welling out and one of the surgeons would say, "I don't want to be melodramatic, Solange, but this is a matter of life and death!" I said, "Okay, okay. I understand, I understand."

At the end of the case the doctors said he had a large hole in one of his common iliac veins. If it had been in his artery he would have been in a real mess. I don't know how many units of blood they kept pumping in. They sewed him up and they sewed the hole closed and at the end of the case everybody said, "Well, we saved his life, but the guy's going to be a paraplegic. Another paraplegic from a gunshot wound."

I followed him after the surgery. I saw him every day. He was an arrogant guy. I asked him, "What happened? How did you get shot?" He said, "I don't know. I was leaving a dance club and somebody shot me." He was the perfect trauma case—a big dramatic mess who obviously would have died without intervention. We saved his life and not only that, he walked out of here a normal guy! I couldn't believe it.

One of the most nerve-wracking experiences a student can go through is presenting a patient at rounds. But you have no choice. So you do it. I presented a guy once on chief-of-service rounds. He was an interesting patient because he was a young man who for all the world looked like he had AIDS, but at the time we didn't have proof. We thought maybe he had disseminated TB. I presented this case because he had a certain type of bacillus growing out of his lungs and his bone marrow. We didn't know if it was TB or not—it turned out that he did have AIDS—and so, nervously, as I stood outside his door, I told about his history and all the lab tests and everything else. Then we all went in to see the patient. The doctors examined him, we discussed his case, and we left to see another patient. Well, it wasn't fifteen minutes later, we were finishing rounds on that floor, and all of a sudden we heard on the loudspeaker, "Arrest STAT, Eleven West." And I remember thinking, "Oh my God!" I went running down the corridor, and within seconds everybody was in his room and they were doing CPR on him. He was dead as a doornail. I felt so shaken by it. Really shaken. I was pretty familiar with him. I wonder how I'll feel when I'm an intern and it's me who has been taking care of the patient.

For the first year or two of med school, I thought I'd eventually go into orthopedic surgery. My dancer friends kept telling me how I'd be so well equipped to take care of them when they get bad knees and stuff. I was actually all hyped up on it. I pictured myself in this glamorous way—Dr. MacArthur, orthopod to the ballerinas! Me and my French twist going to the ballet every night, watching my dancers do arabesques on stage. An elegant grande dame. Of course, I'd have to wear high heels all the time because I'm not tall enough to come across like that otherwise. Then I thought about the surgeon who is presently the star orthopedist of the ballet world. One of the orthopedists here told me that this man really liked ballet more than he liked orthopedics, and in fact I think that's what it is with me, too. I love ballet. I know ballet very well and I know what dancers are like. But it's ballet I love, not so much orthopedic surgery. To me, general surgery is more exciting. So that's what I'll eventually specialize in.

There has never been a time when I questioned my decision to leave the ballet and go into medicine, discounting brief moments, of course, like right before you go into an exam, where you wonder, what am I doing this for? Or the isolated times in the middle of the night where you wake up and you feel completely disoriented and you don't know where you are and somebody has just beeped you to come hold retractors in the OR. Other than that, I never questioned it.

Sometimes I think I should have stayed another year, just to see what it would have been like with Baryshnikov. But in the overall scheme of things, I don't regret my decision. Sure, I could still be dancing *now*, but in two years or so I would have reached my limit. Medicine is something I can do as long as I want to do it. My body's not going to stop me.

Afterword

Books end, but hospitals keep going. A hospital's lights can only be dimmed; they can never be turned off.

The process of medical education is continuous. Students learn from doctors and then in time *become* doctors who teach students. The course is rigorous and regulated. Becoming a licensed doctor takes at least five years and for some specialists it may take as long as ten years. It calls for a commitment of time, energy, and money beyond any other profession. It also asks for a promise to stay with it.

Medical students graduate, become residents, and present themselves as models to the students for whom they are responsible. The residents in turn are taught by the attending physicians. In an arrangement similar to the old apprenticeship system, attending physicians at teaching hospitals devote countless hours, often without pay, teaching younger doctors who will eventually become their competitors.

Doctors never stop being students. The American Medical Association recommends that a certain number of hours a year be spent in continuing medical education. That includes lectures, seminars, programs and meetings where physicians learn about the latest developments in their fields. Even the brightest and most agile minds realize they can never know it all.

New technology builds on the foundations of scientific discovery. New devices and machines are proliferating so fast that yesterday's major breakthrough is tomorrow's old news. For the hospital, this means millions of dollars each year just to keep up. For example, who could have predicted that a piece of electronics the size of two silver dollars stacked one on top of the other, powered by a battery lasting ten years, could be implanted permanently in the body and wired to the ventricle to stabilize the rhythm of an erratically beating heart? A boon to the patient, clearly. But for the hospital, the pacemaker also means providing doctors with operating rooms, radiographic equipment, trained assistants to help with the surgery, and the means to repair or replace the device immediately if it is necessary.

A far more elaborate example is the CAT scanner. Months can pass between the time the need for this multimillion dollar piece of diagnostic equipment is recognized, the decision to acquire it is made, and the money is found to purchase it. More time passes as the best model is determined, ordered, and finally delivered. Then, during installation, just as the last screw is turned, news breaks about a smaller, faster, far superior model. Whether it is a laser or a lithotriptor (a machine that smashes kidney stones), there is no such thing, even in a modern hospital, as having the "latest" of everything.

Scientific research continues. Pediatrician James Wolff spoke of a time in his career when very few children survived leukemia and Hodgkin's disease. Now both are considered curable. Dr. John Driscoll recalled starting practice at a time when two-pound babies could not be saved. Today newborn babies weighing less than one pound come back a year and two years later to play together in the Presbyterian Hospital garden. Dr. Elynne Margulies delivers healthy babies conceived outside the body by way of in vitro fertilization, a procedure developed while she was in medical school. It wasn't long ago that people with end-stage heart disease died because there was no such thing as heart transplantation. Today they die because there are not enough donor hearts. Tomorrow they may live as a result of research currently being done with animal organs.

Research is a vitally important part of a university hospital, and it isn't confined to the laboratories. The ideas for research are most often germinated within the hospital hallways where physicians confer in search of answers to apparently insoluble medical problems. And just as often, ideas are born at the bedside of a patient as the battle to restore him to health is slowly lost.

For many of the people who work there, the hospital day is never over. Something is always left undone. So many of the people interviewed for this book said that they never completely leave their patients behind, that they always take them home in their thoughts. Dr. Wolff, upon leaving a particularly ill child late at night, always wondered if he had done absolutely everything he could to keep the child comfortable until early the next morning when he would see her again. Penny Bushman, like Katherine Rosasko, sees her patients' faces in her dreams.

Like the doctors and the nurses, I found it hard to leave these people behind. Each night, as I left the hospital and headed home across the George Washington Bridge, I thought about them. Occasionally, I would speculate where they might be twenty-five years from now. Perhaps Dr. Bendixen's daughter will be a medical school dean like her father. Maybe one of Dr. Addinizio's heart transplant patients will grow up to design an effective artificial heart. I wondered if Dr. Gomez-Carrion's newborn son would ever hear the words "affirmative action" or if there would still be a need for Dr. Forde's minority recruitment committee in the medical school. Will Jack Rothstein, the baker, ever write his book? Will George Petrosian still think medicine was the right career choice? Will Solange MacArthur put on her high heels and become "Orthopod to the Ballet Stars"?

If history is any indication, twenty-five years from now, many of these people will still be here. And there will be new people with new stories and even new people with the same stories. Students will still enter medicine with imagination and high ideals. There will be technologies we can't even *dream* of today. And, with a little luck, AIDS, like scarlet fever, diphtheria, and polio, may be conquered. One more thing I am sure of: Things will still be moving along. In this sense, the heart of a hospital emulates and even outdoes the human heart. It keeps right on beating.

ABOUT THE AUTHOR

INA YALOF spent ten years as a medical sociologist in a metropolitan hospital. Her numerous articles on health and medicine have appeared in such publications as *GQ* and *Harper's Bazaar*. She is also the author of *Open Heart Surgery*, published in 1983. *Life and Death* is her second book. Ina Yalof lives with her husband, Herbert, in New Jersey and New York City.